The
most
amazing
gardens
in
Britain &
Ireland

PUBLISHED BY
THE READER'S DIGEST ASSOCIATION LIMITED
LONDON • NEW YORK • SYDNEY • MONTREAL

The most amazing gardens in Britain & Ireland

Contents

Introduction

From formal terraces and landscaped parkland to organic wild-flower meadows and modern sculpture parks, discover the sheer beauty and variety of gardens to be found the length and breadth of the British Isles.

Each year, thousands of visitors – from both the UK and abroad – are attracted by the beauty, originality and variety of the gardens in Britain and Ireland, many of which rank among the finest in the world. The gardens featured in this book have been selected for their dramatic setting and vistas, innovative design, intriguing features, rare and unusual species or exemplary plantings. They range from historic landscaped parks to quirky back gardens and include the work of renowned designers such as 'Capability' Brown, Gertrude Jekyll, Tom Stuart-Smith and Christopher Bradley-Hole, as well as highly individual gardens created by amateur enthusiasts.

Some gardens chart changing fashions in design or showcase discoveries of Victorian plant-hunters while others provide the perfect setting for some of the finest houses in Britain and Ireland. Botanic gardens give fascinating lessons in horticultural history, whereas several contemporary gardens combine art and horticulture in innovative ways. Arboretums provide a dazzling display of autumn colours and woodland gardens bloom in spring when they are carpeted with bulbs.

Garden features are often an essential ingredient of a great garden – impressive glasshouses, intricate parterres, magnificent fountains, stylish topiary and atmospheric grottoes add interest and character to many of the gardens in this book.

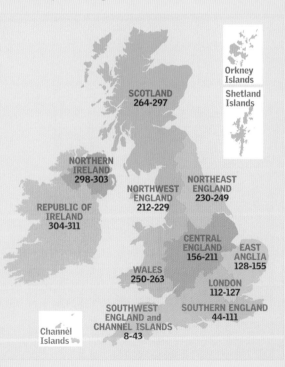

Orkney Islands

Shetland Islands

SCOTLAND
264-297

NORTHERN IRELAND
298-303

NORTHWEST ENGLAND
212-229

NORTHEAST ENGLAND
230-249

REPUBLIC OF IRELAND
304-311

CENTRAL ENGLAND
156-211

EAST ANGLIA
128-155

WALES
250-263

LONDON
112-127

SOUTHWEST ENGLAND and CHANNEL ISLANDS
8-43

SOUTHERN ENGLAND
44-111

Channel Islands

How to use this book

The book is divided into ten regions (see map, left), which are sub-divided by county or, in the case of Scotland and Wales, by area. Ireland appears as Northern Ireland and the Republic of Ireland, with no sub-divisions.

At the beginning of each chapter is a map of the region. Numbers on the map identify the location of the gardens featured in the region. At the start of each entry, directions are supplied along with contact details for the garden – the address, telephone number and website, if available. Also included, where relevant, are the garden grades used by English Heritage. Parks and gardens considered as benchmarks of excellence and worthy of preservation and restoration are listed Grade I, Grade II and Grade II★. Similar grades used by the official heritage bodies in Wales, Scotland and Northern Ireland are given for gardens in these regions.

At the end of each entry, information is provided on opening times, such as 'open all year', 'open main season' and 'open limited season'. Specific dates and times are not given because these are often only confirmed a few weeks in advance of the garden's opening, so always consult the website or telephone before you set out. Details of any special arrangements are also noted, for example if a head gardener should be contacted or if requests must be made in writing for parties of visitors.

The main categories for opening times are as follows:

Open all year – Jan-Dec on most days

Open main season – usually March to late Sept/early Oct on most days

Open limited season – specifically for snowdrops, for example, or June-Aug for summer flowers

Open by appointment – apply to the owners by telephone or by writing to the address given to make an appointment

Open for NGS/charity – these gardens are part of the National Garden Scheme (see below) or only open on special days to raise money for charity

Useful websites

Some gardens are open to the public through the National Gardens Scheme (or the Scottish equivalent). This scheme is a registered charity which opens gardens of quality, character and interest to the public on specific days. If a garden is owned by a heritage or horticultural association, this is stated in the introductory information.

● The National Gardens Scheme (NGS)
www.ngs.org.uk

● Scotland's Gardens Scheme (SGS)
www.gardensofscotland.org

● The National Trust (NT)
www.nationaltrust.org.uk

● The National Trust for Scotland (NTS)
www.nts.org.uk

● English Heritage (EH)
www.english-heritage.org.uk

● Royal Horticultural Society (RHS)
www.rhs.org.uk

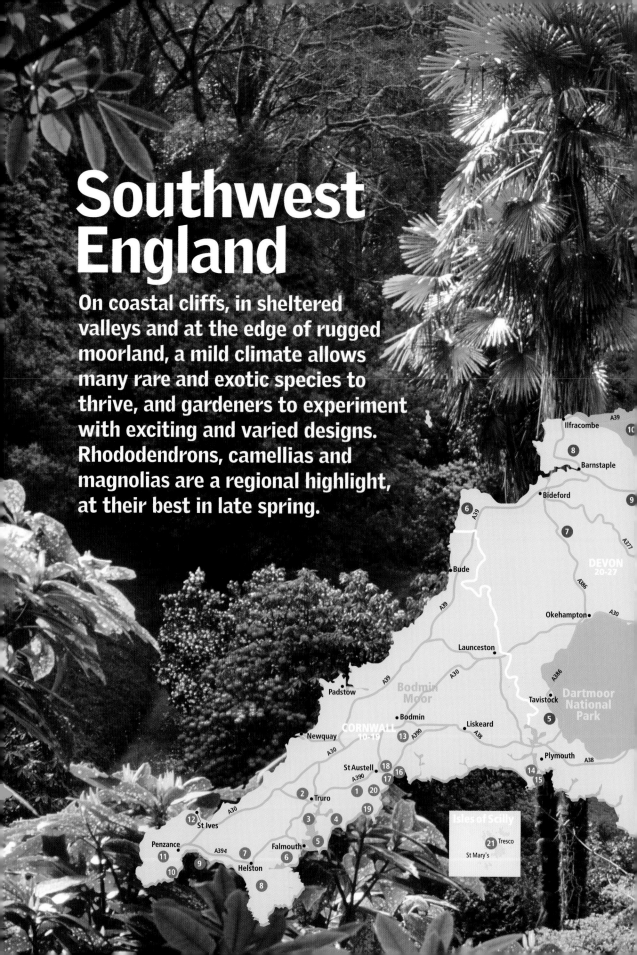

Southwest England

On coastal cliffs, in sheltered valleys and at the edge of rugged moorland, a mild climate allows many rare and exotic species to thrive, and gardeners to experiment with exciting and varied designs. Rhododendrons, camellias and magnolias are a regional highlight, at their best in late spring.

Ilfracombe
A39
10
8
Barnstaple
Bideford
6
A39
9
7
A377
DEVON
20-27
Bude
A386
Okehampton
A30
A39
Launceston
A30
Bodmin Moor
A386
Padstow
A39
Tavistock
Dartmoor National Park
Bodmin
5
CORNWALL 10-19
Liskeard
Newquay
13
A390
A38
A30
Plymouth
A38
St Austell
18
16
14
A390
17
15
2
20
Truro
1
19
St Ives
12
3
4
Isles of Scilly
5
21 Tresco
Penzance
7
Falmouth
St Mary's
11
9
6
10
Helston
8

KEY

1. Garden location
— County boundary
— Motorway
— Principal A road

Bristol

A38
A37
Bath 11
Weston-super-Mare 6 7 9 10

Mendip Hills
Frome
A361
8
A361

Minehead 4

Exmoor National Park

Somerset Levels

Bridgwater
Glastonbury

A39

A361
A396

5
Taunton M5
12
A303
Shaftesbury

SOMERSET 36-41

3
A303
Yeovil
A30

Tiverton 11
12
1
A350
A354

13
2
A37
10 11
Blandford Forum

Honiton
9
DORSET 30-35
1 A31
2 A338

14
Exeter
15 A35
7
8
A35
Dorchester
A348
Poole
Bournemouth

17

16
Exmouth
Lyme Regis
5
4
A35

A38
A380

6 Weymouth
3 Swanage

20 Torquay
A385

Alderney

19 1
Dartmouth 2
3
Salcombe

Guernsey
Herm
3
2 1 St Peter Port
Sark

CHANNEL ISLANDS 42-43

Jersey
4
St Helier

CORNWALL

England's most southerly county basks in the warmth of the Gulf Stream. Its gardens bloom with sub-tropical species, while camellias and rhododendrons put on a spectacular show in spring.

1 Trewithen

The spectacular flowers of the camellia collection can be viewed from platforms that offer a canopy-level perspective.

Grampound Road, Truro TR2 4DD
Tel: 01726 883647
www.trewithengardens.co.uk
Historic Garden Grade II*
LOCATION On A390 between Truro and St Austell

Trewithen is one of the greatest of all Cornish gardens, covering 30 acres, mainly of woodland. It is known internationally for its collections (often grown from wild specimens) of camellias, magnolias and rhododendrons, as well as its many other rare trees and shrubs. Mid March to mid June are rewarding times to visit.

The garden's most striking feature is the long lawn in front of the 1730s house, flanked by borders of mature rhododendrons, magnolias, acers and other shrubs and ornamental trees, and backed by mature hardwoods. The sheer size of many of the rhododendrons and magnolias is particularly remarkable.

To the west, beech and other woodland trees shelter shrub beds and paths. In the southwest is the main camellia collection – with specimens notable for their huge flowers – and many other shrubs; three viewing platforms have been erected to give a different perspective of the camellias from canopy level.

A deep sunken garden contains tree ferns as well as acers and camellias, and a *camera obscura* has been sited in one of the glades, while new rose plantings have been developed in the Deer Park Garden. The 18th-century walled garden (which is not always open) is laid out as a herb and rose garden with herbaceous borders; it features a fish pond, an old summerhouse and a wisteria-clad pergola.

Many hybrid rhododendrons and camellias originated at Trewithen, some of them named by George Johnstone, the garden's creator, after members of his family. The garden's plants were also the inspiration for Tom Leaper's magnolia fountain which adjoins the Beech Wood. The well-stocked nursery has many plants for sale.

▶ *Open main season – telephone or consult website for details*

2 Bosvigo

Among the enclosed gardens near the house are the white and yellow Vean Garden, and a 'hot' garden in red, yellow and orange.

Bosvigo Lane, Truro TR1 3NH
Tel: 01872 275774
www.bosvigo.com
LOCATION ¾ mile W of Truro. From A390, turn into Dobbs Lane next to Aldi sign, just W of Sainsbury roundabout. Entrance is 500m on left

Immaculately maintained, this colourful 2 acre garden consists of several enclosed and walled areas surrounding a Georgian house – a 'hot' garden displaying red, yellow and orange flowers, the Vean Garden in white and yellow, and a walled garden planted in blues, lavenders and mauves. Flowers and foliage are grouped with boldness or subtlety to good effect.

Though not a typical Cornish garden (rhododendrons and camellias do not play a major part), the woodland walk in the spring section contains treasures such as hellebores, epimediums and erythroniums. The garden as a whole can be seen at its best in summer.

A good selection of rare and unusual plants is on offer in the nursery.

▶ *Open main season – telephone or consult website for details*

3 Trelissick

Outstanding in spring, this garden contains a large variety of exotic plants and an area specially devoted to aromatics.

Feock, Truro TR3 6QL	Tel: 01872 862090
www.nationaltrust.org.uk
Historic Garden Grade II*/The National Trust
LOCATION 4 miles S of Truro on B3289 above west end of King Harry Ferry (boat services from Falmouth, Truro and St Mawes, May to September)

Although it is among the most beautiful of Cornish spring gardens, Trelissick also has many summer–flowering shrubs. It covers 40 acres, set amid 400 acres of park and farmland, and offers panoramic views to the sea. The plantings and layout date from 1937. It has fine open lawns and is known for its hydrangeas, camellias, magnolias and rhododendrons in spring, and for its large collection of other tender and exotic plants.

One section is given over to aromatic plants, another houses a collection of fruit trees. An orchard of Cornish apples was planted in 2003. The woodland walks have views of the River Fal in the distance.

▶ *Open all year – telephone or consult website for details*

4 Poppy Cottage

Bursting with a terrific range of plants in every colour, both permanent and seasonal, the garden offers inspiration for all.

Ruan High Lanes, Truro TR2 5JR

Tel: 01872 501411

LOCATION On Roseland Peninsula, 1 mile NW of Veryan, 4 miles SW of Tregony, on A3078 St Mawes Road

A real plantsman's garden, Poppy Cottage is divided into a number of separate but visually linked areas. Such is the design and ingenuity of form and layout that the garden appears much larger than it actually is – a lesson to any garden lover on the intensive use of space.

The owners expanded their small plot – which covers a little less than 1 acre – when they purchased a field that lay 1m (3ft) higher than the original garden. The two areas have been linked with steps and a retaining wall. From the woodchip path at the higher level visitors can wander through many unusual shrubs, all underplanted with ground cover, to look down or over the informal sequence of gardens, each one hidden from the next.

In spring, drifts of bulbs are woven through the beds, and rare and unusual trees, shrubs and herbaceous plants flower in succession to ensure colour and interest right through to autumn. Throughout the garden there are garden seats in many positions that provide a variety of viewpoints from which to appreciate both the detail of the planting and the overall design.

There is also a small orchard where unusual varieties of ducks and chickens wander, and a nursery area where a wide range of herbaceous plants can be purchased.

▶ *Open main season – telephone or consult website for details*

TRELISSICK

5 Lamorran House

Japanese and Italian areas, sculptures and fine views enhance the collections of sub-tropical and temperate plants.

Upper Castle Road, St Mawes TR2 5BZ

Tel: 01326 270800

www.lamorrangardens.co.uk

LOCATION Above St Mawes turn right at garage, continue for ½ mile and house is on left

On a south-facing slope above the sea this intimate 4½ acre garden enjoys a microclimate that supports impressive collections of plants from the Southern Hemisphere, with sub-tropical plants in the lower sections and temperate plants – including rhododendrons and evergreen azaleas – higher up. It also holds a fine collection of palms (more than 30 varieties) and tree ferns.

Paths zigzag down the steep hillside between enclosed compartments, some in Japanese or Italian style, all with views over the sea to St Anthony's Head. There are neo-classical statues and columns, streams and pools. The planting is so dense that the paths are screened from each other and so appear to magnify the total area.

▶ *Open main season – telephone or consult website for details – and by appointment*

6 Trebah

Containing many impressive shrubs and trees on its dramatic slopes, Trebah sustains its vibrant colour throughout the year.

Mawnan Smith, Falmouth TR11 5JZ

Tel: 01326 252200

www.trebah-garden.co.uk

Historic Garden Grade II

LOCATION 4 miles SW of Falmouth. Signed from A39/A394 junction at Treliever Cross

The most remarkable feature of Trebah is the view over its great clumps of rhododendrons, tree ferns and bamboos down into the ravine which runs between towering trees, including the tallest Chusan palms in the country, down to the Helford River. Covering about 25 acres, it has a well-developed collection of trees and shrubs.

There is colour and interest for every season, with an extensive collection of sub-tropical Mediterranean plants. A stream and carp ponds occupy the upper reaches, while in the lower parts is a lake, a plantation of gunnera and acres of blue and white hydrangeas for summer colour.

▶ *Open all year – telephone or consult website for details*

TREBAH

7 Trevarno Estate and Gardens

Formal terracing, a rockery and a grotto testify to the garden's Victorian heritage and it houses the National Garden Museum.

Trevarno Manor, Helston TR13 0RU

Tel: 01326 574274

www.trevarno.co.uk

LOCATION 3 miles NW of Helston off A394 or B3302

During the 1830s, Trevarno was reorganised in the Victorian Gardenesque style, with Italianate terraces, steps and balustrades; later owners added greenhouses and a walled garden. Restoration by the current owners since 1995 has allowed the 70 acre estate to preserve its Victorian heritage.

Features include a bluebell-filled valley, a National Collection of daffodils and a wild-flower garden. A serpentine yew tunnel runs the length of the main lawn and a summerhouse is set on a turntable, which can be cranked around to follow the sun; there are camellia borders and a sedum lawn that flowers in early summer.

In the valley is a Savage Picturesque rockery and rockwork grotto, and lakeside boathouse in the style of a Gothic chapel. The wooded valley includes waterfalls and a bog garden, while a bothy, dovecote and gazebo combine with lush plantings of magnolias and rhododendrons.

The National Garden Museum houses a collection of gardening antiques and ephemera.

▶ *Open all year – telephone or consult website for details*

8 Bonython Estate Gardens

As well as a variety of enclosed gardens, the estate now features a series of atmospheric plantings around its three lakes.

Cury Cross Lanes, Helston TR12 7BA

Tel: 01326 240234

www.bonythonmanor.co.uk

LOCATION 5 miles S of Helston on A3083. Turn left at Cury Cross Lanes, entrance on right

Covering a 20 acre site, this exciting garden is still being developed. The owners began in 1999 with an old walled garden, a few ornamental trees and shrubs, background trees and essential shelter belts (now extended by another 15,000 trees).

In a courtyard of the 1780s house a complex water feature, planted with grasses, herbs and bamboos, is adjoined by a herb parterre; the lawn is surrounded by rhododendrons and azaleas. In the upper part of the large walled garden, herbaceous and shrub borders surround a swimming pool themed with changing blues and purples; below it is a potager garden planted in shades of pink and burgundy.

An orchard where wild flowers grow beneath the trees slopes down to Lake Joy against a background of specimen trees and shrubs, while the sunny bank that dams it has South African and Mediterranean plants, and camassias cluster beside the water course. Below this Lake Sue, planted since 2001 but now mature, is surrounded by ornamental grasses and hot red colours for late summer. From here a stream trickles through the woodland dell, where a path flanked by hellebores leads among dense plantings of dicksonias, young rhododendrons and other spring shrubs to the newly enlarged Quarry Lake, backed by vertical cliffs.

▶ *Open main season – telephone or consult website for details – and for parties of ten or more by appointment*

9 St Michael's Mount

Based on its own tiny island, half a mile offshore, the castle garden houses a surprising variety of exotic plants.

Marazion, Penzance TR17 0EF

Tel: 01736 710507

www.nationaltrust.org.uk

Historic Garden Grade II/The National Trust

LOCATION ½ mile from shore at Marazion, ½ mile S of A394. Access by motor boat (summer only) or walk across causeway

The private 18th-century walled garden of the St Aubyn family rises in terraces from just above sea level at the south-eastern corner of the castle to the foot of its southern wall. Such is the microclimate that, despite constant exposure to salt spray and gales, many tender and exotic sub-tropical plants thrive within the shelter belt of Monterey pines and evergreen oaks. Escallonia hedges also provide some shelter, and much of the planting is among granite boulders.

The private garden, laid out on several terraces near the top, is approached along an informal avenue of kniphofias across rough grass. Both here and above are groups of striking plants: *Agave americanum*, aeoniums, succulents, *Euphorbia mellifera* and yuccas.

Visitors who make the rough, steep climb up to the castle walls will be rewarded by an outstanding view.

▶ *Castle open. Garden open main season (10.30am-5pm) – telephone or consult website for details*

10 Chygurno

Perched high above a cove, this charming terraced garden offers panoramic views as well as a fine collection of exotics.

Lamorna, Penzance TR19 6XH

Tel: 01736 732153

LOCATION 4 miles S of Penzance off B3315. Follow signs for Cove Restaurant; garden is at top of hill on left

The Lamorna valley has long attracted creative men and women to settle in this remote corner of west Cornwall – among them the painters Laura Knight and Alfred Munnings and the authors Derek Tangye and John Le Carré. Now the present owners, a pair of talented gardeners, have transformed a difficult cliff-and-valley site high above Lamorna Cove into a terraced masterpiece.

They started planting the 3 acres in 1998, restricting their palette mainly to Southern-Hemisphere shrubs and exotics. In springtime, the camellias, rhododendrons, bluebells and primroses start to flower among the natural woodland on the lower slopes; turn a corner and huge structural granite outcrops alter the terrain and make a perfect frame for tree ferns, aeoniums, phormiums, agaves and aloes.

Birds abound, as do the butterflies darting in summer between great clumps of agapanthus, lavenders and crocosmias. The steeply winding pathways allow intimate glimpses and wide seascapes, and nothing beats a bird's-eye view of the centre of a huge tree fern; plenty of benches and seats are provided from which to appreciate not only the panorama and the plantsmanship, but also the ingenious methods devised for transplanting soil and gravel down the vertiginous slopes.

▶ *Open main season – telephone or consult website for details – and by appointment*

11 Trewidden

The site of an ancient tin mine now has displays of camellias and magnolias and superlative examples of tree ferns.

Buryas Bridge, Penzance TR20 8TT

Tel: 01736 363021

www.trewiddengarden.co.uk

LOCATION 2 miles W of Penzance on A30

This once-sleeping woodland garden has been rejuvenated and is of interest not only to gardeners and tree specialists but also to those interested in the historic artefacts of the Cornish tin industry, for the 15 acre garden created by successive generations of the Bolitho family in the 18th and 19th centuries has been created on the site of an ancient tin mine.

Woodland paths weave through the 300 varieties of camellias – the second largest collection in the county – past open glades of magnolias, including varieties of *M. campbellii*, *M.* 'Trewidden Belle', *M.* x *veitchii* 'Peter Veitch' and *M. hypoleuca*. Four of them are champions. In spring, visitors can gaze skywards to see the breathtaking vision of a froth of pink waving against a bright blue sky that is created by these huge trees when in bloom.

The fern pit holds the finest stand of tree ferns in Britain, maybe even the Northern Hemisphere, and has a fascinating wartime history, having been progressively deepened by a bomb.

In the south-facing walled garden head gardener Richard Morton is extending the season and broadening the spectrum with tender exotics and new and rare species; he has also discovered inventive ways of using mining artefacts.

▶ *Open most of year – telephone or consult website for details*

12 Barbara Hepworth Museum and Sculpture Garden

A structured, almost architectural style characterises this sloping garden and complements Hepworth's sculptures.

Barnoon Hill, St Ives TR26 1AD

Tel: 01736 796226

www.tate.org.uk/stives

Historic Garden Grade II/Tate St Ives

LOCATION In centre of St Ives. Signposted

Wandering through the narrow streets of St Ives, passers-by cannot imagine the treasure that lies behind the high wall. The house and sloping ½ acre garden once belonged to the sculptor Barbara Hepworth, and both are kept as they were during her lifetime.

The garden has an architectural style, with strong accents and outlines softened by downy underplanting, and the trees shading the upper part reflect the vertical nature of many of the sculptures displayed here.

A ginkgo and a Prunus 'Amanagawa' provide cover for the small pond that separates the upper garden from a small open lawn, and there are other colourful herbaceous beds planted on the lower level. Sun and light dapple the silver-grey paths and glint through the leaves of such plants as *Cordyline australis*, and the sense of nature at play is reinforced by the wind rustling through the bamboos.

▶ *Open all year – telephone or consult website for details. Admission may be restricted in the high season to prevent overcrowding*

13 Lanhydrock

The magnificent house is surrounded by grounds that are a satisfying mix of natural wood and park, and strictly formal gardens.

Bodmin PL30 5AD | Tel: 01208 265950

www.nationaltrust.org.uk

Historic Garden Grade II*/The National Trust

LOCATION 2½ miles SE of Bodmin off A38 and A30, or off B3268

Although the collection of trees was started as early as 1634, the real bones of this superb 30 acre garden in a dramatic woodland and parkland setting were put in place in 1857 by the first Baron Robartes. The architect of his choice was George Gilbert Scott, brought in not only to restore and extend the 17th-century house but also to redesign the garden. The formal gardens remain largely as he conceived them and are complemented by more modern planting.

Behind the original 17th-century crenellated gatehouse is a formal lawn with 29 topiary yews in the shape of truncated cones and with rose beds in between. Beside the house, a Victorian parterre flanked by six similar yews has spring and summer bedding plants. The herbaceous circle is planted to give an appealing display in both spring and autumn.

A shady stream fringed by water-loving plants runs off the hill behind the house, and the Higher Garden, planted with large groups of 'Cornish Red' and other rhododendrons, many camellias, azaleas, magnolias and *Viburnum plicatum*, has a new border planted with perennials.

The hillside woods offer fine walks beneath mature trees underplanted with large-leaved rhododendrons and bluebells.

▶ *House open. Garden open all year – telephone or consult website for details*

IN A WOODLAND AND PARKLAND SETTING

LANHYDROCK

14 Antony

Landscaped by Humphrey Repton during the 18th century, the garden is set in parkland with lawns sweeping down to the river.

Torpoint PL11 2QA | Tel: 01752 812364

www.nationaltrust.org.uk

Historic Garden Grade II*/The National Trust/ Trustees of Carew Pole Garden Trust

LOCATION 2 miles W of Torpoint on A374, 16m SE of Liskeard. From Plymouth use Torpoint car ferry

Antony is a little off the beaten track, but it is well worth the effort to visit one of the country's finest early 18th-century houses in its natural setting. The National Trust owns the house and adjacent formal gardens while the woodland gardens, which lie between the parkland and the River Lynher and are also open to the public, belong to a family trust.

The formal gardens – with a terrace round the house, wide lawns, extensive vistas, yew hedges and old walls – are of the highest quality. A water feature by renowned sculptor William Pye on the west lawn mirrors the yew topiary nearby, and modern sculptures, 18th-century statues, and topiary are features of the yew walk and of the formal compartments of the summer garden. The latter includes a pleached lime hedge, mixed shrub and herbaceous borders with roses, and a knot garden.

The woodland gardens – the central section, which includes Jupiter Hill – are planted with camellias, magnolias and rhododendrons, with the scented rhododendrons outstanding in May. There is a Georgian bath house and a standing stone of Cornish granite has been erected at the highest point in memory of the present owner's parents, who created the woodland gardens.

In the neighbouring woodland walk is a ruined 15th-century dovecote and antiquary Richard Carew's 16th-century Fishful Pond. Other fine walks lead along the riverbanks.

Two National Collections are held here: hemerocallis (610 cultivars) and *Camellia japonica* (300 cultivars).

▶ *House open. Garden open main season – telephone or consult website for details*

15 Mount Edgcumbe House and Country Park

The series of formal gardens has Italian, French and English influences, with recent American and New Zealand additions.

Cremyll, Torpoint PL10 1HZ | Tel: 01752 822236

www.mountedgcumbe.gov.uk

Historic Park and Garden Grade I

LOCATION 8 miles S of Torpoint via A374 and B3247. Signposted from Antony village and Trulefort Roundabout on A38. Access also by ferry from Plymouth

The enterprising Edgcumbe family – who brought back ideas, artefacts and plants from their European travels in the 18th century – created these gardens set in parkland on Cornwall's south coast at the point where the River Tamar meets the sea. Admired by garden designers William Kent and Humphry Repton, and visited by a succession of royals, writers and artists, today the formal gardens offer 22 acres to explore in two contrasting areas.

On the high ground surrounding the house the Earl's Garden has a fine formal east lawn containing flowerbeds, statues and urns; beyond it lies the cedar lawn with its shell-encrusted seat. At sea level are the formal gardens, created from the late 18th century onwards. The Italian, French and English gardens (the latter including a fern dell) all remain true to their original layout, although some of the planting has changed. American and New Zealand gardens are more recent additions, and the Jubilee Garden, a calm green passageway lined with lollipop hornbeams, is sandwiched between the colourful bedding of the French and Italian gardens.

Beyond these is a rose garden planted with old English varieties, and a large amphitheatre is a spectacle in spring when the camellias covering its banks are in full bloom.

The new plant centre stocks young camellia plants propagated from a National Collection held here.

▶ *House open as Earl's Garden. Park and formal gardens open all year. Earl's Garden open main season – telephone or consult website for details*

THE VIEWS INTO THE DELL RANK WITH THE BEST

TREGREHAN

16 Marsh Villa Gardens

Created in the most unpromising location, this well tended garden now brims with examples of inspired and colourful planting.

St Andrew's Road, Par PL24 2LU

Tel: 01726 815920

www.marshvillagardens.co.uk

LOCATION 5 miles E of St Austell. Leave A390 at St Blazey traffic lights, then take first left; garden is 700m on left

This large plantswoman's garden, which has been created since 1986 by the present owner, is all the more remarkable for having been fashioned from a poorly drained meadow. The farmhouse, festooned with clematis and vines, looks across lawns and borders to an old granite barn.

A wide path bordering a stream runs past an area decorated with granite boulders until it meets the hornbeam avenue that forms the main axis of the layout. Here, the garden opens out to a huge natural pond encircled by a path and a more formal square garden with two long borders and a central, diamond-shaped trellis covered with roses and clematis. Both areas are superbly planted, with a wonderful sense of colour, particularly in the vibrant flower borders.

The path then leads on, parallel with the stream, to 14 acres of marshland that has been planted with willows, alders and native irises. Beyond, a boscage – or thicket – of acers stands on a mound created from the spoil of the excavated pond, and a bog garden has been created in a large bowl – the owner's latest 'jungle' project.

▶ *Open April to Sept, Sun-Wed (10am–6pm)*

17 Pine Lodge Garden and Nursery

Come through the woods to discover 12 distinctive gardens with rare and tender plants that thrive in the sheltered setting.

Holmbush, St Austell PL25 3RQ

Tel: 01726 73500

www.pinelodge.co.uk

LOCATION Just E of St Austell off A390 between Holmbush and turning for Tregrehan. Signposted

The entrance to the 30 acre garden – established since the 1980s by the owners with a collection of more than 6,000 plants – is through woodland. This opens out to a pond, spanned by a bridge, with a cottage garden laid out in front of the original house. Here, lawns and more ponds are surrounded by rare plants collected from around the world, which complement magnolias, camellias, rhododendrons and azaleas.

A path leads to a tightly planted arboretum. It is flanked on one side by a 4 acre pinetum, featuring 80 different conifers, and, on the other, by parkland leading down to a lake. An island is home to black swans and waterfowl, and more recently two resident otters and a fat badger.

Passing through a newly planted winter garden, a wild-flower garden with a bell tower and a Japanese garden, the circuit culminates in a tearoom and the well-known and well-stocked nursery. The water gardens near the car park are also attractive.

▶ *Open main season – telephone or consult website for details*

18 Tregrehan

The garden is most glorious in spring when rhododendrons and camellias are in bloom and there is a delightful bluebell walk.

Par PL24 2SJ | Tel: 01726 814389

www.tregrehan.org

Historic Garden Grade II*

LOCATION 2m E of St Austell, on A390 Lostwithiel–St Austell road. Entrance opposite Britannia Inn 1 mile W of St Blazey

The spring garden has been much restored since 1989 by the new owner. The 20 acres are mainly planted as woodland, but there is a 19th-century walled garden that contains a newly restored Victorian glasshouse range, an arch of *Acer palmatum* and interesting spring and summer-flowering climbers. A formal yew walk effectively frames the upper gardens.

The woodland dell is furnished with many species of conifers and native hardwoods. The near, steep side features rhododendrons and camellias, while the cleared areas beside the stream at the bottom and on the opposite bank – beautifully light on a sunny day – glow with young and rare shrubs and trees from the Southern Hemisphere, and there's a bluebell walk in spring. The views into the dell rank with the best in any Cornish garden.

Open for the first time, thanks to an English Heritage grant, is the 18th-century wooded driveway and restored pond and waterfall, planted up with many species from Southeast Asia.

▶ *Open main season – telephone or consult website for details; newly opened wooded driveway open to parties by appointment*

SOUTH WEST ENGLAND

FROM THE TOP TERRACE
VIEWS SLANT DOWN
TOWARDS THE SEA
TRESCO ABBEY

19 Caerhays Castle Garden

From the late 19th century, Caerhays has benefitted from the efforts of plant hunters, who introduced many new species.

Caerhays, Gorran, St Austell PL26 6LY

Tel: 01872 501310

www.caerhays.co.uk

Historic Garden Grade II*

LOCATION 10 miles S of St Austell, on coast by Porthluney Cove between Dodman Point and Nare Head

One of the greatest of all British gardens, Caerhays is a marvellous spectacle in spring. Principally a woodland garden (60 acres in all), it stretches around the hillside above the castle. Its collection of camellias and rhododendrons rank among the finest, and its magnolias are unrivalled. These, as well as many other fine shrubs and trees, are not only huge but bear flowers of a remarkable size and depth of colour.

The extensive replanting in the higher garden after the storm of 1990 has matured with great effect, while the felling of a stand of mature beech trees for safety reasons has revealed new views that look down on many of the magnolias.

Many plants are raised from material brought back by famous planthunters or sent recently from China. It was at Caerhays that the x *williamsii* camellias were originally propagated.
▶ *House and garden open main season – telephone or consult website for details*

20 The Lost Gardens of Heligan

Near abandoned when its gardeners went off to the First World War, Heligan was rediscovered and restored from 1990.

Pentewan, St Austell PL26 6EN

Tel: 01726 845100

www.heligan.com

Historic Garden Grade II

LOCATION 5½ miles S of St Austell off A390. Take B3273 signed to Mevagissey past Pentewan

Started in the late 18th century but neglected since 1914, the 1990s saw a rebirth of the 200 acre gardens at Heligan. The restored productive gardens to the north of the house, a demonstration of horticultural archaeology (the pineapple pits are particularly fascinating), are surrounded by Victorian pleasure grounds laid out as a series of secluded enclosures with fountains and a sundial. Massive, mainly 'Cornish Red' rhododendrons, enclose the large lawn, some collected by botanist Sir Joseph Hooker.

The Jungle, 15 minutes' walk away, is a wild valley where rhododendrons, bamboos, tree ferns and Chusan palms flourish. Further on, woodland walks can be taken in the Lost Valley. A National Collection of camellias and rhododendrons introduced before 1920 are held here.

Beyond the Steward's House, with its magnolias and young, well-planted garden, a pioneering wildlife conservation project has been developed. With the aid of modern technology, visitors can observe the activities of resident barn owls and other inhabitants. There is also an exhibition of ram pumps, an ingenious Victorian device for pumping water around the garden.
▶ *Open all year – telephone or consult website for details. Guided tours by arrangement*

SCILLY ISLES

21 Tresco Abbey

The hillside grounds of a ruined abbey house this sub-tropical garden where Mediterranean and exotic plants thrive.

Tresco, Isles of Scilly TR24 0PU

Tel: 01720 424105

www.tresco.co.uk

Historic Garden Grade I

LOCATION On island of Tresco. By helicopter from Penzance to Tresco heliport (reservations: 01736 363871) or from St Mary's by launch

Tresco, in the Gulf Stream and 28 miles off Land's End, is a world-renowned sub-tropical garden. Within a formal framework of paths, steps, the ruined walls of the old abbey and high hedges, exotic plants soften the outlines and provide striking colour and contrasting shapes.

Set on a south-sloping hillside with horizontal walks, the gardens are visually self-contained. From the top terrace there are views down to the sea, revealing the plantings below, especially those in the more open areas such as the pond where four Mediterranean cypresses form strong verticals. Myrtles, notably various metrosideros, are set among the background trees; aeoniums, cacti, puyas, proteas and huge agaves stand out, while callistemons, banksias, agapanthus and *Geranium maderenese* play a major part.

Just five gardeners plus some student help maintain the 25 acres. The gardens are probably at their peak from March to autumn, and their most colourful from late April to the end of June.
▶ *Open all year – telephone or consult website for details*

SOUTH WEST ENGLAND

DEVON

Woodland walks, herbaceous displays, exotic collections and intriguing architectural planting are some of Devon's great attractions, in which colour and texture combine to create a garden-lover's paradise.

1 Greenway

Camellias and ferns surround the house where crime writer Agatha Christie used to holiday, while a vinery adds extra interest.

Greenway Road, Galmpton, Churston Ferrers, Brixham TQ5 0ES | Tel: 01803 842382

www.nationaltrust.org.uk

The National Trust

LOCATION 4 miles W of Brixham. From A3022 Paignton-Brixham road, take road to Galmpton, then to Greenway quay and ferry. Or park at Dartmouth park-and-ride and take river cruise to Greenway (ferry service 01803 844010). Ferries also from Torquay and Brixham. Allow 4 hours

The 30 acre Devon estate is set high on the bank of the tree-lined Dart River. It offers woodland walks and enclosed flower gardens near the barn and stables, and beyond the sizeable kitchen garden. In high summer, the tree cover from the plethora of mature specimens near the house is so extensive that the river is hidden from view.

There is interest in every season, starting with camellias, rhododendrons, magnolias, davidias and michelias underplanted with narcissus, cyclamen, primroses and bluebells, followed by paulownias, embothriums and *Cornus capitata* with their understorey of campions, foxgloves and ferns. The camellia and fernery gardens and the vinery have been restored, the border in the top garden redeveloped, and collections made of interesting trees and shrubs from around the world, especially South America. The house (Agatha Christie's holiday home from 1938 to 1959) and the area around it are now open.

▶ *Open main season – telephone or consult website for details*

2 Coleton Fishacre Garden

Set in a secluded coastal combe, the terraced garden was carefully designed to complement the architecture of the house.

Brownstone Road, Kingswear, Dartmouth TQ6 0EQ | Tel: 01803 752466

www.nationaltrust.org.uk

Historic Garden Grade II*/The National Trust

LOCATION 3 miles E of Dartmouth, 3 miles S of Brixham off B3205; 2½ miles from Kingswear, take Lower Ferry Road and turn off at toll house

Oswald Milne, a pupil of Edwin Lutyens, designed the house and the architectural features of this 30 acre garden for Rupert and Lady D'Oyly

COLETON FISHACRE GARDEN

Carte; the garden was started in 1926. The mild setting is a steeply sloping Devon combe sheltered by belts of Monterey pines and holm oaks, with streams and ponds providing a humid atmosphere for moisture-loving and sub-tropical plants.

There is a collection of unusual trees, such as dawn redwood, swamp cypress, Chilean myrtle, a tall tulip tree and a tree of heaven (*Ailanthus altissima*) which is the same age as the house. The Paddock Woodland Walk runs from the Gazebo Walk through woodland to a viewing area.

Formal walls and terraces create a framework round the house for a large number of sun-loving tender plants, and there are fine water features, notably a stone-edged rill and a circular pool in the herbaceous-bordered walled garden.
▶ *House and garden open main season – telephone or consult website for details*

3 Blackpool Gardens

This secret woodland garden overlooking Devon's heritage coast is filled with sub-tropical and temperate species.

Blackpool Sands, Blackpool, Dartmouth TQ6 0RG

Tel: 01803 770606

www.blackpoolsands.co.uk

LOCATION 3 miles S of Dartmouth on A379. Parking by beachside café. Entrance through Blackpool Sands car park

Facing south and rising steeply is this hidden garden overlooking the crescent of Blackpool Sands. This chunk of Devon's Heritage Coast

has been in the same family since the late 18th century, but the landscaping of the 3 acre woodland garden was started in 1896.

Four wide parallel paths run the length of the garden, joined by further paths and steps to climb upwards in a gentle zig-zag. The hillside between is filled with sub-tropical, temperate and antipodean trees and shrubs, some of great age, others introduced more recently. An 1848 Monterey pine and an 1896 avenue of cork oaks with pitted bark survive from the earliest period.

The award of a European grant in 2000 enabled the present owner to start regenerating the landscaping and rejuvenating the plantings. Enjoy the view that fades away to distant Start Point, then make your way back to the beach below to enjoy a swim, hire a kayak and return to the real holiday world.
▶ *Open main season – telephone or consult website for details – and for private and school parties by appointment*

4 Overbeck's Museum and Garden

An exotic garden leads down from steep terraces through fuchsias, banana palms, ginger lilies and a rare camphor tree.

Sharpitor, Salcombe TQ8 8LW.

Tel: 01548 842893

overbecks@nationaltrust.org.uk

Historic Garden Grade II*/The National Trust

LOCATION 1½ miles S of Salcombe, SW of South Sands

The palms that grow in this 7 acre garden high above the Salcombe estuary give it a Mediterranean atmosphere. The mild maritime climate encourages exotics such as myrtles, daturas, agaves and a rare camphor tree, *Cinnamomum camphora*. A century-old *Magnolia campbellii* 'Overbeck's', 12m high and wide, is a sight to see in February and March. The steep terraces were built in 1901 and lead down through fuchsia trees, huge fruiting banana palms and ginger lilies to a *Cornus kousa*.

In the centre of the garden, four beds packed with herbaceous perennials, many of them rare and tender, flower from July to September. The parterre of classical design is enlivened in season by orange and lemon trees. The range of unusual and exotic plants is being extended and some of the more hidden areas at the perimeters of the garden made more accessible.
▶ *Open main season – telephone for details*

5 The Garden House

Follow winding paths within the Long Walk to see South African and quarry gardens, an acer glade, birch wood and bulb meadow.

Buckland Monachorum, Yelverton PL20 7LQ

Tel: 01822 854769

www.thegardenhouse.org.uk

LOCATION 10 miles N of Plymouth, 2 miles W of Yelverton off A386

Originally a 2 acre walled enclosure centred around the ruins of a medieval vicarage, the garden was first developed in the 1940s by Lionel Fortescue. He breathed life into its then-derelict terraces, selecting and combining a diverse range of plants and introducing a number of his own varieties of rhododendrons and mahonias.

From 1978, 6 acres of adjacent pasture were transformed into the Long Walk, a garden laid out with winding paths and spectacular vistas. Within this are South African and quarry gardens, a cottage garden and meadow, an acer glade, a birch wood and a bulb meadow. The pioneering planting style known as new naturalism is inspired by natural plant communities in the UK and further afield and features choice trees and shrubs underplanted with thousands of perennials and bulbs.

The garden is now in the hands of the head gardener, who has instigated a programme of replanting and refurbishment that began with the front lawns and South African garden, and now continues in the walled garden and Long Walk. The plant centre offers a wide range of plants to be seen growing in the garden.
▶ *Open March to Oct, daily (10.30am–5pm)*

6 Docton Mill Gardens

Developed over the past 80 years, this woodland garden now has a renowned bog garden and wild-flower gardens.

Lymebridge, Hartland EX39 6EA

Tel: 01237 441369

www.doctonmill.co.uk

LOCATION 14 miles W of Bideford, 12 miles N of Bude off A39. From north Devon travel via Hartland to Stoke or from north Cornwall to West Country Inn, then turn left signed to Elmscott towards Lymebridge in Spekes Valley

Rescued and revived by three sets of committed gardeners, the 9 acre woodland water garden has led a charmed existence since the 1930s.

The Grade II–listed water mill of Saxon origin is hidden away at the bottom of the valley, overlooked by forest trees on one side and a hillside on the other, with stream, ponds and leats making themselves heard throughout the garden. The present owners have continued the woodland tree planting that has enriched the natural landscape, and have also created the one large open space in the whole place: an old donkey paddock, transformed into a magnolia garden with 25 different varieties planted in lawn and fringed by generous herbaceous borders.

In spring, there are displays of narcissi, primulas, camellias, rhododendrons and azaleas, with bluebells carpeting the woods; in summer, the garden is filled with roses, including a bank of 'Felicia' and 'Pax' flanked by another herbaceous border. It is a tranquil place to wander through, absorbing the sounds, scents and shady paths.
▶ *Open main season – telephone or consult website for details*

7 RHS Garden Rosemoor

The south-western outpost of the RHS has striking display gardens and more than 200 rose varieties in bloom in summer.

Great Torrington EX38 8PH | Tel: 01805 624067

www.rhs.org.uk/rosemoor

LOCATION 7 miles SE of Bideford, 1 mile SE of Great Torrington on A3124

Rosemoor was the Royal Horticultural Society's first regional garden, second in importance only to Wisley. Lady Anne Berry created the garden here and the original 8 acres contain more than 3,500 plants from all over the world, many of them collected by her. The 65 acres include a formal garden with 2,000 roses in 200 varieties, colour-themed gardens, a herb garden, a potager, cottage, foliage and winter gardens, an alpine terrace, three model gardens, extensive herbaceous borders. There is also a garden designed by Tom Stuart-Smith with a range of plants grown for their leaves, particularly grasses.

The 18th-century gazebo from the grounds of Palmer House in Great Torrington has been reconstructed in the south arboretum, giving fine views across the garden and the valley. Elsewhere are stream and bog gardens and a large walled fruit and vegetable garden. National Collections of ilex (more than 100 varieties) and cornus are planted throughout.

Lectures, demonstrations, talks and garden walks are held throughout the year.
▶ *Open all year – telephone or consult website for details*

8 Marwood Hill

A crumbling walled garden and pastureland has been transformed into a horticultural paradise with many rare species.

Marwood, Barnstaple EX3 4EB

Tel: 01271 342528

www.marwoodhillgarden.co.uk

LOCATION 4m NW of Barnstaple off A361. Signposted

While the number and range of rare and unusual species amassed in the 20 acres here by the late Dr Smart, who developed the garden from 1949 onward will be of interest to the connoisseur, the impressive trees and setting cannot fail to give pleasure to any visitor. The 5,000 varieties of plants cover collections of willows, ferns, magnolias, eucryphias, rhododendrons and hebes, and many eucalyptus and betulas.

A glasshouse shelters camellias, and other features include a pergola draped with 12 varieties of wisteria, raised alpine scree beds, three small lakes with an extensive bog garden and National Collections of astilbes, clematis, *Iris ensata* and tulbaghias. The garden continues to evolve; new prairie-style plantings of herbaceous perennials, grasses and wild flowers are being developed in a further few acres.

▶ *Open all year — telephone or consult website for details*

9 Castle Hill

Set in a steep valley, the tranquil parkland and woodland areas have been enhanced in recent years by the Millennium Garden.

Filleigh, Barnstaple EX32 0RQ

Tel: 01598 760336 Ext.1

www.castlehilldevon.co.uk

Historic Garden Grade I

LOCATION 7 miles SE of Barnstaple, 19 miles NW of Tiverton off A361. Leave A361 at roundabout after South Molton, heading for Filleigh. Take second right, then after 2½ miles turn right into drive at yellow lodge

The 18th-century landscape garden and park leading away from the Palladian house were created by the 1st Lord Fortescue in 1730 with temples, follies, ponds and, across the valley, a triumphal arch. The unique feature of this landscape is its beautiful valley with steep, rounded hills swooping down to a winding river and up to the castellated folly. The woodland garden shelters magnolias, camellias, rhododendrons, azaleas, a 2 acre daffodil wood and thousands of bulbs. There are also some renowned trees in the Easter Close.

The Millennium Garden by garden designer Xa Tollemache has herbaceous borders planted with lilies, agapanthus, phlox and penstemons edged with box and lavender in gentle curves lining gravel paths. There is an avenue of formal clipped *Quercus ilex* underplanted with *Viburnum tinus* and a water sculpture by artist Giles Rayner.

▶ *Open main season — telephone or consult website for details*

10 Heddon Hall

Featuring imaginative combinations of plants, the garden is awash with colour throughout the gardening year.

Parracombe EX31 4QL | Tel: 01598 763541

www.heddonhallgardens.co.uk

LOCATION 10 miles NE of Barnstaple off A39. Follow A39 towards Lynton, around Parracombe, then turn left to village; entrance 200m on left

In a valley with views of Exmoor, the 4 acre Georgian rectory garden was renovated in the mid 1980s by plantswoman Jane Keatley. Through the cobbled courtyard lies a walled garden with a formal design of box hedges and cordon fruit trees designed by garden writer and designer Penelope Hobhouse; the combination of flowers, fruit, herbs and vegetables between the intricate hedges is the work of *Gardener's World* presenter Carol Klein. Next door, in the rose garden, cordoned and pleached limes line colour-themed beds planted with unusual herbaceous plants brought back from various seed-collecting trips.

On the steeply sloped Himalayan bank bulbs and shade-loving plants, including many unusual epimediums, flower beneath rhododendrons, azaleas, camellias and acers. The young River Heddon flows first through the water garden and then into three ancient stew ponds separated by cascades; a rhododendron tunnel has been planted alongside, and a further bed of rhododendrons includes *R. sinogrande* and *R. rex* subsp. *fictolacteum*.

Snowdrops and hellebores start the gardening year, followed by magnolias, rhododendrons, new English and shrub roses, going out in a blaze of foliage colour from the large collection of specimen acers in the arboretum.

▶ *Open Feb for hellebores and snowdrops; then main season — telephone or consult website for details, and for parties by appointment*

SOUTHWEST ENGLAND

11 Knightshayes

Woodland adjoins formal gardens with animal topiary, and a walled Victorian garden produces fruit and vegetables.

Bolham, Tiverton EX16 7RQ

Tel: 01884 253264 (Garden Office)

www.nationaltrust.org.uk

Historic Garden Grade II*/The National Trust

LOCATION 16 miles N of Exeter, 2 miles N of Tiverton. Turn off A396 at Bolham

The most memorable part of Knightshayes is the Garden in the Wood, an extensive woodland sheltering magnolias, rhododendrons, cornus, hydrangeas and other rare and tender plants, where drifts of pink erythroniums, white foxgloves and cyclamen appear in their seasons. Near the house the terraces are planted with shrub roses, tree peonies and herbaceous plants in silvers and soft colours, and yews enclose a paved garden softened by pink, purple and grey flowers and two standard wisterias. Battlemented hedges frame the pool garden with a backdrop of *Acer pseudoplatanus* 'Brilliantissimum', and topiary hounds endlessly chase a fox on a lower terrace.

The garden and landscaping were originally planned in the late 1870s, but it remained essentially unchanged until Sir John and Lady Amory began replanting in the 1950s. Now the Victorian walled kitchen garden, constructed in tiers with a central ornamental pool, once again provides organic vegetables, fruit and cut flowers.
▶ *House open. Garden open most of year – telephone or consult website for details – and for NGS*

12 Holbrook Garden

Despite heavy clay soil, a host of different habitats have been created that can support the owners' favoured plants.

Sampford Peverell, Tiverton EX16 7EN

Tel: 01884 821164

www.holbrookgarden.com

LOCATION 1 mile NW from M5 junction 27, follow brown signs to Minnows camping site. Garden 300m up Holbrook Hill

In this imaginative 2 acre garden, the owners have recreated the conditions of their favourite plants – a sun-baked mountain track in southern Europe surrounded by *Asphodelius albus*, the lush hills and valleys of the Azores dominated by 2m tall euphorbias and a meadow dotted with tall perennials from across the temperate world. They manipulate habitats to suit the plants, using lots of gravel and stone to reduce humidity and increase the temperature range, and mulching with chopped bark to mimic a woodland floor.

In the stone garden all the plants are self-supporting, starting with small tulips and mountain bulbs, until in late summer the path winds through a 'prairie' of *Ratabida pinnata*, *Salvia uliginosa*, *Rudbeckia subtomentosa* and tall pennisetum grasses. The wet garden is full of irises and primulas, evolving with heleniums (a National Collection) and the late-flowering teasel *Dipsacus inermis* and molinia grasses. The pink garden peaks in July with phloxes, *Filipendula rubra venusta* and Eupatorium 'Riesenschirm'.
▶ *Open main season (telephone or consult website for details), and for NGS*

13 Killerton

An abundance of rhododendrons give the garden its colour, but trees give character, including England's first Wellingtonias.

Broadclyst, Exeter EX5 3LE │ Tel: 01392 881345

www.nationaltrust.org.uk/killerton

Historic Garden Grade II*/The National Trust

LOCATION 7m NE of Exeter on W side of B3181

Surrounded by 6,000 acres of woodland, parkland and farmland, the 18 acre hillside garden was created in the late 18th century. The orange-washed Regency house, hung in summer with purple wisteria and the pale yellow *Rosa banksiae* 'Lutea', makes the most of its views. Near the house is a wide terrace planted with Mediterranean shrubs, a fern *allée*, generous herbaceous borders and island beds; then the land slopes upwards, laid first to lawn planted with bold foliage clumps and groupings before merging into woodland and meadow.

There are 95 species of rhododendrons, many brought from China and Japan, but it is the number and size of the trees – an avenue of beeches, the first Wellingtonias to be planted in England, cedars, conifers, oaks, maples and others – that give the garden its majesty and character.

A charming thatched wooden Hansel and Gretel summerhouse and the Bear's Hut, made from a ragbag collection of artefacts, stands near the ice-house, and the impressive early 20th-century rock garden nearby is being renovated using Himalayan plants.

Peat-free plants for sale in the plant centre have been propagated at the nursery on the estate.
▶ *Park and garden open all year – telephone or consult website for details*

14 Sherwood

The garden is not to be missed in spring, when National Collections of azaleas, magnolias and berberis are in bloom.

Newton St Cyres, Exeter EX5 5BT

Tel: 01392 851216

LOCATION 2 miles SE of Crediton, off A377

Created by the present owners – plant enthusiasts with a passion for learning – the 15 acre garden sits astride two narrow valleys. Woodland paths along the hillsides give unusual perspectives.

The profusion of woodland plants includes more than 500 rhododendrons and National Collections of Knap Hill azaleas, magnolias and berberis, cascading down the steep hillside. Camellias, buddleias, cotoneasters, hydrangeas, cornus, acers, a large heather bank and swathes of wild daffodils help to ensure interest from spring to autumn. After clearance of overgrown laurels another area further down has been planted with epimediums and shade-loving woodland perennials beneath a canopy of ash and oak.

▶ *Open all year – telephone or consult website for details – and for NGS*

15 Burrow Farm Gardens

Over the past 40 years, Mary Benger has created gardens that encompass lawns and borders, woodland and varieties of old rose.

Dalwood, Axminster EX13 7ET

Tel: 01404 831285

www.burrowfarmgardens.co.uk

LOCATION 4 miles W of Axminster off A35

In these 10 acre gardens, an array of azaleas and rhododendrons produce a striking display of colour and foliage. A former Roman clay pit is graded from top to bottom through mature trees and shrubs to an extensive bog garden with a marvellous show of candelabra primulas and native wild flowers from early in the season.

In summer, the pergola walk with its old-fashioned roses and herbaceous borders is a picture, and a courtyard garden and a terraced garden feature late-flowering herbaceous plants. The rill garden has ponds, a classical summerhouse and a ha-ha laid out in a formal design. An azalea glade looks down past a thatched summerhouse towards the lake surrounded by cultivated and wild flowers.

▶ *Open main season – telephone or consult website for details*

BURROW FARM GARDENS

SOUTHWEST ENGLAND

16 Bicton Park Botanical Gardens

The sweeping grounds at Bicton encompass nearly 300 years of garden history including a 180-year-old palm house.

East Budleigh, Budleigh Salterton EX9 7BJ

Tel: 01395 568465

www.bictongardens.co.uk

Historic Garden Grade I

LOCATION 2 miles N of Budleigh Salterton on B3178

Bicton's greatest glory is its palm house, built between 1825 and 1830 and one of the oldest in the country. Cacti and other succulents grow in a naturalistic desert-like landscape in the arid house, and one of Britain's earliest Victorian ferneries has been re-established among the rocks around the shell house; there is also a temperate house and a tropical house for orchids, bananas, bromeliads, figs and bougainvilleas. The formal and informal gardens date from around 1735.

The 64 acres also include a stream garden with a 150-year-old mulberry, collections of azaleas, camellias and flowering cherries, herbaceous borders set against magnolia-clad walls, an American garden established in the 1830s, and a hermitage garden with a lake and water features. The pinetum, first planted in 1839 and extended in 1910 to take the collection of the botanist 'Chinese' Wilson, has rare conifers, including the tallest Grecian fir ever recorded at 41m (135ft).

The Countryside Museum houses a collection of farm machinery, tools and craft exhibits, reflecting changes in rural life since the 1700s.

▶ *Open all year – telephone or consult website for details*

17 Castle Drogo

Set above the Teign Gorge, the formal gardens have fine views over Dartmoor. The rhododendron garden dates from the 1940s.

Drewsteignton EX6 6PB | Tel: 01647 433306

www.nationaltrust.org.uk

Historic Garden Grade II*/The National Trust

LOCATION 5 miles S of A30 or 4 miles NW of Moretonhampstead on A382; follow signs from Sandy Park

The 12 acres at Drogo – the last castle to be built in England and, at 275m (900ft), the National Trust's highest garden – are a testament to the vision of George Dillistone, whose planting skills and stately shelter belts enabled him to create one of the region's most spectacular formal gardens.

At the lower end the view from the rose garden provides the unusual sight of herbaceous borders raised to eye level on top of local granite walls. Curved paths wind between extensively planted beds, while in each corner imposing arbours roofed with *Parrotia persica* are peaceful and secluded. Graceful stone steps and neat gravel paths lead through wisterias, unusually planted as a screen, and along borders of maples and

CASTLE DROGO

spring-flowering shrubs up to the round croquet lawn, surrounded by a tall yew hedge. Beneath the castle, rhododendrons, azaleas, magnolias, cornus and native woodland tumble down from the stone ramparts, from where there are fine views of the distant moor.

▶ *Castle and garden open main season – telephone or consult website for details*

18 Gidleigh Park Hotel

Formal terraced lawns surround the house, leading into a tree-lined landscape set against a backdrop of moorland.

Chagford TQ13 8HH | Tel: 01647 432367

www.gidleigh.com

LOCATION Off A382 11 miles SE of Okehampton. In Chagford Square turn right into Mill Street. After 150m fork right and go to end of road

Set in over 54 acres of secluded grounds and woodland, the mock-Tudor house is surrounded by manicured terraced lawns. Beyond them, azaleas, acers and pieris melt away beneath a canopy of native trees up steep hillsides towards the moor. The recently completed kitchen garden is laid out on semi-circular, granite walled terraces. Neat rows of vegetables radiate out like the spokes of a giant wheel, at the centre of which is an elegant menhir surrounded by herbs.

Below the house, terraces drop away to the North Teign river. Across the bridge are two croquet lawns and an 18 hole putting green. The boundary walk winds its way through the woods, past still ponds and the river. Paths through natural mixed woodland, underplanted with spring bulbs and bluebells, wander up above the house giving striking views of the Dartmoor hills.

▶ *Open most of the year – telephone or consult website for details*

19 Hamblyn's Coombe

On open lawns, topiary and snaking yew hedges complement the owner's sculptures, while foliage predominates elsewhere.

Dittisham TQ6 0HE | Tel: 01803 722228

www.bridgetmccrum.com

LOCATION Between Totnes and Dartmouth off A3122

A unique sculpture garden, with all the works on display carved by the owner. Bridget McCrum and her late husband Robert – a knowledgeable

and inventive gardener – found their 1837 workman's cottage, with its superb setting in a wooded valley of the River Dart, in 1984. They started fashioning a small part of the 7 acres into a garden, leaving the rest as woodland and a wild-flower field running down to the water's edge. Camellias, wild flowers and tree ferns are to be found beside the stream and gently sloping paths in the woodland, but this is above all a foliage garden, with an abundance of different textures and shades of green.

The works on show stand on lawns and in a gravel garden, with topiary and snaking, mounded or fastigiated yew hedges acting as living statues. Some of these, including a row of birds floating in an overflowing bowl, are permanent, but most are temporary residents.

▶ *Open for NGS Sept to June by appointment*

20 Dartington Hall

A strongly architectural garden, that has tiltyard and terraces at its heart, it changes colour with the seasons.

Dartington, Totnes TQ9 6EL | Tel: 01803 862367

www.dartingtonhall.com

Historic Garden Grade II*

LOCATION 2 miles NW of Totnes, E of A384. In Dartington, turn left past church (from London and north) or right before church (from west)

Standing at the crest of its sheltering combe and commanding a green tiltyard, the 28 acre garden is an astonishing piece of theatre. Twelve Irish yews in apostolic procession face a wall of tall and narrow turfed terraces, crowned by a line of chestnut trees and a majestic Henry Moore *Reclining Figure* in Hornton stone. Low, clipped yew screens close the triangle, and a grand stone staircase leads to the upper level. A glade and an azalea dell have been planted, the courtyard transformed and woodland walkways opened up.

There are three walks, each using yew and holly as background plantings for collections of camellias, magnolias and rhododendrons. More recently, the sunny herbaceous border has been redesigned in quiet shades of cream, blue and purple, a Japanese garden has been laid out and the forecourt entrance rationalised.

Over the seasons, the spotlight of colour sweeps around the garden, but the overall effect is strongly architectural, with the tiltyard and terraces at the heart of the garden.

▶ *Open all year – telephone or consult website for details; parties by appointment only*

The fads and fashions of fruit

Far more than just a food,
over the years fruit has been
a symbol of horticultural skill,
political ambition and fashion.

In 1609, spurred by the growing prosperity of the silk industry in France, England's James I ordered thousands of mulberry trees from the continent. His aim was to establish a rival industry in England that would increase 'wealth and abundance' for all. Landowners keen to demonstrate their loyalty set to work, planting in support of the king's ambition, while James himself created a mulberry plantation in London on the site that is now Buckingham Palace. But someone had blundered: silk worms eat only the leaves of the white-berried mulberry, and the imported trees bore luscious black fruit. Around England some of these ancient and erroneous exemplars can still be found, leaning on their elbows or supported by stout props, still bearing the delicious berries.

For the good of all

Social reformers had similar intentions. In the 17th century, Samuel Hartlib idealistically proposed that all waste land in England should be planted with fruit and nut trees 'for the relief of the poor, the benefit of the rich and the delight of all'. Three hundred years later, George Cadbury had fruit trees planted in the workers' gardens at his Bournville model village near Birmingham in 1900. Henrietta Barnet, meanwhile, a moving spirit behind Hampstead Garden Suburb in 1907, followed suit by insisting that every garden in the suburb had an apple tree.

The apple, the most quintessentially English of fruits, has been enjoyed by all social classes from the 15th century onwards, along with pears, plums, quinces, cherries and all kinds of berries and nuts. At Lyveden New Bield in Northamptonshire, the old Elizabethan orchard has been replanted with authentic varieties with evocative names such as Catshead, Doctor Harvey, Shepherd's Bullace and Winter Queening.

For some sectors of society, simply planting fruit trees was not enough. In the 16th century, Southeast England saw a massive influx of Huguenots, Protestant reformers whose beliefs were at odds with the Catholic majority of their native France. Some refugees were nurserymen

WEST DEAN

by trade, and they developed techniques for dwarfing and training trees into espaliers, goblets and fan shapes, forcing them to grow flat against walls. This made the most of light and warmth to ripen fruit, incidentally producing elegant shapes. It became the standard way of growing fruit, especially the more delicate varieties, using south-facing walls, often heated by flues built into the wall. Penshurst Place in Kent, whose walled garden dates back to the 14th century, has fine wall-trained fruit trees, as does West Dean in Sussex, where there is a beautiful pear tunnel as well as espaliered fruit.

Growing under glass

In the 18th century, developing glasshouse technology was used to grow ever more exotic fruit. A well-to-do family would expect to have fresh fruit on the dining table every day of the year, in and out of season – forced strawberries, bunches of some of the 100 available varieties of grapes, and figs that were coaxed into producing two or even three crops a year. But the 'king of fruits' was the pineapple – native to the Brazilian rainforest and unsuitable for growing outdoors in Britain. By the 1730s it was to be found in the gardens of anyone who was anyone.

Every head gardener had his own special method, but essentially pineapples were grown in carefully ventilated, glass-covered pits heated from beneath by fermenting manure, and later by steam. George IV reputedly had a 5kg (10lb 8oz) pineapple at his coronation banquet in 1821. It took an army of gardeners to support this luxury. Boilers had to be stoked – through the night in cold weather – and manure barrowed by the under-gardeners and apprentice boys who lived on site in the 'bothy'.

Such horticultural extravagance did not last. By the 1920s social change, the loss of gardeners in the First World War, the growth of commercial market gardens and imported exotic fruits led to the gardens' rapid decline. Traces of these glory days can be seen in the kitchen gardens at West Dean and at Heligan in Cornwall, where passion fruit, guavas, nectarines and figs are produced in restored pineapple pits and peach houses.

Exotics, however, are still grown today. Goji berries from the Himalayas, blueberries and Aronia from North America are popular for their reputed health properties. With climate change, olives, grown for some time in Southern England as decorative trees, are being considered as a possible crop, while outdoor vines are promoted not just for their wonderful autumn colour but for edible grapes. Kiwi fruit, originally from China, will ripen on a sheltered south-facing wall. Fruit is still fashionable.

A FINE EXAMPLE OF A FORMAL COUNTRY-HOUSE GARDEN

KINGSTON LACY

DORSET

The rugged terrain of the county's steep-sided coombs provides a challenge for Dorset's garden designers, while on gentler ground, handsome manors boast an abundance of fine formal gardens.

1 Kingston Lacy

The gardens surrounding the house reflect a variety of influences, from Egypt to Japan, along with the fernery – a Victorian passion.

Wimborne Minster BH21 4EA

Tel: 01202 883402 | www.nationaltrust.org.uk

Historic Garden Grade II/The National Trust

LOCATION 1½ miles NW of Wimborne on B3082

This is a fine example of a formal country-house garden. Although strongly Victorian in character, the lime avenue – which leads to the Nursery Wood and its colourful collection of rhododendrons and azaleas – was planted in 1668. The terrace displays urns, vases and interesting lions in bronze and marble, as well as an Egyptian obelisk and sarcophagus. The parterre was laid out in 1899 for the house's Edwardian owner Henrietta Bankes in memory of her husband and is still planted in the seasonal bedding schemes designed for her. The Victorian fernery, with 25 different types of fern and a National Collection of *Anemone nemorosa*, leads to the cedar walk.

Snowdrops, daffodils and bluebells abound in spring, and in summer the roses are spectacular. The restored Japanese gardens lie in 7½ acres of the southern shelterbelt; originally laid out in about 1910, they are the largest of their kind in England. The garden holds National Collections of convallarias and anemones.

▶ *House open main season; park and garden open most of year – telephone or consult website for details*

2 Knoll Gardens

With more than 800 grasses, Knoll shows the many ways that they can be displayed, with perennials in a supporting role.

Hampreston, Wimborne Minster BH21 7ND

Tel: 01202 873931 | www.knollgardens.co.uk

LOCATION Between Wimborne and Ferndown, off Ham Lane (B3073). Leave A31 at Canford Bottom roundabout. Signed after 1½ miles

Always at the forefront of changing styles, the garden has become recognised as one of the country's most extensive collections of grasses.

National Collections of deciduous ceanothus, phygelius and pennisetums are also held here.

Planted within an informal English setting, the emphasis is on showing how grasses can work to best advantage with very little maintenance. Perennials play an increasingly important supporting role, combining with both grasses and native plants to create stunning displays and actively encourage wildlife into the garden while requiring minimum upkeep. They are displayed to great effect in the Dragon Garden and the Decennium Border, which is planted with more than 800 grasses and hardy perennials in a modern, naturalistic style.

There are also contrasting areas planted for dry shade and for moisture, a Mediterranean-style gravel garden and a small-scale meadow garden. Although only a little over 4 acres, the many different areas, winding pathways and constantly changing views make the garden seem far larger.

▶ *Open most of year – telephone or consult website for details*

3 Steeple Manor

Curved beech hedges, an *allée* of pleached limes and a crescent of yew create a sense of drama around the historic house.

Steeple, Wareham BH20 5PA

Tel: 01929 480709

LOCATION 5 miles south of Wareham, 1 mile north of Kimmeridge off A351

Set in a remote and lovely valley, and surrounding a historic house of Purbeck stone and slate, the garden was designed in 1923 by the pioneering landscape architect Brenda Colvin. It is one of only three complete gardens by her to have survived.

Colvin's practicality and aesthetic sensibility are shown from the start as two high beech hedges curve to embrace the parking circle and hide all vehicles from view. Streams from the bog garden drop to a rill in the formal lily pond garden where the flat, formally trained lime hedges are backed by escallonia, and from there to a meadow with ponds and trees, then to the countryside beyond.

The walled garden to the south has a terrace crammed with pots and urns of tender plants. The gate leads to a theatrical space where ▷

SOUTH-WEST ENGLAND

lawn is bordered by a crescent of yew backed by a taller hedge of beech, giving the layered effect beloved by today's *fashionistas*.

By extending the garden, the present owners have combined Colvin's rigour and sense of drama with generous and varied plantings of their own. The west borders are planted in shades of blue and white, while the raised grass terrace is punctuated by five-pillar cypresses. Primulas and irises are followed by the roses and clematis and, later, by *viticella* clematis, a profusion of dahlias, buddleias and much more, while the wall borders are filled with cistus, helianthemums, rosemary and salvias.

▶ *Open by written appointment only*

4 Kingston Maurward Gardens

A grand Edwardian garden overlooks the lake, with a Grecian temple and statuary loaned by the Palace of Westminster.

Dorchester DT2 8PY | Tel: 01305 215003

www.kmc.ac.uk/gardens

Historic Garden Grade II

LOCATION E of Dorchester off A35. Turn off at roundabout at end of bypass

Three distinct periods coexist harmoniously here. In 1720, the handsome house was built, dignified by a contemporary landscape park with 50 acres of fine trees, water and woodland. Then, between 1918 and 1920, the formal gardens to the west of the mansion were laid out by the Hanbury family. Within splendid stone terraces, balustrading, steps and yew hedges, they made a series of intimate enclosures, including water features, topiary, a yew maze and other requisites of a grand Edwardian garden. Positioned on a steep hillside overlooking an 8 acre lake, the views are outstanding.

The most recent phase has been a determined restoration since 1990 by the present incumbents, the staff and students of Kingston Maurward College. The formal gardens are resplendent once more, with National Collections of penstemons and salvias held here, together with a large collection of herbaceous perennials. In spring, drifts of bulbs occupy the sweeping lawns and the margins of the lake. Of particular interest is the statuary on long loan from the Palace of Westminster and the restored Grecian temple at the lake's edge.

There is also a Japanese-style garden with Chusan palms, bamboos and maples, a tree trail with 65 different species to discover, and an animal park for children.

▶ *Open most of year – telephone or consult website for details. Guided tours by appointment*

5 Athelhampton

Striking obelisk shaped yews surround the Great Court, while the river services pools, fountains and a canal lined with water lilies.

Athelhampton, Dorchester DT2 7LG.

Tel: 01305 848363 | www.athelhampton.co.uk

Historic Garden Grade I

LOCATION 5 miles NE of Dorchester, 1 mile E of Puddletown off A35 at Northbrook junction

Visitors will take away with them an abiding memory of some of the most stylish architectural topiary in England. Also, the River Piddle, which girdles the garden, has been cleverly harnessed within it to service pools, fountains and a long canal studded with water lilies.

The four gardens and two pavilions of the Tudor manor house were designed in 1891 by landscape designer F. Inigo Thomas, and the garden was extended with great sensitivity during the 1960s and 1970s. Courts and walls follow the original plan with beautiful stone and brickwork arches; a 15th-century dovecote on the lawn facing the west wing and a pleached lime walk behind the Pyramid Garden are major features. Here, 12 massive yews are fashioned to echo the obelisks on the raised terrace walk, which has a matching pair of pavilions at each end. The toll house to the south has been restored, and a raised boardwalk extends over 200m (650ft) along the river. The planting, including tulips, rambling roses, clematis and jasmine, is big boned, low key and sophisticated. A remarkable interpretation of the late-medieval ideal.

▶ *House open as garden but from 11am; gardens open all year – telephone or consult website for details*

6 Abbotsbury Subtropical Gardens

Set in 20 acres of a wooded valley, the sheltered aspect has fostered an exotic garden redolent of tropical climes.

Abbotsbury, Weymouth DT3 4LA

Tel: 01305 871387

www.abbotsbury-tourism.co.uk

Historic Garden Grade I

LOCATION 9 miles NW of Weymouth, 9 miles SW of Dorchester off B3157

Proximity to the sea and shelter from the north create the microclimate that has turned Abbotsbury into a botanical treasure trove.

The nucleus of the place is the walled garden established by the 1st Countess of Ilchester in 1765 as a kitchen garden for the castle, which burned down in 1913. In 1899, a catalogue of 5,000 plants was produced; today, there must be many more within the 30 acres, which has been restored and replanted over the past two decades.

Rare trees abound. A Mediterranean bank displays exotics from Australia, South Africa and Mexico, including proteas, banksias and olive trees. Bamboo groves, bog gardens, bananas from Ethiopia, masses of hydrangeas, azaleas, hostas and more can be seen on the woodland walk, where peacocks, golden pheasants and other exotic birds may be spotted among the trees. A waterside planting of primulas, hostas, rogersias and other moisture-lovers is maturing well. A new magnolia walk, 250m (820ft) long, leads out of the garden up to a high point giving spectacular views of the World Heritage Jurassic coast.

The nearby swannery at the eastern end of the village should not be missed.

▶ *Open all year – telephone or consult website for details*

7 Mapperton

From the great lawn, the gardens descend through formal topiary down to a woodland garden and the valley floor arboretum.

Beaminster DT8 3NR

Tel: 01308 862645

www.mapperton.com

Historic Garden Grade II

LOCATION 5 miles NE of Bridport, 2 miles SE of Beaminster between A356 and A3066

Dorset's coombs are famously intriguing, and Mapperton offers one of the county's most atmospheric gardens which is set into a unique stepped valley. It begins on the first of three levels with the courtyard garden at the front of the 16th and 17th-century manor house, which introduces a cast of old roses and clematis.

To the east, beyond the 17th-century house and below the main lawn, the land falls towards the Fountain Court with its sculptured topiary and Italianate features. Pools of water, carved stone steps, a pergola and massed Mediterranean borders face the classical orangery built by the current owner's father in 1968. A golden hamstone wall shows off a living wallpaper of pink *Erigeron karvinskianus* and a tree poppy, *Romneya coulteri*. The Baroque-inspired fountain, beautifully restored, is surrounded by box and yew to

evoke the original 1920s design. Below are deep fishponds that reflect walls of yew – with niches displaying evocative statuary – and the tower house rising above.

Down on the third level – the floor of the valley – is a small arboretum, which opens into the countryside beyond with views of cattle roaming. Throughout the visiting season, the gardens offer flower and leaf colour from the first magnificent pink flowers of *Magnolia campbellii* to the fruits and berries appearing in summer and early autumn in the valley garden.

Mapperton is a draw for garden lovers and for photographers and watercolourists in particular, because of the play of light across the planes of this extraordinary north-south valley.

▶ *House open. Garden open main season – telephone or consult website for details*

8 The Old Rectory, Netherbury

A formal courtyard garden with rose arch, yew *allée* and central fountain, drops to a bog garden and wild-flower meadow.

Netherbury DT6 5NB | Tel: 01308 488757

LOCATION 6 miles N of Bridport, 3 miles SW of Beaminster off A3066, next to parish church

Since 1994, the present owners have transformed a 5 acre pine forest into a marvellous amalgam of formal and wild spaces, sparing only some majestic oaks, a splendid ginkgo and other mature trees. They have divided up the valley beyond the house into a series of small gardens.

Heading out from an enclosed courtyard with box-edged beds and a central fountain, a series of paths create a processional way with a rose arch, four pairs of yew pyramids and a taller yew *allée*. To give variety and a change of rhythm, the central path changes from patterned cobbles to mown grass and back again. Blocks of *Geranium clarkei* 'Kashmir White', ribbons of *Iris pallida* var. *dalmatica* and other herbaceous perennials are used tellingly to add colour and lightness to each enclosure.

To the side of this formal layout the land drops sharply to the left, opening out to a bog garden threaded by a wandering stream, where irises, primulas, hostas and arum lilies carpet the ground, revelling in the moist conditions; a pointed-roofed summerhouse marks the transition to a wild-flower meadow.

To the east of the house is a well-stocked kitchen garden with a castellated hedge leading the eye to the church tower at the far end.

▶ *Open for NGS*

SOUTH WEST ENGLAND

9 Forde Abbey

The gardens are full of interest, from Victorian lawns and yews to the monks' Great Pond and an impressive fountain.

Chard TA20 4LU | Tel: 01460 221290

www.fordeabbey.co.uk

Historic Garden Grade II*

LOCATION 8 miles NW of Beaminster, 7 miles W of Crewkerne, 4 miles SE of Chard off A30

This former Cistercian abbey, inhabited as a private house since acquiring a castellated face-lift in 1649, is set in a varied and attractive garden.

An early 18th-century canal at the end of the long and stately range of abbey buildings, lime and walnut avenues and a large lake some distance away are major features of the garden, which extends over 30 acres. Old walls and colourful borders, sloping lawns, ponds (don't miss the unusual pleached beech pavilion overlooking the Great Pond), graceful statuary and huge mature trees combine to create an atmosphere of timeless elegance. The Centenary Fountain with a jet that spurts 50m (164ft) into the air celebrates the Roper family's 100 years in residence.

The bog garden, at its peak in July, displays a large collection of primulas and other Asiatic plants; the shrubbery contains rhododendrons, magnolias, and other lovely specimens; the rock garden has a magnificent display of cyclamen coum and naturalised widow iris in spring; and a fine arboretum has been built up since 1947.

At the back of the abbey is an extensive walled kitchen garden and a nursery selling rare and unusual plants.

▶ *House open. Garden open all year – telephone or consult website for details*

10 Stanbridge Mill

The stylish gardens with iris and herbaceous borders, a white walk and wisteria-clad pergola were created in the 1990s.

Gussage All Saints BH21 5EP

Tel: 01258 841067

LOCATION 7 miles N of Wimborne on B3078 Cranborne Road

Designed in its initial stages in the 1990s by Chelsea Flower Show 'Best Garden' winner Arabella Lennox-Boyd, with sensitive later additions by the present owner and head gardener, the summer visitor is greeted with clouds of white oxeye daisies on either side of

the drive. This wild theme prevails throughout. Extensive water meadows, managed as a nature reserve, attract bird life and wild flowers, and grass drives meander alongside streams towards an elegant thatched summerhouse.

The house, formerly a water mill, is surrounded by more formal areas although the millstream remains a key part of the design. A particular feature is the Mound Garden, from where tiers of hedges – ranging from diminutive box through yew and beech to pleached lime – lead up to a higher level with a swimming pool and pavilion. The design is rectangular, with clever planting edged by neat box.

A white-flowered *allée* lies beneath a series of iron archways and the ensuing wisteria walk with herbaceous borders stretches for some 60m (197ft). Everything is well maintained and shown off to perfection by paving and steps created in patterns by up-ended tiles, flints and bricks.

▶ *Open for NGS, and for parties of five or more by written appointment*

CRANBORNE MANOR GARDEN

11 Cranborne Manor Garden

Set around this ancient manor are a series of themed gardens, some of them formal 'rooms', others more casual and naturalistic.

Cranborne, Wimborne Minster BH21 5PP

Tel: 01725 517248

www.cranborne.co.uk

Historic Garden Grade II*

LOCATION 10 miles N of Wimborne on B3078. Entrance via garden centre

Surrounding what has been called 'the most magical house in Dorset', this garden embraces the visitor with its secrecy and charm. John Tradescant, a former keeper of Chelsea Physic Garden, established the basic framework in the early 17th century, but little remains of his work. The past four generations of the family who own the Manor have rectified a long period of neglect and stamped their own imprint on the garden as they developed certain areas, altered others, replanted borders and created new vistas. Clipped yew hedges surround formal beds and a large croquet lawn to the west, and the walled north garden is planted with white flowers and shrubs.

Approached through two Jacobean gatehouses (sometimes closed), the high-walled entrance courtyard to the south has a circular lawn on which a fountain by leading British sculptor Angela Connor sits, surrounded on all four sides by shrubs and old-fashioned flowers.

The long grass on either side of the south drive contains a thriving collection of orchids throughout the early part of summer and leads through three more yew-lined rooms to the garden centre and car park. The excellent nursery specialises in traditional rose varieties and carries a wide selection of clematis, herbaceous perennials and flowering shrubs.

▶ *Open main season – telephone or check website for details – for NGS, and some weekends for charity*

SOMERSET

Several celebrated garden designers have left their mark in this county, where traditional, formal designs mix with imaginative, contemporary planting, often set in dramatic landscapes.

1 Yews Farm

A blank canvas in 1996, this garden is now a contemporary design that focuses on tall plants – often in unusual combinations.

East Street, Martock TA12 6NF

Tel: 01935 822202

LOCATION 6 miles NW of Yeovil off A303. Turn off main street through village at Market House onto East Street; garden is 150m on right after post office

Located on the edge of the Somerset Levels in the small, picturesque town of Martock, this dramatic garden lies behind a 13th-century cruck-framed house. Surrounded by walls and buildings built using golden Hamstone and sheltered by its setting, it has a strong outline set off by a long season of natural plantings, mainly of perennials.

Inspired by shape, height and texture, block planting in a restricted but imaginative palette has been used to achieve skilful effects, with colourful head-high plants complemented by self-seeding and formal clipped box shapes.

The heavy accent on soil fertility comes courtesy of the farmyard pigs and chickens, with the healthy and intensive plantings and superb organic vegetable garden as proof of its benefits. Visitors leave with memories of a contemporary garden of personal inspiration and discovery.
▶ *Open June-Aug for parties of 15 or more by appointment*

2 Wayford Manor

A formal upper terrace leads down to an Edwardian loggia before descending to a rockery and woodland below.

Crewkerne TA18 8QG | Tel: 01460 73253

Historic Garden Grade II

LOCATION 3 miles SW of Crewkerne off B3165 at Clapton

The 4 acres of south-facing, multi-layered gardens surrounding the manor house (13th century with Elizabethan and Victorian additions) are a fine example of the work of Edwardian landscape designer Harold Peto, who redesigned them in 1902. The formal upper terrace with yew hedges and topiary fronting the house has panoramic views over west Dorset. Steps down to the second terrace lead to a new stone-pillared pergola complementing the loggia designed by Peto, which in turn complemented the Elizabethan porch to the house.

Below the rockery and grass tennis court is an area of semi-wild woodland gardens planted with a variety of mature trees and shrubs, including fine maples, cornus, magnolias, rhododendrons and spring bulbs. Colourful displays of candelabra primulas, arum lilies, gunneras and other moisture-lovers fringe the lower ponds. Natural spring water is used throughout, and widespread planting continues apace.
▶ *Open for NGS and for parties of ten or more by appointment at other times*

COTHAY MANOR

3 Cothay Manor

Many garden rooms and a river walk in the grounds of the ancient manor are shown off to best advantage in summer.

Greenham, Wellington TA21 0JR

Tel: 01823 672283

www.cothaymanor.co.uk

LOCATION 5 miles W of Wellington. From west (M5 junction 27), take A38 signed to Wellington then, after 3½ miles, turn left to Greenham. From north (junction 26), take Wellington exit; at roundabout take A38 signed to Exeter. After 3½ miles turn right to Greenham (1½ miles) and right again on left-hand corner at bottom of hill. House is 1 mile further

There can be few more evocative settings for a historic house than the 15 acres of garden and wild-flower meadows that surround the medieval manor of Cothay. The gardens were laid out in the 1920s, with the original 200m (656ft) long, yew-hedged walk still forming the backbone of the present layout.

During the 1990s, the present owners remade the garden as a series of rooms and courts within the original framework, each with a different character and atmosphere – from the Bishop's Room, where the colour scheme of reds and purples reflects the rich fabric of episcopal robes, to the Green Knight Garden, which is essentially a white garden. The planting everywhere is discerning and sensitive, revealing a keen sympathy for old and well-loved shrubs and climbers. At every turn there is a new delight, from the stone-paved terrace bursting with flowers and foliage (including a large wisteria umbrella) and many imaginatively planted pots, to formal pools, a cool shady enclosure with ferns, exuberant herbaceous beds and avenues of decorative trees.

Beyond the formal *enfilade* of rooms, a quietly flowing river weaves through mature trees and long grass, and a bog garden made from an old river course is lushly planted with lysichitons, gunneras and other waterside plants. The wild-flower meadow, sprinkled with tulips and camassias in season, rises to a little hill with mown paths that spiral to its summit – the perfect spot for an overview of the ancient house and its imaginative setting.

▶ *House open for parties by appointment. Garden open main season – telephone or consult website for details – and for parties by appointment*

4 Greencombe

In a dramatic setting that overlooks Porlock Bay, this colourful organic garden includes immaculate beds and an ancient woodland.

Porlock TA24 8NU

Tel: 01643 862363

LOCATION 7½ miles W of Minehead, ½ mile W of Porlock off B3225

Set on a dark hillside overlooking the Bristol Channel, the garden glows with colour, especially in spring and summer.

Created in 1946, it has been extended by the present knowledgeable owner over the past three decades. The formal lawns and beds round the house are immaculate, brimming with roses, lilies, hydrangeas, maples and camellias.

The woodland area, which is traversed via a maze of narrow paths, offers attractions of a different character; here, a wide variety of rhododendrons and azaleas flowers in the shelter provided by mature trees, and ferns and woodland plants flourish.

No sprays or chemicals are used in the cultivation of this garden, which is run on organic principles, and contains National Collections of erythroniums, gaultherias, polystichums and vacciniums.

▶ *Open main season – telephone for details*

5 Hestercombe Gardens

A Georgian landscape garden, Victorian terrace and Edwardian formal garden reflect three eras of garden design history.

Cheddon Fitzpaine, Taunton TA2 8LG

Tel: 01823 413923

www.hestercombe.com

Historic Garden Grade I

LOCATION 4 miles NE of Taunton off A361, just N of Cheddon Fitzpaine. Signposted

This is a superb product of the collaboration between legendary garden designers Edwin Lutyens and Gertrude Jekyll between 1904 and 1908, blending the formal art of architecture with the art of planting. The detailed design of steps, pools, walls, paving and seating is Lutyens at his most accomplished, and the rills, pergola and orangery are also fine examples of his work. Replanting in the formal garden continues as closely as possible to mirror Jekyll's original plans.

To the north of the house are the landscaped gardens of the Combe, a splendid example of 18th-century pleasure grounds that were laid out two centuries earlier than the main gardens; they remained unchanged until the timber was felled in the 1960s. Major work has also been undertaken in the glorious parkland designed between 1750 and 1786 by garden designer

Coplestone Warre Bampfylde, including the restoration of his Great Cascade.

The Victorian terrace is once again planted twice a year, and the shrubbery – created in around 1880 in the style of Arts and Crafts advocate William Robinson – has also been restored to incorporate a 19th-century yew tunnel with views towards a Victorian tower.

Other features of interest are the Doric temple, the Gothic alcove, the octagonal summerhouse and the Chinese seat – which commands views of Taunton Vale – and the recently restored watermill tea garden.

▶ *Open all year. Parties by written appointment only*

6 Holt Farm

A striking purple glasshouse is the new centrepiece of this organic ornamental garden that has recently been overhauled.

Bath Road, Blagdon, Bristol BS40 7SQ

Tel: 01761 461650

LOCATION 12 miles S of Bristol off A368 between Blagdon and Ubley. Entrance to Holt Farm, through Yeo Valley Farms, is ¼ mile outside Blagdon on left

This interesting modern garden has been closed for the past 18 months while undergoing the Soil Association's organic conversion process; it will be reopening in June 2010 as one of only a handful of organically certified ornamental gardens in the country. The young and dynamic team has taken the opportunity to rework some of the existing plantings and undertake new projects – the centrepiece of the redevelopment is a new purple glasshouse set within a formal design, framed by hedging and pleached *Malus* 'Red Sentinel'.

The more informal parts retain their relaxed and contemporary feel, with colour-themed borders and perennial and annual wild-flower meadows. In high summer the streamside walk and gravel garden are filled with colour, shape and movement achieved by bold and imaginative repeat-planting on a generous scale, and autumnal fireworks are provided by late perennials, dahlias and grasses.

Grasses are also used extensively to link the garden to the Mendips country to the north of the house, while the simple sweep of lawn leading down to pastureland gives a view over Blagdon Lake to the south. Charming wrought-iron gates and quirky sculptures are other personal statements.

▶ *Open for NGS, and by appointment*

7 Ston Easton Park

Master landscaper Humphry Repton's park surrounds the house, while the kitchen garden provides produce for hotel guests.

Ston Easton, near Bath BA3 4DF

Tel: 01761 241631 | www.stoneaston.co.uk

Historic Garden Grade II

LOCATION 11 miles SW of Bath, 6 miles NE of Wells on A39

The 18th-century park – the only surviving landscape in Somerset designed by Humphry Repton – surrounds a Palladian mansion (now a hotel). The drive winds through the park to a large, flat lawn laid out before the front façade, giving a taste of the elegance of his landscape, and the wide terrace behind the house is the perfect place to view the series of cascades and two bridges over the River Norr (one with a sham castle folly) that he designed.

Repton's Red Book of ideas and plans has been used as a guide during restoration. Attention has also been lavished on the large walled garden; today, as well as being a feast for the eye, it provides fruit and vegetables for the hotel's chefs and flowers for its florist on a daily basis.

▶ *Open all year – telephone or consult website for details*

8 Milton Lodge

The imaginatively planted terraced garden with views of Wells Cathedral has numerous fine trees on display in its arboretum.

Wells BA5 3AQ | Tel: 01749 672168

www.miltonlodgegardens.co.uk

Historic Garden Grade II

LOCATION ½ mile N of Wells. From A39 turn north up Old Bristol Road; first gate on left

The fine terraced garden, planted around 1914 in Arts and Crafts style and replanted in the 1960s, is cultivated down the side of a hill overlooking the Vale of Avalon, affording magnificent views of Wells Cathedral. The spacious levels are imaginatively planted with a wide variety of plants, many of them tender and all suitable for the alkaline soil, giving a succession of colour and interest from March to October.

Many fine trees can be seen both in the garden and in the separate 7 acre arboretum, which has a good range of native and exotic trees.

▶ *Open main season – telephone or consult website for details – and for parties and coaches by appointment*

SOUTH WEST ENGLAND

9 Ammerdown House

Yew, sculpture and parterre cleverly link this Bathstone house to the orangery, while fountains and statues add interest.

Radstock, Bath BA3 5SH.

Historic Garden Grade II*

LOCATION 10 miles S of Bath, ½ mile off A362 Radstock-Frome road on B3139

The Bathstone house was designed by Georgian architect James Wyatt, with panoramic views on one side and a garden on the other; the 15 acre garden was conceived by celebrated garden designer Edwin Lutyens, who wanted to link the house with the orangery. While walking through the Italianate rooms of yew, sculpture and parterre, most visitors will be unaware of the tricks of space that are being played on them.

Massive yew hedges, now mature and nearly 4m (13ft) high, create enclosed formal areas that lead irresistibly one from another, and fountains and statues add architectural interest in all seasons.

There has been much replanting in the garden in recent years, and beautiful meadows and ponds now link the formal gardens with the fine surrounding parkland.

▶ *Open for charities, and for parties by appointment*

10 Brewery House

The established organic garden is set on two levels, with contrasting plantings that include grasses, bamboos and euphorbias.

Southstoke, Bath BA2 7DL | Tel: 01225 833153

LOCATION 2½ miles S of Bath, off A367 Bath-Radstock road. At top of dual carriageway, turn left onto B3110 to double roundabout, then next right into Southstoke; house on left behind high wall by white railings

Tightly packed with interesting plants, the garden is set on two levels and has magnificent views over rolling countryside to the south. The planting is dramatic, aimed at achieving strong contrasts in shape and size as well as colour, with perennials appearing next to huge specimens of phyllostachys or miscanthus. The owners are keen on bamboos, the more unusual hydrangeas, euphorbias and grasses, and have collected many varieties of each. Among the many roses, *Rosa* 'Kiftsgate' and *R. soulieana* make their presence felt.

In the top garden, enclosed by a high stone wall, roses and clematis jostle for space with wall fruit and other climbers. There are many mature trees, including davidia, ptelia, medlar, apple and pear, and large specimens of walnut and mulberry. At the far end the swimming pool has been converted into a water garden with water lilies, gunneras and other aquatic plants. The garden has been run organically since 1983.

▶ *Open by appointment*

11 Prior Park Landscape Garden

A serpentine lake and sham Rococo bridge create a theatrical effect around the Cabinet, which has a cascade and grotto.

Ralph Allen Drive, Bath BA2 5AH

Tel: 01225 833422

www.nationaltrust.org.uk

Historic Garden Grade I/The National Trust

LOCATION No parking at garden; catch bus from city centre or walk up A3062 from Widcombe

This romantic garden is a superb example of the landscape movement at its height. The Palladian mansion, designed by architect John Wood from 1735 for Bath's leading entrepreneur and philanthropist, Ralph Allen, dominates the steeply sloping landscape and provides stunning views of the city. While the mansion is presently owned by Prior Park College and is not open to the public, the grounds are well worth the circular walk from the entrance gate off Ralph Allen Drive.

Allen landscaped and planted from 1734 to 1764, helped by several renowned gardeners, notably 'Capability' Brown, who eliminated areas of formality, and Alexander Pope, who inspired the Wilderness. The serpentine lake that stretches out from the Rococo sham bridge has been restored and a great deal of new planting of shrubs and herbaceous perennials is taking place in this area in order to achieve the theatrical effect beloved of 18th-century landscapers, especially around the Cabinet – a gravel clearing at the base of the main cascade and the grotto. The grotto, directly influenced by Pope, is the next feature to be restored.

The walk continues from the mansion viewpoint down the east side of the valley to the lakes and the Palladian bridge of 1755, returning by the west side of the valley via the Rock Gate. Undoubtedly two-star are the views of the Palladian bridge, the mansion from the bridge and the city of Bath; the 'Priory path' leading into the field next to the garden gives a panoramic view over the city.

▶ *Open main season – telephone or consult website for details*

12 Yarlington House

Crab apples in the shape of a bandstand and a romantic Italian garden that celebrates Napoleon are among features of interest.

Yarlington, Wincanton BA9 8DY

Tel: 01963 440344

LOCATION In village of Yarlington S of Castle Cary, signposted off A371

This varied formal garden is blessed with an ideal mix of good design and planting. The fine pleached lime square surrounding the rose garden and the romantic sunken Italian garden – complete with classical statuary and balustrades, and awash with scent and soft colours – complement the scale and style of the distinguished 1780s house.

Created by the present owners over more than 40 years, the garden is now at a satisfying stage of maturity within the setting of the fine surrounding parkland. Within an area of just 2½ acres it achieves a series of skilful mood changes, moving gradually from the more formal areas towards an unusual circle of crab apples that have been trained into the shape of a bandstand (this feature was termed the 'apple house' by the garden designer and writer, J.C. Loudon) and down towards a dell that is replete with ferns and shade-loving specimens.

A number of vegetables and fruit trees are grown within a walled garden that is approached through impressive gates. Early in the year the daffodils make an impressive display before the laburnum walk comes into full flower over a Gothic-arched pergola.

The Emperor Napoleon is commemorated in the sunken Italian garden, surrounded by roses – that include, of course, 'Empress Josephine' and 'Souvenir de la Malmaison'. A dovecote is stationed within the small children's garden.

▶ *Open for parties of ten or more by appointment*

PRIOR PARK LANDSCAPE GARDEN

CHANNEL ISLANDS

Blessed with the warmest climate in the British Isles, bamboos, tree ferns, banana and palm trees thrive in the islands' gardens, alongside fragrant British favourites such as honeysuckle, lilies and lavender.

1 La Petite Vallée

Mixed borders, shrubberies and terraced gardens descend to the sea in this garden, one of the most admired in these isles.

Rue de Putron, St Peter Port, Guernsey GY1 2TE

Tel: 01481 238866
(or to book an appointment 01481 726611)

LOCATION 2 miles S of central St Peter Port

This 3 acre valley garden facing the sea is full of surprises and excitement, reflecting the passion lavished on it by its knowledgeable and enthusiastic owner. It encompasses many styles, levels and views, and a wealth of rare and unusual plants, sourced and remorselessly tracked down.

Water plays an important role: a rill flows down a staircase and along the lower terrace before winding around the garden to a canna-fringed lily pond and splashing down a waterfall to a koi pond, surrounded by a blue and burnt-orange garden. A summer bed is planted with psoraleas, *Iochroma grandiflorum*, deutzias, philadelphus and daturas, and there are wild-flower meadows, shrubberies, herb, water and rose gardens, all flowing into each other with ease.

A sub-tropical garden has replaced the former lilac grove, a rock bed in front of the house now includes an enticing mix of deep purple and lime-green gladioli, and the latest projects are a shade garden and a dry border next to the terrace.
▶ *Open for charities, and by appointment*

2 Mille Fleurs

Giant gunneras, tree ferns and arum lilies surround two ponds, while there is a Mediterranean feel to the pool area.

Rue du Bordage, St Pierre du Bois, Guernsey GY7 9DW

Tel: 01481 263911 | www.millefleurs.co.uk

LOCATION 6 miles SW of St Peter Port, 100m down lane from Rue de Quanteraine/Rue du Bordage junction

Set in a peaceful, wooded conservation valley this garden is informal, with a naturalistic design, and much of the planting has been chosen with wildlife in mind. The areas around the house and holiday cottages are a profusion of roses, clematis, penstemons and other herbaceous perennials, with sweetly scented honeysuckles and jasmines framing arches and doorways.

Paths flanked by lilies, lavender and other fragrant plants meander down to the bottom of the valley, where more tender, sub-tropical plants flourish in the sheltered microclimate. A natural spring feeds into two ponds surrounded by mature tree ferns and giant gunneras amid huge stands of arum lilies.

A large mature fig tree and a host of terracotta pots brimming with red pelargoniums and cordylines, together with banks of crocosmias, phormiums and euphorbias, lend a Mediterranean feel to the swimming-pool area.
▶ *Open for limited season – telephone or consult website for details*

3 Sausmarez

Collections from the Mediterranean and sub-tropics mix with wild flowers, and the work of 90 artists features in the Art Park.

St Martins, Guernsey GY4 6SG

Tel: 01481 235571

www.sausmarezmanor.co.uk

LOCATION 1½ miles S of St Peter Port

Set around two small lakes in an ancient wood, the garden has been crammed with unusual and rare species to give it an exotic feel. It is strewn with plants from many parts of the world, particularly the sub-tropics and the Mediterranean, which also enjoy Guernsey's mellow maritime climate.

Collections of yuccas, ferns, camellias (more than 300), bamboos, hebes, bananas, echiums, lilies, palm trees, fuchsias, as well as hydrangeas, hostas, azaleas, pittosporums, clematis, rhododendrons, cyclamens, impatiens and giant grasses all jostle for space with indigenous wild flowers. No pesticides are used so wildlife flourishes. A poetry trail winds through the wood.

MILLE FLEURS

There is also an art gallery and the Art Park, displaying around 200 pieces of sculpture by 90 British, European, African, American and local artists, all of which is for sale.

A pitch-and-putt course, small children's play area and ride-on trains add to the holiday atmosphere here.

▶ *Garden open all year – telephone or consult website for details. Guided tours for parties by appointment*

4 Domaine des Vaux

The camellias here are of particular note, and a varied collection of conifers and other trees provide year-long foliage colour.

Rue de Bas, St Lawrence, Jersey JE3 1JG

Tel: 01534 863129

LOCATION 2 miles N of St Helier

This delightful garden, which is continually being added to and improved, is in two contrasting parts. At the top lies an Italianate garden, set around and above a sunken rectangular lawn, with borders that are a riot of unusual and familiar perennials and shrubs. This perfect formal area, with grey and silver borders facing yellow, gold and bronze ones, has clearly been planted with a sure eye for foliage as well as for flower colour.

The present generation have planted a small formal herb garden on a triangular theme, and they have created a *jardinière* and a pair of long flower borders.

The lower garden is a semi-wild and quite steep valley with a string of ponds connected by a stream. The valley and wood are at their best in spring, when a carpet of wild Jersey narcissi spreads under camellias, azaleas and rhododendrons; a magnificent *Magnolia campbellii* has reached maturity and flowers abundantly during March.

Of particular note are the camellias in both gardens, and an interesting collection of conifers and other trees planted to give year-round foliage colour in a small arboretum. Here the trees are complemented by maples and ericaceous plants and shrubs like pieris and azaleas to give an added burst of colour in spring and autumn, while July brings a riot of blue from a now-mature planting of agapanthus.

A Mediterranean garden stands at the top of the valley, which includes a collection of pots planted to reflect the colours of the south of France and Italy.

▶ *Open by appointment*

Southern England

Rolling hills and downlands, the sheltered south coast and broad river floodplains define the region and contribute to its successful cultivation. The result is a clustering of superb gardens, from magnificent landscapes to those epitomising the country idyll.

WILTSHIRE
105-111

KEY

- ① Garden location
- County boundary
- Motorway
- Principal A road

BEDFORDSHIRE 46-47

BUCKINGHAMSHIRE 51-55

OXFORDSHIRE 72-81

BERKSHIRE 48-50

HAMPSHIRE and Isle of Wight 56-61

HERTFORDSHIRE 62-63

SURREY 84-91

SUSSEX 92-104

KENT 64-71

The Chilterns

The North Downs

The South Downs

The South Downs

Bedford

Biggleswade

Milton Keynes

Buckingham

Leighton Buzzard

Stevenage

Hertford

Luton

St Albans

Watford

High Wycombe

Maidenhead

Reading

Windsor

Tring

Aylesbury

Oxford

Didcot

Newbury

Basingstoke

Winchester

Southampton

Petersfield

Haslemere

Woking

Guildford

Farnham

Dorking

Reigate

Crawley

Haywards Heath

Chichester

Bognor Regis

Worthing

Brighton

Lewes

Eastbourne

Bexhill-on-Sea

Hastings

Rye

Royal Tunbridge Wells

Crowborough

Gravesend

Rochester

Chatham

Maidstone

Canterbury

Margate

Ashford

Dover

Folkestone

Portsmouth

Newport

Banbury

BEDFORDSHIRE

From the chalk hills of the Chilterns to the clay of the vales, the county's gardeners have worked with nature to create designs that take their influence from around the world, as well as art and science.

1 Seal Point

A tiny bonsai garden, topiary in fun shapes and a wildlife copse are among the many unusual features in this town garden.

7 Wendover Way, Luton LU2 7LS

Tel: 01582 611567

LOCATION In NE Luton. Turn N off Stockingstone Road into Felstead Way and take second on left

This sloping, wildlife-friendly town garden just gets better as it matures, displaying interesting plants and gorgeous colour schemes from spring right through the summer. A hardy standard fuchsia is now over 3m (9ft) high, and 20 or more different grasses are integrated into the borders.

There is something unusual at every turn – a wildlife copse, a tiny bonsai garden, three pools (one with a waterfall), yin and yang beds, amusing topiary, original ornaments, and much more. The garden is run organically, and log piles, ladybird lodges, bumblebee nests and nectar plants place the accent on nurturing wildlife throughout.

▶ *Open for NGS, and by appointment*

2 Toddington Manor

This themed garden includes many scented roses as well as hostas, delphiniums, peonies and a handsome pleached lime walk.

Park Road, Toddington LU5 6HJ

Tel: 01525 872576

www.toddingtonmanor.co.uk

LOCATION 8 miles NW of Luton, 1 mile NW of Toddington, 1 mile W of M1 junction 12

Although maintained to the highest standards, the shrubs and plants at Toddington are allowed to grow, flower and seed in abundance. Each area has been given its own theme. The attractive pleached lime walk is paved and surrounded by large herbaceous borders that show off an exuberance of hostas with many variations of leaf, blue delphiniums, white astilbes and hellebores, euphorbias and angelicas.

Inside the walled garden are borders with dramatic sweeps of delphiniums, peonies, clematis and grasses, backed by shrubs. In the rose garden

the air is scented by yellow and white floribunda roses and philadelphus, pierced by spikes of eremurus. A stream flows through the garden and feeds the ponds and the fountain. There is a good herb garden and greenhouse, and beyond the walls a wild-flower meadow, orchards and woodland.

▶ *Open main season – telephone or consult website for details – and for parties by appointment*

3 The Manor House

Rothko and Hepworth are just two of the artists who have influenced the planting and colour schemes in this striking garden.

Church Road, Stevington, Bedford MK43 7QB

Tel: 01234 822064

www.kathybrownsgarden.homestead.com

LOCATION 5 miles NW of Bedford off A428, through Bromham. In Stevington, turn right at crossroads; garden is on left after ¼ mile

This atmospheric and imaginatively planted garden has 20 distinct areas within its 4½ acres. The summer container garden planted in and around the old fish pond is colourful and strongly Mediterranean, with a variety of succulents and imposing echiums, followed by a fine display of aeoniums, agaves and dasylirions. An olive grove underplanted with lavender, rosemary, dianthine and Californian poppies also creates a Mediterranean atmosphere beside the tennis court.

In contrast is the more understated avenue of *Betula utilis* var. *jacquemontii* 'Grayswood Ghost' underplanted with acanthus, which leads to a flowery meadow through beds of grasses.

The French garden is an essay in formal design, and the 12 yew 'jurors' that back the box parterres commemorate the trial in 1661 of Fouquet, Louis XIV's finance minister.

Moving forward in time, a 'Rothko room' glows with purple beech, berberis and prunus, an airy 'Hepworth room' has grasses mingling with herbaceous plants, and other gardens draw inspiration from the works of artists Hokusai, Monet and Mondrian.

There are also major collections of late spring and summer bulbs, clematis and roses.

▶ *Open for NGS, and for parties by appointment*

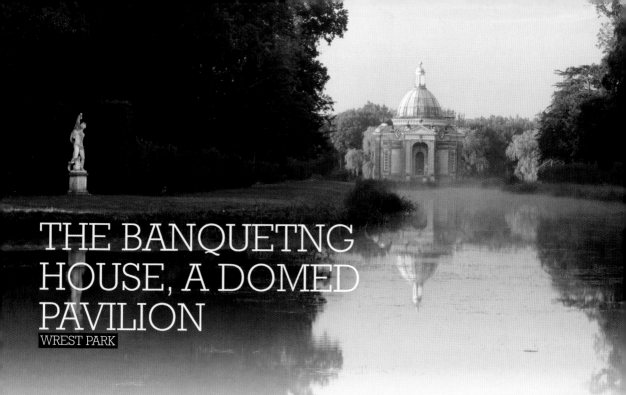

THE BANQUETNG HOUSE, A DOMED PAVILION
WREST PARK

4 Tofte Manor

The grass labyrinth is based on one in the floor of Chartres Cathedral; crystals mark key points around the geometric design.

Souldrop Road, Sharnbrook MK44 1HH

Tel: 01234 781425

www.toftelabyrinth.co.uk

LOCATION Exit A6 at roundabout to Sharnbrook, and go through village towards Souldrop. At Y-junction take right fork; house is ahead on left

With its walls covered with magnolias, wisterias, roses and jasmine, the striking Jacobean manor is accompanied by an uplifting 5 acre garden. One of the highlights is a grass labyrinth inspired by the one set into the floor of Chartres Cathedral. Water is piped below in the same circular pattern, and there is a tap from which to drink. The soothing journey around its sacred curves takes 20 minutes or more to complete.

The huge old well is followed by the sunken garden which has terraces and soaring clipped yews. Beds of yellow roses form the centrepiece, with variegated honeysuckle and yellow clematis tumbling over the arbour above. To the left, deep herbaceous borders sit astride a watery crystal ball that gleams in the sunshine, while a clipped box garden lies round the corner, crowned by a graceful statue. Geometry is ever present here and crystals mark significant points around the garden.
▶ *Open for NGS, and by appointment*

5 Wrest Park

In this exemplary Baroque formal garden, the Long Water canal forms the main axis with an elegant pavilion at its head.

Silsoe, Bedford MK45 4HS | Tel: 01525 860152

www.englishheritage.org.uk

Historic Garden Grade I/English Heritage

LOCATION 10 miles S of Bedford, ¾ mile E of Silsoe off A6

Formal Baroque gardens from the early 18th century are rare. At Wrest, the Long Water, a canal flanked by hedges, dominates the 'Great Garden' and provides the main axis of the grounds, cutting through thick blocks of woodland. At its head lies the Banqueting House, a domed pavilion designed by Baroque architect Thomas Archer.

The great landscaper 'Capability' Brown worked here later, creating a naturalistic river to surround the grounds at their perimeter. The woods are intersected by avenues and dotted with interesting features, including a delicate Chinese pavilion and giant urns set in grassy glades. The 1770 Bath House was built as a romantic classical ruin. Water catches the eye in every direction.

The 1830s house (limited access) is fronted by terraces and box-edged parterres tightly packed with vibrant annuals. The large orangery was designed by French architect Cléphane.
▶ *Open main season – telephone or check website for details*

GLORIOUSLY SCENTED BY
OLD VARIETIES OF SHRUB
ROSES UNDERPLANTED WITH
HERBACEOUS PERENNIALS

BERKSHIRE

The River Thames winds through much of the county and many great houses fringe its banks. In addition, downland gardens offer magnificent vistas, often framed by innovative planting schemes.

1 Englefield House

Despite its size, the garden feels intimate, an effect achieved through the careful balancing of formal and more natural areas.

Englefield, Theale, Reading RG7 5EN

Tel: 0118 930 2221

www.englefield.co.uk

Historic Garden Grade II

LOCATION 5 miles W of Reading. Entrance on A340, near Theale

Dating back to the 17th century and designed on a grand scale, the special charm of this 9 acre garden lies in its feeling of intimacy and the rare and successful balance between cultivated garden and natural landscaping. The land rises steeply upwards from the house and its discreetly elegant stone terraces overlook the deer park. The terrace balustrades are artfully garlanded with climbing roses that weave over and in between the stonework.

The formal garden appears to blend seamlessly into the woodland garden on the higher slopes, where mown grass rides stretch out between mature trees and meadow grass spattered with wild flowers and bulbs. A handkerchief tree, breathtaking in season, soars among its neighbours.

The woodland area makes outstanding use of associations between different shapes and colours of foliage, with a rich variety of shrubs. In autumn there is a magnificent display of bronze and red-leaved maples. A stream, fringed generously with hostas and bog-garden plants, winds its way down the slope.

Throughout are many corners and bowers with seats to surprise and delight the visitor, including a small ivy house and a grotto with an interior lined with fir cones and a mirror reflecting the planting outside. An imaginative garden on a small hill is surrounded by a cordon of giant gunneras, with a seat at the top in a cobbled mosaic circle surrounded in turn by evergreen hedging. Touches of humour include a carved wood bear rearing from the undergrowth and an area with a water trick device triggered by entry through a child-sized yew arch.

▶ *Open all year – telephone or consult website for details*

2 Mariners

Clever planting makes the most of this site's gradient while the main highlight in summer is a delightful sunken rose garden.

Mariners Lane, Bradfield RG17 6HU

Tel: 0118 974 5226

fenjaanderson@aol.com;
www.mariners-garden.com

LOCATION 10 miles W of Reading. From M4 junction 12 take A4 W; at roundabout take A340 signed to Pangbourne, then turn left after ⅓ mile signed to Bradfield. After 1 mile turn left again signed to Bradfield Southend, then after 1 mile turn right opposite signpost to Tutts Clump; house is on left at bottom of hill

This sloping site has been planted with intelligence and imagination, and the owners are constantly fine-tuning their planting and colour schemes.

On the bank above the broad terrace, two borders have been contoured so that the colour and texture of the flowers and foliage may be enjoyed at close quarters. One is planted in a predominantly wine-and-red colour theme, the other in soft blues, creams and yellows.

The main herbaceous border and the bank border opposite, which incorporates a bog garden, forms the backbone of the garden. Lawns planted with unusual trees link the various areas and lead the eye upwards, past a small area of meadow, where a succession of bulbs – daffodils, camassias and *Gladiolus byzantinus* – and perennials mingles with the grasses.

At the highest level there is an orchard, along with a sundial garden and a hexagonal arbour that supports vines and clematis. Beyond lies a 1 acre wild-flower meadow with a charming 'borrowed' tower terminating the view.

The most atmospheric part of the garden is the sunken rose garden, which is a fabulous sight in June and is gloriously scented by the many old varieties of shrub roses underplanted with herbaceous perennials; a moon gate is festooned with rambling roses and an arbour with roses and clematis. From here a path leads down under trees to a varied walk by the side of a stream.

▶ *Open for NGS, and by appointment*

SOUTHERN ENGLAND

49

3 The Old Rectory, Farnborough

Once home to poet John Betjeman, today the Rectory's gardens flourish with fabulous and unexpected combinations of plants.

Farnborough, Wantage OX12 8NX

Tel: 01488 638298

LOCATION 4 miles SE of Wantage off B4494

This award-winning garden with superb views has been created over 30 years, based on an original structure of large trees and hedges. Deep, parallel herbaceous borders backed by yew hedges include groupings of rare and interesting plants, selected for colour and texture.

The owner is a talented garden-maker and plantswoman, with a masterly eye for unusual combinations. The planting by the front of the house is subtle and effective, and smaller areas have been laid out for sun or shade-loving plants. Woodland contrasts with shrubs and lawns, and the growing arboretum now contains more than 150 trees.

The swimming pool is surrounded by a large *Hydrangea sargentiana* and potted lilies, with mixed roses and clematis around the outside walls. There is a collection of old roses and small-flowered clematis, and wild flowers line the front lawn by the ha-ha. The tennis court has been turned into a shady and delightful *boule à drôme* garden, with four large beds, pretty wrought-iron gates and a gazebo. The vegetable garden is neat and productive.

The poet John Betjeman lived here from 1945 to 1950, and visitors can look for the ghost of his muse, Miss Joan Hunter Dunn, in the shrubberies.
▶ *Open for NGS, and by appointment*

4 Waltham Place

The naturalistic design features ground elder and bindweed while yew hedges have been cut into billowing forms.

Waltham Place, White Waltham, Maidenhead SL6 3JH | Tel: 01628 825517

www.walthamplace.com

LOCATION 3½ miles S of Maidenhead. From M4 junction 8/9 take A404M and follow signs to White Waltham. Turn left to Windsor and Paley Street. Parking signposted at top of hill

This garden is a source of inspiration to many visitors. When the owners called in the Dutch designer Henk Gerritsen, renowned for a particular kind of naturalistic planting, he filled a small enclosed garden mainly with plants to attract butterflies, another with herbs and native species. The Square Garden combines lawns and generous sweeps of gravel dotted with grasses in a freely drawn design separated by box hedges. A large area of herbaceous planting holds some surprises, such as the invasive ground elder, here chosen for its striking leaves and subtle flowers.

Beyond the potager, the knot garden and Japanese garden, are long, densely packed herbaceous borders, where beech alcoves shelter half-moon-shaped beds filled with tall weeds, including native bindweed, and stipa grasses. Old yew hedges have been artfully cut into swirling forms, as if by a creative giant with hedgecutters.

The ornamental gardens lie within a walled enclosure of mellow brick; substantial brick-pillared pergolas support an abundance of roses and climbers and provide shady walks. The 40 acre grounds include a lake, woodlands and a maze.
▶ *Open for NGS, and by appointment*

5 Scotlands

Although they are modern additions, the walled garden and sunken courtyard evoke the house's 17th-century origins.

Cockpole Green, Wargrave, Reading RG10 8QP

Tel: 01628 822648

LOCATION 4 miles E of Henley-on-Thames, off A4 at Knowl Hill

The elegant country garden surrounding the 17th-century house was landscaped and developed during the 1980s. The pretty flint-and-brick tool shed and stone urns on either side of the gate in the formal walled garden and the white-painted bower are all in character with a period house; even the duck house looks like a gentleman's residence from an earlier age.

The house sits above the garden's slopes with views over the pool and a woodland copse. To one side is the original 17th-century kitchen garden, planned with neat and formal lawns, paved paths and box topiary; on the other side a charming sunken courtyard is planted with sun-loving plants and an outstanding ceanothus.

Elsewhere the design is more relaxed, with herbaceous beds, attractive shrubs and fine trees that rise above areas of lawn and swathes of uncut grass. At the garden's lower level, beyond the large pool and woodland, is a network of interlinked ponds, a waterfall and a rich mixture of primulas, lysichitons, ferns and waterside plants that combine with azaleas, rhododendrons and other shrubs under a canopy of trees.
▶ *Open for charities, and by appointment*

BUCKINGHAMSHIRE

Glorious gardens and historically important landscapes sit amid the beech woodlands of Buckinghamshire. More than 1,000 acres of this beautiful county is protected by the National Trust.

1 Cliveden

Superbly sited overlooking the Thames, Cliveden's gardens, fountains, temples and statuary have an air of classical formality.

Taplow, Maidenhead SL6 0JA	
Tel: 01628 605069	
www.nationaltrust.org.uk	
Historic Garden Grade I/National Trust	
LOCATION 6 miles NW of Slough, 2 miles N of Taplow off A4094	

The setting of the house is one of the most beautiful in Britain. The flamboyant Duke of Buckingham found the site in 1666 and architect William Winde exploited it, excavating the grounds and moving earthworks to raise the house onto a platform so that, according to diarist John Evelyn, it 'stands somewhat like Frascati on the platform… a circular view of the utmost verge of the Horizon, which with the serpenting of the Thames is admirably surprising… The Cloisters, Descents, Gardens, and avenue through the wood august and stately.'

The present house (now a hotel) was designed by Sir Charles Barry and incorporates a terrace with a balustrade brought by the 1st Viscount Astor from the Villa Borghese in Rome in the 1890s. There are deep herbaceous borders, formal gardens and many fountains, temples and statues.

Among the famous designers who have worked on the 376 acre grounds are Bridgeman (walks and the amphitheatre), Leoni (the Octagon Temple), John Fleming (the glorious flower-filled parterre, currently being restored) and Geoffrey Jellicoe (the well-named Secret Garden, shortly to be reinstated). New plantings by the National Trust are starting to take effect, and vistas are being opened up to make the most of the river setting, but it would require the wealth of a latter-day Duke of Buckingham to return the garden entirely to its 'august and stately' heyday.

▶ *House open. Garden open all year – telephone or consult website for details*

CLIVEDEN

2 Old Thatch

This delightful cottage's setting inspired the author Enid Blyton and its rose and clematis walk and water gardens continue to charm.

Coldmoorholme Lane, Bourne End SL8 5PS

Tel: 01628 527518

www.jackyhawthorne.co.uk

LOCATION 3 miles E of Marlow, 1 mile NW of Bourne End off A4155

The 17th-century thatched house, once the home of *Famous Five* creator Enid Blyton, has been enlivened with a series of vibrant and informal gardens, some traditional, others revealing of the owner's unusual and skilful approach to design and planting.

Moving from the formal garden and the pretty rose and clematis walk, the garden becomes more intriguing as it fans outwards. In the water garden, numerous small beds enclosing the large pool and fountain are surrounded by large borders in shades of turquoise, blue, silver and bronze. Elsewhere is a circular garden with a tapestry bed, two shady secret spaces, and a bed bouncing with balls of *Lonicera nitida* 'Baggesen's Gold' and architectural foliage plants.

There are two modern enclosures. One has small groups of acers and malus planted among herbaceous perennials; the other, lined by eight standard *Prunus* 'Chanticleer', is charmingly light-hearted and planted with bright pink geraniums.

Tall perimeter trees give seclusion throughout and grass paths form a graceful link between the different spaces. The central part of the house has been made into an attractive tearoom.

▶ *Open main season – telephone or consult website for details – and by appointment for parties of 15 or more*

3 West Wycombe Park

The 18th-century Rococo landscape gardens are perfectly preserved and include fine statues, temples and an ornamental lake.

West Wycombe HP14 3AJ

Tel: 01494 513569

www.nationaltrust.org.uk

Historic Garden Grade I/The National Trust

LOCATION 2 miles W of High Wycombe, at W end of West Wycombe, S of A40 Oxford road

The gardens and park at West Wycombe were created by the second Sir Francis Dashwood, the founder of the notorious Hellfire Club.

They were influenced by his experiences on the Grand Tour in the early years of the 18th century, which included visits to Asia Minor and Russia. The first phase involved the creation of the lake, with meandering walks, completed by 1739. Numerous classical temples and statues were subsequently added, as well as the charming little flint and wooden bridges that span the streams.

Later still, in the 1770s, the park was enlarged; architect Nicholas Revett was employed to design yet more temples and follies, including a music temple on one of the three islands. Thomas Cook, a pupil of the famous landscaper 'Capability' Brown, was entrusted with the planting of trees and alterations to the landscape. There are several fine vistas, especially looking towards the swan-shaped lake.

▶ *House open. Grounds open limited season – telephone or consult website for details*

4 The Manor House, Bledlow

Water features and modern sculptures embellish the main grounds, while across the lane is a wild water garden.

Bledlow, Princes Risborough HP27 9PE

LOCATION 8 miles NW of High Wycombe, half a mile E of B4009 in middle of Bledlow

With the help of the renowned landscape architect Robert Adams, an elegant English garden of an exceptionally high standard has been created here.

The productive and colourful walled vegetable garden has Yorkshire-stone paths and a central gazebo. Tall yew and beech hedges enclose the formal spaces, one of which has a water feature by sculptor William Pye – whose *Slip Stream* and *Jet Stream* water sculptures can be seen at Gatwick Airport's North Terminal – at its centre. Mixed flower and shrub borders around the immaculate lawns feature many roses and herbaceous plants.

Another garden, approached through a yew and brick parterre, was planned around the existing mature trees on a contoured and upward-sloping site with open views. It is now well established, with its trees and lawns fulfilling the original landscaping design, and incorporates several modern sculptures.

The Lyde Garden, across the lane, is a wild water garden of great beauty and tranquillity. However, children do need careful watching here.

▶ *Manor House Garden open for NGS, and main season for parties by written appointment. Lyde Garden open all year*

5 Turn End

In this stylish marriage of design and architecture, carefully crafted vistas and mini-gardens create an illusion of space.

Townside, Haddenham, Aylesbury HP17 8BG

Tel: 01844 291383/291817

LOCATION 7 miles SW of Aylesbury. From A418 turn to Haddenham. From Thame Road turn at Rising Sun pub into Townside; garden is on left

Peter Aldington, one of the few 20th-century architects to have had two buildings listed Grade II★, turned his hand later in life to making gardens. His own garden is an excellent example of how the two disciplines can combine.

Creating a sense of space is one of Aldington's strengths – and it is an achievement here in just over half an acre. Divided loosely into different sized and shaped areas and enclosures – which make attractive mini-gardens in their own right – curving fingers of grass splay out from the central island bed to point to the far ends of the garden.

Part of the delight is in the detail, with carefully crafted vistas throughout. A gravel path running round part of the perimeter switches to mossy paving and then to mown lawn, introducing changes of mood and planting.

The choice of plants is idiosyncratic, with tree peonies, fuchsias, bamboos and alliums taking over from snowdrops and primroses outside the main door, and gravel and railway sleepers in the summer garden making an excellent foil for yuccas, tumbling roses and a collection of sempervivums in pots.
▶ *Open for NGS, and for parties of ten or more by appointment*

6 Wotton House

The replanted lime avenue, recontoured lake and repaired paths have all helped to restore 'Capability' Brown's fine landscape.

Wotton Underwood, Aylesbury HP18 0SB

Tel: 01844 238363

Historic Park and Garden Grade II★

LOCATION 8 miles W of Aylesbury off A41

The 200 acre pleasure grounds and 32 acres of water surrounding the 18th-century house have been restored by the owner, who has carefully and sensitively unpicked the secrets of the landscape shaped after 1750 by 'Capability' Brown. The lime avenue has been replanted, the contours of the lakes and the serpentine canal that links them redefined, the paths restored and the woodland on the far side of the garden thinned out to re-establish the ascendancy of native trees.

Above all, he has reintroduced the Arcadian elements of the landscape – the sense of anticipation created by a grass path lined with yews and crab apples at the start of the lakeside walk; the well-placed shrubberies along the path; and the exclusion of man-made features at certain points and carefully crafted vistas of bridges, temples and statues at others. The park remains a harmonious vision, and a work in progress on a huge scale.
▶ *Open for limited season – telephone or consult website for details – and for parties by written appointment*

7 Waddesdon Manor

Fountains, vistas, terraces, statuary and a Rococo-style aviary of exotic birds are as grand as the house they surround.

Historic Garden Grade I/National Trust

Waddesdon, Aylesbury HP18 0JH

Tel: 01296 653226

www.waddesdon.org.uk

LOCATION 6 miles NW of Aylesbury, 11 miles SE of Bicester on A41. Entrance in Waddesdon village

Baron Ferdinand de Rothschild's grandiloquent château at Waddesdon (built 1874-1889) is set in 165 acres of grounds with fountains, vistas, terraces and walks laid out by his landscape designer Elie Lainé. There is an impressive collection of Italian, French and Dutch statuary. The extensive parterre and fountains to the south require thousands of plants for the main summer display alone, and the theme changes every year.

To the west of the parterre, an ornate, semi-circular aviary of 18th-century French Rococo style, erected in 1889, houses many exotic birds. It also acts as an exedra (an outdoor seat), from which to view the pleasure grounds and the landscape beyond. The area in front of it has been restored to its original bedding-plant scheme.

The gardens undergo changes almost annually, with old features restored and new ones added. Wildflower Valley has daffodils in spring and cowslips, oxeye daisies and a range of orchids in summer, which are encouraged to seed. Close by, more than 20,000 camassias, colchicums, lilies-of-the valley and wild garlic have been naturalised in grassland and in the woodland garden.
▶ *House (including wine cellars) and grounds open most of year – telephone or consult website for details*

SOUTHERN ENGLAND

8 Ascott

This opulent late Victorian garden includes grandiose bedding schemes, a serpentine walk and a remarkable topiary sundial.

Wing, Leighton Buzzard LU7 0PS

Tel: 01296 688242

www.ascottestate.co.uk

Historic Garden Grade II*/The National Trust

LOCATION 7 miles NE of Aylesbury, ½ mile E of Wing, S of A418

Ascott began life as a 17th-century farmhouse. Acquired by Baron Mayer de Rothschild in 1873, it was transformed by his nephew, Leopold, into the 'palace-like cottage' we see today.

The garden is 30 acres of Victorian designs and planting at their best, laid out with the aid of nurseryman Harry Veitch and overlaid with more recent schemes. It is notable for its collection of mature trees set in rolling lawns. Intriguing topiary includes an evergreen sundial with a yew gnomon and the inscription 'Light and shade by turn, but love always' in golden yew – a celebration of Leopold's marriage.

Wide lawns slope away to views across the Vale of Aylesbury, glimpsed between towering cedars. Formal gardens include the Madeira Walk with sheltered flower borders and the bedded-out Dutch garden. The stately fountains of Venus and Cupid were sculpted by Thomas Waldo Story in the 19th century. The Long Walk leading to the lily pond has been reconstructed as a serpentine walk with beech hedging, and there's a wild garden in Coronation Grove. Spring gardens feature massed carpets of bulbs.
► *House and gardens open main season – telephone or consult website for details*

9 Stowe Landscape Gardens

A hugely influential landscape garden now being returned to its 18th-century origins, Stowe has 25 listed garden buildings.

Buckingham MK18 5EH | Tel: 01280 822850

www.nationaltrust.org.uk

Historic Garden Grade I/The National Trust

LOCATION 3 miles NW of Buckingham via Stowe Avenue off A422 Buckingham-Brackley road

This is garden restoration on a heroic scale. Stowe has had a huge influence on garden design from the mid 17th century onwards under a succession of distinguished designers, including 'Capability' Brown. What remains today is a *locus classicus* of 18th-century landscaping, with a 19th-century overlay that diversifies the landscape into distinct 'scenes', each with its own character. The aim over the past 20 years has been to reinstate these.

The restoration was brilliantly planned, using the National Trust's considerable resources to bring back lost plantings and remove recent inappropriate additions. Visitors can now wander through the gardens enjoying the wonderful views, the water, the splendid trees and autumn colour, the historic buildings – Stowe has more than twice as many listed garden buildings as any other garden in England – and the statuary. Alternatively, they can step back in time and try to understand the underlying political and philosophical significance of the designs pioneeered by the Landscape Movement.

Over the past decade, 320 acres of land has been bought back, including the home farm and deer park, embellished by the Wolfe obelisk (erected to honour Major General James Wolfe), the Gothic umbrello and a superb set of 1790s farm buildings. Recently completed projects include the Sleeping Wood, where orchids are now springing up, the statue of Friga (one of the seven Saxon deities) and the pebble alcove inscribed with the motto '*Templa quam delicta*' (How beautiful are thy temples).
► *House (Stowe School) open (tel: 01280 818166). Garden open most of year – telephone or check website for details (last admission 90 minutes before closing)*

CHENIES MANOR HOUSE

10 Gipsy House

Fans of the children's author Roald Dahl will enjoy the gipsy caravan that inspired one of his books, and the hut where he wrote.

Whitefield Lane, Great Missenden HP16 0BP

Tel: 01494 890465

www.roalddahlfoundation.org

LOCATION 5 miles NW of Amersham on A4128, off A413

Roald Dahl admirers can make a pilgrimage to the 1 acre garden enfolding the Georgian farmhouse in which he lived and wrote for 36 years. But don't expect the inspired anarchy of his books; the garden is grown-up and sophisticated.

Set in unspoilt countryside, it is divided into a sequence of spaces protected by tall hedges or walls. Four large *Quercus ilex* lollipops in the Sundial Garden, raised beds outlined by sturdy railway sleepers in the terraced kitchen garden, an avenue of pleached limes underplanted with alliums and hostas, an airy gazebo guarded by two stone eagles – these and other details are handsome and self-confident, softened by planting schemes that change in mood and colour.

There are a few Dahl footprints – his little white writing hut with its bright yellow door, a low maze in which the Yorkstone slabs are carved with extracts of his writings, and the brightly painted gipsy caravan that spawned the book *Danny Champion of the World*. Beyond, a wild-flower meadow merges into the surrounding land.

▶ *Open for NGS, other charities, and by appointment*

11 Chenies Manor House

Among many special features in Chenies' garden are an historic turf maze, a white garden and a medicinal physic garden.

Chenies WD3 6ER | Tel: 01494 762888

www.cheniesmanorhouse.co.uk

LOCATION 3 miles E of Amersham off A404

Decorative and maintained to the highest standards, the fine linked gardens are in perfect keeping with the brick manor house. Planted for a long season of colour, spring sees the mass flowering of tulips in the sunken garden, followed by vibrant annual bedding that is matched by colourful herbaceous plantings; old-fashioned roses and cottage plants are favoured, too.

There is plenty to enjoy here, including formal topiary in the white garden, medicinal and poisonous plants in a physic garden, a parterre, a historic turf maze and intricate yew maze, and a highly productive kitchen garden.

▶ *Open main season – telephone or consult website for details*

HAMPSHIRE

Visitors to this county can enjoy some superb collections of plants, such as the glorious, fragrant Mottisfont roses, Sir Harold Hillier's arboretum and Bramdean's vibrant herbaceous borders.

1 Mottisfont Abbey Garden

Enjoy the remarkable sight and scent of the historic roses, some dating as far back as the Middle Ages, during June and July.

Mottisfont, Romsey SO51 0LP

Tel: 01794 340757 | www.nationaltrust.org.uk

Historic Garden Grade II/The National Trust

LOCATION 15 miles NW of Southampton, 4¼ miles NW of Romsey, ½ mile W of A3057

The walled garden of historic roses, based on the collection of rose specialist Graham Thomas, caused a sensation when it first opened in the 1970s. Today, two walled gardens contain medieval gallicas, albas and damasks, moss roses and centifolias of the 18th century, the earliest Chinas and hybrid perpetuals from the 19th century, and collections of rugosas, early teas and hybrid teas.

The best time to visit is an evening in the first few weeks of June, when peace has descended, perfume drenches the air and the gardens stay open until 8pm. The climbing and rambler roses are at their peak in July and the herbaceous borders look good throughout the season.

The gardens are worth visiting at any time of year and offer fine cedars and sweet chestnuts, a huge plane and woodland walks. Water welling at the font (hence the name Mottisfont) flows on to the River Test.

▶ *House open. Garden open most of year – telephone or consult website for details*

2 The Sir Harold Hillier Gardens

With 12,000 species and cultivars and 11 National Collections, this garden has something to impress at any time of year.

Jermyns Lane, Ampfield, Romsey SO51 0QA

Tel: 01794 369318 | www.hilliergardens.org.uk

Historic Garden and Arboretum Grade II

LOCATION 2 miles NE of Romsey, 9 miles SW of of Winchester, ¾ mile W of A3090

The collection of hardy trees and shrubs amassed after 1953 by the late Sir Harold Hillier is the largest in the world. The gardens cover around 180 acres and include approximately 12,000 different species and cultivars, many of which are rarities. There are 11 National Collections, including those of quercus and hamamelis, held here – more than any other garden.

The garden produces weekly lists that guide visitors to plants of particular interest for the season, whether in the herbaceous, scree, heather or bog gardens. With about 42,000 plants in the garden, it is impossible to come away without learning something about what, where and how to plant.

MOTTISFONT ABBEY GARDEN

Notable among the trees are *Eucalyptus nitens* and *E. niphophila, Magnolia cylindrica* spp. *zanthoxylum* (the prickly ash or toothache tree) as well as acers and sorbus. Among the shrubs there is a wide range of rhododendrons, azaleas, camellias and hydrangeas. The winter garden specialises in plants at their best from November to March, and includes gold-and-black stemmed bamboos and the white-stemmed *Rubus thibetanus*.

A curved walk of *Metasequoia glyptostroboides* leads to the education pavilion and the approach to the arboretum gives a view of rare trees merging with the Hampshire countryside beyond. Much more than just an arboretum, these attractively laid-out gardens can be enjoyed at many levels.

▶ *Open all year – telephone or consult website for details*

3 Longstock Park Water Garden

Voted 'the finest water garden in the world', no fewer than 48 different kinds of water lilies are grown in the ponds here.

Longstock, Stockbridge SO20 6EH

Tel: 01264 810904 | www.longstockpark.co.uk

LOCATION 5 miles S of Andover, 2 miles N of Stockbridge. From A30 turn N on A3057

The 7 acres of these superb water gardens, created in 1948 by John Spedan Lewis, the founder of the John Lewis Partnership, are fed from the River Test and surrounded by acid-loving trees and shrubs. They form an archipelago connected by narrow bridges and causeways.

Gunneras and swamp cypresses, surrounded by stilts, royal ferns and *Aralia elata,* are just a few of the plants reflected in the waters teaming with gold carp. Aquatics include 48 different water lilies. A walk along the paths gives a succession of views followed by more intimate spaces.

Do not miss Longstock Park Nursery nearby, which has a fine herbaceous border and an extensive collection of *viticella* clematis.

▶ *Open main season – telephone or consult website for details – and by appointment for parties*

4 Bere Mill

This riverside site is modelled on a Japanese stroll garden, with mirror borders, a teahouse and modern sculptures.

London Road, Whitchurch RG28 7NH

Tel: 01256 892210

LOCATION 9 miles E of Andover, 12 miles N of Winchester

The early 18th-century mill house is where the French emigré Henri de Portal started a 200 year dynasty of printers to the Bank of England. The garden, surrounded by tributary streams of the River Test, was inspired by Japanese stroll gardens.

It is approached by a well-planted gravel garden. Mirror-image herbaceous borders behind the house lead to a lake and a teahouse, and there are water meadows beyond. The mill stream is lined by low wooden corridors planted with varieties of *Iris ensata*.

Modern sculpture is placed at focal points and in the sculpture garden, approached by an avenue of swamp cypress. There is also a wisteria garden, a walled orchard and a vegetable garden.

▶ *Open for NGS, and for parties of ten or more by appointment (Friday only)*

5 Farleigh House

Metallic seagulls soar above species roses in this romantic modern garden, transformed from playing fields 20 years ago.

Farleigh Wallop, Basingstoke RG25 2HT

Tel: 01256 842684

LOCATION 3 miles SE of Basingstoke off B3046. Leave M3 at junction 7, signed from Dummer

Complementing the knapped-flint house, this is an exemplary modern garden in the classic tradition. The large kitchen garden has a herbaceous border with blue *Clematis durandii*, and culminates in a conservatory – with a pond – scented by various brugmansias, rare passion flowers and other choice plants. The quadripartite fountain garden, planted with roses, nepeta and alchemilla, is followed by an area of species roses with silver metallic seagulls wheeling overhead. A simple maze leads, via two topiary peacocks pecking at strawberries, to a rectangular waterlily garden. Beyond this, at the end of the Scots pine walk, wrought-iron gates open onto a lake.

There are some delightful details to observe: a huge smooth granite apple in woodland lit by a shaft of light; another pair of wrought-iron gates decorated with flowers and abstract geometrical patterns; hedges dipping to give glimpses of gardens beyond; the little barrel seat above the well-house. There are also many fine shrubs and trees, including a fine *Cornus controversa* 'Variegata'.
▶ *Open for NGS, and for parties by appointment*

6 West Green House Garden

A grand water garden, fanciful topiary, Chinese pagodas and Neoclassical follies are among the garden's many striking features.

West Green, Hartley Wintney, Hook RG27 8JB

Tel: 01252 844611

www.westgreenhouse.co.uk

LOCATION 10 miles NE of Basingstoke, 1 mile W of Hartley Wintney, 1 mile N of A30

Nestling in a wooded corner of Hampshire is this attractive 1720s manor house, where busts of gods, emperors and dukes look down from the walls over a series of remarkable gardens and a Neoclassical park.

The inner gardens, enclosed by 18th-century walls, are all devoted to parterres – one is filled with water lilies, another is of classical design with box topiary while a third enacts the whimsy of *Alice in Wonderland*. The main walled garden is planted in subtle hues of mauve, plum and blue, contained in beds that have been restored to their original outlines, and groups of tulips echo the colour schemes. A decorative potager is centred around berry-filled fruit cages where herbs, flowers and unusual vegetables are designed into colourful patterns that change every year.

All this is surrounded by the park, which is studded with follies, birdcages and monuments designed by Neoclassical architect Quinlan Terry. The entrance is through a tunnel of hornbeams, which have been pleached to direct the eye to two Chinese pagodas and the Dragon Garden.

Water is everywhere. A tree-fringed lake is especially attractive in spring with its drifts of fritillaries and other bulbs. A grand water garden, the Nymphaeum, spills down rills and steps from a devil's mouth into serene ponds. Between the two lies a geometric parterre of moated trees and grass rectangles. A winding ribbon of blue *Iris sibirica* borders a fern-fringed stream, which is crossed by five Chinoiserie-inspired arches to form the new Garden of the Five Bridges.

A green theatre, a picturesque orangery and long green *allées* are also fine features.
▶ *Open main season – telephone or consult website for details – and by appointment*

7 Bury Court

Naturalism and grasses dominate the walled garden, while in front of the house there is a modernist grid design of raised beds.

Bentley, Farnham GU10 5LZ

Tel: 07989 300703

LOCATION 6 miles NE of Alton, 5 mile SW of Farnham, 1½ miles N of Bentley on road signed to Crondall

This important garden incorporates designs by two contemporary masters of the plantsman's art. The walled garden, entered through three oast houses, is the work of Dutch garden designer Piet Oudolf and displays both his naturalism and characteristic use of grasses. It opens onto a swirling tapestry of asymmetrical beds, dominated by robust perennials and grasses, clipped hedges, two mirror pools and an outstanding gravel bed with mounds of silver-leaved Mediterranean species.

At the front of the main house is a modernist grid design by Christopher Bradley-Hole. It is laid out in geometric raised beds edged with rusted steel and planted with drifts of grasses that are shot through with accents of colour from unusual varieties of perennials.
▶ *Open for parties by appointment*

8 The Manor House, Upton Grey

Planned in 1908 by the legendary designer Gertrude Jekyll, this is now the most faithfully restored of all her gardens.

Upton Grey, Basingstoke RG25 2RD

Tel: 01256 862827

www.gertrudejekyllgarden.co.uk

Historic Garden Grade II*

LOCATION 6 miles SE of Basingstoke in Upton Grey, on hill immediately above church

In this 5 acre living museum to Gertrude Jekyll – The Manor House has the most authentic Jekyll garden now in existence – every plant is laid out as prescribed in her original plan. Visitors can explore her use of reds, yellows, greys and blues, the proportions of steps, the width of paths and everything else that goes to make up her distinctive schemes.

The garden is at its peak in May and June, but its delights continue for longer. On the upper terrace, twin herbaceous borders stretch from the tile-hung house and a central pergola leads to steps descending to the formal rose garden. This is planted with *Paeonia* 'Sarah Bernhardt', hybrid tea roses and *Lilium regale*. On the lowest terrace are a tennis court and bowling lawn.

Today, a door in the rose-hung wall leads to an Arts and Crafts style rotunda with views over downland – an innovation Jekyll would have welcomed. Her only surviving wild garden, with its rambling roses, wild flowers and water-lily pond, is located on the other side of the house.

▶ *Open main season – telephone or consult website for details – and by appointment*

9 Bramdean House

Behind a yew and box cloud hedge lie mirror-image herbaceous borders and a superb walled kitchen garden.

Bramdean, Alresford SO24 0JU

Tel: 01962 771214

Historic Garden Grade II

LOCATION 9 miles E of Winchester, 9 miles W of Petersfield on A272 in middle of Bramdean

A real plantsman's garden, Bramdean is full of interest all year round but especially from April until October. The 18th-century red-brick house is protected from the road by a cloud hedge of yew and box. Behind the house 5 acres of garden slope up through the exemplary mirror-image herbaceous borders, planted with more than 100 genera and reaching their peak in June with nepetas, geraniums, tradescantias, *Clematis* x *diversifolia* 'Hendersonii' and galegas, followed by yellows and then the russets of late summer.

The way forward, towards dianthus and roses, leads to the wrought-iron gates of the walled kitchen garden, filled with well-ordered fruit and vegetables, old-fashioned sweet peas and a mass of herbaceous flowers. Beyond a second gate lies the orchard with its curving tapestry hedge of box and yew, beehives, flowering cherries and fruit trees underplanted with daffodils.

The ancient blue door of a lovely apple house and belfry signals the top of the garden. Trees on the eastern side include *Ginkgo biloba*, *Maytenus boaria*, *Liriodendron tulipifera* and *Davidia involucrata*, magnolias and *Staphylea colchica*. Spring brings to the garden carpets of aconites, snowdrops, crocuses and other early bulbs, and autumn a large collection of tender and hardy nerines.

▶ *Open for NGS, and Mon-Fri by appointment*

10 Hinton Ampner

Once described as 'a classical beauty of layout and ornament', it has fine topiary, terracing and a range of unusual plants.

Hinton Ampner, Bramdean, Alresford SO24 0LA

Tel: 01962 771305 | www.nationaltrust.org.uk

The National Trust

LOCATION 8 miles E of Winchester, 1 mile W of Bramdean on A272

This classic country-house garden of lawns and avenues, deep borders and secret places was created by Ralph Dutton, later Lord Sherborne, who inherited the estate in 1935. The terraces below the Georgian-style house command fine views over downland. Their cross-axes, revealing glimpses of urns, statues or an obelisk, add an Italianate dimension to a quintessentially English garden.

The yew and box hedging and topiary are dense and neat, while the giant yew mushrooms look surreal. Among the wide range of unusual plants are *Syringa* x *laciniata*, *Abelia triflora* and *A. floribunda* with its raspberry tubes, *Amorpha fruticosa* and the Kentucky coffee tree, *Gymnocladus dioica*.

The old walled kitchen garden is now laid out as a formal orchard. A rose garden has been planted, while salvias and autumn crocuses, and the late-flowering *Heptacodium miconioides*, keep interest going to September and beyond.

▶ *House open; garden open main season – telephone or consult website for details – and for parties of 15 or more by appointment*

SOUTHERN ENGLAND

11 Osborne House

Italianate designs created for Victoria and Albert have been restored and the period flavour recaptured with Victorian planting.

East Cowes, Isle of Wight PO32 6JY

Tel: 01983 200022

www.english-heritage.org.uk

Historic Garden Grade II/English Heritage

LOCATION 1 mile SE of East Cowes off A3021

Built from 1845 to 1851 as a family retreat for Queen Victoria, the 20 acre gardens, designed jointly by the royal couple in the formal Italianate style, are now being restored and replanted to the original designs. Old cultivars have been used for the Victorian-style bedding on the terraces, and the borders are filled with plants of the period. Both the park and gardens are notable for their magnificent trees.

The Swiss Cottage Garden, where the gardens of Victoria and Albert's children once stood, has nine plots, each with 14 beds, planted with old varieties of soft fruit, flowers and vegetables. The museum has replicas of the royal children's wheelbarrows, and other curiosities include a mock fort and Queen Victoria's bathing machine.

There is also a wild-flower meadow and an orchard. The 1 acre walled garden has been restored sympathetically using historic plants within a modern design. Olive, orange and lemon trees complement the wall-trained fruit – vines, figs, pears, plums and cherries.

Multiple plantings in the garden ensure a continuous display of striking colour throughout summer, and broad rows of herbaceous plants

are offset by extensive plots of annually sown flowers, herbs and vegetables. The glasshouses commissioned by Prince Albert have been restored and house collections of plants from South Africa and those introduced to Britain during the Victorian period. The entwined V&A motifs to be seen in the furnishings of the house are also used here on ironwork arches, garden benches and terracotta pots.

▶ *House open. Garden and grounds open most of year – telephone or consult website for details*

12 Apple Court

Hemerocallis and hostas are the stars here, but the elegant white and tranquil Japanese gardens are equally appealing.

Hordle Lane, Hordle, Lymington SO41 0HU

Tel: 01590 642130 | www.applecourt.com

LOCATION Just N of A337 between Lymington and New Milton

Created within the abandoned walled kitchen garden of nearby Yeatton House in 1988, the garden comprises a series of themed spaces laid out on a grid. Although a lot is packed into just over an acre, it retains an open feel. Specialising in hemerocallis and hostas, the garden is at its peak in July and August, but given the range and interest of the planting and the charming layout, it is well worth visiting at any time.

The theatrical white garden with its elliptical border of white flowers and silvery foliage, framed by a screen of pleached hornbeams and backed by yew hedging, imparts an air of elegant

classicism, while the impressive Japanese garden maintains a tranquil atmosphere.

The planting along the main axes is colour-themed, with cool pastels moving from east to west and hot tones from north to south. Other features include an elegant rill running down the central axis, a fern path, a sub-tropical border, an impressive selection of grasses and rose and clematis-laden rope swags.

The garden is artfully designed and features some interesting and complementary sculptures among the planting. Many of the unusual plants are available to buy in the nursery.

▶ *Open main season – telephone or consult website for details*

13 Exbury Gardens

Winding woodland paths meander through this superb collection of many-coloured azaleas, rhododendrons and camellias.

Exbury, Southampton SO45 1AZ

Tel: 023 80 891203 │ www.exbury.co.uk

Historic Garden Grade II*

LOCATION 15 miles S of Southampton. From M27 west junction 2 take A326 then B3054 2½ miles SE of Beaulieu, after 1 mile turn right for Exbury

Established between the wars by Lionel de Rothschild, these extravagant gatherings of acid-loving rhododendrons and azaleas are the most outstanding of their kind in the south. Exbury has become renowned worldwide as a spectacular example of a lavish woodland garden. A number of paths lead visitors through the gardens' 200

acres and proceed under a light canopy of trees, mostly oak and pine, over a bridge and beside ponds to the Beaulieu River.

Many rhododendrons and azaleas, such as *R. yakushimanum* and *R.* (Hawk Group) 'Crest', were introduced here and are to be found growing beside purple Japanese maples and candelabra primulas. At times the colour associations can seem brash – harsh orange beside blush, metallic magenta next to pale blue – but a glade of towering white blooms, pink in bud, provides a delicate contrast.

Early rhododendrons, camellias and the daffodil meadow flower in March. In April, the rock garden – miniature mountain scenery with screes and valleys – is at its peak with alpine rhododendrons flowering among 'Skyrocket' junipers. Summer is the high season, when the herbaceous and grass garden is a mass of colour with a wide variety of plants on show, and the recently planted exotic garden is full of unusual species. For autumn interest there is a magnificent collection of deciduous trees, shrubs and, most notably, acers, which exhibit fiery hues next to the ponds.

The Summer Lane Garden, planted in a contemporary design inspired by Dutch expert Piet Oudolf, combines huge swathes of herbaceous plants, grasses, bulbs and wild flowers, and includes an apple orchard, a pumpkin patch and a sunflower meadow. It is accessed via a steam railway that has opened up the southeast corner of the gardens, offering visitors a 20 minute journey in comfort.

The well-stocked plant centre is worth a visit.

▶ *Open most of year – telephone or consult website for details*

SOUTHERN ENGLAND

HERTFORDSHIRE

Conveniently accessible from London and its outer reaches, the county boasts several impressive gardens with historical connections, including royal links to Elizabeth I and the late Queen Mother.

1 Hatfield House

Elegant parterres and the knot garden where Henry VIII's children once played are highlights of the house's splendid grounds.

Hatfield AL9 5NQ | Tel: 01707 287010

www.hatfield-house.co.uk

Historic Garden Grade I

LOCATION 2 miles from A1(M) junction 4 off A414 and A1000, opposite Hatfield railway station

Laid out originally in the early 17th century by Robert Cecil – the 1st Earl of Salisbury and Chief Minister to James I – and planted by gardener and plant collector John Tradescant the Elder, the garden has evolved over the centuries, particularly in the Victorian era and again during the 20th century at the hands of the Dowager Marchioness of Salisbury.

The many delights include a charming herb garden in the scented garden and the formal East Garden with its parterre, topiary, herbaceous borders and vegetable garden. The renowned knot garden, filled with species used from the 15th to 17th centuries, adjoins the Old Palace where Elizabeth I spent much of her childhood. There is also a wild garden around the New Pond (originally formed in 1607).

Up to 20,000 bulbs are planted each year in the wilderness garden, which transforms into a mass of bluebells and daffodils in spring. The park has also extensive walks and picnic areas.

▶ *House open. Park, West Garden, restaurant and shop open main season, East Garden Thurs only – telephone or consult website for details*

HATFIELD HOUSE

2 Knebworth House

Enjoy the restored Edwardian designs of Edwin Lutyens and Gertrude Jekyll, and the Dinosaur Trail in the wild garden.

Knebworth, near Stevenage SG3 6PY

Tel: 01438 812661 | www.knebworthhouse.com

Historic Garden Grade II*

LOCATION Direct access from A1(M) junction 7

In 1909, Edwin Lutyens remodelled the elaborate Jacobean-style design into a scheme that included a sunken lawn with pollarded lime walks, rose gardens and pools. Beyond a tall yew hedge lie his Green, Gold and Brick Gardens (the last with a blue and silver theme), and a pergola covered with clematis and roses. To one side is a pets' cemetery, to the other a crab-apple walk.

The herb garden, designed by Gertrude Jekyll in 1907, was laid out in 1982 and the Victorian maze replanted in 1995. The redeveloped walled garden now boasts a collection of culinary herbs and vegetables. The Wilderness is a carpet of daffodils in spring followed by blue alkanet, foxgloves and other wild flowers. Life-size dinosaurs are to be found around the 7 acres.

▶ *House and garden open main season – telephone or consult website for details*

3 St Paul's Walden Bury

One of only a few English gardens based on a *patte d'oie* or 'goose foot' design, it is set amid woodland with many fine viewpoints.

Whitwell, Hitchin SG4 8BP | Tel: 01438 871218

Historic Garden Grade I

LOCATION 5 miles S of Hitchin, ½ mile N of Whitwell on B651

The childhood home of the late Queen Mother, the formal 60 acre landscape garden was laid out in 1730. Influenced by French tastes, it is based on a *patte d'oie* design: three radiating avenues round a central point.

From the house, the landscape is ravishing. The long mown rides or *allées* are lined with clipped beech hedges and fan out from the 18th-century house through bosquets, or groves, to temples, statues, ponds and a medieval church. In one of the bosquets is a green theatre. There are fine seasonal displays of snowdrops, daffodils, rhododendrons, magnolias, cowslips and lilies.

Not to be missed is a walk around the lake, with wonderful vistas and two impressive temples.

▶ *Open for NGS, and by appointment*

4 Benington Lordship

In spring, snowdrops fill the old moat and its surrounds and visitors can enjoy lovely views from the Victorian folly all year.

Benington, Stevenage SG2 7BS

Tel: 01438 869668

www.beningtonlordship.co.uk

Historic Garden Grade II

LOCATION 5 miles E of Stevenage

A romantic hilltop garden spreads around the manor house and Victorian folly with fine views over the lake and open countryside. The massive and well-filled herbaceous double borders are designed with a glorious feeling for texture and colour, backed by the old kitchen garden wall and a sloping bank planted with an informal mixture of foliage and flowering plants.

A lavender-edged rose garden is set in a square in the centre of the old bowling green, and the kitchen garden has ornamental borders as well as functional rows of vegetables. In the moat and the adjacent grounds, the display of snowdrops followed by drifts of scillas is outstanding.

▶ *Open Feb for snowdrops – telephone or consult website for details – for NGS, and by appointment*

5 Vineyard Manor

Beyond a sophisticated terrace border lies a large and colourful secret garden with intriguing modern sculptures.

Much Hadham SG10 6BS | Tel: 01279 843761

LOCATION 5 miles W of Bishop's Stortford off A120

At its peak in high summer, this garden of both imagination and humour has been developed since 1995. Visitors enter up a slope planted with ferns, hostas and shade-loving plants under mature trees, passing an amusing man's head with two clutching hands peering from the grass by modern sculptor Mark Hall and a tall bronze of fighting hares by animal artist Paul Jenkins.

Behind the house a terrace with a wide border set into the hillside is planted in gold, silver and bronze. Hidden behind yew hedging, a large secret garden with an old dew pond has been taken into the garden and planted in generous drifts of colour, with ligularias, euphorbias, geraniums, veronicastrums, thalictrums, monardas, *Rheum palmatum*, scented *Telekia speciosa*, *Gunnera manicata*, eupatoriums and tall grasses.

▶ *Open May to Aug by appointment*

SOUTHERN ENGLAND

KENT

A mild climate makes Kent the garden capital of the country and encourages impressive displays – from the heavenly flowers of Sissinghurst to the spectacular yew hedges of Doddington Place.

1 Wykehurst

Curving beds help to achieve a sense of space, which is filled by a potager, parterre and walnut orchard – all in miniature.

Mill Road, Aldington TN25 7AJ

Tel: 01233 720395

LOCATION 5 miles SE of Ashford off A20, leaving M20 at junction 10

Set high above Romney , the charming, inventive, 1 acre garden surrounds a 17th-century farmhouse. Flowing spaces, defined by beds curving around mature trees, are divided and screened by hedges and linked by rose and ivy-covered arches. A tiny thatched summerhouse beside a sunken bog garden, a diminutive potager and parterre, a miniature walnut orchard and a secret golden garden are punctuated by witty topiary.

Those interested in learning how to achieve the same effects should enquire about the topiary courses held here.
▶ *Open for NGS, and June, July and Sept by appointment*

2 Old Place Farm

A number of elegant spaces have been created here, including a herb parterre, cutting garden and philadelphus walk.

High Halden, Ashford TN26 3JG

Tel: 01233 850202

LOCATION 10 miles SW of Ashford. From A28, opposite Chequers pub in High Halden, take Woodchurch road and follow for ½ mile

In the superb gardens surrounding the Tudor farmhouse are a series of stylish spaces, some enclosed and intimate, others opening into the wider pastoral landscape, created with the help of designer Anthony du Gard Pasley. Throughout, a strong sense of style combines profuse planting and restrained decoration. Burgeoning herbaceous borders lead to a sheltered herb parterre and a charming cutting garden, where vines and roses screen a decorative potager. Hellebores, bulbs and ferns cluster under an avenue of topiary hawthorn, and the lake is overlooked by a delightful gazebo against a backdrop of blue, purple, cream, apricot and silver. Woodland areas, a philadelphus walk and ponds contrast with the croquet lawn, which is near an imaginative and playful topiary garden.
▶ *Open by appointment*

3 Sissinghurst Castle Garden

Romantic compartments of floral displays planted with an artist's eye for colour are a highlight of this celebrated garden.

Sissinghurst, Cranbrook TN17 2AB

Tel: 01580 710700/710701 (Infoline)

www.nationaltrust.org.uk

Historic Garden Grade I/The National Trust

LOCATION 13 miles S of Maidstone, 2 miles NE of Cranbrook, 1 mile E of Sissinghurst on A262

One of Britain's most renowned gardens, the series of stylised outdoor rooms created among the ruins of a moated Tudor manor in the 1930s by poet and novelist Vita Sackville-West and her husband, writer and diplomat Harold Nicolson, is still beloved by gardeners today. The much-emulated colour palettes and the plantings of the highest subtlety and quality continue to inspire.

Spring in the Lime Walk is spectacular, with drifts of bulbs creating a tapestry based on Nicolson's meticulous records. High summer in the incomparable White Garden and the heady delight of the old roses is followed by fiery and exuberant planting schemes in the cottage garden, lush ferns and foliage carpeting the nuttery, aromatic scents wafting across the herb garden, tall meadow grasses in the orchard and rustling poplars beside the moat. For many, this is the definitive English garden, evoking the poetic sensibility of its creators, their deep feeling for history and rural tradition and the influence of their aristocratic travels.
▶ *Open main season – telephone or consult website for details – and for parties of 11 or more by appointment*

MUCH-EMULATED
COLOUR PALETTES
AND PLANTINGS OF
THE HIGHEST QUALITY
CONTINUE TO INSPIRE
SISSINGHURST CASTLE GARDEN

4 Marle Place

A peaceful garden appealing to artists and plantsmen, it has a formal framework, acres of woodland and some surprising sculptures.

Brenchley, Tonbridge TN12 7HS

Tel: 01892 722304 | www.marleplace.co.uk

LOCATION 9 miles E of Tunbridge Wells, 1 mile SW of Horsmonden, W of B2162. Follow tourist signs

The vision of several generations of enthusiastic gardeners has created a special atmosphere in the tranquil gardens surrounding the early 17th-century Wealden ironmaster's house. Sweeping lawns, tree-lined avenues, intimate walled spaces and enclosed walks along profusely planted borders provide the framework for the garden, while a croquet lawn, restored Edwardian rockery and Italianate scented garden evoke the long summer days of yesteryear.

However, it is an artistic sensibility that creates surprise and intrigue today. The gardens and surrounding woodlands are the setting and inspiration for painting days and land art workshops. Observant visitors may discover subtle sculptures made from natural materials and objects that have been found. These include a witty mosaic terrace, eccentric gates, thrones, benches and bridges, and a gallery with exhibitions inspired by the wild.

Picnics may be enjoyed in the woodland surrounding the original marl pond where clay was dug. Streams meander through an exotic bog garden and bamboo grove, while the wild-flower-strewn arboretum and allium meadow are spectacular in June. A stylish potager with a box parterre and traditional greenhouse echo the days when nine gardeners tended this idyllic site.

▶ *Open main season – telephone or consult website for details – and by appointment*

5 Nettlestead Place

The rose garden, gravel terrace, herbaceous beds and arboretum of acers are arranged on different levels and all are grand in scale.

Nettlestead, Maidstone ME18 5HA

Tel: 01622 812205

www.nettlesteadplace.co.uk

LOCATION 6 miles SW of Maidstone off B2015. Next to church

Built on an ancient site mentioned in the *Domesday Book*, the 13th-century house commands fine views of the River Medway and the surrounding farmland. Approached through a gatehouse and an avenue of Irish yews, the gardens have been developed since the hurricane of 1987, when 46 mature trees were lost.

Terraced to accommodate the sloping site, the grounds are divided into distinct areas, all on a grand scale. The magnificent house is reflected in a large and tranquil pool fringed by willows and gunneras, and a gravel terrace is planted with alpines and dwarf bulbs.

Below, a spring-fed canal runs into a deep valley planted with wetland plants. The formal rose garden, with lavender-edged turf paths, holds a profusion of roses of every variety, and a huge herbaceous garden has island beds that have been planted with bold-leaved shrubs and grasses, as well as perennials.

Other parts of the garden are linked by paths and borders filled with unusual plants, shrubs and bamboos – look out for the 600-year-old walnut tree and other fine specimens, including a newer arboretum of acers from around the world.

▶ *Open for NGS, and by apppointment*

6 Southover

The owners' dual love of plants and wildlife is highlighted by abundant cottage flowers, eco-hedges and a wild-flower meadow.

Grove Lane, Hunton, Maidstone ME15 0SE

Tel: 01622 820876

LOCATION 6 miles S of Maidstone between A229 and B2010. From Yalding take Vicarage Road to Hunton. Almost opposite school turn left into Grove Lane; house is about 180m (600ft) on right. From Coxheath turn down Hunton Hill to Hunton; Grove Lane is immediately past school

The gardening partnership of the present owners, both trained horticulturists, combines botanical knowledge and imagination to great effect. Around their 15th-century Kentish yeomans' house, the garden reflects both their love of plants and a sensitive awareness of nature and the needs of wildlife.

Divided into contrasting rooms by old walls, brick paths and high hedges, the house emerges above a sea of flowing foliage and flowers. Colours are muted and textures soft, with plants self-seeding and jostling companionably together. Large curving borders filled with bold perennials are underplanted with hellebores. A profusion of old roses and drifts of unassuming cottage flowers and herbs scent a sunny, sheltered terrace, and the adjacent meditation garden is filled with cushions of *Alchemilla mollis* in a box parterre.

Produce fills the potager, which has compost bins built from locally recycled apple tree stakes. On the field boundary of the potager ingenious 'eco-hedges', created by packing offcut branches within a framework of vertical stakes, provide wildlife habitats in the shady copse. A wild-flower meadow has been established and moisture-loving plants and many species of snowdrops thrive near a winterbourne. Other spring bulbs feature strongly in a separate grassy area naturalised by cowslips, fritillaries, martagon lilies and *Veratrum nigrum*. There is also a sunken shady walk and a fern bank.

An autumn border of grasses and colchicums, a restored pond for moorhens and old oaks left for woodpeckers complete the pleasing balance of man in harmony with nature.

▶ *Open for NGS, and by appointment*

7 Groombridge Place

An aerial walkway leads from the formal grounds to an Enchanted Forest, designed to entertain and intrigue both young and old.

Groombridge, Tunbridge Wells TN3 9QG

Tel: 01892 861444 | www.groombridge.co.uk

Historic Garden Grade I

LOCATION 4 miles SW of Tunbridge Wells. Take A264 towards East Grinstead, then after 2 miles B2110 to Groombridge

Within the ancient walls of the original 1230 moated castle, the gardens have been developed over centuries and recently the 17th-century formal gardens have been imaginatively and entertainingly restored. From a magnificent border on the highest terrace, a gravelled path leads between a striking double procession of 24 drum-shaped yews. On either side are garden rooms of differing character – the Oriental Garden inspired by the colours of an oriental rug, the Drunken Garden of misshapen junipers and the former kitchen garden now a white-flowered rose garden. A canal feeds a tranquil lake, originally the village millpond, and there are newer features such as the Giant Chessboard, the Golden Key Maze and a knot garden.

An exciting aerial walkway leads to the Enchanted Forest, created by land artist Ivan Hicks and designer Myles Challis, where extraordinary sculptures and mysterious pools provide imaginative challenges for children and adults. The moated manor house, built in 1662 and half hidden in a broad wooded valley, is not open.

▶ *Open main season – telephone or consult website for details*

8 Hever Castle and Gardens

The Italian Garden – which displays a collection of classical sculpture – is not to be missed in these spectacular grounds.

Hever, Edenbridge TN8 7NG | Tel: 01732 865224

www.hevercastle.co.uk

Historic Garden Grade I

LOCATION 3 miles SE of Edenbridge off B2026, between Sevenoaks and East Grinstead

The gardens laid out between 1904 and 1908 to statesman William Waldorf Astor's designs were conceived on a majestic scale. One thousand men were employed for the job, 800 to dig out the 35 acre lake. Steam engines shifted rock and soil to create apparently natural new features, and teams of horses moved mature trees from Ashdown Forest.

Today, the gardens have reached maturity and are teeming with colour and interest all year long. Among the many superb features is an outstanding 4 acre Italian garden, the setting for a large collection of classical statuary; opposite is a magnificent pergola supporting camellias, wisteria, crab apples, Virginia creeper and roses. It fuses into the hillside beyond, which has shaded grottoes of cool, damp-loving species such as hostas, astilbes and polygonums.

Less formal areas include the rhododendron walk and Anne Boleyn's orchard and walk, which extends the length of the grounds. A Tudor herb garden has been added, and the Sunday Walk nearby runs beside a stream past newly created borders in mature woodland. The 110m (360ft) herbaceous border has been re-created and the water maze on Sixteen-Acre Island is planted with a wide range of interesting aquatic plants. From the maze there are walks down to the millennium fountain.

▶ *Castle open. Gardens open most of year – telephone or consult website for details*

SOUTHERN ENGLAND

TEEMING WITH COLOUR AND INTEREST ALL YEAR
HEVER CASTLE AND GARDENS

9 Penshurst Place

Visitors can enjoy the splendours of the formal walled gardens, which retain their Elizabethan flavour after 600 years.

Penshurst, Tonbridge TN11 8DG

Tel: 01892 870307 | www.penshurstplace.com

Historic Garden Grade I

LOCATION 5 miles SW of Tonbridge on B2176, 7 miles N of Tunbridge Wells off A26

The scale and complexity of the 600-year-old gardens still convey the status and prestige they were designed to embody. The 11 acres of walled and hedged spaces form one of the oldest gardens in private ownership. Though much restored, they retain their Elizabethan patina.

The formal parterre of the huge Italian Garden is matched in the restored Union Flag Garden by lavender, roses and tulips and in the Heraldic Garden by its fretwork of painted medieval beasts. In between lie yew-hedged rooms with individual characters and planting schemes. In contrast are the nut plat, where coppicing of old cobnuts has encouraged the flowering of crab apples, drifts of bluebells and cow parsley, and an orchard where spring flowers spangle the long grass.

The current big project is the re-creation of the double herbaceous border leading from the original entrance gates to an ingenious design by garden specialist George Carter. Over the past two years, the land has been cleared and prepared for the planting of resplendent new borders with plantings inspired by Gertrude Jekyll. Due to open in 2011, the borders will be divided by benches set in topiary bays and framed by historic apples.

▶ *House open. Gardens open most of year – telephone or consult website for details*

PENSHURST PLACE

10 Great Comp

Long-flowering salvias are a speciality among the many rare and beautiful plants that provide interest for every season.

Comp Lane, Platt, Borough Green, Sevenoaks TN15 8QS | Tel: 01732 886154

www.greatcomp.co.uk

LOCATION From M20 junction 2, take A20 towards Maidstone. At Wrotham Heath take B2016. Signposted

Several hours may be required to do justice to the imaginatively planned 7 acre garden that is the fine setting for the 17th-century house. It has been developed by the present owners since 1957 and succeeds in being a garden for all seasons.

Spring sees the flowering of magnolias, azaleas, hellebores and early bulbs; then herbaceous perennials, masses of roses and an Italianate garden designed to set off a collection of Mediterranean plants see the summer season through. Salvias, dahlias, crocosmias, knifophias and other exotics follow on, and a flourish of turning leaves leads the garden into autumn. Mature acers, *Ginkgo biloba* and magnolias, liquidambars and liriodendrons make a fine backdrop during the growing season and a pleasing skeleton in winter; large tonsured balls of golden yew also add to the structure.

Dotted around the garden, a series of ironstone 'ruins', enclosing seats and plantings of perfumed shrubs and flowers, provide delightful secret areas for rest and contemplation. From the Italian garden with its statuary and small stream a path leads towards the outer reaches of the garden, densely planted with geraniums and a variety of ground-cover plants.

Alternatively, the visitor can make for the open lawn in front of the house, flanked on one side by a long herbaceous border – a good place

to take in the contrasting and complementary shapes and colours of the trees, shrubs and huge variety of plants.

▶ *Open main season – telephone or consult website for details*

11 Restoration House

This house, immortalised by Dickens, has a split-level garden with Gothic arches, topiary shapes and an intricate parterre.

17-19 Crow Lane, Rochester ME1 1RF

Tel: 01634 848520

www.restorationhouse.co.uk

LOCATION In centre of historic Rochester

The owners of this historic house and its immaculate walled garden have achieved an imaginative re-creation of what might have been. Lying within the walls of the city of Rochester, the late 16th to early 17th-century house had, as its name implies, strong Royalist connections and was later immortalised by novelist Charles Dickens in *Great Expectations* as Miss Havisham's

doomed dwelling. In the split-level garden, which is divided longitudinally by a mellow brick wall, the different components have been blended perfectly, and nothing jars the beauty of the fine composition.

In the upper garden, the lawn near the house is edged with low box hedges and brick and stone paths – a feature of the garden as a whole – flanked by herbaceous borders. Roses and hydrangeas abound, together with many elegant box and yew topiary shapes, and an intricate central parterre replicates a Jacobean door in the house.

The north side of the wall, pierced by substantial Gothic arches, drops to a lawn and an ornamental pool. Beyond are prolific and well-stocked vegetable, fruit and cutting gardens. An elegant oak-framed greenhouse shelters against the wall at the end of the garden, while an ingeniously camouflaged potting shed is carefully incorporated into the main bisecting wall. At the far end a mound overhung by a magnificent *Catalpa bignonioides* is the ideal spot from which to view this oasis of calm.

▶ *House open. Garden open main season – telephone or consult website for details*

12 Leeds Castle

In the landscaped grounds of the medieval castle lie a Mediterranean-style garden and a striking grotto in the centre of a maze.

Maidstone ME17 1PL

Tel: 01622 765400 | www.leeds-castle.com

Historic Garden Grade II*

LOCATION 7 miles E of Maidstone on B2163 near M20 junction 8

Visit the medieval, moated castle and grounds for its romantic, wooded setting, covering some 500 acres, and its gardens for the areas developed by painter and garden designer Russell Page.

The woodland garden, with its old and new plantings of shrubs, is especially beautiful when the daffodils are in flower. The attractive Culpeper Garden in a secluded area beyond the castle is not, as the name implies, a herb garden – although a small area does include some herbs – but is named after a 17th-century owner. The garden was started by Page for the current owner Lady Baillie in 1980 on a slope overlooking the River Len (he also flooded the valley to make a new lake) and is surrounded by high brick walls. It consists of a simple pattern of paths lined with box containing old roses riotously underplanted with herbaceous perennials. The terraced, Mediterranean-style Lady Baillie Garden overlooking the Great Water has stunning architectural plants. Not to be missed is the modern maze with a spectacular grotto at its heart; the rockwork is by grotto expert Diana Reynell and the sculptures by artist Simon Verity.

The garden is complemented by some rare and attractive birds in the duckery and aviary, which are well placed amid Page's planting of numerous shrubs and small trees.

▶ *Castle open. Grounds open all year – telephone or consult website for details*

13 Boyton Court

The garden, which has breathtaking views over the Weald, harnesses water from a natural spring to create ponds and a rill.

Sutton Valence ME17 3BY | Tel: 01622 844065

LOCATION 5 miles SE of Maidstone, off A274 at Kings Head. Go through Sutton Valence, then leaving chapel/art centre on right, go ½ mile to crossroads; turn right and garden is on right

This is a garden of style and distinction, developed since the late 1980s on 3 acres of the Greensand Ridge with wonderful southerly views

across the Weald to Tenterden and Sissinghurst. From the house, stretches of lawn lead the eye down past a flourishing bog garden to a small lake with a floating duck house that is bounded by several species of willow underplanted with a succession of waterside plants. Box and yew has been used extensively, providing additional form and structure.

A parterre on the west side incorporates a fountain, and two knot features pick out the family initials in three kinds of box, with olive bushes in pots and bands of lavender lending an Italian feel. Water from a natural spring links all the ponds in the garden and feeds a stepped rill that leads down from the parterre garden past beds set in gravel and filled with irises, astilbes and less common types of perennial geranium.

To the east of the house an eye-catching rectangular bed of box-edged lavender slopes steeply downwards, with seven different varieties planted in lines within it. A seat is judiciously positioned at the bottom of the slope to catch the full impact of its heady scent. Here, too, is a garden fragrant with David Austin roses and an intimate 'privy garden' that is shaded by *Albizia julibrissin rosea*.

Notable among the trees are the black mulberry (*Morus nigra*) and the Judas tree (*Cercis siliquastrum*), a liquidambar, a paulownia, a dawn redwood and *Cedrus atlantica* 'Glauca'. The pure white trunks of *Betula utilis jacquemontii* and the copper bark of *Prunus serrula* provide additional winter interest.

▶ *Open for NGS, and by appointment*

14 Doddington Place Gardens

Giant, cloud-like yew hedges, backing a mirrored obelisk sundial, have become an outstanding feature in their own right.

Doddington, Sittingbourne ME9 0BB

Tel: 01795 886101

www.doddingtonplacegardens.co.uk

Historic Garden Grade II

LOCATION 6 miles S of Sittingbourne. From A20 turn N at Lenham, from A2 turn S at Teynham. Signposted

Seldom are hedges the most memorable element in a garden, but the extraordinary amorphous yews that define the sweeping lawns and *allées* of Doddington have evolved, in the words of garden writer Dan Pearson, 'into giant mounds like a range of cumulus clouds… soft and full of character'. Kept formally clipped until the

Second World War, they are a living reminder of the changes that occurred in many great British gardens as a direct result of the war years. Today they frame natural glades filled in spring with tulips and camassias, with a mirrored obelisk sundial as a modern focal point.

Earlier eras are evoked by the Wellingtonia avenue, which is in keeping with the 19th-century house, that leads to 3 acres of woodland planted with rhododendrons, camellias, acers and azaleas.

From the handsome brick-and-flint Gothic folly that celebrates the life of the owner's first wife, the route leads back to the formal terraces near the house which provide views into the peaceful Kent countryside. A sunken garden, well planted with perennials, provides soft colour through into autumn.

Since 2003, an Edwardian rock garden has been subject to much restoration and clearance. This is still a work-in-progress and, at present, the new plantings struggle to complete with the harsh realities of the hard landscaping.

▶ *Open limited season – telephone or consult website for details – for NGS, and by appointment*

15 Goodnestone Park

Set in historic parkland, the highlight here is a stunning walled garden full of roses, summer flowers and kitchen produce.

Goodnestone, near Wingham, Canterbury CT3 1PL

Tel: 01304 840107

www.goodnestoneparkgardens.co.uk

Historic Garden Grade II*

LOCATION 5 miles E of Canterbury. Take A2 signed to Dover, turn left at junction B2046 for Wingham/Aylesham, then E after 1 mile

Since the 1960s, the gardens surrounding the house have gradually been restored and expanded, and the overall effect is spectacular.

Built in 1704, the Palladian-inspired house commands a panoramic view of 18th-century parkland, complete with estate cricket pitch. Below the terrace, a box parterre marks the millennium and, rising from the porticoed west entrance, a grass amphitheatre leads to a majestic lime walk. Mature woodland contains fine specimen trees underplanted with magnolias, cornus, hydrangeas and spring bulbs. Beyond is the Golden Arboretum planted in 2001.

The latest project is a gravel garden created by artist gardener Graham Gough on the site of the old tennis court, where a shingle path curves gracefully between waving grasses and drought-tolerant perennials.

The *pièce de résistance* is the wonderful walled garden, with an enchanting vista towards the Norman church through three profusely planted enclosures. The first has old-fashioned roses, clematis and early colour; the central room includes a new rill; and beyond, fruit and vegetables mingle with flowers for cutting.

▶ *House open. Garden open main season – telephone or consult website for details*

16 The Pines Garden

Run on organic principles, the coastal garden has fine trees, a lush bog garden, waterfalls and a grass labyrinth.

Beach Road, St Margaret's Bay CT15 6DZ

Tel: 01304 851737

www.baytrust.org.uk

LOCATION 3 miles NE of Dover off A258, through St Margaret's at Cliffe, just before beach

Sheltered among trees down a winding road leading to the white cliffs of Dover, this tranquil garden is immaculately maintained and run in adherence to organic principles. The Calyx Centre, constructed from excavated chalk, promotes sustainable living and a pathway in the garden uses recycled materials, including seashells from Whitstable's oyster beds.

It is hard to believe that this was a patch of scrubland until 1970, when Fred Cleary, founder of the Bay Trust, started to transform the original 6 acre site – known as the Barrack Field from its days as the quarters and training ground for soldiers during the Napoleonic Wars. Now it has a good variety of trees, gently undulating lawns, well-planted beds and a lush bog garden. The lake, with its cascading waterfalls, provides further interest and adjoining it is a grass labyrinth.

A bronze statue of Churchill by Oscar Nemon looks across the garden to the cliffs, matched at the other end by a 17th-century façade from a London Cheapside property.

A roundhouse provides shelter for picnics if the weather is breezy.

▶ *Open all year – telephone or consult website for details*

OXFORDSHIRE

History and horticulture combine in a county where the elegant grounds of stately homes sit alongside Britain's oldest botanical garden, some cutting-edge creations and exceptional plant collections.

1 Greys Court

A Tudor donkey wheel and symbolic maze enliven these ornamental grounds, which can be viewed from a medieval tower.

Rotherfield Greys, Henley-on-Thames RG9 4PG

Tel: 01491 628529 | www.nationaltrust.org.uk

Historic Garden Grade II/The National Trust

LOCATION W of Henley-on-Thames, E of B481. From town centre take A4130 towards Oxford, at Nettlebed mini-roundabout take B48. Signposted to left shortly after Highmoor

Six acres of beautiful and varied walled gardens are set against the ruins of a 14th-century fortified house. An ancient wisteria forms a canopy over one garden room, an ornamental kitchen garden is packed with unusual vegetables and a tamed wild-flower meadow stretches out under the old apple orchard. Billowing herbaceous borders and fragrant shrub roses herald the summer season.

The grass Archbishop's Maze, by leading maze designer Adrian Fisher, is interesting for its symbolism. Other modern touches include decorative ironwork and statues. Seek out the donkey wheel – used to draw water from a well – and the restored icehouse, and climb the 13th-century tower to view the garden from above.
▶ *Open main season – telephone or consult website for details*

2 Ashdown House

Snowdrops line the avenues and carpet woodland in spring, with views of the Downs and ancient Ridgeway beyond.

Lambourn, Newbury RG16 7RE

Tel: 01488 72584

www.nationaltrust.org.uk

Historic Garden Grade II*/The National Trust

LOCATION 3½ miles NW of Lambourn on W side of B4000

The exquisite hunting lodge built by Lord Craven for Elizabeth of Bohemia and set in a hauntingly beautiful valley may have lost its large formal park, but it is perfectly framed by two lime avenues radiating outwards from the house and its matching pavilions. The intricate scroll parterre in front of the house was laid out in the 1950s to replace one destroyed by troops during the Second World War, when the square was used as a parade ground.

Spring sees the mass flowering of snowdrops along the avenues and in the woodland rising from the house, which is planted in an hour-glass shape with a mile-long avenue running down the centre. From here rides and glades lead off and wonderful views open up to the ancient Ridgeway and the Berkshire Downs.
▶ *House open. Garden open main season (parties must pre-book) and woodlands open all year – telephone or check website for details*

GREYS COURT

3 Woolstone Mill House

Tree ferns and swamp cypresses meet country-garden favourites here, while topiary sheep guard the vista beyond.

Woolstone, near Faringdon SN7 7QL

Tel: 01367 820219

LOCATION 7 miles W of Wantage, 7 miles S of Faringdon off B4507 below Uffington White Horse Hill; ⅓ mile from White Horse Inn in Woolstone take road signed to Uffington

When the present owners came here in 1976, this wonderful 2 acre garden was little more than a field. Luckily both have gardening in their blood and now, within sheltering yew hedges, delightful spaces are planted with a sure eye for colour, form and juxtaposition. Some of the plants used are traditional country garden favourites, others – tree ferns, swamp cypresses, the highly poisonous such as Indian pokeweed, *Davidia involucrata* and *Schizophragma hydrangeoides* – are more unusual.

The main area behind the house is light and airy in feeling, with a wide terrace and box parterres opening out to a large circular lawn that is surrounded by generous curving herbaceous borders in a palette that changes colour from season to season. These give way in their turn to open countryside, where two amusing sheep with bodies made from topiary box and carved stone heads stand boldly in view.

The clever and interesting parts of the design are the secret, densely planted pathways leading off this space, and the element of surprise that awaits in each enclosure. There is a small white garden in gravel sandwiched between the stream and an old barn and dovecote, a mound planted with medlars and purple lace-cap hydrangeas, and a barn walk leading to a vegetable garden. Each one would make a charming small garden in its own right.

▶ *Open main season, Wed (2pm-5pm), for NGS and by appointment at other times*

4 Buscot Park

These pleasure grounds include one of Britain's finest water gardens, designed by Harold Peto and reached through woodland.

Faringdon SN7 8BU | Tel: 01367 240786

www.buscotpark.com

Historic Park and Garden Grade II*/
The National Trust

LOCATION On A417 between Lechlade and Faringdon

The huge walled estate is situated in the flatlands of the Thames, with a house built between 1780 and 1783 and a grand country-house garden developed during the 20th century.

The water garden within a wood was created by Edwardian garden designer Harold Peto in 1904. Later, avenues linking lake to house were cut through, branching out from a three-pronged goose-foot near the house, with fastigiate and weeping varieties of oak, beech and lime.

The Egyptian avenue is guarded by sphinxes and embellished with Coade-stone statues copied from an original from Hadrian's Villa. Two new gardens at *allée* intersections – the Swinging Garden and the Citrus Bowl – provide enclosed areas of great charm.

The walled kitchen garden was rearranged in the mid 1980s and is now intersected by a fine pleached avenue of *Ostrya carpinifolia* (hop hornbeam) and a Judas tree tunnel. Deep borders under the outside walls showcase unusual and skilled planting, mixing old roses and climbing ▷

BUSCOT PARK

vegetables (gourds, marrows, beans, cucumbers), which lay themselves out over the rose bushes after their flowering is over.

Walkways both outside and inside the kitchen garden lie between wide borders, with the exterior and interior walls and trellises acting as screens. In the latter, the planting by the late author and garden designer Peter Coats and imaginative development by the present Lord Faringdon, who administers the property, is exceptionally effective.

▶ *House open. Garden open main season − telephone or consult website for details*

5 Kingston Bagpuize House

Reminders of past glories survive alongside new plantings in this garden, which boasts a wide variety of rare and unusual plants.

Kingston Bagpuize, Abingdon OX13 5AX

Tel: 01865 820259

www.kingstonbagpuizehouse.org.uk

LOCATION 5½ miles W of Abingdon off A415

The beautiful mellow brick Baroque house, set in its compact park, was owned by Miss Marlie Raphael, an enthusiastic and much-travelled plant collector, from 1939 until her death in 1976. With the help of nurseryman Sir Harold Hillier and other friends, she created a 10 acre garden planted with a mind-boggling variety of rare and unusual trees, shrubs and plants. The present owner, together with her late husband, successfully uncovered and restored much of the original planting, complementing it with their own innovative ideas.

Within the framework of old brick walls and hedges of yew, beech and laurel (and even of brachyglottis), there is an air of informality. An enormous mixed border 10m (33ft) deep is packed with tall perennials covering a broad spectrum of harmonious colours.

At every turn in the 3 acre woodland garden there are rare and interesting trees and shrubs, including several spectacular magnolias. Beneath the jungle canopy are carpets of snowdrops and other bulbs, followed by drifts of geraniums, astrantias, campanulas, vincas, hellebores, lilies and other shade-loving perennials.

In spring, Church Copse is a mass of naturalised snowdrops, native woodland bulbs and perennials. Along the edge of the Garden Park with its beech avenue, Wellingtonias and other specimen trees, the shrub border reveals yet more rarities.

The terrace walk has a growing cistus collection and provides an excellent vantage point from which to enjoy a view of the house and different aspects of this informal and fascinating garden.

▶ *House and garden open main season − telephone or consult website for details − and for parties by appointment. Guided tours available*

6 Lime Close

Clever colour combinations define the cottage garden, while the potager displays more than 100 varieties of tall bearded iris.

35 Henleys Lane, Drayton OX14 4HU

LOCATION 2 miles S of Abingdon off B4017

Entering this welcome oasis, the visitor is greeted by an asymmetrical parterre quartered in box-edged beds of roses and lavender – the first of the many delights to be found in the plantsman's garden created by its garden-designer owner.

At the far side of the 16th-century house (not open) lies a herb garden laid out by garden designer Rosemary Verey, and then a sun-drenched lawn with a subtly coloured herbaceous border including, in early summer, poppies from pink to buff, alliums and purple foliage.

The potager, its Italianate crossing pergolas softened by clematis, has in its four beds a fine collection of tall bearded irises, each centred on an obelisk of golden hop. The beds in the recently planted cottage garden have been carefully colour graded from pink and purple through blue and white to fiery hot shades, all surrounding a cool, circular water tank.

Lawns stretch away beyond, with fine mature trees defining the boundary of the garden and groups of shrubs, favourite trees and shade-loving plants outlining the curvilinear lawn. There is also topiary and masses of bulbs and hellebores.

▶ *Open for NGS, and Feb to June for parties of ten or more by written appointment*

7 Appleton Manor

Since 2000 an award-winning garden designer has created a lavender courtyard, topiary and luxuriant summer wall border.

Appleton OX13 5JR | Tel: 01865 861614

LOCATION In Appleton, 6 miles W of Oxford on A420; drive is on right next to church

Traces of antiquity linger here in the house of great character, the remains of a moat on three sides and some magnificent trees. The garden, laid out since 2000, is an inspiring mixture of sophistication and informality.

In 2000, the present owners called in Chelsea Flower Show winner Arne Maynard to rescue the then-dilapidated 15 acres. He placed a gravel and box enclosure beneath the front façade, shielded by a screen of pleached crab apples and furnished now with lavenders, *Verbena bonariensis*

and self-seeded verbascums. To the rear he made a courtyard with more lavender and a large flat box table; a weeping willow presides over this sunny, butterfly-haunted spot. He joined the two with a lush summer wall border, and down the slope towards the moat placed a tactile group of caterpillar-like box topiary shapes.

Maynard's imprint is now being supplemented by those of the owners and head gardener. The wall separating the garden from the Norman church has been planted with a cloud hedge of yew, the beds in the vegetable garden are filled to bursting with many old varieties of fruit and vegetables, and plans are afoot for a woodland walk, a new orchard and more spiral hedging.

▶ *Open all year – telephone or consult website for details*

8 Cotswold Wildlife Park

A wide range of planting styles has been used to give drama and atmosphere to the setting and to tie in with the enclosures.

Burford OX18 4JP | Tel: 01993 823006

www.cotswoldwildlifepark.co.uk

LOCATION 2 miles south of Burford on the A361

In these varied and extensive grounds, it is the twin demands of the birds, mammals and reptiles and their imaginatively planted enclosures that create the dynamic environment.

In the walled garden hot colours and the largest collection of tender perennials in the country grow alongside traditional bedding displays and a range of containers and hanging baskets. The animal enclosures are given appropriate plantings that range from arid to jungle, savannah to rainforest and are intended, with their winding paths and sudden spaces, to create a sense of theatre – meerkats peer out from their stumpery towards a landscape of cacti, while penguins can be glimpsed in an attractive glade shaded by grasses and tall banana trees.

The terrace beside the listed Victorian Gothic manor house, which has a formal pond and parterre, forms a cool contrast, featuring blues and mauves, and masses of white roses. In the parkland, studded with mature and ancient trees, lions, zebras and wolves roam in an approximation of their native habitats, and bolder plantings are exemplified by the huge swathes of grasses punctuated in autumn by orange kniphofias that rear up beyond the ha-ha in the rhino paddock. There are delights for all ages.

▶ *Open all year – telephone or consult website for details*

9 Westwell Manor

Highly individual garden rooms include a memorable Cotswold enclosure, a moonlight garden, an auricula theatre and a nut walk.

Westwell, Burford OX18 4JT

LOCATION 10 miles W of Witney, 2 miles SW of Burford off A40

The exceptional garden of noted designer Anthea Gibson is well on its way to becoming a period piece. Seven acres of characterful outdoor rooms are laid out in an interlocking pattern beside and behind the house. Some are traditional while others, including a black-dyed *pièce d'eau*, are surprising and original.

Especially notable, in classic Cotswold style with a twist, is a long enclosure on two levels. On the upper storey an avenue of standard *Quercus ilex* gives height to a rose garden where each of the eight square, box-ball-edged beds is occupied by a different rose, all underplanted with tulips followed by a variety of perennials.

Continuing the axis on the lower level is a pergola draped with clematis and wisteria, flanked by well-planted borders. At the far end, a double rill terminates in a raised lawn surrounded by a pretty 'moat' of hostas, irises and moisture-lovers.

Then comes another splendid composition – twin rectangles of standard hornbeams are set in grass, with a fringe of long grass left under the trees, and separated by deep herbaceous borders.

Other areas of interest include a lavender terrace, a sundial garden, a moonlight garden, an auricula theatre, a knot garden, a nut walk, a grass amphitheatre.

Mid May to early July is the best time to visit.
▶ *Open for NGS, and by written appointment for horticultural parties of 20 or more*

10 Asthall Manor

The garden blends formal and natural styles, from box-edged parterres to wild woodland, with sharp wedges of yew at its core.

Asthall, near Burford OX18 4HW

Tel: 01993 824319 | www.onformsculpture.co.uk

Historic Garden Grade II

LOCATION 3 miles E of Burford off A40. At roundabout take turning to Minster Lovell; turn immediately left signed to Asthall

Set in the unspoilt Windrush valley with an early 17th-century Cotswold stone manor house at its heart and a Norman church peering over the wall, this garden is a beguiling mix of traditional and contemporary. The plants in the herbaceous borders around the house are country-garden favourites, while the paving stones in the broad courtyard are all but obliterated by tussocks of alchemilla and dianthus.

On the steeply sloping bank facing the courtyard, however, a gently subversive element has been at work. Two yew-edged squares flanked by twin box parterres filled with vibrant perennials slope downwards from way above head height; higher still are solid and substantial wedges of yew set in short mown rides. This inspired modern core is the creation of garden designers Julian and Isabel Bannerman.

A large and long flat lawn is punctured at both ends by sextets of *Prunus* 'Taihaku', with mighty trees – a silver birch, a cut-leaved black walnut and two copper beeches – leading the eye down over a bank of wild flowers to the countryside beyond. Here, too, is a delightfully unkempt area of wild woodland with two treehouses, a shady pond and a sculptured turf mound. Try not to miss the well-regarded sculpture exhibition.
▶ *Open for NGS*

ASTHALL MANOR

11 Brook Cottage

Although full of interest in every season, 200 species of rose and more than 50 varieties of clematis are summer highlights.

Well Lane, Alkerton, Banbury OX15 6NL

Tel: 01295 670303/670590

www.brookcottagegarden.co.uk

LOCATION 6 miles NW of Banbury. From A422 turn W signed to Alkerton, follow signs in village

There is much of interest packed into every season in this garden. From 1964 the owners have transformed four sloping acres of west-facing pastureland into an intriguing and characterful series of spaces. These combine the natural slopes with level areas of terrace and lawn, yew and beech-hedged enclosures and groups of trees and shrubs in an intricate yet seemingly casual framework, before finally merging into the surrounding countryside.

There are rarities to be found among the bulbs, perennials and shrubs, and the wide range is further extended by waterside and bog plants, and alpines, in the gravel garden. Colour combinations are especially effective – *Euphorbia griffithii* 'Fireglow' and marsh marigolds around the lily pond dazzle in May; deep purple and white variegated lunaria run riot above the house in a wonderfully natural display; and, borders ring the changes from pink and blue, silver and white, to hot-coloured schemes.

It is worth revisiting the garden in spring, summer and autumn to catch the bulbs and blossom, followed by the primulas, irises, astilbes and daylilies in the water garden in the valley, before the 200 species of old-fashioned and modern shrub roses start to bloom in the renowned 'hanging' rose garden. They are joined by more than 50 varieties of clematis, many of them late-flowering, clambering over walls and shrubs and around the tennis court to complement the herbaceous colour. Blue and white agapanthus interspersed with lemon and lime kniphofias then carry the flag until the visiting season ends on a high note with hips, berries and flaming autumn foliage.

▶ *Open main season – telephone or consult website for details – and by appointment*

PETTIFERS

12 Pettifers

A superb array of dahlias, agapanthus and roses bloom on the lower terrace, with a 'Gustav Klimt' inspired border below.

Lower Wardington, Banbury OX17 1RU

Tel: 01295 750232 | www.pettifers.com

LOCATION 5 miles NE of Banbury on A361 Daventry Road (from M40 junction 11)

The narrow, sophisticated garden in front of the 17th-century house does not prepare visitors for the beautifully planted garden and stunning landscape that lie behind. A rectangle of lawn is flanked by deep borders, resplendent in spring with tulips and alliums, followed later in the season by grasses and perennials.

The lower terrace is different in character – a parterre with four yews and domes of *Phillyrea angustifolia* forms the centrepiece of an area planted in summer with dahlias, agapanthus and roses. A flight of steps descends to a border honouring artist Gustav Klimt, which peaks in July. At the bottom of the garden is a colourful autumn border. Finally comes the tranquillity of a long paddock with an avenue of *Malus transitoria* – a sea of camassias in early summer.

The owner's travels in India have liberated her sense of colour. She uses many plants that are rare or unusual and has an instinctive talent for combining them well. A horticultural feast for plant lovers, July, August and September are the peak months to visit.

▶ *Open by appointment*

13 Broughton Castle

***Fleur-de-lys* shaped beds in the Ladies' Garden surrounding this moated castle are lined with box and brimming with roses.**

Broughton, Banbury OX15 5EB

Tel: 01295 276070 | www.broughtoncastle.com

Historic Garden Grade II

LOCATION 2½ miles SW of Banbury on B4035

In the most romantic of settings, the garden encircles a moated castle and is itself surrounded by open parkland grazed by sheep and cattle. The delightful walled Ladies' Garden, where box-edged *fleur-de-lys* beds are filled with floribunda roses and climbing roses cascade down the walls, was laid out in the 1880s. The two magnificent west and east-facing borders in front of the battlemented wall are planted in subtle shades – blues, yellows and whites for one, reds, mauves and blues for the other. Another wonderful border rises up to the house wall, with everywhere a profusion of fragrant old-fashioned roses.

The effect throughout the garden, particularly in midsummer, is quite breathtaking. The castle, for six centuries the home of the Fiennes family and immortalised in William Fiennes' best-selling 2009 memoir, *The Music Room*, is well worth visiting, not least for the splendid views of the garden from the upper windows.

▶ *Castle open. Garden open main season – telephone or consult website for details – and for parties by appointment*

14 Broughton Grange

View the walled garden from a special platform, which looks out over the three terraces, a rill and *parterres de broderie*.

Wykham Lane, Broughton OX15 5DS

Tel: 07701 098161

LOCATION From Banbury take B4035 to Broughton. At Saye and Sele Arms turn left up Wykham Lane (one way) and follow road for ½ mile out of village; entrance is on right

Set in mature parkland, this is a garden grand in both scale and vision. To begin, a knot garden anchors the front façade of the Cotswold manor house into its surroundings. Beyond, a rose garden and parterre lead on to a generous herbaceous border, which in turn introduces a succession of gardens concealed further below the house.

First comes a shady woodland garden devoted to ericaceous plants confined within black peat retaining walls, then a young grove of rare and rustling bamboos and, most unexpected of all, a great stumpery that straddles the woodland path like a fortress gateway. After all these theatrical effects, the land opens out to light, space and height – an 80 acre arboretum with more planting to come over the coming years.

At one apex is a grass terrace with Mediterranean planting, from where the eye is led down two grand avenues of chestnut and lime to the river, where a wet garden is being established. Back within the garden proper, a spring walk passes a turreted treehouse and ends in a series of high-hedged rooms sheltering the tennis court, swimming pool and open-air jacuzzi, planted with perennials and grasses by landscape designer Tom Stuart-Smith. He was also responsible for the exceptional walled garden created in 2001. It is screened on one side by architect Ptolemy Dean's striped, stepped and buttressed wall, and descends on its longest axis between a pleached lime *allée* and a beech tunnel.

Stuart-Smith divided the vast sloping space into three broad terraces, with a greenhouse and viewing platform occupying the top level, a rill and water tank crossed by stepping stones the centre ground, and at the lowest point three *parterres de broderie* tracing in box the veins of a beech, an ash and an oak leaf. If the design is ingenious, the planting is masterly – a controlled explosion of colour, texture and height that wells down the slope in crests and troughs. It is worth visiting on both open days to see the garden in its remarkably different spring and summer attire.
▶ *Open for NGS, and for guided parties by appointment*

15 Blenheim Palace

One of the greatest of Britain's 18th-century landscaped parks surrounds the palace, with a lake and Versailles-style water terraces.

Woodstock, Oxford OX20 1PP

Tel: 01993 811091

www.blenheimpalace.com

Historic Park and Garden Grade I

LOCATION 8 miles NW of Oxford. At Woodstock on A44

Walking through Nicholas Hawksmoor's Triumphal Arch of 1723, the visitor is greeted by one of the greatest contrived landscapes in Britain, comprising a 2,100 acre park and 100 acres of formal gardens.

The 1st Duke of Marlborough, who received the estate as a reward for his victories over Louis XIV, entrusted this grand project to the esteemed architect Sir John Vanbrugh. Vanburgh enlisted in his turn the help of royal gardener Charles Bridgeman and Henry Wise, Queen Anne's master gardener and the last of the British formalists. Wise constructed a bastion-walled 'military' garden, laid out kitchen gardens, planted immense elm avenues and linked Vanbrugh's impressive bridge to the sides of the valley. The gardens were ready when the Duke moved into the palace in 1719.

Major alterations were made by the 4th, 5th and 9th Dukes, one of the earliest of which was the removal of Wise's formal and military gardens by renowned landscaper 'Capability' Brown. After 1764 he also landscaped the park, installing the lake, which was created by damming the River Glyme, and the cascades.

Today, the gardens include areas established by French garden designer Achille Duchêne in the early 19th century to replace those destroyed by Brown. He made formal gardens to the east and west, the latter as two water terraces in the Versailles style.

To the east of the palace is the elaborate Italian garden of patterned box and golden yew, interspersed with various seasonal plantings, and beyond the terraces to the southwest lie the rose garden and arboretum. A grove of venerable cedars, laurel shrubberies and a box and yew exedra beckon from the vast south lawn. A maze was planted in part of the kitchen garden in 1991, and the former garden centre has been redeveloped as a lavender and herb garden.
▶ *House and park open all year. Garden open most of the year – telephone or consult website for details*

SOUTHERN ENGLAND

16 Rousham House

William Kent's masterpiece of English landscaping remains largely as he left it, alongside superb walled gardens.

Near Steeple Aston, Bicester OX25 4QX

Tel: 01869 347110

www.rousham.org

Historic Park and Garden Grade I

LOCATION 11 miles N of Oxford, 2 miles S of Steeple Aston off A4260 and B4030

Before landscape architect William Kent's design of 1738 effectively froze the garden in time, poet Alexander Pope had already described it as 'the prettiest place for water-falls, jetts, ponds, inclosed with beautiful scenes of green and hanging wood, that ever I saw'. The enchanting setting, and the use Kent made of it, exercise a powerful impression on every visitor.

Influenced perhaps by stage scenery, he set out to create a series of effects, choreographing splendid small buildings and follies, fine sculpture, water, seats and vantage points. The best way to view the garden is to follow these in the guidebook one by one in the order he intended.

This was also one of the first places where the garden took in the whole estate, 'calling in' the surrounding countryside, to use Pope's phrase.

Walled gardens next to the house, which pre-date Kent, are a major attraction in their own right, with a parterre, a rose garden, a fully tenanted dovecote and a productive vegetable garden; particularly attractive are the exuberant herbaceous borders spilling out over their box edging.

▶ *House open for parties by appointment. Garden open all year — telephone or consult website for details*

ROUSHAM HOUSE

17 St Catherine's College

Danish designer Arne Jacobsen's impressive grid system successfully links the college's buildings with its garden spaces.

Manor Road, Oxford OX1 3UJ

Tel: 01865 271700 | www.stcatz.ox.ac.uk

Historic Garden Grade I

LOCATION In city centre, near Holywell Cemetery

The college is a shrine for Danish visitors eager to see the finest work in Britain of the late Danish architect and designer Arne Jacobsen. He immersed himself in the challenges of the 9 acre site – a former flood plain between two arms of the River Cherwell. His solution was to impose a grid system to connect the buildings, using brick walls, covered walkways, beech and yew hedging and blocks of clipped yew to articulate the design, reflect the lines and detailing of the architecture and act as wind shields.

The most emphatic statements are the majestically long and wide water-lily canal that runs the length of the main building complex, and the square courtyard with a huge circular lawn at its heart. The river is shut away behind tall hedges, and it is the open spaces that count, along with the mature and splendid trees. Other specimen trees and shrubs have been chosen for their flowers, berries, bark or autumn colour.

Other incidents in the landscape are the academic equivalent of 18th-century follies and temples – a circular bike shed, a scalloped music house and a little yew-backed amphitheatre.

▶ *Open all year – telephone or consult website for details. Please report to Lodge on arrival; tours by appointment only (email simon.horwood@stcatz.ox.ac.uk)*

18 University of Oxford Botanic Garden

No fewer than 7,000 types of plant in Britain's oldest botanic garden have been arranged to educate and excite visitors.

Rose Lane, Oxford OX1 4AZ | Tel: 01865 286690

www.botanic-garden.ox.ac.uk

Historic Garden Grade I

LOCATION In city centre, opposite Magdalen College near bridge

This is the oldest botanic garden in Britain, which was founded in 1621 for physicians' herbal requirements. It is surrounded by a Grade I listed wall and entered through a splendid archway by 17th-century architect Nicholas Stone. Nowhere else on earth, it is claimed, are so many different plants clustered in 4½ acres. There are 7,000 types of plant in all, representing more than 90 per cent of the families of flowering plants.

One yew survives from the 1650 plantings, and there is a series of family beds containing herbaceous and annual plants in labelled systematic groups. The old walls back beds with tender plants, including roses and clematis. To the left is a collection of glasshouses, with modern ones replacing those built in 1670. A rock garden has been renovated, as has the water garden and late summer/autumn borders, and a series of vegetable beds has been added recently. A National Collection of euphorbias is held here.

Garden designers Nori and Sandra Pope were commissioned to plant autumn borders, and they have used dark and silver shrubs with spectacular autumn foliage at the back of the border.

▶ *Open all year – telephone or consult website for details. Guided tours available*

19 Waterperry Gardens

The well-labelled plants will delight collectors, along with a fine herbaceous border that flowers from May to October.

Waterperry, near Wheatley OX33 1JZ

Tel: 01844 339254

www.waterperrygardens.co.uk

LOCATION 9 miles E of Oxford, 2½ miles N of Wheatley off M40 junction 8 from London, or 8A from Birmingham. Signposted

The fine, well-planted gardens – which date back to the 1930s, when a small horticultural school was opened here – are of both historical and horticultural interest. The herbaceous nursery stock beds lie within the ornamental gardens and form a living catalogue, with the plants grown in rows and labelled. Intermixed with this are major features of the old garden – lawns and a splendid herbaceous border; beds containing collections of alpines, dwarf conifers and other shrubs; a rose garden; a formal knot garden; a water-lily canal; and a clay bank planted with shade-lovers. A National Collection of *Kabschia saxifrages* is held here.

There is a garden centre in the walled garden, a renovated glasshouse that is home to a 100-year-old Seville orange tree, and orchards that yield thousands of bottles of apple juice.

▶ *Open most of year – telephone or consult website for details – for NGS and Art in Action (020 7381 3192)*

SOUTHERN ENGLAND

Painting with plants

Garden colourists of the past sought to contain plants within formal schemes. Today's artists take a more relaxed approach.

Some garden designers are professional artists and craftsmen – Gertrude Jekyll, renowned for her rainbow borders, was an expert embroiderer; John Hubbard, creator of the garden at Chilcombe House in Dorset, is a painter – but all gardeners are essentially painters with plants.

A number of the most vibrant pictures are created by massed displays of low-growing flowers and foliage plants. Popular since the 16th century, they are especially eye-catching when laid out as parterres – beds outlined with low clipped hedging to form a pattern. These were initially infilled with coloured gravel, later with low-growing spring and summer flowers and then with exotics used as annual bedding.

At their best, these strictly conceived schemes can be breathtaking. At Hanbury Hall in Worcestershire, George London's large sunken parterre dates from the 18th century. From spring to autumn the four substantial box-edged squares, held together by narrow paths and a central roundel, flower continuously with varieties of plants from that period, such as *Armeria maritima*, *Pulsatilla vulgaris* (the Pasque flower), marigolds and alyssums, London pride and *Dianthus barbatus*.

In the following century, the activities of the great plant collectors brought many showy exotics into play: zinnias, dahlias, heliotropes, begonias, petunias, clarkias, mimulus and many more. Gardeners were trained to arrange them

GREAT DRIFTS OF COLOUR CREATE A PAINTERLY BUT NATURALISTIC EFFECT

PENSTHORPE

by colour in plantings that towards the end of the 19th century started to resemble elaborate mosaics or costume jewellery. Formal parterres and curvaceous beds were designed to show off a seasonal palette of richly coloured flowers; at Drumlanrig Castle in Dumfries and Galloway, a Scottish variation saw heather used as an infill instead of bedding plants.

Formal schemes

One of the largest and most splendid examples of this kind of carpet bedding scheme can be seen at Waddesdon Manor in Buckinghamshire. The parterre in front of the south façade was designed on a massive scale for Baron Ferdinand de Rothschild by the Frenchman Elie Lanié in the ten years following the Baron's purchase of the house in 1874. In 2000, when the garden was revived, the painter John Hubbard was chosen to design the first scheme; followed by the couturier

Oscar de la Renta and three other celebrity plant-painters. Designs are based on an aspect of the Baron's life, with the family colours of blue and gold predominating; in 2009 an equestrian theme had Bomber, the winner of the Ascot Gold Cup a century earlier, depicted centre-stage in 8,000 leafy alternantheras.

At around the same time, Lord Armstrong was developing the gardens at Cragside, his house in Northumberland. The formal garden on a south-facing terraced slope consists of two complex beds, 2m wide and 18m long. Runners as opposed to carpets, they dominate the middle terrace, framed by substantial sandstone edging. Like the early Victorian bedding schemes, they are filled only with foliage plants, including some succulents. The annually changing designs often reflect aspects of the house and family – including details of carpets, stained-glass windows, even door knobs and drain covers.

Modern casual

In complete contrast to such formal schemes is the late Christopher Lloyd's garden at Great Dixter in East Sussex. A major exponent of exploratory colour in gardening, he clashed seemingly unrelated colours to stunning effect. 'I have no segregated colour schemes,' he wrote, 'In fact I take it as a challenge to combine every school of colour effectively ... if I think a yellow candelabrum of mullein will look good rising from the middle of a quilt of pink phlox, I'll put it there – or let it put itself there'.

Even more visually relaxed is the Millennium Garden at Pensthorpe in Norfolk, where great drifts of colour create a painterly but naturalistic effect in every season. Designed by Piet Oudolf, it was first planted in 1999. In spring, bulbs such as irises and puschkinias and shrubs including *Viburnum bodnantense* 'Dawn' are at their subtle best. Later, foliage predominates, followed by more brilliantly hued perennials such as the deep red *Astrantia major* 'Claret' and the golden fountainheads of *Deschampsia cespitosa* 'Goldtau' in summer when the garden is at its peak. In early autumn, flowers such as asters and vernonias appear and the colours of perennial foliage and grasses contribute a vivid show.

Another example of Oudolf's approach to colour is in the walled garden at Scampston Hall in North Yorkshire, where the perennial meadow successfully combines deceptively casual planting with a more formal outline in a scheme that is a superb picture at any time of year.

Whether designed with a limited palette, set on an almost mathematical grid, or allowing nature to have the upper hand, gardens where colour is key are a sensual and artistic delight.

SURREY

This verdant county is home to many grand houses, historic parks and gardens of special interest, including an arboretum, imaginative planting schemes, and the RHS's flagship garden at Wisley.

1 Wotton House

A striking mound lies at the heart of this garden created by diarist John Evelyn, along with a classical temple, pool and fountain.

Guildford Road, Dorking RH5 6HS

Tel: 01306 730000

LOCATION 3 miles W of Dorking on A25 Dorking-Guildford road. Entrance by Wotton Hatch pub

Wotton House was the birthplace, in 1620, of the diarist and gardening writer John Evelyn, who created the garden. Greatly influenced by his travels in Europe during the Civil War, he designed it originally for his elder brother, George, but inherited the estate at the age of 79.

The dominant feature, set against a backdrop of mature trees, is the spectacular mound rising on three levels. It has a classical temple at its base, a circular pool with a fountain in front, and it is surrounded by a parterre of interlocking box triangles filled with a variety of plants.

Near the house are two fake stone Pulhamite grottoes, one with a pool, and a fernery. Hidden away in a walled enclosure is a tortoise house in the style of an Italian temple and rectangular pools, intended originally for terrapins. A drained lake is currently being transformed into a water meadow.
▶ *Open for NGS, and by appointment*

2 Hannah Peschar Sculpture Garden

This valley garden is the perfect setting for the sculptor's contemporary works, which are displayed against plants or water.

Black and White Cottage, Standon Lane, Ockley RH5 5QR | Tel: 01306 627269

www.hannahpescharsculpture.com

LOCATION 6 miles S of Dorking, 1 mile SW of Ockley off A29

Winding along the narrow paths that criss-cross the 10 acres of valley garden here, looking down on streams, lakes and precarious wooden bridges, is to escape the real world for a while. The effect is enhanced by the romantic buildings lying at the heart of the garden. When Hannah Peschar and her husband, the landscape designer Anthony Paul, came here in 1977, the place had been neglected for years. He kept the old trees, and under their canopy has encouraged some 400 native species to spread among his favourite architectural plants – dynamos such as gunneras, *Ligularia* 'The Rocket', vast groups of petasites, giant hogweed, grasses and stands of bamboo.

But the garden is only half the story. It has been designed primarily as a showcase for Hannah Peschar's contemporary sculpture, placed among vegetation or against water to bring out the character and quality of each piece.
▶ *Open for limited season – telephone or consult website for details – and for parties of four or more by appointment*

3 Winkworth Arboretum

Glorious views, vibrant spring and autumn colour and more than 1,000 species of trees and shrubs, many rare, can be enjoyed here.

Hascombe Road, Godalming GU8 4AD

Tel: 01483 208477 | www.nationaltrust.org.uk

The National Trust

LOCATION 2 miles SE of Godalming, E of B2130

Visit Winkworth not only for its superlative trees but also for its setting, on a sloping hillside with glorious views over the lake to the hills beyond. Dr Wilfrid Fox, an amateur gardener and botanist, bought the 110 acres in 1937. Aided by his connections with Kew and Hilliers, he set about establishing extensive collections of trees – among them birch, holly, magnolia and a National Collection of sorbus.

Eucryphias, glorious in August, stand sentinel on either side of Fox's memorial with views down the valley. Carpets of bluebells in spring are followed by cherries, rhododendrons and azaleas in bright splashes, and in autumn acers, liquidambars and nyssas provide colour. After problems with the dams, the lower lake has been drained to form a wetland area, crossed by a handsome bridge with a viewing platform – it is the highpoint of a new woodland walk.
▶ *Open all year – telephone or consult website for details*

IN AUTUMN ACERS, LIQUIDAMBARS AND NYSSAS PROVIDE LUMINOUS COLOUR

WINKWORTH ARBORETUM

4 Vann

Art and nature combine in this enchanting garden, with an Arts and Crafts pergola and a woodland water garden.

Hambledon, Godalming GU8 4EF

Tel: 01428 683413 | www.vanngarden.co.uk

Historic Garden Grade II*

LOCATION 11 miles S of Guildford, 6 miles S of Godalming. Take A283 to Chiddingfold; turn left after Winterton Alms pub into Skinners Lane and left again at T-junction signed to Hambledon. Garden is 1½ miles on right

The Grade II-listed house (not open), standing in 5 acres of garden, dates from 1542 – the name is derived from the word 'fen'. The oldest part of the garden is at the front, enclosed by clipped yew hedges, divided by paths and planted in cottage-garden style. Behind the house, a stone pergola erected in 1907 by W.D. Caröe – a major figure in the Arts and Crafts movement – is underplanted with shade-lovers and leads out towards an old enlarged field pond.

The woodland water garden was designed in 1911 with the help of Gertrude Jekyll, who supplied the plants. It has a winding stream, crossed and recrossed by Bargate stone paths and swathed in lush planting; above the pond a narrow, stone-walled stream is enclosed by a yew walk planted in 1909. A serpentine crinkle-crankle wall supports fruit trees, and there are two mixed herbaceous borders in the vegetable garden and island beds in the orchard.

▶ *Open for NGS, and by appointment (parties of 15 or more by written appointment)*

5 Munstead Wood

A remarkable piece of horticultural history, Gertrude Jekyll's garden has been lovingly restored using her colour palette.

Heath Lane, Busbridge, Godalming GU7 1UN

Tel: 01483 417867

Historic Garden Grade I

LOCATION From Godalming take B2130 to Busbridge. Heath Lane is on left opposite church

Thanks to an authentic restoration begun in the early 1980s, garden designer Gertrude Jekyll's own garden now provides a fascinating insight into her horticultural credo. It was strongly influenced by her art college training and travels in Europe and remains highly respected and widely copied today. The formal beds and lawns in front of the house become increasingly relaxed as they pass through stands of silver birch, drifts of daffodils, massed azaleas and banks of rhododendrons cleft by a wide path, melting finally into woodland. Across the wide lawn the fern-filled sunken rock garden glimmers with flowering bulbs in spring. A grass path leads through shrubs to the main flower border which is 60m (200ft) long and 4m (13ft) deep and was designed by Jekyll according to her famous colour palette – bright reds and oranges in the centre shading out through yellow, blues and mauves to white at either end.

Through the arched doorway in the Bargate wall, the triangular summer garden and sheltered spring garden lie side by side. Passing back through the wall again, the visitor comes upon a rose pergola and nut walk, each tree now reduced to five stems and underplanted with hellebores. The aster garden glows with pinks and purples in late summer, and paths edged with lavender and pinks lead to the tank garden, topiary and the courtyard at the back of the house, where the walls support *Hydrangea petiolaris* on the shady side and *Rosa banksiae* 'Lutea' opposite. To the left the primula garden is laid out in curving lines under nut trees.

In Jekyll's day, the gardens extended down to the end of Heath Lane and were tended by a staff of eight. The fruit, vegetable and cutting gardens and the barn and gardener's cottage were sold off after the Second World War, and now just two people maintain the 10 remaining acres.

▶ *Open by appointment*

6 Knowle Grange

This hilltop garden, created from scratch in 1990, blends traditional planting with an architectural framework to great effect.

Hound House Road, Shere GU5 9JH

Tel: 01483 202108

LOCATION 8 miles SE of Guildford off A25. Go through Shere and after railway bridge, continue 1½ miles past house on right to end of lane

A garden of strong architectural lines softened by planting, it was created only recently but is traditional in style. The house, which sits on a hilltop with a wide and verdant view to the north, was built in 1928. The gardens were started in 1990, following a clear-up after the great storm of 1987, and were inspired by the owner's visits to gardens in this country and abroad.

Eighteenth-century French stone steps lead down to a circular lawn with a long curve of French Gothic balustrading. Behind the house the ground has been levelled to make a wide lawn with flower borders; a Burgundian fountain and pool are at one end, a belvedere at the other. To the west the land slopes down to a series of outdoor rooms – an Italianate garden with columns and pencil cypresses, and woodland, Japanese and knot gardens. A charming stone gazebo is festooned with roses. To the south, a mile-long Universal Path of Life is being created; it will encompass a hilltop with distant views, a bluebell valley and a holly labyrinth.

▶ *Open for NGS, and for parties of 15 or more by appointment Mon–Fri in May, June and Sept*

7 Chilworth Manor

Three terraces were cut into the hillside to form a walled garden, which features box balls, wavy parterres and a lavender walk.

Halfpenny Lane, Chilworth GU4 8NN

LOCATION 3½ miles SE of Guildford on A248. From centre of village turn into Blacksmith Lane, then first driveway on right in Halfpenny Lane

This is one of those interesting amalgams that do the county proud: a historic garden sympathetically restored, then touched up with some bold contemporary accents.

The three terraces cut into the hillside in the 18th century by Sarah, Duchess of Marlborough to make a walled garden are now edged with box balls, clouds of *Alchemilla mollis* and pink peonies. The lower terrace has neat box parterres in a contemporary wavy design, and on the upper level the original lavender walk has been retained, accompanied by plantings of aquilegias, pink peonies and draping wisteria. The old roses, miraculously regenerated, climb the walls above herbaceous borders planted with pink Oriental poppies, foxgloves and hollyhocks.

In the old vegetable garden, the swimming pool is surrounded by restored glasshouses and a dramatic water feature, with a mature olive and specimen trees in pots for horticultural interest.

The 11th-century stewponds have been linked to a new Japanese-style garden by a leat (water channel), crossed by a bridge and granite stepping stones, with a waterfall cascading down. The path leads between mounds carpeted with sedums and dramatic rocks to a stream and Japanese azaleas.

In the peaceful water garden, modern sculpture stands among mature trees and flowering shrubs. An old Judas tree is propped beside the ha-ha and there's a herd of alpacas roaming in the paddock beyond.

▶ *Open for NGS*

8 Painshill Park

The stunning 18th-century park includes a serpentine lake, spectacular waterwheel and an island grotto lined with stalactites.

Portsmouth Road, Cobham KT11 1JE

Tel: 01932 868113

www.painshill.co.uk

Historic Garden Grade I

LOCATION 4 miles SW of Esher, W of Cobham. From M25 junction 10, take A3 and A245. Entrance 200m (650ft) from A245/A307 roundabout

Landscape designer Charles Hamilton created the 158 acre landscaped park – contemporary with Stowe and Stourhead – between 1738 and 1773, when it had to be sold after he ran out of funds. The garden was well maintained until the Second World War then, in 1948, it was sold off in lots and all but lost. Between 1974 and 1980 Elmbridge Council bought up most of the land; the following year the Painshill Park Trust was formed and began the task of restoration.

To the north is a crescent of parkland with clumps of trees, and the ornamental pleasure grounds to the south were designed around a serpentine 14 acre lake and spectacular waterwheel fed from the River Mole. The restored Chinese bridge, opened in 1988, leads to an island and grotto, the main chamber of which is 12m (40ft) across, hung with stalactites and lined with shards of glistening felspar. The mausoleum, near the river, was depicted on one of the plates of Catherine the Great of Russia's 'Wedgwood Frog' dinner service; a further reach of the lake reflects an abbey ruin.

The focal point of the garden is the elegant Gothic temple on higher ground. It is approached across a grassed amphitheatre encircled by formal 18th-century-style shrubberies. A dramatic blue and white Turkish tent with a gold coronet stands on a plateau among informal plantings; in the distance is the Gothic tower. The great cedar of Lebanon, 36.5m (120ft) high and with a girth of 10m (33ft), is reputedly the largest in Europe.

The vineyard has been replanted on a southern slope and the hermitage rebuilt, while the restoration of the grotto and rebuilding of the Temple of Bacchus are ongoing. The acclaimed American Roots exhibition continues within the old walled garden, and a National Collection of North American trees and shrubs is held here.

▶ *Open all year – telephone or consult website for details – and by appointment for parties of ten or more*

SOUTHERN ENGLAND

9 Savill Garden

One of Britain's finest ornamental gardens, it has superlative herbaceous borders and a temperate house for tender species.

Wick Lane, Englefield Green TW20 0UU

Tel: 01753 847518

www.theroyallandscape.co.uk

Historic Park Grade I

LOCATION 4 miles W of Staines, 5 miles S of Windsor. Follow signs

One of the largest and most important natural gardens to be created during the 20th century, Savill Garden was begun in the late 1930s for George VI by Sir Eric Savill, deputy ranger of Windsor Great Park.

In spring, carpets of naturalised miniature daffodils thrive in a meadow, and a fine collection of rhododendrons, magnolias and camellias flower under rare trees. The curving Golden Jubilee garden is planted in summery pinks and blues around a water sculpture; a dry garden was added following the hot summers of the 1970s.

Dramatic double herbaceous borders 100m (330ft) long lead at one end to the Queen Elizabeth Temperate House, which shelters tree ferns and tender plants. At the other end lies a rose garden, which is reopening in 2010; a raised walkway will allow it to be viewed from above.
▶ *Open all year – telephone or consult website for details*

10 The Valley Gardens

A flowering forest interspersed with meadows, the tiers of azaleas in its Punch Bowl amphitheatre are a dazzling sight.

Wick Road, Englefield Green TW20 0UU

Tel: 01753 847518

www.theroyallandscape.co.uk

LOCATION 4 miles W of Staines, 5 miles S of Windsor. Follow signs

When Sir Eric ran out of space in the Savill Garden (see above), he began to plant the 250 acres of undulating mature woodland area created in the 18th century with the spoil resulting from the excavation of the vast Virginia Water lake. In his celebrated Punch Bowl amphitheatre evergreen azaleas are arranged in tiers and shaded with acers; a further valley is banked with deciduous azaleas, a blaze of colour in spring and autumn, and a cool beech wood rises behind.

GREAT FOSTERS

The main valley, planted with magnolias, Japanese cherries and hydrangeas, has views over the lake.

In March and April the Daffodil Valley is spectacular, with carpets of dwarf daffodils backed by collections of dwarf and slow-growing conifers, and there is also a camellia garden and a National Collection of species rhododendrons. The overall feeling is natural, the only ornaments being a totem pole given to HM the Queen by the people of Canada in 1958, a Palladian memorial shelter and a pillared colonnade imported in the 19th century from Leptis Magna.
▶ *Open all year – telephone or consult website for details*

11 Great Fosters

Striking formal gardens are framed on three sides by a Saxon moat, but the grassed amphitheatre is the most impressive feature.

Stroude Road, Egham TW20 9UR

Tel: 01784 433822 | www.greatfosters.co.uk

Historic Garden Grade II

LOCATION 1 mile SW of Staines off M25 junction 13, 1 mile S of Egham

This garden is a remarkable marriage between the classic and the contemporary. Although the house was built in the late 16th century, the topiary

designed the castellated belvedere. Charles Bridgeman made a turf amphitheatre overlooking a formal pool. William Kent shaped a serpentine ha-ha and turned the pool into a naturalistic lake with an island, where he placed a classical pavilion. 'Capability' Brown even diverted the London to Portsmouth road to enlarge the grounds and improve the viewpoints.

But in 1922 the property was broken up and a school bought the house and belvedere. The National Trust purchased the remaining 49 acres and started the restoration in 1975. Although much of its past has gone, there are tantalising glimpses of former glory – behind the camellia terrace an avenue of limes leads to a yew-framed bowling green, and beyond it the grassy slope up to the handsome two-storey belvedere.

The belvedere, which offers splendid views, can be visited on certain weekends in summer, and tranquil walks may be taken at any time of year through banks of rhododendron and laurel, with a bird's-eye view of the amphitheatre available from the terrace above.

▶ *House and belvedere open. Garden open all year – telephone or consult website for details*

parterres – recently restored – were created in 1918 within a U-shaped moat. A Japanese bridge, festooned with wisteria, leads to a pergola and a circular, sunken rose garden with an octet of steps descending to a lily pond and fountain. Nearby are two modern gardens, a vista garden with serpentine hedges, a lake fringed by marginals and a woodland area. The most innovative development is the vast amphitheatre at the end of the lime avenue, carved out against a *bund* (embankment) made to block out the M25.

▶ *Open all year – telephone or consult website for details*

12 Claremont Landscape Garden

Some of the garden's 18th-century glory remains, including many delightful vistas, a camellia terrace and a belvedere.

Portsmouth Road, Esher KT10 9JG

Tel: 01372 467806

www.nationaltrust.org.uk/claremont

Historic Park Grade I/The National Trust

LOCATION E of A307, just S of Esher

This landscape garden was created by some of the great names in garden history. Sir John Vanbrugh

13 Dunsborough Park

Recently restored elements are the Victorian palm house and glasshouses and newly replanted double herbaceous borders.

Ripley, Woking GU23 6AL │ Tel: 01483 225366

www.sweertsdelandas.com

LOCATION 3 miles NE of Guildford. Take A247 or A3 to Ripley. Entrance across Ripley Green

The restoration of the splendid 10 acre garden, together with its Victorian glasshouses and palm house, is virtually complete and makes a fitting showcase for the extensive collection of statuary and ornaments displayed among the plants.

Double herbaceous borders have been replanted with blue and white perennials, and a colour-themed border replaced with vibrant late-summer herbaceous perennials. There are two walled gardens. One has been divided into separate rooms and filled with unusual plants; the other shelters shrub roses and, behind a unique ginkgo hedge, a display of garden ornaments.

The main part of the water garden, crossed by stepping stones, has been restored and replanted, and can be viewed from the delightful belvedere on the bridge. An ancient, spreading mulberry dominates the secluded white garden.

▶ *Open for limited season – telephone or consult website for details – and by appointment*

SOUTHERN ENGLAND

14 RHS Garden Wisley

The RHS's leading garden is an expertly executed mix of ornamental planting and trial beds, offering interest all year round.

Wisley, Woking GU23 6QB | Tel: 01483 224234

www.rhs.org.uk

Historic Garden Grade II/RHS

LOCATION 7 miles NE of Guildford, on A3

The Royal Horticultural Society's flagship garden is a maze of plantings, open spaces and specialist areas that spread across 200 acres and provide hours of interest for visitors in every season.

There is no fixed route but there are definite honeypots. These include the lily canal and loggia that form the first spectacle on entry; the colourful rock garden bisected by a fanfare of steps to allow close inspection of the plants; and, on the far side of Battleston Hill, the trial beds that include permanent trials of hot favourites such as dahlias and chrysanthemums. In spring, the flowering rhododendrons, azaleas, magnolias and camellias on Battleston Hill and the shrubs and trees in the wild garden draw the crowds. In summer, they include the romantic planting in the country garden and the superb, deep herbaceous borders where plants are grown in generous drifts. In autumn, the Glasshouse Borders of grasses and perennials reach a crescendo of colour. In winter, seedheads in the grass beds lining the path to the restaurant add colour and the heather garden comes into bloom.

Another specialist area is the alpine house, where a tufa rock landscape has been created to allow the plants to form naturalistic cushions of foliage and flowers. For the tree lover, the 1,400 specimens in the 32 acre Jubilee Arboretum can be explored via a network of paths cut through rough grass.

For the fruit grower, there are the 16 acre fruit fields where it is easy to compare varieties of apples, plums, pears, quinces, medlars and nut trees grown in rows. Other fruits and vegetables, and methods of cultivation, can be inspected in the model gardens. The eight urban plots on Witan Street, which is beyond the model gardens

and easy to miss, are imaginatively designed and crisply maintained.

Since 2007, a well-trodden route leads across Seven Acres to the bicentenary glasshouse, a soaring, curved construction of steel and glass divided into four climatic zones plus an interactive root zone, a fun place for children to explore the secret life of plants beneath the soil. The surrounding landscaped garden is a matrix of terraced arcs and squares filled with perennials and grasses, with beech hedges linking the glasshouse to its borders. On the far side of the glasshouse the small teaching garden in the Clore Learning Centre has been designed to show sustainable gardening. The riverside walk leads to an area where wildlife is encouraged.

No RHS garden is complete without its roses, and the new Bowes-Lyon rose garden on the slopes of Weather Hill, due to be finished in 2012, combines roses with shrubs, herbaceous plants and bulbs. Visitors can make use of the well-stocked plant centre and excellent bookshop.

▶ *Open all year – telephone or consult website for details*

RHS GARDEN WISLEY

15 Cherkley Court

Set in 400 acres of parkland with views over the Mole Valley, the gardens have a series of grand terraces at their heart.

Reigate Road, near Leatherhead KT22 8QX

Tel: 01372 380980 | www.cherkleycourt.com

LOCATION 3 miles NE of Dorking off B2033

Surrounded by parkland and woodland, the mansion was bought in 1910 by publishing tycoon Max Aitken, later Lord Beaverbrook. The 16 acres of garden have been redesigned to reflect Cherkley's glory days. The planting is elegant, the hard landscaping is beautifully done and new sculptures and garden buildings blend in perfectly.

The main garden lies on two terraces behind the house. A broad path flanked by a row of tulip trees drops to a lawn with a rill, two pavilions and a grotto. This lower terrace is backed by a long, boldly planted herbaceous border.

Elsewhere there's an Italian garden around a formal pool, an exotic planting of lilies, bananas, dahlias and cannas, and an area behind the house that is Mediterranean in planting and atmosphere.

▶ *Open main season – telephone or consult website for details*

16 Gatton Park

This 'Capability' Brown landscape, with its Japanese and Rock Gardens and lake, can be enjoyed again following restoration work.

Reigate RH2 0TW

Tel: 01737 649068 | www.gattonpark.com

Historic Park Grade II

LOCATION 3 miles NE of Reigate. From A23 or Gatton Bottom, turn into Rocky Lane

During the 18th century, 'Capability' Brown landscaped the parkland and created the 28 acre lake. Next, mustard magnate Jeremiah Colman built a dramatic rock and water garden, topping it off with a Japanese garden complete with thatched teahouse, bridge and lanterns.

The Gatton Trust has been restoring the gardens since 1996. Now the ponds, cascades and serpentine river feeding the lake run clear again, the rock garden displays alpines and small shrubs, and the dry-stone arch has been restored.

To mark the millennium, ten Caithness stones 3m (10ft) high have been engraved with texts from the past 1,000 years.

▶ *Open for limited season – telephone or consult website for details – and for NGS for snowdrops*

SUSSEX

Many botanically rich gardens steeped in gardening history and showcasing the finds of renowned plant collectors are found here among the unspoilt countryside of the South Downs and the Weald.

1 Arundel Castle Gardens

Restoration has made the walled garden and lean-to peach house grand again, and a new formal area boasts topiary and sculpture.

Arundel BN18 9AB | Tel: 01903 882173/884581

www.arundelcastle.org

Historic Garden Grade II*

LOCATION 10 miles E of Chichester on A27

Since 1996 the neglected gardens surrounding this romantic castle have been returned to their Victorian splendor. The delightful walled vegetable garden is based around a formal Victorian design of small paths and square beds. Its central point is a lead fountain viewed through arches of apple trees, while flowers among the vegetables add to the tapestry of colour. An 1850 lean-to iron peach house once again has peaches on its wall with citrus and other exotic fruits.

The remaining third of the walled garden is being transformed into a series of enclosures, terraced on two levels, that pay homage to the long-lost Renaissance garden created at Arundel House in London by the 14th Earl of Arundel. The design, by garden designers Julian and Isabel Bannerman, is at once formal and contemporary, employing topiary, water devices and sculpture.

In the small white garden of the Fitzalan Chapel, an atmosphere of stillness and reflection prevails. The rose garden is also worth a visit.
▶ *Castle and garden open main season – telephone or check website for details*

2 Denmans Garden

Designed to showcase foliage plants, the garden is a tamed wilderness of euphorbias, yuccas, phormiums, thistles and bamboos.

Denmans Lane, Fontwell BN18 0SU

Tel: 01243 542808 | www.denmans-garden.co.uk

LOCATION 5 miles E of Chichester. Turn S off A27, W of Fontwell racecourse

John Brookes, one of Britain's most influential designers, moved here in 1980 and turned the 4 acre garden into a stage for foliage plants. Even in spring, visitors are seduced by euphorbias, yuccas, phormiums and mounds of clipped box.

The centre of the garden is a river of pebbles and gravel against which the leaves of thistles and bamboo show up dramatically. There are some choice tulips and other spring bulbs, interesting primulas and spring-flowering shrubs. In late summer a large border of *Romneya coulteri*, the Californian tree poppy, is at its best, while autumn and winter interest are given by the stems of willow and cornus, and by the leaves of staphylea and *Parrotia persica*.

The sheltered walled garden contains many old roses mixed with perennials. Outside the house tender species grow surrounding a circular pond, and John Brookes' studio has its own terrace surrounded by palms and other exotica.
▶ *Open most of year – telephone or consult website for details – and for parties of 15 or more by appointment*

3 Rymans

A pretty walled garden is the highlight here with a fine display of roses backed by lime trees and a wisteria-clad arbour.

Apuldram, Dell Quay, Chichester PO20 7EG

Tel: 01243 783147

LOCATION 1 mile SW of Chichester. Turn off A259 at sign to Dell Quay, Apuldram; garden is on left

The beautiful early 15th-century house and its tower stand next to the church at Apuldram. In front of the house, two formal box parterres flank beds of *Rosa odorata* 'Mutabilis'.

The avenue leading from the house to the parish church is lined with black poplars underplanted with daffodils. An archway leads into a charming walled garden, where double borders of old hybrid musk roses are backed by an avenue of pleached limes underplanted with *Tulipa* 'Beauty of Apeldoorn' and forget-me-nots, and spanned by a fine wooden arbour draped with white wisteria. High brick walls shelter mimosas, spiraeas and *Trachycarpus fortunei*, and a pretty white dovecote is the centrepiece of a box spiral scattered with lavender, thyme and rosemary.

With the church as a striking backdrop, island beds are filled with unusual trees and shrubs, including *Magnolia stellata*, winter-flowering

DENMANS GARDEN

Sophora microphylla 'Sun King', a weeping pear and many ornamental grasses; beyond, a wilder area is reached through wrought-iron gates.

In the Paradise Garden, a long rill links two octagonal ponds on different levels and gravelled paths run around the upper pond past giant terracotta urns brimming with *Euphorbia characias*, phormiums and cordylines.

▶ *Open for NGS, and by appointment*

4 West Dean Gardens

The productive kitchen garden with its spectacular pergola leads to parkland walks and an arboretum overlooking the Downs.

West Dean, Chichester PO18 0QZ

Tel: 01243 818210 │ www.westdean.org.uk

Historic Garden Grade II*

LOCATION 6 miles N of Chichester on A286

If you want to see fruit and vegetables growing in profusion, this is the garden to visit. The restored Victorian glasshouses are immaculate and the regimented rows of fruit and vegetables excellently labelled. In the charming orchard, backed by an old crinkle-crankle wall, are several fruit trees trained in a variety of shapes and an unusual circular thatched apple store. The potting sheds now house interesting garden-themed exhibitions.

Outside the 3½ acre walled garden you can explore the 35 acres of ornamental grounds – designed around the house (now an Arts and Crafts College). The property was bought in 1891 and designer Harold Peto was commissioned to create the magnificent 100m (330ft) pergola. Stroll the length of the pergola and admire the lush planting designed to flower from spring through to early autumn, then relax in the sunken garden, a mass of tulips in spring, before taking the woodland walk.

The west end of the garden has been restored and replanted. The spring garden, with its enchanting summerhouse, laburnum tunnel and flintwork bridges over the River Lavant, is given an exotic jungle atmosphere by a planting of Chusan palms and bamboos.

Beyond is the wild garden, which has some unusual trees and is planted in more naturalistic style. From here there is an enjoyable walk through the park to St Roche's Arboretum, carpeted in spring with wild daffodils, where the college's founder Edward James is buried beneath the trees he loved so much.

▶ *Open all year – telephone or consult website for details – and for parties by appointment*

SOUTHERN ENGLAND

93

LEONARDSLEE LAKES AND GARDENS

5 Cass Sculpture Foundation

Exceptional works by leading British sculptors are displayed against a leafy backdrop of ancient woodland.

Goodwood, Chichester PO18 0QP

Tel: 01243 538449

www.sculpture.org.uk

LOCATION 7 miles N of Chichester, 3 miles S of East Dean, between A286 and A285

Twenty-six acres of woodland have been shaped to provide the perfect setting for 21st-century British sculpture. The quality of the work is outstanding, with the trees acting as screens to give each piece its own stage, and sometimes opening out to views of the Sussex countryside.

Beautiful gates by Wendy Ramshaw, a well-known British designer of jewellery, herald the entrance to the park, while at the end of one walk the spire of Chichester cathedral is borrowed sculpture of the most majestic kind. More than 70 large, ever-changing outdoor works are on show at any one time, including pieces by sculptors such as Steven Gregory, Bill Woodrow and Tony Cragg.

▶ *Open most of year – telephone or consult website for details*

6 Parham House

In the pleasure grounds a maze replicates 16th-century embroidery and a grove of white-flowering cherries dazzles in spring.

Near Pulborough RH20 4HS

Tel: 01903 742021/744888

www.parhaminsussex.co.uk

Historic Garden Grade II*

LOCATION 4 miles SE of Pulborough on A283, equidistant from A24 and A29

Set in the heart of a medieval deer park on the slopes of the South Downs, the award-winning gardens surrounding the Elizabethan house are approached through Fountain Court. A broad gravelled path leads down a gentle slope through a wrought-iron gate guarded by a pair of Istrian stone lions to a walled garden of about 4 acres. Retains its original quadrant layout, this walled garden is divided by broad walks and includes an orchard and a teak walk-through greenhouse.

The scope and character of this garden have evolved through progressive replanting, with huge herbaceous borders of Edwardian opulence to ensure a long season of interest. There are also cut-flower borders, a potager, a rose garden and a green border, planted along the outer west wall, and a lavender garden. In one corner is an enchanting miniature house with its own garden, a delight for both children and adults. The 7 acre pleasure grounds provide lawns and walks under stately trees to the lake, with views over the cricket ground to the South Downs. A brick and turf maze is a feature here.

This is a garden for all seasons, dominated in spring by carpets of bulbs and the splendid 'sacred' grove of white-flowering 'Mount Fuji' cherries, which are more than 50 years old.

▶ *House open. Gardens open main season – telephone or consult website for details – and by appointment for private parties and guided tours*

7 Petworth House

Immortalised on canvas by Turner, the fine landscaped park surrounding the house offers year-round colour and interest.

Petworth GU28 0AE | Tel: 01798 342207

www.nationaltrust.org.uk

Historic Park Grade I/The National Trust

LOCATION 6½ miles E of Midhurst on A272 in Petworth

The stately palace, with one of the finest late 17th-century interiors in England, sits in a magnificent park. This has been developed from what was a small enclosure for fruit and vegetables in the 16th century to its present size of more than 700 acres. It is enclosed by an impressive stone wall 5 miles long.

Garden designer George London worked here at the end of the 17th century, and from 1751 to 1763 'Capability' Brown was employed by the 2nd Earl of Egremont to modify the contours of the ground, plant cedars and many other trees, and construct the serpentine lake in front of the house – one of his earliest designs. Turner painted fine views of the park (as well as the interior of the house), and it is interesting to be able to compare them with the original.

This is not a place for the keen botanist, but it is a splendid experience all year round with a fine show of daffodils and bluebells in spring and glorious colour in autumn. The individual trees and shrubs, including Japanese maples and rhododendrons, deserve close study, and majestic veteran trees now tower over wild-flower meadows and ornamental shrubs, providing interest throughout the year. It is worth noting that at the turn of the century Petworth employed more than two dozen gardeners (they were always counted in dozens). Far fewer staff

have, since the storms of 1987 and 1990, planted in the region of 40,000 trees and continue to replant the pleasure grounds in Brownian style.

▶ *House open. Park open all year. Pleasure grounds open most of the year – telephone or consult website for details*

8 Leonardslee Lakes and Gardens

One of the largest woodland gardens in England, its stunning rhododendrons and azaleas are internationally renowned.

Lower Beeding, Horsham RH13 6PP

Tel: 01403 891212

www.leonardsleegardens.com

Historic Garden Grade I

LOCATION 4 miles SW of Handcross and M23 on B2110/A281

Covering 200 acres, this is one of the most extensive woodland gardens in England. The serenity evoked by woodland walks, grassy glades and stretches of water (there are seven lakes here with many species of dragonfly) is counter-balanced by dramatic sweeps and vistas of vibrant colour.

Some of the largest and oldest rhododendrons can be found in the Dell. Although the first ornamental plantings here date from the turn of the 19th century, the development of the gardens as they are seen today was the work of Sir Edmund Loder, the Victorian plant collector who acquired the property in 1889. Retaining the natural character of the site, he planted in large groups for maximum dramatic impact.

The flowering season begins in April and May, when rhododendrons, camellias and magnolias make the woodland garden and valley glow, swathes of bluebells flower beneath the blooms of the rhododendrons, and strong-hued azaleas fill the two-tiered rock garden and cast their reflections on the lakes. As the season progresses the hydrangeas along the pathways and oriental dogwoods introduce a subtler note infused with splashes of colours. In autumn the valley assumes a cloak of russet, orange and yellow.

Other attractions include a temperate greenhouse and an alpine house, a collection of Victorian cars and the 'Beyond the Dolls House' exhibition – and, of course, the present generation of wallabies that have lived semi-wild in parts of the valley since the late 19th century.

▶ *Open main season – telephone or consult website for details*

SOUTHERN ENGLAND

9 Selehurst

**Bluebell and larch woods, a gothic folly
and six ponds contribute to the romantic
atmosphere in this charming garden.**

Lower Beeding, Horsham RH13 6PR

Tel: 01403 891501

LOCATION 4½ miles SE of Horsham on A281

Once part of the Leonardslee estate (see page 95),
the original 'Loderi' rhododendrons can still be
found at Selehurst and the tallest *Eucalyptus gunnii*
in the country. The rest of this romantic landscape
garden has been created since 1976 by garden
designer and novelist Sue Prideaux.

It is a place of glorious views and large-scale
planting. Near the house the picture is classic
and traditional – walled garden, Italian borders,
laburnum and rose tunnel, herb knot, herbaceous
borders and topiary. But if you cross the meadow
down to bluebell woods and a stand of copper
beeches there is a crinkle-crankle hornbeam
hedge, a 'magnolia axis' underplanted with
bluebells, an amphitheatre and a 5,000–year-old
petrified Irish yew root set on a mound within
a copper beech circle.

In the larch wood a walk is lined with
columnar cypresses and *Cornus* 'Eddie's White
Wonder'. There are six ponds, each different
in outline and atmosphere. In one, a Gothic
folly tower is reflected, and from here the path
meanders through magnolias, azaleas, cornus and
tree ferns to a hornbeam *allée*. Alternatively, you
can take the original 1890s woodland walk back
to the topmost pond and Chinese pavilion.

On the other side of the house are plantings
of eucryphia, stewartia and camellia, and a lime
walk leading to a wild-flower meadow.

▶ *Open for parties by appointment*

10 Nymans

**Ruins draped in climbing plants overlook
a colourful walled garden surrounded by
woodland in one of Sussex's great gardens.**

Handcross RH17 6EB | Tel: 01444 405250

www.nationaltrust.org.uk

Historic Garden Grade II/The National Trust

LOCATION 4 miles S of Crawley, off A23/M23
and A279, at southern end of Handcross

When he bought the 600 acre estate in 1890,
stockbroker Ludwig Messel began the creation
of one of Sussex's most important gardens. On
the main lawn the ruins of the 1920s house

are romantically clad in clematis and wisteria;
restored family rooms overlooking the knot
garden and forecourt are open to the public.

Messel devoted himself first to laying out the
walled garden, where the summer borders are
now a riot of annual and perennial colour and
the summer-flowering trees include *Magnolia
sieboldii*, *Styrax hemsleyanus* and *S. japonicus*. The
rose garden, created in the 1920s, was renovated
in 1987 and planted with more than 150 old-
fashioned roses, including 'François Juranville',
'Debutante' and 'Henri Martin'.

The top garden is an area of grass surrounded
by shrubs and trees – magnolias, rhododendrons
and a magnificent *Cornus kousa* acquired in China

NYMANS

11 High Beeches Gardens

Among the rare trees and plants are Britain's only naturalised willow gentian and a National Collection of stewartias.

Handcross RH17 6HQ | Tel: 01444 400589

www.highbeeches.com

Historic Garden Grade II*

LOCATION 5 miles S of Crawley, 1 mile E of Handcross, S of B2110

Walks meander like the streams through this delightful woodland and water garden of over 25 acres with its rare trees and unusual shrubs. Alongside a National Collection of stewartias are glades of rhododendrons, azaleas and magnolias.

Originally designed in 1906, the garden is always extending its well-labelled collection. Bluebells begin the year, followed by stunning cornus, a wild-flower meadow, a glade of *Gentiana asclepiadea* (the only naturalised site of willow gentian in Britain) and *Eucryphia glutinosa* in late August. A carpet of *Cyclamen hederifolium* at Centre Pond adds to the autumn colours.

▶ *Open main season – telephone or consult website for details*

12 Borde Hill

Shrubs collected from around the world form a botanically rich garden, boasting several award-winning collections.

Balcombe Road, Haywards Heath RH16 1XP

Tel: 01444 450326 | www.bordehill.co.uk

Historic Garden Grade II*

LOCATION 1½ miles N of Haywards Heath on Balcombe-Haywards Heath road

The fine planthunter garden was created from 1893 with trees and shrubs collected from Asia, the Andes, Tasmania and Europe. It has award-winning collections of azaleas, rhododendrons, magnolias and camellias, surrounded by 220 acres of parkland and bluebell woods.

The classic rose and Italian gardens are the work of garden designer Robin Williams, and lottery funds were used to restore the glasshouse area and create a series of small rooms filled with rare Southern Hemisphere shrubs around the old potting sheds. In the Long Dell, Sino-Himalayan species surround Chusan palms, while the Round Dell has Chusan palms, bamboos and huge gunneras. A white garden was created in 2002.

▶ *Garden open main season – telephone or consult website for details. Parties must pre-book*

by plant collector E.H. Wilson. In summer, its branches are smothered in white bracts and in autumn it is covered in strawberry-like fruits.

Borders flanking the path towards the garden are planted with lupins, delphiniums, oriental poppies, deutzias and other favourites for a June display. The garden is at its peak in summer but every season brings its pleasures, from the white narcissi and snake's-head fritillaries in early spring to the magnificent autumn colour in the natural woodland. A recent addition is a jungle of bamboos that will form a green and yellow screen hemming in the twisting wooden paths.

▶ *House open main season. Garden open all year – telephone or consult website for details*

SOUTHERN ENGLAND

13 Clinton Lodge

A romantic planting includes an arcade adorned with white roses and lilies, and knots of box infilled with aromatics.

Fletching, Uckfield TN22 3ST

Tel: 01825 722952

LOCATION 4 miles W of Uckfield off A272. Turn N at Piltdown and continue for 1½ miles to Fletching. House is in main street surrounded by yew hedge

The distinguished early 17th-century house that faces the village street conceals the six complex and exuberantly planted acres that lie behind. Developed by a passionate gardener, they illustrate the combination of restraint and romanticism so evident in the best English gardens.

Smooth lawns framed by tall hornbeam flow into the deer park, with an obelisk on a distant wooded hill. Classical formality continues with interlocking yews that frame pools and lead to an Italian marble cistern. The potager follows the medieval plan, laid out with fruit, vegetables, herbs and cutting flowers, pleached apple trees and vine-clad arbours, while the Elizabethan love of pattern is the inspiration for the walled herb garden, with its camomile paths and knots infilled with sweet cicely, lovage and lavender.

An arcaded cloister walk, inspired by a Pre-Raphaelite painting, is swagged in white roses and perfumed by lilies, leading to a wild garden with a flowery meadow of oxeye daisies. Later Victorian tastes are reflected in double herbaceous borders where drifts of delphinium, monkshood and iris take their places alongside *Crambe cordifolia*, punctuated by box topiary.

A walled garden of fragrant old roses surrounding a formal arbour and a swimming pool encircled by an arcade of apples are further instances of gardening with a sense of history.

▶ *Open limited season – telephone or consult website details – for NGS, and by appointment*

SHEFFIELD PARK GARDEN

14 Town Place

Walk through the apple tunnel, dell and orchard to a 'circus' garden, surrounded by a circular, striped conifer hedge.

Ketches Lane, Freshfield, near Scaynes Hill
RH17 7NR | Tel: 01825 790221

www.townplacegarden.org.uk

LOCATION 3 miles E of Haywards Heath. From A275 turn W at Sheffield Green into Ketches Lane (signed to Lindfield); garden is 1¾ miles on left

Visitors enter this wonderful 3 acre garden, created since 1990, through wrought-iron gates onto a lawn enclosed by low walls and old brick paths. The path to the left leads up steps to an apple tunnel and herb garden, then down to the dell with its freeform raised pond and fountain. Across the main lawn in front of the 1650s house (not open) is a long herbaceous border backed by a flame tapestry hedge. A rose pergola shields a sunken rose garden, replanted in 2005 with more than 140 English roses, and this in turn leads into the orchard and an area by the pool with gravel paths and beds block-planted with box, screened by a line of *Rosa* 'Excelsa'.

Walk through the orchard, which is carpeted with daffodils in spring, to the Circus, where beds of grasses and shrubs are surrounded by the circular, clipped, striped conifer hedge. Beyond lies the English rose garden, box-edged and planted with more than 400 roses of 36 different cultivars. Follow the sound of water to find a spring garden and a hidden garden. Other highlights include copper beech hedges, a hornbeam walk, a potager and cutting garden and the New Territories, where hornbeam hedges re-create the outline of a fantasy ruined priory.
▶ *Open for NGS, and June and July for parties of 20 or more by appointment*

15 Sheffield Park Garden

Four lakes in a valley are linked by cascades and surrounded by towering specimen trees that provide fabulous autumn colour.

Sheffield Park TN22 3QX | Tel: 01825 790231

www.nationaltrust.org.uk/sheffieldpark

Historic Park Grade I/The National Trust

LOCATION 5 miles NW of Uckfield, midway between East Grinstead and Lewes E of A275

Laid out in 1776 for the Earl of Sheffield by 'Capability' Brown and further developed in the early 20th century, the 265 acre park is a fine example of the work of the Landscape Movement. What impresses most is the sheer scale. Two lakes, created in a valley below the neo-Gothic house and later increased to four, are linked by cascades and surrounded by towering mature specimen trees that provide superb autumn colour.

But a visit here is rewarding at any time due to the beauty and diversity of foliage, the continuing programme of tree and shrub planting, and the drifts of daffodils and bluebells followed by displays of rhododendrons and azaleas. Bold waterside planting shelters swans, moorhens and mallards, with elegant water lilies on the lakes.
▶ *Open all year – telephone or consult website for details*

16 Latchetts

This imaginative garden is continually evolving, with features that include a giant sundial and a Christian millennium garden.

Freshfield Lane, Danehill, Haywards Heath
RH17 7HQ | Tel: 01825 790237

LOCATION 7 miles S of East Grinstead on A275. In Danehill, turn at war memorial into Freshfield Lane. House is 1 mile further (not Latchetts Farmhouse)

Remarkable in its diversity, the 8 acre garden is filled with assured planting for every situation. This includes 3 acres of woodland with wooden sculptures, a fern stumpery and a 'scary path'.

Set high above a Wealden valley, the house is surrounded by 5 acres of grounds. Smooth lawns are outlined by mature trees and huge shrub borders slope to raised beds massed with sun-loving perennials. A rill trickles from a water garden fringed with giant gunneras into a cool, wild wood sheltering tree ferns and bamboo. Bold swathes of prairie planting provide late colour, sheltered by a high bank of shrub roses.

At every turn there is something new – a mysterious pool with mist rising from the water and sculptures creating sound; a rose-laden tunnel leading to a vegetable garden; an intimate millennium garden filled with Christian symbolism and the soothing sound of water; a desert garden laid out around a giant sundial with a mound to climb to look out over a wild-flower meadow with a labyrinth cut into it.

In 2006, a sunken garden was created with a mural and a water lily pond. Everywhere are benches, summerhouses and vantage points from which visitors can enjoy the varying views.
▶ *Open for NGS, and by appointment*

17 Wakehurst Place

Rare orchids, Japanese irises and Himalayan species are among the many collections in an extremely varied botanic garden.

Ardingly, Haywards Heath RH17 6TN

Tel: 01444 894066 (Infoline) | www.kew.org

Historic Garden Grade II/The National Trust

LOCATION 5 miles N of Haywards Heath on B2028. From London take A(M)23, A272, B2028 or A22, B2110

Mature plantings in a glorious setting of valleys, lakes and woodlands create an air of stability and pleasure at every turn. The 465 acre estate is divided into gardens, woodland walks and the Loder Valley Nature Reserve, with parkland and woodland on the perimeter.

The 1590 mansion was built by Sir Edward Culpeper, a distant relative of the renowned herbalist, but the gardens were not developed until 1902 when the estate was bought by Gerald Loder (later Lord Wakehurst), a passionate and knowledgeable plantsman who sponsored many of the great expeditions. He built up an impressive collection of rhododendrons, conifers and Southern-Hemisphere plants, and National Collections of betulas, hypericums, nothofagus and skimmias are also held here.

Well-signed pathways lead to a multitude of areas and varied plantings. A glade containing species that grow at above 3,000m (1,000ft) in the Himalayas is the only one of its kind in the country, and a fine collection of Japanese irises is part of the extensive and fascinating water gardens.

For the first-time visitor, there is no better place to start than the front of the house, where on a summer's day the large pond is full of water lilies and the reflection of the architecture can be seen in the water. The spring border provides wonderful early colour, enhanced by the magnolias and rhododendrons planted nearby. A short distance from the house are two walled gardens. One is cottage-garden in feel, planted with pastel flowers interspersed with grey and also silver-leaved artemisias. The other holds a fine array of late-flowering summer shrubs and a surprise element in the shape of a small lawn enclosed by a yew hedge.

Conservation is an important part of the work of Wakehurst, and so the meadow includes two rare native orchids, *Orchis morio* and the taller *O. laxiflora,* in flower in April and May. The millennium Seed Bank, futuristic in appearance and masterly in design and presentation, is tastefully surrounded by beds showing different native UK habitats.

▶ *Part of house open. Garden open all year – telephone or consult website for details. Guided walks available. Garden is leased from the National Trust, so members entitled to free entry*

18 Gravetye Manor

Designed by William Robinson, pioneer of the English natural garden, this restored garden remains true to his ideals.

Vowels Lane, East Grinstead RH19 4LJ

Tel: 01342 810567

Historic Garden Grade II*

LOCATION 4 miles S of East Grinstead between M23 and A22. Via M23, take exit 10 onto A264 towards East Grinstead. After 2 miles, at roundabout take 3rd exit on B2028; 1 mile after Turners Hill fork left and follow signs

This historically important garden has been carefully and sensitively restored in the naturalistic style pioneered by William Robinson, author of the bestselling 1883 book *The English Flower Garden*. Robinson lived in the house for 50 years before his death in 1935 and used the garden as a testing-ground for his ideas.

Near the house (now a luxury hotel) he introduced a scheme of formal beds and enclosed garden rooms filled with many of the flowers – shrub roses, violas and pinks, set off by the feathers of perovskias and bolder outlines of silybums and cardoons – that he praised in his book. Only guests staying or eating at the hotel can enjoy these now, but other visitors can view them from the strategically placed perimeter path that passes through the woodland and meadow to the north and south.

His ambitions for these wilder areas were set down in *The Wild Garden*, published 13 years earlier. Scots pines, birches, parrotias and rhododendrons form part of the naturalistic

A LONG AVENUE OF PLEACHED BOX GIVES A VIEW THROUGH TO

PASHLEY MANOR GARDENS

woodland plantings, and his meadow is still scattered with the offspring of the 'several hundred thousand bulbs and roots' he recorded planting here over five years.

The path down the magnolia walk, bordered by shrubbery and large camellias, leads down through Smugglers Lane to a lake, continues along the water's edge and completes the circuit back to the entrance.

▶ *Open all year to hotel and restaurant guests; perimeter footpath for members of the public open Tues and Fri*

19 Merriments Gardens

Deeply curved, colour-themed borders provide inspirational plant combinations for every situation and season.

Hawkhurst Road, Hurst Green TN19 7RA

Tel: 01580 860666

www.merriments.co.uk

LOCATION 7 miles N of Battle, on A229 (formerly A265) between Hawkhurst and Hurst Green

In this 4 acre garden, pools and pergolas surrounded by boldly curving beds of impressive colour-themed planting create a rich source of inspiration for modern gardeners. Well-designed and labelled schemes show off plants for every situation, from a tropical border to a wild area, a shady bog garden filled with lush marginals to the sun-baked gravelled garden.

Between these extremes are imaginatively stocked borders in every colour combination, filled with herbaceous plants and shrubs underplanted with tulips, alliums and hostas. Specimen trees such as *Gleditsia triacanthos* 'Sunburst' and *Catalpa bignonioides* 'Aurea' have been chosen specially for their decorative foliage.

Benches, arbours and summerhouses afford good vantage points throughout, while handsome containers and sculptures make effective focal points. The health and vigour of the plants, which include many excellent varieties of clematis, are remarkable at all times of year.

A welcoming tearoom and a shady terrace combine with a superbly stocked nursery.

▶ *Open main season – telephone or consult website for details*

20 Pashley Manor Gardens

Sensitive landscaping, imaginative plantings and fine collections of tulips, lilies and roses provide spring and summer colour.

Ticehurst TN5 7HE | Tel: 01580 200888

www.pashleymanorgardens.com

LOCATION 16 miles N of Hastings, 10 miles SE of Tunbridge Wells on B2099 between Ticehurst and A21. Signposted

The beautiful Grade I-listed house – with its 1550 timber-framed front façade and 1720 rear elevation – is pivotal to the handsome gardens that surround it. The entrance drive leads through elegant parkland, and there are fine views of the surrounding countryside from all sides. But the garden proper, stretching over 11 acres, lies mainly to the rear.

Near the house, festooned with a mighty wisteria, is a progression of large, curving borders and, stretching eastwards, a series of enclosed formal gardens, each different but all immaculately maintained. In one, golden flowers and foliage dominate; another is given over to roses; in a third a long avenue of pleached pears is underplanted with box, arranged to give a view through to a magnificent hydrangea hedge. Major collections of tulips, lilies from growers Bloms Bulbs and the renowned Peter Beales' roses ensure a spectacular progression of colour and scent from May through to early August, when the hot-coloured herbaceous borders facing outwards to the grazing fields take centre stage.

Sweeping lawns and water are the other key elements, enticing visitors down towards the perimeter of the garden, to the medieval moat and its island and to a string of ponds falling away into the distance, the top one with a magnificent fountain. Gravel paths lead through camellia and rhododendron shrubberies and a collection of azaleas in an intriguing circuit, and in every part of the garden there are sculptures to discover.

A visit here is enjoyable for many other reasons: the restaurant is excellent, the plants for sale well grown, the staff welcoming and, if the owners are in residence, the whole place bubbles with enthusiasm.

▶ *Open main season – telephone or consult website for details. Coach parties by appointment*

PEARS UNDERPLANTED WITH A HYDRANGEA HEDGE

SOUTHERN ENGLAND

21 Great Dixter

This experimental garden has carpets of meadow flowers and bulbs, yew topiary and borders bursting with riotous colour.

Dixter Road, Northiam, Rye TN31 6PH

Tel: 01797 252878 | www.greatdixter.co.uk

Historic Garden Grade I

LOCATION 10 miles N of Hastings, ½ mile N of Northiam. Turn off A28 at Northiam post office

Enfolded by its glorious gardens, the medieval house at Great Dixter appears historically authentic. It was in fact reinvented after 1910 by the designer Edwin Lutyens, who enlarged it in the local vernacular and designed the gardens.

Garden expert Christopher Lloyd lived and gardened here with his inimitable passion and flair for planting until his death in 2006. He left behind a garden that is inspirational at every turn, and is now being taken in new and exciting directions by the current head gardener.

Meadow gardening is a striking feature, with the entrance flanked by long grass filled with *Camassia quamash*, and colonies of bulbs and early purple orchids in the orchard. The Long Border is a spectacular mixture of shrubs, climbers, perennials and annuals, reflecting Lloyd's determination to combine colours unconventionally to exuberant effect, while the sheltered Exotic Garden is a riot of tropical colours and unfamiliar shapes.

In the High Garden, approached through superb topiary, stock plants and vegetables grow together in intriguing combinations. Many of the plants are propagated *in situ* and for sale in the attractive nursery.

▶ *House open. Garden open main season – telephone or consult website for details*

22 Bateman's

Author Rudyard Kipling's garden running down to the River Dudwell has a reflecting pool, a pear *allée* and a mulberry garden.

Burwash, Etchingham TN19 7DS

Tel: 01435 882302

www.nationaltrust.org.uk

Historic Garden Grade II/The National Trust

LOCATION 14 miles E of Uckfield, 10 miles SE of Tunbridge Wells, ½ mile S of Burwash off A265

The spirit of Edwardian England pervades the tranquil gardens surrounding the Wealden ironmaster's house that was bought by author and poet Rudyard Kipling in 1902. Elements

GREAT DIXTER

of his original plan include the formal lawns surrounding a reflecting pool, emphasised by pleached limes, the pear *allée* he planted in the walled kitchen garden now bounded by a fine herb border, the sheltered Mulberry Garden in the former farmyard and the wild fringes of the little River Dudwell running to the working mill. These all combine to evoke the atmosphere of privacy and permanence that he created here in the three decades leading up to his death in 1936.

The house and garden are rich in associations with his stories and poems, especially *Puck of Pook's Hill* and *Rewards and Fairies*, which were both set here; the mill that featured in these stories is only a short walk away.

▶ *House and mill (which grinds flour most Saturdays in open season) open. Garden open main season – telephone or consult website for details*

23 Sarah Raven's Cutting Garden

The presenter's inspirational flower and vegetable gardens provide an effective mix of colour, structure and inspiration.

Perch Hill Farm, Willingford Lane, Brightling, Robertsbridge TN32 5HP

Tel: 0845 050 4849

www.sarahraven.com

LOCATION 5 miles E of Heathfield on A265. In Burwash village turn S at war memorial; after 3 miles turn R at crossroads into Willingford Lane (signed Burwash Weald). Garden is ½ mile on right (only suitable for small vehicles)

At Perch Hill Farm, set high on a windy Sussex hillside, TV presenter Sarah Raven has developed a successful business brand from writing and broadcasting, growing food and flowers, and organising short courses that range from floristry to animal husbandry. Providing inspiration for both students and visitors, her gardens are imbued with a spirit of change and experiment.

In the vegetable and cutting garden, where students are instructed in crop rotation, raised beds are filled with flowers grown for their striking colours and forms. The vegetable garden burgeons with produce and a sculptural element is introduced through the many ingenious plant supports that have been used, including tunnels, obelisks, hurdles and arbours fashioned from hazel, birch and willow.

The more intimate spaces nearer to the farmhouse are filled with a profusion of fruit, planted alongside peonies, foxgloves and tulips,

and herbs, grown loosely around a structure of box balls. A new gravel garden surrounds a sunny terrace where olive trees and grasses, followed by perennials, provide movement, soft texture and muted shades.

In contrast, the sheltered oast garden is planted with extravagant and architectural foliage and vivid flower combinations – intense lime greens, deep clarets, purples and oranges – that Sarah has developed as her signature palette.

Although the owner is fashionable and media-savvy, the garden feels authentic, with a sense of connection to the Sussex landscape and the agricultural life beyond.

▶ *Open for NGS, and for guided tours Mon-Fri main season – telephone or consult website for details*

24 Hailsham Grange

In just an acre, a gentleman's estate has been created in miniature, with a series of stylish rooms and colour-themed plantings.

Hailsham BN27 1BL

Tel: 01323 844248

www.hailshamgrange.co.uk

LOCATION 8 miles N of Eastbourne off A22. Turn off Hailsham High Street into Vicarage Road and park in public car park

Theatrical and elegant behind its formal façade, this vicarage garden is a box of delights. Light and shade is created through the use of graphic, three-dimensional hornbeam and box hedging, which divides the 1 acre space into a series of stylish rooms, creating vistas and enclosures in what resembles a perfect gentleman's estate in miniature.

The textures of clipped foliage, gravel and brick make neat and pleasing contrasts with the luxuriant, colour-themed planting. The central turf path leading to a rose-swagged gazebo reveals a *coup de théâtre* of twin borders that have been planted in a warm and inspired palette of cream, yellow and apricot perennials, with bronze, burgundy and claret shrubs to provide a dramatic background contrast.

Throughout the garden, texture and form are carefully balanced, yet plants are often allowed to lean companionably together or flow onto paths in counterpoint to the perfection of the classical parterre.

A tiny, cool white garden, a ferny wilderness and a bulb-filled spinney complete this perfect little paradise sheltered by trees that frame or disguise the world beyond.

▶ *Open for NGS, and for parties by appointment*

25 Michelham Priory

These tranquil gardens on a moated island combine wild flowers and formal planting, with a potager and physic garden.

Upper Dicker, Hailsham BN27 3QS

Tel: 01323 844224 | www.sussexpast.co.uk

LOCATION 10 miles N of Eastbourne off A22 and A27

Founded by Augustinian canons in 1229 and protected by the longest water-filled moat in Britain, the Priory's gardens reflect its past and are a reminder of the vital role plants played in medieval life. The moat has a rich diversity of flora and fauna, including swans, wildfowl and kingfishers. A variety of native wild flowers fringing the moat influence the style of planting elsewhere – broad swathes of meadowsweet, cow parsley and angelica are echoed in the scale of the sweeping borders, where huge clumps of inula, spiky cardoons, echinops, eryngiums, phormiums and foxtail lilies combine with swaying grasses.

The physic garden contains native medicinal plants, and an enclosed cloister garden illustrates medieval techniques for growing food crops and herbs. A flowery mead is summer-bright with poppies, cornflowers and cowslips.

The magnificent mature trees, flower-strewn orchard and restored Victorian potager with its pleached apple tunnel and burgeoning produce complete the picture of timeless tranquillity. The only discordant note is struck by some rather extraneous sculpture.
▶ *House, museum and gardens open main season – telephone or consult website for details*

26 Marchants Hardy Plants

Ornamental grasses are cleverly positioned to highlight diverse and extensive plantings of colourful herbaceous perennials.

2 Marchants Cottages, Mill Lane, Laughton BN8 6AJ | Tel: 01323 811737

www.marchantshardyplants.co.uk

LOCATION 6 miles E of Lewes. From Laughton crossroads on B2124 (at Roebuck Inn), travel E for ½ mile. At next crossroads turn S, signed to Ripe, down Mill Lane; entrance is on right

Specialising in herbaceous perennials and ornamental grasses, this well-designed and diversely planted garden is enhanced by wonderful views of the South Downs. Although it covers only 2 acres, the space is used intensively, providing a fine show garden for the well-known nursery established in 1998.

The main and spring gardens have curving pathways and borders, with sweeps of herbaceous planting of varied texture and tone giving a depth of interest. Treating gardening as an art, the owner paints with plants, responding to the seasons so that early snowdrops and hellebores move on through campanulas and hemerocallis of summer to the rich autumn tapestry provided by late crocosmias and sanguisorbas. As the colour of the perennials is interspersed with the structure and texture of the grasses, the nursery drifts into the garden and the garden on into the countryside.
▶ *Garden open main season – telephone or consult website for details. Nursery open as garden, but from mid March*

27 Ringmer Park

Continuous colour is the emphasis in this densely planted garden, with midsummer roses followed by autumn favourites.

Ringmer, Lewes BN8 5RW

LOCATION On A26 Lewes-Uckfield Road, 1½ miles NE of Lewes, 5 miles S of Uckfield

Sheltered by the South Downs, this glorious garden of 8 acres is the vision of the present owner, who has developed it with a plantsman's eye and a sure sense of scale. Robust and healthy plants flourish in the deep compost mulch made from grass cuttings, and well-considered planting extends the season from spring to late autumn.

The roses are spectacular in midsummer. They include blowsy hybrid teas filling the traditional rose garden, old shrub roses skilfully trained into extravagant and fragrant domes, and climbers clothing a long pergola bordered by glamorous peonies. A double herbaceous border awash with soft pinks and mauves is punctuated by vigorous spires of delphinium and eremurus. Elegant white and silver planting frames a yew-hedged pool garden, contrasting with a hot garden filled with strong colours and the varied shapes of autumn favourites such as crocosmias, ligularias and heleniums beneath dahlias, cannas and ricinus.

A nuttery with paths mown through a flower-filled meadow leads to the old orchard, now transformed with beds of unusual shrubs and grasses flowing around a venerable apple trees and a contemporary thatched shade house. This is bounded by a wave-cut blackthorn hedge.
▶ *Open for NGS, and by appointment*

WILTSHIRE

The undulating countryside has many inspiring gardens adjoining its charming mills and historic manors. It is also home to Stourhead, considered to be one of the world's finest landscape gardens.

1 Stourhead

In this exquisite English landscape garden, vistas around the lake reveal temples, a pantheon, grotto, cascade and much more.

Stourton, Warminster BA12 6QF

Tel: 01747 841152 | www.nationaltrust.org.uk

Historic Garden Grade I/The National Trust

LOCATION 3 miles NW of Mere via A303 at Stourton off B3092

This outstanding example of an English landscape garden was designed by owner Henry Hoare II between 1741 and 1780. A paragon in its day, it is one of the greatest surviving gardens of its kind.

Walk along the top path from the house, which gives inspiring views of the lake below, then follow a route anti-clockwise around the lake and gradually the sequence of arcadian images is revealed. There are tantalising glimpses of classical temples across the water, which appear almost mirage-like and unattainable, but on reaching them other architectural visions attract the eye. To gain a better idea of how these buildings would have looked had the surrounding planting remained as it was originally, take a walk by Turner's Paddock Lake below the cascade.

Between 1791 and 1838 Hoare's grandson, Richard Colt Hoare, planted many new species, particularly from America, including tulip trees, swamp cypresses and Indian bean trees. He also introduced *Rhododendron ponticum*. From 1894 the 6th Baronet added to these with the latest kinds of hybrid rhododendrons and scented azaleas, and a large number of copper beeches and conifers, of which many are record-sized specimens.

In the early 19th century, Stourhead boasted one of the finest collections of pelargoniums in the world, with more than 600 varieties, and the latest effort to emulate Richard Colt Hoare's passion consists of more than 100 varieties, to be found in a 1910 lean-to greenhouse. The garden is especially atmospheric in the quiet of winter when more views are afforded through the bare trees.

▶ *House open. Garden open all year – telephone or consult website for details*

2 Wilton House

Set in majestic landscaped parkland, the formal gardens include a lavender-bordered parterre and an Oriental water garden.

Wilton, Salisbury SP2 0BJ

Tel: 01722 746720

www.wiltonhouse.com

Historic Garden Grade I

LOCATION 3 miles W of Salisbury on A30

The home of the 18th Earl of Pembroke, the house built by Inigo Jones in 1647 is surrounded by quintessentially English parkland dotted with statues and eye-catchers – the Whispering Seat, which has special acoustic properties, is a good vantage point looking down towards the Tudor entrance of the house. Formal gardens were created by garden designer Isaac de Caus in 1633, sweeping over 300m (985ft) to the south. When this style fell from favour, one of the earliest examples of English landscaping took its place.

The River Nadder runs right through the park, beneath the 1736 Palladian bridge. When walking along the riverside today, visitors come across a loggia and an avenue of liquidambars. The woodland walk leads along a tributary of the River Wylye, overlooking the arboretum. Cedars of Lebanon, some introduced in the 1630s, others newly planted, appear throughout the park.

After he succeeded to the title in 1969, the 17th Earl commissioned four gardens. The one in the north courtyard incorporates pleached limes within formal box hedges. Before the foliage becomes a feature, colour comes from white and pink tulips, followed by standard honeysuckles and lavenders. A box-hedged parterre is bordered by cotton lavender, echoing designs from the central 9th-century wellhead. The Oriental water garden and a hedged garden of old roses complete the quartet, and a Miz-maze of crushed white stone and turf is a work in progress. A large adventure playground provides entertainment for children.

▶ *Open main season – telephone or consult website for details*

IFORD MANOR

3 The Old Vicarage, Edington

A National Collection of evening primroses provides fragrance after dusk, and dierama species are a highlight in the hot garden.

Edington, Westbury BA13 4QF

Tel: 01380 830512

LOCATION 4 miles NE of Westbury on B3098 to West Lavington. Signposted

Set on a 3 acre escarpment on the north side of Salisbury Plain, this scented garden holds a wide variety of different plants, with new additions every year. Swags of clematis, cistus and mahonias enliven the plain façade of the former vicarage; a wide croquet lawn leads to a meadow artful with wild flowers beneath rare varieties of chestnut, sorbus and maple. Stunning views towards Edington Church lift the visitor's eyes through well-planted vistas.

Dividing the garden is a yew hedge, an *allée* of fastigiate hornbeams points the view towards Devizes, and brick walls create rooms and shelter exotic plants and trees. Waves of dierama species mark the hot garden, while a sunken garden to the rear of the house is romantically planted in cool shades around a 15m (50ft) well. Nepetas, which are a particular passion, run riot and a National Collection of evening primroses gives special pleasure after dusk.

Towards the end of the tour, a gravel bed is a sea of agapanthus and eryngiums, and everywhere seedlings push through the gravel.

▶ *Open for NGS, and by appointment*

4 Iford Manor

The Italianate hillside garden of landscape designer Harold Peto is characterised by pools, colonnades and columnar cypresses.

Bradford-on-Avon BA15 2BA

Tel: 01225 863146 | www.ifordmanor.co.uk

Historic Garden Grade I

LOCATION 2 miles S of Bradford-on-Avon off B3109, 7 miles SE of Bath via A36. Signposted

The Edwardian landscape designer Harold Peto found himself a near-ideal house in the steep valley through which the River Frome flows languorously towards Bath. Here, he created for himself a garden that is now renowned for its beauty. The topography lends itself to the strong architectural framework he favoured and to the creation of areas of differing moods. The overriding inspiration in the 2½ acres is Italianate, with a preponderance of cypresses, junipers, box and yew, punctuated at every turn by sarcophagi, urns, terracotta, marble seats and statues, columns, fountains and loggias.

In a different vein is a meadow of naturalised bulbs, with spectacular martagon lilies. A path leads from here to the cloisters – an Italian-Romanesque building of Peto's confection made with fragments collected from Italy. From here one can admire the whole garden, and the breathtaking valley and walled kitchen garden on the other side. Peto's hand is also evident in the artefacts and planting of the Japanese garden; however, the central pond and rockwork were created later.

▶ *Open main season – telephone or consult website for details – and for parties by appointment*

5 The Old Malthouse

Sculpture abounds in this garden, where the scene changes constantly, from a cloister garden and terrace to potager and orchard.

Lower Westwood, Bradford-on-Avon BA15 2AG

Tel: 01225 864905

LOCATION 1½ miles NW of Trowbridge, 1½ miles SW of Bradford-on-Avon off B3109

In this 1 acre garden created by a film producer and his former-actress wife, drama and wit are at the forefront of the design. A work-in-progress since 1995, its level has been raised to create vistas of Westwood Manor and the church of the medieval village.

Within the garden, the scene shifts constantly, from the Arts and Crafts mood at the front of the house with its dry-stone walls, water rills and spouts, sedums and English roses, to a stretch of lawn overlooking fields and a long herbaceous border in shades of green and white. An old orchard with long grass and daisies merges into a potager, where fruit and vegetables are presented with panache.

The main garden includes a stream and a view into the cloister garden, where espaliered fruit trees and roses roam over pergolas. On the paved terrace above, silver, white and blue planting makes a soft background for sculpted furniture; the enclosing walls support wisterias and ramblers in drifts, and self-seeding plants are encouraged to rampage.

Above all, there is sculpture – carvings, seats, fountains, cages and surreal details – setting and stealing the scene in every part of this original and inspiring garden.

▶ *Open for NGS, and by appointment*

SOUTHERN ENGLAND

6 Ridleys Cheer

Split over two levels, the informal garden features a wealth of usual shrubs and roses, an arboretum and a wild-flower meadow.

Mountain Bower, Chippenham SN14 7AJ

Tel: (01225) 891204 | www.ridleyscheer.co.uk

LOCATION 8 miles W of Chippenham off A420. Turn N at The Shoe pub, take second left, then first right

This stylish garden, filled with treasures, has been created since the early 1980s. It covers some 14 acres, two of which hold an attractive and interesting arboretum, and the wild-flower meadow is a splendid sight in July and August.

The garden is on two levels, connected by a broad flight of steps with a wrought-iron rose arbour at the top and a grass walk, and contains many fine examples of rarer shrubs and trees. Spring is ushered in with bulbs, some 15 varieties of magnolia and 20 different daphnes and deutzias. The shrub roses, including some 125 species and hybrids seldom encountered, are a major summer feature; notable too are the displays of white martagon lilies and *Meconopsis betonicifolia*. There is a small potager, and outside the conservatory a gravel garden planted with box and yew. Autumn colour is given by a growing number of maples, beeches, tulip trees and oaks.

The garden is full of appeal for plantsmen who can derive much information from the knowledgeable owners. A small nursery sells trees, shrubs and perennials propagated from the garden.
▶ *Open for NGS, and coach parties by appointment*

7 Hazelbury Manor

Medicinal herbs and plants have been added to this architectural garden, with its fine topiary, laburnum tunnel and archery walk.

Box, Corsham SN13 8HX | Tel: 01225 865322

Historic Garden Grade II

LOCATION 5 miles SW of Chippenham. From Box take A365 towards Melksham, turn left onto B3109, next left, then right into private drive

Richly architectural in character, the gardens are entirely in keeping with the history and scale of the 15th-century fortified manor house they surround. Following an Edwardian renaissance, they were largely rescued in the 1970s by Ian Pollard – co-author of *The Naked Gardener* – who reconfigured them on a lavish scale with 8 acres

of formal gardens around the house and 10 acres of landscaped grounds. Since 1997, the present owner has restored and improved them, and added a profusion of organically grown medicinal herbs and plants. The glory of the garden is the main lawn, dramatic in its proportions and framed by impressive yew hedges and compartmented colour-themed borders. The borders are backed by grassy banks leading to mature beech *allées*. A topiary chess set and a richly underplanted laburnum tunnel and lime walk add extra dimensions to the garden.

The front of the house is seen across lawns and borders ablaze with spring bulbs, while behind is an historic archery walk – exactly 40 paces long. To the west of the house the mood becomes more relaxed and intimate, with informal plantings of shrubs and perennials opening onto the surrounding landscape.

There is a fine organic vegetable garden and a flowery mead sprinkled with crocuses, fritillaries and martagon lilies. Beyond the garden lies a mound and circle of seven megaliths that pay homage to the prehistoric monuments nearby.
▶ *Open for NGS, and by appointment*

8 Bolehyde Manor

A series of colourfully planted garden rooms surround the manor, with vibrant pots of tender plants, topiary and a pear walk.

Allington, Chippenham SN14 6LW

email: amcairns@aol.com

LOCATION 1½ miles W of Chippenham on A420 Bristol road. Turn N at Allington crossroads

This 4 acre garden is steeped in tradition yet bursting with innovative ideas. The 15th-century manor house is of weathered Cotswold stone, and this is reflected in the linked garden rooms around the house. Artists and gardeners admire the pond garden, and the potager is immaculate.

Within a semi-formal framework are splendid contrasts, gracefully achieved – courtyards filled with brilliantly coloured flowers and flamboyantly planted pots, a pear walk, and some lovely wild-flower meadow planting. Sheltered and sunny formal areas are edged with colourful narrow beds and topiary abounds.

Planted for year-round interest, the garden is nevertheless at its stunning best in midsummer, when masses of roses bloom on the old walls and the half-hardy planting of the courtyard – much of it in darkly glowing jewel colours – is nearing the peak of a brilliant display.
▶ *Open for NGS, and for parties by appointment*

9 The Priory, Kington St Michael

Hundreds of blooms line the stone walls in the classic rose garden, while a sun garden in white and silver is a striking new feature.

Kington St Michael, Chippenham SN14 6JG

Tel: 01249 750360

LOCATION 3 miles N of Chippenham off A350. Drive through village, turn left down lane opposite stud farm on right at bottom of hill

Since 1994, the owner, Mme Anita Pereire, a respected writer and garden designer, has created a satisfying and elegant 2 acre garden around the buildings of an ancient priory, combining a firm overall structure and lavish planting.

Radiating from a central patchwork stone path lined with an avenue of weeping silver pears (her signature tree) are well-defined and separate areas. These include a breathtaking 'French' garden of topiary and standard roses (the long-lasting 'The Fairy' and 'Ballerina'), an exquisite water garden, a ha-ha ablaze with rock plants, perennials and flowering shrubs, and a classic rose garden filled with colour and scent from masses of old-fashioned varieties.

Beyond the hedge-enclosed part of the garden lies a meadow with mown paths forming a maze. In the wild garden, grass paths edged with wild roses lead down to a gravel garden that blends into the surrounding meadowland. The latest additions are a white and silver sun garden full of artemisias and cistus, and a rose garden planted unusually into pockets of earth set between stones.
▶ *Open by appointment only*

10 Abbey House Gardens

Alongside an amazing knot garden in the form of a Celtic cross is the largest private collection of roses in the country.

Malmesbury SN16 9A │ Tel: 01666 827650

www.abbeyhousegardens.co.uk

LOCATION In town centre next to abbey

This remarkable garden has been created since 1996 with passion and enthusiasm, reflected in the exuberant planting schemes. The 5 acres set around a late Tudor house beside the abbey feature an enormous arcade-encircled herb garden, a laburnum tunnel, a knot garden in the shape of a Celtic cross to echo its historic surroundings and huge herbaceous borders in riotous colours. There is also a waterfall, river and woodland walk (with kingfishers and water voles) – foliage and maple walks, and a scree garden. In all there are more than 10,000 different species and varieties of plants here.

The season starts with a dazzling display of 100,000 tulips and meconopsis, followed by roses (the largest private collection in the country), clematis and rhododendrons, and continues right through to autumn. There is a large and well-chosen collection of cordon fruit trees around an arcade, with sweet peas for added colour.

The owners are indefatigable, adding to the collections and planting new areas year on year.
▶ *Open main season – telephone or consult website for details – and for parties by appointment*

11 Bowood House

One of the county's hidden treasures, its pinetum, fine cascade, Doric temple and rhododendron walks should not be missed.

Bowood House, Derry Hill, Calne SN11 0LZ

Tel: 01249 812102 │ www.bowood.org

Historic Park and Garden Grade I

LOCATION 3 miles SE of Chippenham, 2½ miles W of Calne off A4, 8 miles S of M4 junction 17. Separate rhododendron walks off A342

The house and its 100 acre pleasure grounds lie in the centre of 'Capability' Brown's enormous park, where thousands of daffodils herald the arrival of spring. Other highlights include a tranquil lake, an arboretum and a pinetum, a Doric temple, a cascade waterfall and a hermit's cave. The Robert Adam orangery (now converted into a gallery) is particularly fine, and in front of it are formal Italianate terraces with rose beds, standard roses, fastigiate yews and a large variety of unusual climbers along the full length of the two terraces. The 62m (200ft) long herbaceous border along the east lawn was planted in 2008. The upper terrace was laid out in 1817 and the present fountains were added in 1839.

New planting has ensured that the flowering season continues from early spring through to late summer, with early tulips followed by alliums, as the forerunners to a blaze of perpetual roses. In the 19th century it was the aim of every garden to be 'as clean as a drawing room' and Bowood is in this class once again.

The rhododendron walks are situated in a separate 60 acre woodland garden.
▶ *House, garden and pleasure grounds open most of year – telephone or consult website for details. Rhododendron walks open daily end April to early June (depending on flowering season)*

SOUTHERN ENGLAND

12 Home Covert Gardens and Arboretum

Together the garden and woodland form a tranquil arboretum with numerous specimen trees, rare shrubs and a bog garden.

Roundway, Devizes SN10 2JA

Tel: 01380 723407

LOCATION 1 mile N of Devizes. Turn off A361 NE of town, signed to Roundway. Signposted

This is a garden of wonderful contrasts and year-round colour. The owners carved the 33 acres out of amenity woodlands in the 1960s and built themselves a house facing the splendid wide view that opens up from a large lawn on a plateau edged with grasses, herbaceous plants and alpines. Beyond this, grass pathways meander through a collection of trees and rare shrubs.

A steep path drops to a water garden, lake, waterfall and bog garden, rich with colour from bog primulas, and shaded by fine specimen trees. Excellent collections of magnolias, camellias, erythroniums and hydrangeas are scattered throughout, and roses and clematis scramble over walks and through trees. The garden is at its best from mid April to the end of July.

▶ *Open by appointment. Guided parties (12-40) welcome*

13 Broadleas Garden

Reminiscent of a Cornish garden, a number of tender species such as parrotias, azaleas and magnolias thrive in the acidic soil.

Broadleas, Devizes SN10 5JQ

Tel: 01380 722035

LOCATION 1 mile S of Devizes on A360

Set in a combe below Devizes, this 9½ acre garden is stuffed with fine plants that one would think too tender for these parts – large specimens of *Paulownia fargesii*, *Parrotia persica* and all manner of rare and notable magnolias, azaleas, hydrangeas, hostas, lilies and trilliums.

It is a garden of tireless perfectionism, at its most stunning in spring when carpets of bulbs stretch out beneath the flowering trees; rarely seen in such quantities are the erythroniums or dogtooth violets. Mature and semi-mature magnolias grow on each side of a steep dell and there is a woodland walk, a sunken rose garden and a silver border. Some of the more unusual plants are grown for sale.

▶ *Open main season – telephone or consult website for details*

14 The Old Mill, Ramsbury

The River Kennet divides the formal and natural areas, while colour and plants have been chosen to complement the mill itself.

Ramsbury SN8 2PN | Tel: 01672 520266

LOCATION 5 miles NE of Marlborough. Go down High Street, turn right at The Bell pub

It would be hard to imagine a more idyllic setting than this garden, with the River Kennet running through it. The formal areas near the house on one side of the river have views of a wilder and more natural landscape across the water. The pool, mill stream, mill race and numerous channels, all once part of the original working mill, dominate and shape the 5 acres.

The design never intrudes on the natural beauty of the site, due to the colour and choice of plants. The entire garden is experimental, and new features and buildings spring up all the time.

There are numerous spring bulbs and good autumn colour, but summer is the garden's high point. Close to the house are ebullient salvias, colour-themed borders and an attractive area combining an arrangement of pots with planting in gravel. Wooden bridges span streams to extend the garden in different directions, and an enclosure of lawn and herbaceous borders leads into a green garden backed by an old brick wall.

▶ *Open for NGS, and by appointment*

15 Chisenbury Priory

A clematis-covered curving steel pergola makes a dramatic feature in the mature garden surrounding this medieval priory.

East Chisenbury, near Pewsey SN9 6AQ

Tel: 07810 483984

LOCATION 3 miles SW of Pewsey. Turn E off A345 at Enford, then N to East Chisenbury

In this traditional English garden, broad-ranging vision and attention to detail have produced an atmosphere of controlled exuberance within an ancient framework. A fine avenue of mature chestnuts and sycamores leads to the 18th-century house, with two 30m (100ft) herbaceous borders on each side of the lawn. The rest of the priory is much older and 400 years of history have been enriched by skilful and imaginative planting in its surrounding 4 acres of garden.

A great curving pergola in galvanised steel by landscape blacksmith Paul Elliott, dripping with roses and late-flowering *Clematis viticella*, forms a

CHISENBURY PRIORY

unique feature. The fine bridge over the leat in the wild garden, an offspring of the River Avon, is also Elliott's work.

Water was an important element in the redesign of the garden in the 1960s, when many of the mature shrubs and trees were planted. Now mown paths wander past iris-fringed pools, down a nut walk and through flowery orchards offering glimpses of striking modern sculptures. Sheltered enclosures nearer the house are ablaze with colour from early spring to the end of July – successive waves of alliums and aquilegias followed by superb delphiniums, lilies, campanulas and masses of roses.

▶ *Open for NGS, and by appointment*

16 Heale Garden

The tranquil ambiance of the Japanese water garden and thoughtful planting thoughout provides a timeless appeal.

Middle Woodford, Salisbury SP4 6NT

Tel: 01722 782504 | www.healegarden.co.uk

Historic Garden Grade II*

LOCATION 4 miles N of Salisbury between A360 and A345

This is an idyllic garden with mature yew hedges, much of it designed by Harold Peto. A tributary of the Avon meanders through, providing the perfect boundary to the 8 acre site, and a sealing-wax red bridge and thatched teahouse straddle the water. The teahouse was brought over from Japan and assembled in 1910 with the help of four Japanese gardeners; it extends under the shade of *Magnolia* × *soulangeana* along the boggy banks planted attractively with moisture-lovers.

There are two terraces to the west of the house linked by a Yorkstone path rampant with alchemilla. The topmost has beds containing aged wisterias among tall herbaceous plants, backed by clipped yew. The other has two stone lily ponds and two small borders given height by tall wooden pyramids bearing roses, clematis and honeysuckles. The Long Border contains dark-leaved plants, including *Sambucus* 'Black Beauty', *Physocarpus* 'Diabolo' and interesting herbaceous perennials; behind is a border of musk roses.

It is tempting to linger in the tranquil walled kitchen garden, which perfectly marries practicality and pleasure. The wonderful flint-and-brick wall provides protection for many plants, including *Cytisus battandieri* and an ancient fig tree. Look out for the ancient mulberry, the very old *Cercidiphyllum japonicum* (the second tallest in Europe), and the *Magnolia grandiflora*.

The plant centre is comprehensive and the shop appeals to the discerning – unique wrought-iron plant supports can be bought here.

▶ *Open main season – telephone or consult website for details*

London

The capital's rapid growth and metropolitan bustle have not left it bereft of green space. Landscaped parks provide peace amid the traffic, while city gardeners make the most of unpromising sites to create their own oases in back gardens and even on rooftops.

LONDON 114-127

see panel opposite

M25

A110   Enfield

M 1

A1

A10

A406   LONDON 114-127

A409

A5

A410

A4180   Harrow

Hampstead Heath

19 20

8

A40

A10   Barking

A4020   see panel opposite

A13   Thames

21   A201

M4   A102   A220

A4   A4   18

A30   17   A2   22

Richmond upon Thames   A205   A223

A316   13   10   9

Richmond Park

15 16 11   A3   A20

Kingston upon Thames   A21   Bromley

A308   14   A23   A22

12   A2A A17   A232

A243   Croydon   A232   A21

A3   A23

A2 2   A233

23

KEY

1 Garden location

County boundary

Motorway

Principal A road

LONDON

The capital and its environs have a long history of creative planting. Botanic gardens, exotic rooftop retreats, landscaped squares and traditional schemes number among its many attractions.

1 The Inner Temple Garden

A site of historic interest, its borders are boldly planted with echiums and cardoons and there is a garden of peonies.

Crown Office Row, Inner Temple EC4 7HL

Tel: 020 7797 8243

www.innertemple.org.uk

LOCATION Between Fleet Street and Victoria Embankment

The iron railings enclosing the 3 acre communal garden – overlooked by lawyers' chambers and the 12th-century Temple Church – are festooned with roses, clematis, wisteria and fuchsias. Invitingly so, since the Society of the Inner Temple is generous in welcoming residents and those who work locally to enjoy the sweeping lawns, mature trees and flower-filled borders of this tranquil green space.

The site has had a varied and, at times, chequered history. There were fruit trees here in medieval times and roses in Shakespeare's day. It became a formal garden after being gifted to the society by James I in 1608, and acquired its striking avenue of plane trees in 1871. Flower shows are often held in the grounds and during the Second World War the beds were used to grow vegetables.

Since the arrival of a new head gardener in 2007, bold successional planting has been introduced into the garden, particularly in the 70m (230ft) long herbaceous border on the south-facing terrace. This is characterised by cardoons, echiums, melianthus and miscanthus, with blocks of late-flowering perennials providing a striking autumn crescendo of colour and foliage.

The hoop-shaped peony garden is a relaxed mix of herbaceous and tree peonies threaded with foxgloves and delicate *Thalictrum* 'Elin'. Nearby, a woodland planting combines strong textures and shapes beneath a *Prunus sargentii* and *Metasequoia glyptostroboides*.

The old avenue of plane trees has been underplanted with more than 13,000 *Liriope muscari* for autumn interest, and a thick buffer of native hedging screens the newly established propagation area.

▶ *Open most of year – telephone or consult website for details – for NGS, and for Open Squares Weekend*

THE INNER TEMPLE GARDEN

2 Roots and Shoots

This impressive wildlife garden with a summer meadow and planted roofs provides inspiration for urban biodiversity.

The Vauxhall Centre, Walnut Tree Walk
SE11 6DN

Tel: 020 7587 1131/7582 1800

www.rootsandshoots.org.uk

LOCATION Off Kennington Road; main entrance in Walnut Tree Walk, pedestrian access off Fitzalan Street

Lambeth's hidden green lung – a ½ acre wildlife garden within earshot of the chimes of Big Ben and 5 minutes' walk from the Imperial War Museum – was built on the rubble of a demolition site. Walking up to the entrance, traffic sounds seem to fade away as waving echiums greet you from the Mediterranean garden and a spreading walnut tree provides welcome shade in summer.

The cutting-edge learning centre has solar electricity and water heating, planted roofs, a 'brown-field' roof and a rainwater collection system. Local schools come here to experience pond-dipping, observe the abundant wildlife and listen to stories around the solar-powered dragon's well. A shelter hung with passion flowers, clematis and wisteria provides a tranquil resting place away from the hustle and bustle of the city.

Honeybees labour in an apiary and beehives stand in the long grass. Beekeeping courses are held throughout the year. Robinias, *Acacia dealbata* and espalier-trained apple trees provide shade and interest and a Yorkstone terrace is surrounded by pineapple guavas, passion vines and other tender exotics.

In June, roses are allowed to flower freely among shrubs and grasses and over meandering stony paths; in July, the wild-flower meadow steals the limelight, and during National Apple Week in October, single-variety apple juices are pressed in the oak barn.

▶ *Open all year, but some closures during school holidays – telephone or consult website for details*

LONDON

115

3 The Ismaili Centre

An unusual rooftop garden in four parts, it reflects Islamic tradition through the use of running water and colour-themed planting.

1 Cromwell Gardens SW7 2SL

Tel: 020 7581 2071

LOCATION Opposite V&A Museum. Entrance on corner of Thurloe Place and Exhibition Road

In this serene courtyard garden on the top floor of the Ismaili Centre, the sound of water running along rills masks the roar of traffic three storeys below. Designed by Japanese firm Sasaki Associates in the 1980s, its geometrical design and sense of enclosure recall the ancient Islamic *chahar bagh*, or four-fold garden, common in Persian and Indian Muslim architecture.

The 60m² (200sq ft) garden symbolises the celestial paradise found in the Koran, which is divided into quarters by rivers flowing with water, milk, honey and wine. The central fountain, an octagon of dark blue marble, feeds narrow channels set in the granite floor, and these lead to more fountains, one at a slightly raised level and all four in the shape of circular pools within a square.

The planting is in shades of green with white, silver and blues, in keeping with the traditional Muslim idiom. Structural plants include a fig tree, two silvery-grey weeping pears and cylinders of *Ilex aquifolium* 'J.C. van Tol' in beds 80cm (30in) deep. Roses and jasmine provide scent and white oleanders in pots frame the main doorways.

▶ *Conducted tours hourly on London Gardens Day in June and London Open House in Sept. Also open by appointment at other times*

4 Chelsea Physic Garden

Britain's second oldest botanic garden provides a fascinating demonstration of the medicinal use of plants through the ages.

66 Royal Hospital Road, Chelsea SW3 4HS

Tel: 020 7352 5646

www.chelseaphysicgarden.co.uk

Historic Garden Grade I

LOCATION Entrance in Swan Walk, off Chelsea Embankment and, for wheelchair users only, in Royal Hospital Road

A wrought-iron gate in Swan Walk opens on to one of London's most fascinating secret gardens. The only garden to retain the title 'physic', it was founded in 1673 as a place to train apothecaries'

apprentices in plant identification. Now the 3½ acre garden offers visitors an opportunity to stroll through the ages of plant classification and discoveries and, in the Garden of World Medicine and the Pharmaceutical Garden, to discover their many uses worldwide.

The walled garden's microclimate enables tender plants to flourish, including towering echiums and the largest outdoor fruiting olive tree in Britain. The beds radiate from an imposing statue of Sir Hans Sloane, who leased the land in perpetuity to the Society of Apothecaries in 1722. It also features a rock garden dating from 1773 and two ponds.

In one glasshouse is the rare *Musschia aurea* with starry cream flowers that, in the wild, are pollinated by lizards living on the volcanic slopes of Madeira. Another glasshouse contains an exceptional collection of species pelargoniums.

▶ *Open main season – telephone or consult website for details*

create three distinct illusions – a formal Spanish garden with a canal, an English woodland garden, and a Tudor garden.

Nowhere is the soil deeper than 1.5m (5ft), so it is remarkable that more than 500 varieties of trees and shrubs, including palms, figs and vines, survive up here. Ducks swim in their high-rise ponds watched over by flamingos, and there is a delightful maze of small paths, bridges and walkways, with peepholes in the outer walls giving glimpses across the city skyline.

▶ *Open by appointment – telephone or consult website for details*

6 The Royal College of Physicians Medicinal Garden

Present-day remedies mix with ancient cures in this living library, which has 800 species arranged geographically.

11 St Andrews Place, Regent's Park NW1 4LE

Tel: 020 7224 1539

www.rcplondon.ac.uk/garden

LOCATION On SE corner of Regent's Park, at junction of Outer Circle and Park Square East. Nearest underground station Regent's Park and Great Portland Street

When leading garden writer Mark Griffiths was asked to design and plant a physic garden for the 21st century, his brief was to make it a place of visual appeal as well as a living library and research resource. Retaining the best of earlier plantings, including a magnificent pomegranate, he replanted the small garden during 2005 and 2006, using thousands of plants from some 800 species.

The result is an inspiring design based on a fascinating range of plants, including some that are the source of current remedies such as *Illicium anisatum* (an ingredient of Tamiflu), some, such as *Veratrum nigrum*, long used in medicines, and others taken by different peoples through the ages.

The planting follows geographical regions and is split between the borders at the front (most colourful in spring and late summer) and those that encircle the undulating lawn to the rear. Here you will find plants associated with famous doctors, from the ancient Greek Dioscorides to 18th-century physician Mead, and a range of dramatic exotics in a gravel bed.

In 2007, eight new beds were planted with species from the *Pharmacopoeia Londinensis* of 1618 that were used in medicine at that time.

▶ *Open all year by appointment (telephone Paula Crosier on 020 7034 4901)*

CHELSEA PHYSIC GARDEN

5 The Roof Gardens

Palms and flamingos create a fantasy world in three themed rooftop gardens high above the streets of Kensington.

99 Kensington High Street W8 5ED

Tel: 020 7937 7994

www.roofgardens.virgin.com

Historic Garden Grade II*

LOCATION In Derry Street off Kensington High Street by lift

It is well worth making an appointment to visit this fantastical garden 30m (100ft) above ground on the sixth floor of what was once Derry and Toms department store. Now a private members' club with restaurant facilities, the 1½ acre gardens surrounding the bar and dining room are also used for functions and conferences. Horticultural visionary Ralph Hancock designed them to

LONDON

7 The Holme

Colourful formal planting stands in stark contrast to a lush rock garden in this well-maintained garden overlooking Regent's Park.

Inner Circle, Regent's Park NW1 4NT

LOCATION In Regent's Park, just W of Inner Circle

This garden, which is attached to one of the best-positioned houses in Regent's Park, is essentially in two parts. The first is a south-facing formal garden, with a sunken lawn and circular pool ringed by generous beds of statuesque herbaceous perennials. The second is an expanse of lawn dotted with fine specimen trees, including several mature willows and a *Taxodium distichum*, and beds planted with shrubs, grasses and swathes of herbaceous flowers.

Four gardeners keep the 4 acre site in immaculate order, cutting the lawn in summer several times a week in stripes that run the full width of the garden. By contrast, the rock garden is a secret dell where ferns, bamboos, reeds, ivies and other water-loving plants are allowed to grow in profusion. The two parts of the garden are linked by a strip of woodland, heady with scent in spring from *Syringa microphylla* and viburnums.

Throughout, bedding plants are used in adundance to add elegant swathes of colour. The garden won the 2005 award from BALI (British Association of Landscape Industries) for best-maintained domestic garden.

▶ *Open for NGS, and by appointment*

8 Little House A

The design of these gardens reveals an Arts and Crafts influence that appeals to both plant lovers and architects.

16a Maresfield Gardens, Hampstead NW3 5SU

LOCATION Off Fitzjohn's Avenue, near Freud Museum. Nearest underground Swiss Cottage or Finchley Road (5 mins)

These front and back gardens are superb modern interpretations of Arts and Crafts design and plantsmanship. Created in 2002 to link with the 1920s house built by Danish artist Arild Rosenkrantz, both gardens have been designed with an eye for symmetry and attention to detail.

The elegant front garden is centred on an octagonal bed set in stone paving. This is punctuated by squares of brick and sinuous roof tiles laid on their sides that echo motifs on the house itself.

There is a similar attention to detail in the back garden, where curving steps flanked by pots lead from a flagstone terrace to a lawn at a higher level. Here, a dark yew hedge set with niches for sculptural pots makes a dramatic backdrop to the garden's crowning glory – a stainless-steel water feature that feeds a narrow stone rill running across the garden. In the centre it widens into a rectangular basin and then flows into a little stream that disappears beneath a *Dicksonia fibrosa* before trickling through colourful plantings down one side of the garden. On the other side a pergola is smothered with glorious roses, wisteria, clematis and vines.

▶ *Open for NGS*

9 29 West Hill

Bold planting and artistic touches – an Indian wardrobe door links two areas – have resulted in a garden of great originality.

London SW18 1RB

Tel: 020 8874 2590

LOCATION On A3 close to Wandsworth High Street. Nearest underground station Putney East

This walled garden, at the back of the handsome Georgian house fronting a busy main road, is a leafy box of delights that displays the owner's artistic flair and originality. From the Yorkstone terrace a gravel path winds through bold plantings of *Melianthus major*, *Echium pininana*, bay and yucca, with an underplanting of white foxgloves and herbaceous plants specially chosen to attract birds.

The backdrop is an ivy-clad wall, topped by huge clay pots filled with foliage plants. An off-centre painted filigree door – a wardrobe door from Rajasthan – leads into the next part of the garden.

Under birches and a eucalyptus festooned with a 'New Dawn' rose is a seating area with a small raised pond. Ivy-edged steps reveal further plantings at the topmost level of the garden. Continue through a clematis-covered archway to a small herb parterre and return through a charming garden room shaded by roses, clematis and a vine.

Adding impact throughout the year are artistic touches – a terracotta head decorated with a crystal wreath and a ruff of vibrant oxalis, and containers planted with twigs, stems and colourful foliage, like so many giant outdoor flower arrangements.

▶ *Open on certain dates for charity, and by appointment*

10 5 Garden Close

Different moods are achieved with the help of exuberant and varied planting in this calm, green-themed garden.

London SW15 3TH

LOCATION Off Putney Heath, ½ mile E of Roehampton. In cul-de-sac off Portsmouth Road

This remarkable modern walled garden can be enjoyed on several levels. With a profusion of clipped and foliage plants and a vertical accent provided by black-stemmed bamboos, the strongly structured space is a perfect complement to the architecture of the award-winning steel-and-glass house surrounded by timber decking and overlooking two ponds.

It is also a tranquil, predominantly green garden where groves of white-stemmed birch on either side of the central front path create a sylvan mood and link the garden to the heath outside. Finally, it is an inspired combination of four discrete areas different in mood.

The first impression is of woodland edge, but with a difference. Tall birch trees and conifers are underplanted with glossy-leaved *Fatsia japonica* and phormiums, and backed by a screen of *Phyllostachys nigra* that runs the width of the garden.

It is all highly controlled – shrubs and trees, including the fine *Catalpa bignonioides* on the front lawn, are clipped regularly, while the box edging is elegantly offset by a strip of bark bordered by pale stone setts. Yet the garden has a relaxed rhythm, achieved by the repeated use of certain plants, such as cloud-pruned *Hebe rakaiensis* and ribbons of lavender.

The shrubs that fill the beds in the front garden are subtly tiered, as are the plants that ring the gnarled apple tree to the right of the pools. Other old fruit trees link the planting on the south border, which is backed by a beech hedge. Here the greens of the front garden give way to an explosion of summer colour from geraniums, alliums, daylilies and, alongside the deck, clumps of kniphofia, crocosmia and nasturtiums in pots.

Box edging continues round the back of the house, enclosing a productive vegetable bed and leading to a silver-leaved *Pyrus salicifolia* rising above a dark green carpet of *Hedera hibernica*. Ivy runs the length of the border on this side, punctuated by a single dramatic clump of green-stemmed *Phyllostachys* 'Castillonii', a superb contrast to the exuberance of the planting opposite. Leave yourself time to sit on the deck and surrender to the garden's different moods.

▶ *Open for NGS*

11 Isabella Plantation

An ornamental woodland garden and bird sanctuary full of exotic plants is home to a National Collection of Kurume azaleas.

Richmond Park, Richmond TW10 5HS

Tel: 020 8948 3209

www.royalparks.org.uk

Hidden away behind a wrought-iron gate within the sweeping tracts of Richmond Park is a remarkably rich wooded plantation of 40 acres. Fine native trees – including oaks, beeches and birches – provide flaming autumn leaves and shelter spring-flowering bulbs, colourful magnolias, camellias, rhododendrons, azaleas (a National Collection of Kurume azaleas is held here) and scented winter-flowering shrubs. Ponds, streams and a bog garden are planted with irises, daylilies and candelabra primulas.

The garden is also a notable bird sanctuary – nuthatches, tree-creepers, kingfishers, woodpeckers and owls have all been spotted – and an atmosphere of secrecy and seclusion makes it a sanctuary for human visitors, too.

▶ *Open all year – telephone or consult website for details*

12 239A Hook Road

Attention to detail is a hallmark of this creative four-part garden, which makes good use of colour combinations.

Chessington, Kingston-upon-Thames KT9 1EQ

Tel: 020 8397 3761

www.gardenphotolibrary.com

LOCATION On Hook road (A243) close to Hook underpass and A3. Opposite recreation ground

The narrow side entrance dressed with containers leads to an explosion of creative planting in this 45m (150ft) long suburban garden. It is divided into four interconnecting areas, all circular in shape. There is a brick-edged patio, a small lawn encircled by lollipop *Ilex aquifolium* and a deep pool. Hidden behind a tall yew hedge that creates a false end to the garden, a potager is filled with crisply angled beds for vegetables and fruit, and newly planted cordon apples along the wall.

The garden photographer owner and his wife have a flair for plant combinations – the whites, purples and wines of the upper border give way to blue and mauve perennials further down – and have also devised a series of artistic solutions to the unwelcome activities of visiting wildlife.   ▷

119

Where foxes were starting to tunnel they have mulched with pebbles, and to stop herons from snatching up the resident Koi carp they have deepened the sides of the pool.

In the same vein, they have transformed a dead plum tree in the potager into a sculptural eye-catcher by painting the limbs white and stringing them up with gold and silver baubles. A gravel garden links the patio and lawn, providing a dining area that is wafted with the scent of roses and nicotiana under the developing canopy of a golden catalpa.

Another fragrant seat, this time a wooden arbour planted with *Trachelospermum jasminoides* and *Rosa* 'New Dawn', and flanked by terracotta pots brimming with marguerites, catches the evening sun in the potager.

This garden offers a lesson in attention to detail and style. There is also a night-time charity opening, during which the garden is lit by flares and hundreds of tealights in home-made containers that are strung from trees or float in the pool. This accentuates the architectural shapes of many of the plants, including the poolside planting of gunnera, phormium and bamboo.

▶ *Open for NGS, and by appointment*

13 7 St George's Road

A wide variety of planting is packed into a limited space and a Mediterranean garden leads to bog and knot gardens.

7 St George's Road, St Margaret's, Twickenham TW1 1QS

Tel: 020 8892 3713

www.raworthgarden.com

LOCATION Off A316 between Twickenham Bridge and St Margaret's roundabout

If you are a new owner of a London garden or seek inspiration to revamp your own, make an appointment to visit this ½ acre site, where a wide variety of plantings are enclosed by formal clipped hedges. Among the striking features is a large north-facing conservatory, a rose and clematis-covered pergola and wide borders that give shape and colour for nine months of the year.

Visitors enter through a sunken Mediterranean garden and an area filled with container plants. A tiered variegated cornus leads the eye to the bog garden with its decked walkway, on the far side of the lawn, and then to the newest part, a charming knot garden.

▶ *Open for NGS, and for parties of ten or more by appointment*

14 Hampton Court Palace

Careful attention has been paid to historical and horticultural accuracy in the parts of this superb garden that have been restored.

East Molesey KT8 9AU | Tel: 0844 482 7777

www.hrp.org.uk

Historic Park and Garden Grade I

LOCATION On A308 at junction of A309 on N side of Hampton Court Bridge over Thames

The gardens, which provide the setting for the palace, are an exciting and eclectic mixture of styles and tastes. They are renowned worldwide for the Great Vine planted in 1768 – officially the largest vine in the world, probably the oldest and still producing hundreds of 'Black Hamburg' grapes each year (for sale to the public when harvested in late August) – and the maze, the oldest hedge-planted maze in Britain.

The sunken Pond Gardens offer a magnificent display of bedding plants. Originally created as ornamental ponds for Henry VIII in the 1530s, they then held carp and other fish. There is also a 1924 knot garden with interlocking bands of dwarf box, thyme, lavender and cotton lavender infilled with bedding plants.

On a grand scale, the Great Fountain Garden, an immense semi-circle of grass and flower beds with a central fountain, is probably the most impressive element, but the Wilderness Garden in spring, with its mass of daffodils and spring-flowering trees, has the most charm.

The restored Privy Garden of William III is a spectacular example of the Baroque style, with parterres, cutwork, clipped yews and spring and summer displays of 17th-century plants. A more recent restoration is William III's unique Orangery Garden, containing hundreds of exotics planted in ornate pots.

A double row of 544 lime trees has been planted to flank the Longwater in Home Park, bringing Charles II's Long Walk Avenue back to its 1661 glory. An area of the gardens that is sometimes missed by visitors is the secluded Twentieth-Century Garden with contemporary plantings in an informal setting, located next to the Fountain Garden.

There's too much to see in one day, so plan at least two trips – one in spring and one in summer – to take in different sections of the 60 acres of gardens.

▶ *Palace open. Gardens and park open all year – telephone or consult website for details*

AN EXCITING AND
ECLECTIC MIXTURE OF
STYLES AND TASTES
HAMPTON COURT PALACE

From wilderness to wildlife haven

Four hundred years ago, a wild garden was surprisingly formal in style, but nowadays informal meadow plantings are all the rage.

When the earliest gardens were created in Britain, much of the land was covered by forest. A moat, fence or hedge formed a protective mantle around a house, providing shelter for herbs, fruit and flowers. By the 17th century, much of the forest had been cleared, and the gardens of grand houses expanded out into the landscape, where the gentry would venture beyond the formal gardens surrounding the house into the 'wilderness'.

These 17th and 18th-century wildernesses were actually quite formal – they were walled and consisted of several compartments enclosed by clipped hedges and planted with trees and shrubs. In the restored wilderness at Ham House in London, 2m (6½ft) high hornbeam hedges make up 16 compartments laid out in a symmetrical pattern, eight of them closed and eight with openings that allow them to be explored. Four are planted with wild-flower meadows, the rest with trees, shrubs, climbers and other flowering plants. Mown paths radiate from the centre point of the wilderness where originally, eight lead statues on pedestals stood, ringed by shell-backed chairs and Versailles boxes containing citrus trees.

Return to the wild

Eventually these so-called wildernesses became more relaxed and many reverted to woodlands. Gardeners focused instead on exotic imported plants and the formal designs they inspired. From 1832 mechanical lawnmowers transformed grassy areas into manicured lawns. But some gardeners wanted to retain a wilder and more natural look. In *The Wild Garden*, published in 1870, William Robinson, advocated using native wild flowers alongside hardy foreign plants in rougher parts of the garden. This style of gardening can be seen at his garden at Gravetye Manor in Sussex. He planted thousands of narcissi in the grass and advised that to achieve a natural effect they should be planted in groups, not scattered.

WIDE MOWN PATHS CUT THROUGH THE LONG GRASS FILLED WITH WILD FLOWERS

CHISENBURY PRIORY

Robinson's wild garden was based on aesthetic considerations, but in the later 20th century, it became clear that intensive agriculture had led to the destruction of many of Britain's wild-flower meadows and the creatures dependent on them. Many gardeners, such as the influential writer Christopher Lloyd, began to create wild-flower meadows as a way of conserving wild flowers and providing a habitat for insects. Though sometimes tricky to establish as they require a poor, light soil, once the right mix of grasses and flowers is achieved, insects and invertebrates will move into a meadow, even in the middle of a city.

A refuge for wildlife

At London's Roots and Shoots garden in Kennington, the ½ acre wildlife meadow is home to countless creatures, including two species of grasshopper, two rare crickets, solitary and social bees, hoverflies, butterflies and moths. Two ponds are inhabited by newts, frogs and damselflies, while several beehives, log piles and a green roof support yet more insects and invertebrates.

Elsewhere, wild gardens have been designed with specific kinds of animals in mind. Badgers roam freely at night in Blakenham Woodland Garden near Ipswich in Suffolk, which has welcomed wildlife since it was begun in 1951.

A fusion of unusual specimen trees and shrubs and native wild flowers, it is a perfect example of how wildlife and beautiful gardens can coexist.

A recently created meadow at Coton Manor in Northamptonshire is filled with wild flowers including oxeye daisies, ragged robbin and common vetch. Yellow rattle, used to keep the grasses down, has attracted common blue butterflies and burnet moths. The meadow is awash with colour from early June until late July when it is cut for hay and grazed by sheep thereafter.

At Chisenbury Priory in Wiltshire, a leat originating from the River Avon flows through the wild garden, which is planted with moisture-loving species. Wide mown paths cut through the long grass filled with wild flowers allow close up views. At Marle Place in Kent a host of alliums create a purple haze in early summer in the meadow, while at Garden House in Devon a bulb meadow provides colour from spring to autumn, with snowdrops followed by wood anemones and corydalis, and finally finishing with cyclamen, colchicums and autumn crocus.

Alhough they may appear delightfully casual, these modern wild-flower meadows are in fact as highly designed and managed as the formal wildernesses that preceded them.

15 Ham House

The 17th-century layout has been restored using only plants from the period, with formal parterres and a wild garden.

Ham Street, Richmond TW10 7RS

Tel: 020 8940 1950

www.nationaltrust.org.uk

Historic Garden Grade II*/The National Trust

LOCATION On S bank of Thames, W of A307 at Petersham

The formality of the clipped bays, yew cones and box hedging at the front of the magnificent 17th-century house provides a clue to the garden stretching behind. Instead of wide borders packed with colourful shrubs and herbaceous perennials, the landowners of the time who created this garden favoured clipped shrubs, espaliered trees and pots planted up with citrus trees, exotics and annuals. The garden also features narrow borders where the plants are arranged in repeat lines and expensive foreign imports given plenty of bare soil to enhance their display.

The plant species used throughout the 109 acre garden were all introduced to Britain before 1700. This is emphasised in new information panels that give a clear feel of the garden in its 1760s heyday.

After entering the main gate, turn left to avoid missing the much-photographed Cherry Garden and the exquisite all-seasons parterre. Here the box-edged beds are filled with clipped santolina and lavender, while paths defined by box cones converge on a central statue of Bacchus.

Next follow a shady hornbeam *allée* to a wide south terrace that runs the length of the house and overlooks the square lawns known as plats, surrounded by gravel walks. These lawns were originally cut by scythe and would probably have sported central statues.

Beyond them is the Wilderness, a fascinating 17th-century feature where trees and shrubs are enclosed in 16 compartments, concealed from the promenader by head-high hornbeam hedges resembling a maze.

Wander along the grassy paths in this tranquil garden or sit in one of the four summerhouses, listen to birdsong and admire the tree canopies in the Wilderness beyond. On the west side of the plats is the entrance to a 17th-century walled kitchen garden, where you can take tea in the earliest surviving orangery in the country.

The historic plans reproduced on the information boards show the original kitchen garden as twice its current size. The four plots now in cultivation are planted with annual heritage vegetables, flowers for cutting and permanent plantings of fruit and vegetables. A conservation plan outlines further cultivation in the kitchen garden and the reinstatement of some of the pots (327 are listed in a contemporary inventory) that once lined the paths between the plats.

▶ *House open main season. Garden open most of year – telephone or consult website for details*

16 Petersham House

A country garden that complements its setting perfectly, it has riotous borders, stylish yews and an Antony Gormley statue.

Church Lane, Petersham Road, Petersham TW10 7AG | Tel: 020 8940 5230

www.petershamnurseries.com

LOCATION Entrance in Church Lane, off Petersham Road. Nearest station Richmond. Or take Hammerton Ferry from Marble Hill Park to Ham House

The best way to approach this stylish 2 acre garden, which is blessed with a glorious semi-rural setting and furnished with exemplary borders by garden writer and designer Mary Keen, is to walk along the river from Richmond Bridge, past the tranquil water meadows of Petersham.

The wide lush lawns that lead out from the house give time for the eye to take in the many delights. Under an old yew tree is an Antony Gormley statue and crisp clipped yews stand in sentinel fashion on the lawn. The massed double borders running down from the lawns are packed with colour and texture. There is also a well-designed vegetable and small cutting garden with a stylish abode alongside for bantams.

Allow time to visit the nursery with its well-maintained plants, restored propagation house filled with conservatory plants and original pieces of garden furniture and equipment. A café serves delicious lunches (booking advised).

▶ *Open for NGS*

CRISP CLIPPED YEWS

17 Royal Botanic Gardens

The historic landscaped gardens are home to the largest living plant collection in the world as well as many fine listed buildings.

Kew, Richmond TW9 3AB | Tel: 020 8332 5655

www.kew.org

Historic Park Grade I

LOCATION Kew Green, S of Kew Bridge

There are many reasons to visit these magnificent gardens, but the two that top the list must be the 14,000 or so trees that form stately avenues, woods and towering specimens, and the wealth of magnificent buildings (40 of them listed, including glasshouses, follies, the orangery, the Dutch palace and the ten-storey Victorian pagoda) that punctuate the grounds.

Started in 1750 as a 9 acre private garden, Kew now extends to 300 acres and became a UNESCO World Heritage site in 2003. It is a place of records and superlatives. It possesses the world's largest living plant collection, the oldest pot plant in the UK, the biggest indoor plant in the world, the largest Victorian plant conservatory in existence, the most extensive collection of mature hollies in cultivation and the world's first gallery dedicated to botanical art.

But it is also a place where garden lovers can while away hours identifying and admiring plants in the more intimate areas, such as the sunken Nosegay Garden, the Secluded Garden, the rhododendron dell and the Mediterranean, azalea garden and grass gardens. The primary purpose of the gardens is plant conservation and all plants are given clear, detailed labels.

Entering via the main gate, the first-time visitor will be drawn to the southern section where the elegant new glasshouses, the Princess of Wales conservatory and the Davies alpine house are located. Here, too, are the established rock garden, the order beds and the superb Victorian glasshouses – the renowned palm house, the steamy waterlily house and the vast, tranquil temperate house where date palm fronds brush the underside of the roof.

From here it's a short walk to the most recent structure, an 18m (60ft) high Xstrata Treetop Walkway that makes a discreet circuit through the canopy layer of sweet chestnut, oak, lime and beech trees, offering superb views. Further north is the lake commissioned by Sir William Hooker, Kew's first official director, with four wooded islands, spanned now by the sinuous bridge of John Pawson. The western boundary encloses the wildest part. Here, native species are encouraged, dead wood is left standing and the bluebells form a vivid carpet in spring.

At every season Kew offers blooms and colourful foliage, and the map provided with the entry ticket indicates the highlights to seek out.
▶ *Palace open April to Oct (10am-5.30pm). Gardens open all year – telephone or consult website for details*

18 Chiswick House

Grand vistas and hidden pathways combine in these elegant gardens, the birthplace of the English Landscape Movement.

Burlington Lane, Chiswick W4 2RP

Tel: 020 8995 0508

www.english-heritage.org.uk

Historic Park and Garden Grade I/English Heritage

LOCATION 5 miles W of central London on A4

The celebrated gardens, now stretching over 66 acres, were created in four stages between 1715 and 1858. Over the years the gardens have expanded outwards from the house, which is the finest example of Palladian architecture in Britain.

In the 1720s garden designer William Kent was employed to create a garden based on the ancient classical model, planting groves of trees, making sweeping lawns, opening up views, adding an exedra lined with statuary and a *patte d'oie* with three architectural focal points. He also gave the canal a more sinuous shape and created a cascade at one end designed to mimic an underground river flowing from a rocky hill.

An Italian garden with parterres and a conservatory (built to house a famous camellia collection) was constructed after 1811.

The current programme of restoration includes planting 16,000 new trees, renewing miles of paths and restoring the conservatory. Watch for the changes in the formal hedges, admire the improved views from the western lawn, and continue to seek out the hidden pathways and beautiful specimen trees.
▶ *House open main season. Gardens open all year – telephone or consult website for details*

STAND IN SENTINEL FASHION

PETERSHAM HOUSE

19 The Hill Garden and Pergola

The lengthy pergola constructed from oak beams and stone columns is one of the capital's most dramatic garden structures.

Inverforth Close, North End Way NW3 7EX

Tel: 020 8455 5183

Historic Garden Grade II*

LOCATION From Hampstead pass Jack Straw's Castle on left-hand side of road to Golders Green. Inverforth Close is off North End Way (A502)

From the entrance a spiral staircase climbs up to reveal a striking garden structure – a 250m (820ft) long classical pergola with oak beams and stone columns planted with a wide variety of climbers. Designed by landscape architect Thomas Mawson in the early 20th century to link the garden to that of Inverforth House, it is at ground level on one side but supported by a red-brick colonnaded structure 5m (16ft) above ground on the other.

There are views across the tree tops and down onto the old kitchen garden of the house, laid out in sweeping beds containing cherries, magnolias, shrub roses, geraniums and bergenias, with a stand of birch in one corner. At the lower end, the many mature climbers include what may be a wisteria from the original planting. A belvedere looks out to distant Harrow on the Hill.

Steps descend past an ancient sweet chestnut into the Hill Garden proper – a peaceful retreat with lawns unfurling down the hill, mature trees, a long formal lily pond and well-maintained shrub and perennial borders.

▶ *Open all year – telephone or consult website for details*

20 Kenwood

A picturesque landscape with views across London where visitors can enjoy walks through woodland and alongside lakes.

Hampstead Lane NW3 7J │ Tel: 020 8348 1286

www.english-heritage.org.uk

Historic Park Grade II/English Heritage

LOCATION On N side of Hampstead Heath, on Highgate-Hampstead road

This attractively landscaped garden was laid out by Humphry Repton at the end of the 18th century. Sweeping lawns run down from the terrace of Kenwood House and give fine views over Hampstead Heath and the city.

Large-scale shrubberies are dominated by rhododendrons. The pasture ground slopes down towards two large lakes, and woods to the south of the lakes fringe the heath, accessible through a number of gates.

THAMES BARRIER PARK

The 112 acres here are a good place to walk at any season, but particularly when the trees are turning in autumn. Look out for the ivy arch, which opens out on to the lakes (one of Repton's famous 'surprises'), the sham bridge on the Thousand Pound Pond and sculpture by Barbara Hepworth and Henry Moore. Chelsea Flower Show winner Arabella Lennox-Boyd has designed the terraced garden behind the café.

▶ *House and park open all year – telephone or consult website for details*

21 Thames Barrier Park

This urban oasis includes London's largest sunken garden, in which yew and maygreen hedges replicate the ripples of the river.

Barrier Point Road, off North Woolwich Road, E16 2HP | Tel: 020 7476 3741

www.thamesbarrierpark.org.uk

LOCATION On N bank of River Thames, between North Woolwich Road and Thames Barrier in Silvertown. Nearest underground station Canning Town or DLR Pontoon Dock

Opened in 2000, this exciting modern park is at once a brave act of regeneration and a landscaping *tour de force*. The distinguished French designers Alain Provost and Alain Cousseran of Groupe Signes teamed up with English architects Patel Taylor and engineers Ove Arup to transform a contaminated brownfield site into a 22 acre park on the north bank adjacent to the river's most significant modern work of engineering – the giant stainless-steel 'cockleshells' of the Thames Flood Prevention Barrier.

The river promenade gives a setting to the barrier, and a raised walkway opens up views along and over the river. The flatness of the high-level plateau emphasises its spaciousness. A vast area of lawns and wild-flower meadows – the size of ten or more football pitches – is framed by bands of shrubs and interspersed with broad mown paths.

The greatest surprise and pleasure is, however, the Green Dock, the largest sunken garden in London. Stretching the length of the park, this simulation of a marine dock is a glorious, accessible garden dug deep and crossed by two viewing bridges. Look down and the planting is a tidal flow of wave-cut hedges alternating with beds of perennials. And 32 water jets play in the fountain plaza.

▶ *Open all year – telephone or consult website for details*

22 Hall Place

On the banks of the River Cray, these formal gardens feature magnificent topiary modelled on statues at Hampton Court.

Bourne Road, Bexley DA5 1PQ

Tel: 01322 526574 | www.hallplace.com

Historic Garden Grade II*

LOCATION Just N of A2 near A2/A223 junction

The Tudor mansion house is surrounded by 50 acres of award-winning grounds. A raised walk overlooks the topiary lawn where the Queen's beasts – modelled on the original statues at Hampton Court – stand against a mature Solanum 'Glasnevin' on a red-brick wall.

Further on, rose beds give way to a hedge-enclosed secret garden with wide herbaceous borders. A wisteria-covered bridge leads to Italianate and herb gardens. A wildlife meadow, a time-garden – which explores the history of plants through the ages – and a dipping pond are good places for budding young environmentalists.

The horticultural area has sub-tropical plant houses, a nursery, display gardens and a sales area.

▶ *House open. Garden open all year – telephone or consult website for details*

23 Cottage Farm

A cottage garden of great individuality that includes rustic pergolas, fuchsia displays, a stumpery and tropical plants.

Cacketts Lane, Cudham TN14 7QG

Tel: 01959 532506

www.cottagefarmgardens.com

LOCATION 5 miles NW of Orpington on A21

This is a delightful series of intimate garden spaces around a row of brick-and-flint cottages. Visitors enter through an immaculate kitchen garden laid out in sturdy raised beds. Rustic pergolas clothed in scented roses provide shade, seclusion and seating, old-fashioned sweet peas scramble up tripods, clematis and honeysuckles festoon old apple trees and the cottage-garden planting spills over narrow paths. A sheltered terrace blooms with exotics such as daturas, strelitzias, palms, cordylines and cannas.

Tropical plants and fruits flourish in heated glasshouses, and there is a well-stocked fruit cage and greenhouse. Fuchsia displays, a vine-covered dome, a wildlife pond and a stumpery planted with ferns add further interest.

▶ *Open for NGS, and for parties by appointment*

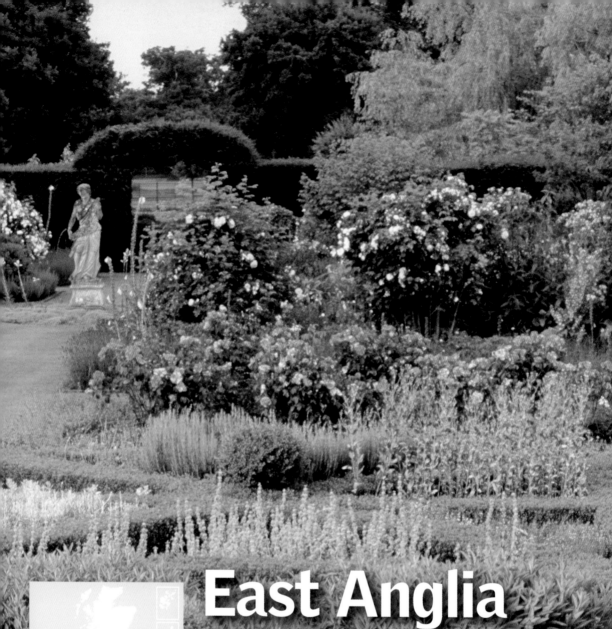

East Anglia

Still largely rural, England's eastern corner is its flattest region, often windswept and bounded by the cold North Sea. Shelterbelts and walled gardens provide welcome refuge from the chilly breezes, while lime-rich soil encourages herbaceous variety as well as wild-flower meadows.

KEY

1 Garden location
— County boundary
— Motorway
— Principal A road

ABBOTS RIPTON HALL

CAMBRIDGESHIRE

Great gardeners, past and present, have created many of the fine gardens in this county, using imagination and skill to shape the grounds in a variety of unusual and attractive ways.

1 Crossing House Garden

Plenty of interesting features are packed into a tiny site, including ponds, an alpine house and an extensive range of plants.

78 Meldreth Road, Shepreth, Royston SG8 6PS

Tel: 01763 261071

LOCATION 8 miles SW of Cambridge, ½ mile W of A10

This small garden, started by the present owners in 1967, is crammed full of plants and shows just what can be achieved in a restricted space – two pools, excellent dwarf box edging, an arbour in clipped yew, rockeries and a lawn, and two tiny glasshouses full of orchids and alpines. There are thousands of different plants here, so a visit at any time of year will be rewarding.

▶ *Open all year*

2 Abbots Ripton Hall

With many rare trees and historic roses, this garden showcases the work of several leading 20th-century gardeners.

Abbots Ripton, Huntingdon PE28 2PQ

Tel: 01487 773555

www.abbotsriptonhall.co.uk

Historic Garden Grade II

LOCATION 2 miles N of Huntingdon, approached from B1090

Many of the last century's greatest gardeners have had a hand in this 8 acre garden. In the 1950s, gardener and painter Humphrey Waterfield designed a ring of historic roses with a circular lawn at its centre and planted a grey border with alpines and sun-loving perennials. Unfortunately, his work ended abruptly when he was killed in a car crash in 1971. An inscription at the foot of a memorial urn commemorates his life.

Between 1960 and 1970, landscape gardener and journalist Lanning Roper also advised on planting and design. The follies are the work of Peter Foster, Surveyor of the Fabric at Westminster Abbey. They range from two large Gothic screens in the herbaceous borders stretching from the 18th-century house, which are backed by columns of yew and philadelphus, to the Chinese pagoda at the end of the lake.

Garden designer Jim Russell advised on trees and added a plantation along the earth bank. Sculptor Peter Coates and gardening journalist Tony Venison also worked here.

The present owner, with the help of rose specialist Peter Beales, has replanted the rose circle and many of the borders, and there is a collection of rare oaks from acorns gathered from around the world.

▶ *Open for charities, and by appointment*

3 Chippenham Park

A formal water garden with a tadpole-shaped lake is one of many original elements retained in this impressive garden.

Chippenham Park, Ely CB7 5PT

Tel: 01638 720221/721991

www.chippenhamparkgardens.info

LOCATION **5 miles NE of Newmarket, 1 mile off A11**

This is one of the county's most original gardens, and it improves year on year. William Emes, known both as a landscaper and an enthusiast for garden flowers, created the perimeter drive and tadpole-shaped lake and island. Many of the original features have been retained, including the old formal water garden and trees planted by the 17th-century owner Admiral Russell to echo the formation of ships drawn up at the battle of La Hogue.

The present owners have created a 15 acre garden within the park, embellishing Emes's work. The great canal has been strengthened by the introduction of a copper beech avenue and in Adrian's Walk (named after a still-serving gardener of 53 years) colourful plantings are reflected in the waters of the lake. The long south border produces peonies and alliums, while the Victorian box walk preserves an air of mystery at the entrance to the woodland garden.

The old vegetable garden, which is divided into four, includes a mound and a quince garden, a Spanish garden with olive trees and a green

theatre, and a fine memorial garden to Admiral Russell planted around a magnificent statue of a sitting hare.

With more than 750 rose bushes and a wide selection of acers and other rarer trees, this garden never gives the feeling of being too large or too busy. Spires of eremurus in season reflect the grandeur of the gables on the house, which dates to 1895.

▶ *Open last weekend in Jan and first three weekends in Feb for snowdrops, for NGS, and for parties of 20 or more by appointment*

4 Anglesey Abbey Gardens and Lode Mill

An outstanding garden with a wildlife discovery area, outdoor art and working watermill, it is renowned for its snowdrops.

Quy Road, Lode CB25 9EJ

Tel: 01223 810080

www.nationaltrust.org.uk/angleseyabbey

Historic Garden Grade II*/The National Trust

LOCATION **6 miles NE of Cambridge off A14, on B1102**

This tranquil National Trust garden is noted for its collection of statues, urns and columns. The formal gardens around the house were part of the original 1860s layout. They were redesigned, with the addition of a statuary, by the 1st Lord Fairhaven in the 1930s. A mile-long winter walk was created by the National Trust in 1998.

For wildlife interest, visit the new Hoe Fen wildlife discovery area. Snowdrops, hyacinths, narcissi and leucojums appear in their thousands, equalled in density and diversity by the wild flowers in the meadows. Lode Mill, a restored 18th-century watermill, is situated on the edge of the gardens.

The huge curving herbaceous borders and gardens filled with modern bush roses and dahlias keep the garden alive at the close of summer, while a splash of *Amaryllis belladonna* against the grey stone walls ushers in autumn and the arboretum trees start to tint red and gold. Then it is the turn of white-stemmed birches and black-stemmed *Cornus alba* 'Kesselringii' in the winter walk to make a final flourish before the snowdrops begin the year again.

▶ *House and garden open all year – telephone or consult website for details. Mill machinery operates first and third Sat of month*

EAST ANGLIA

131

5 Murray Edwards College

Colourful seasonal plantings of flowers, vegetables and herbs enliven the landscaped grounds of this Cambridge college.

Storey's Way, Cambridge CB3 0DF

www.newhall.cam.ac.uk/grounds/gardens

LOCATION Off A1303 Madingley Road and Huntingdon Road

The unprepossessing, albeit Grade II-listed, buildings of the Soviet-style campus of this renamed college (formerly New Hall) have inspired the head gardener and her team to create a unifying vision of colour against its monochromatic walls, vaults and domes. Using naturalistic northern European-style plantings on a south-facing slope, each part of the garden is thought-provoking. Some beds contain vegetables for consumption by students, while others are planted with herbs, flowers and even the bearded wheat 'Soissons' for breadmaking.

To fit in with the academic year, the self-propagated, colour co-ordinated plantings reach their peak during the last week of June, the third week of September and the first week of October.

The entrance has a central bed that blazes in spring and is followed by a profusion of sub-tropical bedding. The Planet Garden – a tribute to the college's founder Dame Rosemary Murray – is also filled with tulips, followed in autumn by chrysanthemums and grasses.

Nora Barlow, Charles Darwin's granddaughter, gave the house and garden to New Hall, and the aquilegia named for her is naturalised throughout the garden. The 1880 greenhouse used by her grandmother, Emma, has been fully restored and now shelters half-hardy plants through winter. The greenhouse overlooks a pawlonia grove and a border of scarlet salvias and dahlias that screen the tennis courts.

The grounds also showcase works of art, including the prize-winning 'Transit of Venus' garden that the college presented at the Chelsea Flower Show in 2007.

▶ *Open most of year – telephone or consult website for details – and for NGS*

6 University Botanic Garden

A collection of habitat displays, ranging from tropical rainforest to alpine, is just one of the garden's many highlights.

Bateman Street, Cambridge CB2 1JF

Tel: 01223 336265

www.botanic.cam.ac.uk

Historic Garden Grade II

LOCATION In S of city, on E side of A1309 (Trumpington Road). Entrances at Brookside Gate at corner of Bateman Street and Trumpington Road and Station Road

This diverse garden covering 40 acres fulfils its three remits: research, education and amenity. Even in winter a visit is worthwhile to see the red, black, green and yellow-ochre stems of the dogwoods contrasting with *Rubus biflorus* and the pale pink trunks of *Betula albo-sinensis* var. *septentrionalis*.

The garden has the best collection of trees in the east of England, with limes, chestnuts, willows and conifers featuring prominently. Exotic trees include pawpaw and specimens of madrona, black walnut and dawn redwood. Historic beds display the hardy representatives of 90 families of flowering plants, and there are both limestone and sandstone rock gardens.

The glasshouse displays have recently been restored and replanted to highlight plant diversity under conditions ranging from tropical rainforest to arid desert. In the alpine house, plants are changed regularly as they come into flower. The new borders in front of the glasshouse aim to inspire visitors to introduce more bee-friendly plants into their own gardens.

The Dry Garden investigates how design and careful selection of plants can eliminate the need for watering in a typical city garden. Local habitats are re-created nearby, including a fenland display.

The Genetics Garden shows how the huge variety of flowering plants results from genetic variation due to mutation, while the figure of 'Healthy Herbie' and a display about compost and compost-making highlight current concerns about chemicals, drugs, recycling and sustainable living.

In the new Cambridge Border, mixed shrub and herbaceous planting focuses on species that originated in the garden, including *Rosa* 'Cantabrigiensis' and *Epimedium* x *cantabrigiensis*, together with prize-winning stalwarts such as *Viburnum* x *bodnantense* 'Dawn' and *Mahonia* x *media* 'Lionel Fortescue'.

▶ *Open most of year – telephone or consult website for details*

ESSEX

Rural Essex has many delightful gardens, created and nurtured by influential gardeners. Traditional sites are expertly tended and restored, while modern plots thrive under innovative direction.

1 RHS Garden Hyde Hall

This beautiful garden, unforgettable in any season, displays a wide range of both formal and naturalistic planting styles.

Rettendon, Chelmsford CM3 8AT

Tel: 01245 400256 | www.rhs.org.uk/hydehall

LOCATION 7 miles SE of Chelmsford, signed from A130

The cultivated area, covering more than 24 acres, is perched above the East Anglian wheatfields. Very low rainfall and the exposed nature of the site combine to make it a challenging place to cultivate. However, by choosing the right plants for the right places the RHS has demonstrated that it is possible to create a garden of beauty and year-round colour and interest even in adverse conditions.

The garden demonstrates an eclectic range of horticultural styles, from the formality of clipped hedges in the Hilltop Garden to the naturalistic planting of perennials and grasses on Clover Hill.

A renowned dry garden boasts many thousands of healthy looking plants in hundreds of varieties. The original rose garden contains a number of species roses interplanted with naturalised *Eremurus robustus*, while the newer rose beds, surrounded by low yew hedging, are given added height by tall obelisks supporting climbing roses. The colour-themed herbaceous borders are at their best in late summer, and the gardens hold a National Collection of viburnums.

The 2 acre Robinson Garden, completed in 2007, is a dell garden planted with more than 150 perennials and numerous shrubs. The stone walls are clad in ferns and ivy, and visitors can look down into the garden from two oak bridges.

Vegetable plots demonstrate alternative systems of cultivation, such as the 'no dig system', and showcase a wide selection of vegetables from around the world. During the past few years hundreds of thousands of bulbs have been planted, and 12 acres of wild-flower meadow were sown in 2008

▶ *Open all year – telephone or consult website for details*

RHS GARDEN HYDE HALL

2 The Gibberd Garden

Glades, groves, pools and *allées* provide the ideal backdrop for a collection of modern sculpture and architectural artefacts.

Marsh Lane, Gilden Way, Harlow CM17 0NA

Tel: 01279 442112

www.thegibberdgarden.co.uk

Historic Garden Grade II

LOCATION E of Harlow between A414 and B183. From M11 junction 7 take A414 to Harlow, follow signs to Old Harlow onto B183 (Gilden Way) and continue for 1 mile; Marsh Lane is on left

The creation of the architect and art collector Sir Frederick Gibberd from the 1950s until his death in 1984, this is an outstanding example of 20th-century garden design. The sloping 7 acre site comprises a series of rooms designed to display his collection of modern sculpture and architectural artefacts. He was a consummate manipulator of what he called 'the art of space', and so the structure is not restrictive; drama but also tranquillity are provided by glades, groves and *allées* as they open up vistas or focus on sculpture.

A tapestry hedge flaunts its bold blocks of colour in autumn, while in the woodland area to the east of the garden a waterfall, quiet pools and lushly planted channels of water have been incorporated into a small brook with a moated castle at one end. There is also a tree house and a gazebo.

The garden is now in the enthusiastic hands of a trust that, with the initial help of a Lottery grant, is keeping alive Sir Frederick's wish that it remain open to the public in perpetuity.
▶ *Open for snowdrops, then main season – telephone or consult website for details*

3 Audley End

This 'Capability' Brown landscape includes an 1830s parterre, now faithfully restored, a cascade and an organic kitchen garden.

Saffron Walden CB11 4JF | Tel: 01799 522842

www.english-heritage.org.uk

Historic Garden Grade I/English Heritage

LOCATION 1 mile W of Saffron Walden on B1383

A ten-year restoration project is reuniting the house – the relic of an extraordinary Jacobean mansion – with its early parterre garden. English Heritage has introduced irises, martagon lilies, roses, peonies, astrantias, violas and hypericums,

all staples of the period, along with spring and summer bedding set out in some 170 beds. The generous herbaceous borders leading into the parterre have been planted with a wide variety of perennials.

The design was inspired by classic 17th-century French parterres but with sheltering shrubberies to relate to the contemporary (1830) interiors. It follows the plans developed by the 3rd Lord Braybrooke and his wife around 1830, with advice from landscape designer William Sawrey Gilpin.

The restoration has been completed without interfering with the surrounding 'Capability' Brown landscape, the park buildings – which include a circular temple, a bridge, Lady Portsmouth's Column by leading country architect Robert Adam – and a cascade constructed in the same year on the site of an ancient mill dam. There are fine planes, oaks and tulip trees, and a pond garden, laid out in 1868, containing many scented old roses and sub-tropical bedding, with a Pulhamite rock garden at one end.

The walled kitchen garden includes a 52m (170ft) long vine house, a full set of service buildings, a gardeners' bothy and an orchard house. It has been developed into a working organic kitchen garden laid out in the Victorian style, including fruit trees on the walls and a wide variety of period vegetables, which are also for sale in season.
▶ *House open. Garden open main season – telephone or consult website for details*

4 Spencers

A glorious walled garden contains the county's oldest greenhouse, while nearby wilder plantings predominate.

Great Yeldham CO9 4JG

Tel: 01787 238175

www.spencersgarden.net

LOCATION 7 miles W of Sudbury on A1017. In Great Yeldham turn at Domesday Oak and keep left signed to Clare and Belchamp St Paul. Past first entrance to Spencers and after ¼ mile turn left at Spencers Lodge

With the aid of landscape designer Tom Stuart-Smith, the current owners have spent 20 years restoring and reinterpreting the garden that was originally laid out in the second half of the 18th century. The results are impressive. The walled garden is quite different from the cutting-edge design and plantings of today.

SPENCERS

The visitor is greeted by oblong beds divided by pebble paths, which in early summer are full of foxgloves, sweet peas, roses and armies of true-blue *Delphinium* 'Lord Butler' (named after politician Rab Butler by the Royal Horticultural Society), set against a backdrop of climbers including honeysuckles and more roses.

Ahead is an elegant timber-framed greenhouse built in the 1760s and said to be the oldest in Essex, which is filled from spring through summer with the flowers and heavy scents of jasmine, stephanotis, orchids, bougainvillea and datura. At the back the lines of the swimming pool are softened by a number of excellent plants in pots, including two fine *Pittosporum tobira*, and by a huge wisteria that covers an entire wall and rambles in and out of yew trees rising above.

Outside the walled garden the grass paths are wider and show off the borders to perfection. Beds surrounded by circular paths around a central sundial display *Rosa* 'Graham Thomas', while others are filled with a wide range of plants providing an exuberant display of colour throughout spring and summer.

There are also wilder areas. A spring garden is a brilliant green floor of clover with a grass path wandering through, surrounded on three sides by espaliered pear trees. An adjoining meadow is smothered in oxeye daisies in June. A tranquil woodland walk passes among a mass of wild flowers, carpets of bright blue comfrey, fragrant shrub roses and blossom in spring and early summer.

▶ *Open for NGS, and by appointment – telephone or consult website for details*

5 Marks Hall

One highlight is the stunning walled garden that shelters both exotic plants and the region's longest double border.

Coggeshall CO6 1TG | Tel: 01376 563796

www.markshall.org.uk

LOCATION 1½ miles N of Coggeshall on B1024. Signposted from Coggeshall by-pass

A walled garden is the jewel of the 200 acres of gardens and arboretum here. The sloping 2 acre space is enclosed on three sides by 18th-century brick walls and open to one of two lakes on the fourth. The resulting microclimate allows unusual and exotic plants, such as giant echiums and oleanders, to feature in the 160m (525ft) double border, the longest in East Anglia.

The five distinct areas below are linked by the threads of a pittosporum hedge, balls of stone and box, curling paths and slate-topped walls. In some places the planting is dense and feathery, in others simple and structured. Similarly, the colour themes range from quiet and gentle to dazzling.

The remaining acres include tree collections representing temperate areas of the world. One of the most recently planted is Gondwanaland, with a collection of Southern Hemisphere species that includes the largest planting in Europe of Wollemi pine, which grows happily alongside its near-relative, the monkey puzzle, with hundreds of white agapanthus nearby.

Water plays a large part in the garden – a tributary of the River Blackwater runs down in a series of gentle waterfalls, linking the two lakes. Trees and shrubs are massed along their banks to reflect their glowing autumn colours in the water, with vast numbers of Fothergilla major making an impact at the water's edge. Winter-flowering shrubs and early bulbs carry the interest on through to the high point of summer.

▶ *Open most of year – telephone or consult website for details*

6 The Beth Chatto Gardens

Well-designed water gardens and a gravel garden created from wasteland show how to plant to best advantage.

Elmstead Market, Colchester CO7 7DB

Tel: 01206 822007

www.bethchatto.co.uk

LOCATION 3 miles E of Colchester, ¼ mile E of Elmstead Market on A133

Beth Chatto, more than anyone else in the world of horticulture, has influenced gardeners through her choice of plants for any location and her ability to show them off to perfection. Her planting is a masterclass on how to use both leaf and flower to best advantage. She designed her own gardens, 7 acres of which are open to the public, in the 1960s from a neglected hollow that was either boggy or exceedingly dry. The large gravel garden, which she planted to replace the old car park, is a home for plants that can thrive in very dry conditions. Part of the original Mediterranean garden has been given over to scree beds – a setting for the smaller plants in the form of five irregular islands.

Five large ponds, each slightly lower than the other, lie at the heart of the garden, and on the perimeter a patch of woodland nurtures shade-loving plants. Adjoining the garden is the excellent Unusual Plants Nursery.

▶ *Open all year – telephone or consult website for details – and for parties by appointment*

7 Olivers

This tranquil garden makes bold use of bulbs and bedding, and overlooks woodland, lakes and a natural meadow.

Olivers Lane, Colchester CO2 0HJ

Tel: 01206 330575

LOCATION 3 miles SW of Colchester off B1022 Maldon road. Follow signs to Colchester Zoo. From zoo continue ¾ mile towards Colchester and at roundabout turn right. After ¼ mile turn right again into Olivers Lane. From Colchester pass Shrub End church and Leather Bottle pub then turn left at second roundabout

Surrounded by woodland originally planted in the 17th century with rides cut through, many ancient trees survive in this atmospheric garden. The Georgian-fronted house is sited on a hill with a fine view of the gardens and woodland. In spring, the borders on the generous Yorkstone terrace in front of the house blossom into a display of tapestry bedding, with tulips, white myosotis and wallflowers planted closely together. Wicker fighting-cock baskets used as frost protectors early in the year are an amusing feature.

Yew hedges divide the well-planted borders below the terrace into small sections, each with a different colour theme, and the *Ceanothus repens* is a wonderful sight in full bloom. A 'willow pattern' bridge crosses the first of a succession of pools dropping down to an ancient fishpond, with a *Taxodium distichum*, metasequoia, ginkgo and tree ferns flourishing by the waterside.

Beyond, an orchard and a collection of quinces and medlars merge into a natural meadow – cut only to encourage wild flowers and grasses – which spreads out to the trees bordering the river. There is also a delightful woodland walk, where mature native trees shelter rhododendrons, azaleas and shrub roses.

▶ *Open by appointment*

THE BETH CHATTO GARDENS

EAST ANGLIA

A taste for the exotic

Tender species from around the world thrive in many parts of Britain, enhancing gardens with sub-tropical displays.

Following the Ice Age, Britain was left with the smallest natural flora in the world – just a few hundred plants. To compensate for this, garden designers turned to an intrepid band of plant-hunters to increase diversity and add a touch of the exotic to their gardens. As a result, Britain now has some of the most diverse and species-rich gardens in the world.

The Victorian era was the golden age of plant-hunting, and the legacy of these botanical explorers has transformed the landscape in parts of Britain. Among these adventurers was George Forrest, who returned from China, Tibet and Burma with more than 600 species, including rhododendrons, magnolias, camellias and primulas. Botanist Joseph Hooker further increased the craze for rhododendrons following his expeditions to the Himalayas. And the Lobb brothers from Cornwall introduced species from North and South America, such as the monkey puzzle tree and wellingtonia.

Housing tender plants

Plants have been brought to Britain from every corner of the world, and names such as *tradescantia*, *forrestii*, *wilsonii* and *hookeriana* bear witness to their importers. Many adapted and flourished in the temperate climate, while others needed special care. Orangeries were built for citrus trees, botanic gardens nurtured tender plants and as glasshouses developed they provided environments for a wider range of exotics. Huge glasshouses such as the Palm House at Kew and, more recently, the biomes of the Eden Project in Cornwall can house whole plant colonies.

In the mid 19th century many tender plants were collected and the warm, sheltered valleys of the southwest provided ideal conditions for them. Heligan's jungle is the perfect environment for palms and tree ferns. The mild climate of Caerhayes Castle, also in Cornwall, nurtured plants from Ernest Wilson's Chinese expeditions.

Inevitably, this desire for the new and exotic has led to experimentation and the introduction of diverse planting schemes. In the 1890s, several influential books on Japan were published and later the Japan exhibition of 1910 fuelled a brief craze for Japanese gardens with their clipped shrubs, moss, rocks, lanterns, bridges, tea-houses and temples. Some were designed and installed by Japanese experts, with the plants, buildings and even rocks imported from Japan.

Without specialist maintenance most of these gardens fell into disrepair, however, one of the best surviving gardens, renovated in 2001, is at Tatton Park in Cheshire. Designed in the style of a tea garden, it contains an authentic Shinto shrine.

Victorian gardeners are responsible for many of the plants found in contemporary exotic gardens and also the penchant for mass bedding. During the 1850s, John Gibson – the first superintendent of Battersea Park in London and a former pupil of renowned architect and designer Joseph Paxton – introduced the use of mass bedding with tropical and sub-tropical leafy plants. He created sheltered beds and had his gardeners dig special holes lined with bricks to provide heat and drainage to keep plants growing

into autumn. The most tender had to be brought in under cover in winter. The costs and labour required to maintain this style of planting meant that it had all but vanished by the end of the First World War, although some less tender planting lived on in park bedding schemes. The Battersea garden was restored in 2004.

Countrywide experiments

It is no coincidence that many of these gardens are in the east of England, where well-drained soil and the low rainfall mean that many sub-tropical shrubs will survive outside with little or no protection. During the 1980s, gardening writer Will Giles began experimenting with planting exotic species in his Norwich garden. He grew plants that had been used by the Victorians – musa (bananas), cannas, ricinus, caladiums, dracaenas, hedychium (ginger), yuccas and tetrapanax. The result was the lush Exotic Garden, a paradise of hardy and tender species growing beautifully in a 1 acre microclimate.

On the north Norfolk coast, Alan Gray and Graham Robeson have developed the gardens of East Ruston Old Vicarage. They whisk you through a whole series of different small gardens. A Mediterranean garden brings together plants from Mexico, the Canaries, and South Africa while the Desert Wash with its rocks and stones replicates parts of Arizona where succulents and cacti flourish.

However, exotic gardens can be found anywhere with a sheltered microclimate and a wide range of plants are grown, not just sub-tropical species. These gardens may contain desert areas with cacti, aloes, agave or Mediterranean areas with cistus, rosemary, lavenders, grasses, agapanthus, aeoniums and echiums. Some exotic gardens create a jungle atmosphere with bamboos, tree ferns, bananas, astelia and large ferns. Exotic gardens have even been produced in urban settings, where, with the right plants, many small, dank, shady gardens have been transformed into an exotic paradise.

THE WALLED GARDEN IS
IMAGINATIVELY DIVIDED
BY YEW AND BEECH HEDGING
HOUGHTON HALL

NORFOLK

The county has an impressive selection of gardens, many of them walled and containing fragrant and colourful planting. Features to be found include secret gardens, willow sculptures and a grass labyrinth.

1 Stow Hall Gardens

Majestic trees overlook cloisters wreathed in climbers and a kitchen garden with a tunnel of arched apple and pear trees.

Stow Bardolph, King's Lynn PE34 3HU

Tel: 01366 383194/382162

LOCATION 2 miles N of Downham Market, E of A10

A lawned park surrounded by ancient trees forms the backdrop to a series of imaginative gardens in the 20 acres here, all linked by a central path. Three courtyard gardens have high, warm walls swathed in climbers, with many tender plants thriving in the shelter they provide.

Leading from the main path are small formal gardens – a sunken Dutch garden, cloisters with scented climbers, formal perennial borders that frame the summerhouse, crisp yew hedges and topiary. Beyond the croquet lawn, the walled kitchen garden includes a rose border stretching either side of the main gate, box-edged beds of fruit and vegetables, an arched tunnel with gnarled apple and pear trees, a mulberry and an orchard containing many local apple varieties.

Surrounding the greenhouse is a cottage garden with scented plants and herbs, and another area is planted with ferns and shade-loving species. Wild-flower areas and a formal avenue of clipped standards underplanted with native species and bulbs are planned for 2010.
▶ *Open main season – telephone or consult website for details – and for parties by appointment*

2 Narborough Hall

This romantic and quirky garden includes hedges clipped to resemble dragons, a white garden and a border of speckled plants.

Narborough PE32 1TE | Tel: 01760 338827

www.narboroughhallgardens.com

LOCATION 10 miles SE of King's Lynn, NW of Swaffham off A47

Water, colourful borders and an old kitchen garden combine to give an atmosphere of romance in this riverside garden. The owner stumbled on the house in 2002 and set about transforming its surroundings. The garden is fed by the River Nar and a 'blue' terrace runs down to a lake. On a misty morning a planting of nepeta, irises and rosemary seems to melt into the water.

Recent developments include a contemplative white garden and walks through the 80 acres of grounds. The borders, colour-themed in shades of chocolate and plum, pastel and white, are a triumph. Quirky areas include hedges clipped into dragons, willow sculptures and a freckled border where only speckled plants are included. A café offers homemade vegetarian food, including cakes made with flowers and other produce from the organically run kitchen garden.
▶ *Open main season – telephone or consult website for details – and by appointment*

3 Houghton Hall

The award-winning walled garden was recently redesigned as a series of innovative ornamental gardens in various styles.

King's Lynn PE31 6UE | Tel: 01485 528569

www.houghtonhall.com

Historic Garden Grade I

LOCATION 13 miles NE of King's Lynn off A148

In recent years the grounds around the magnificent house have been enhanced by the planting of impressive trees. In 2003 leading designers Isobel and Julian Bannerman were brought in to redesign the 5 acre walled garden, which has won several awards. It is imaginatively divided by yew and beech hedging into a potager, a rose garden, a croquet lawn, an Italian garden, a pool garden and the Laburnum Garden. This has a new 3 minute water wonder – a moving jet of water surmounted by a ball of flame. The centrepiece is a double herbaceous border, leading the eye to a 'temple' with rustic oak columns and deer antlers. At the opposite end stand some restored glasshouses and an unusual water feature.

In the park, grazed by a herd of white deer, are modern sculptures by James Turrell and Richard Long. Make time for lunch in the elegant restaurant, or tea looking over the park.
▶ *Hall open. Park and gardens open main season – telephone or consult website for details*

EAST ANGLIA

4 Sandringham

A dramatic lakeside rockery and grotto, elaborate parterres and woodland walks make this one of the finest royal gardens.

Sandringham, King's Lynn PE35 6EN

Tel: 01553 772675

www.sandringhamestate.co.uk

Historic Garden Grade II*

LOCATION 9 miles NE of King's Lynn on B1440 near Sandringham Church

The garden manages to combine grandeur with intimacy, thanks in part to the friendliness and enthusiasm of the attendants. The huge Victorian house stands among broad lawns with an outer belt of woodland. A path runs past the magnificent cast-iron and wrought-iron Norwich Gates of 1862 and plantings of camellias, hydrangeas, cornus, magnolias and rhododendrons, with some fine specimen trees. Set in open lawn are specimen oaks planted by Queen Victoria and other members of the royal family.

To the southwest of the house the eastern side of the upper lake is built up into a massive rock garden using blocks of local carrstone, now largely planted with dwarf conifers. Below the rock garden, opening onto the lake, a cavernous grotto was once used as a boathouse, and above is a small summerhouse built for Queen Alexandra. There are thick plantings of hostas, agapanthus and various moisture-loving plants around the margin of the lake. The path passes between the upper and lower lakes, which are set in wooded surroundings.

To the north of the house is a garden designed by landscape architect Sir Geoffrey Jellicoe for King George VI. It is a long series of box-hedged beds, divided by gravel and grass paths and flanked by avenues of pleached lime, one of which is centred on a gold-plated statue of a Buddhist divinity.

Set within the 600 acre park, the 60 acres of garden are immaculately maintained throughout.
▶ *House open. Garden and park open main season – telephone or consult website for details*

5 Norfolk Lavender

From July hundreds of acres of lavender, including more than 120 varieties, stretch into the distance in a blaze of purple.

Caley Mill, Heacham, King's Lynn PE13 7JE

Tel: 01485 570384

www.norfolk-lavender.co.uk

LOCATION 3 miles N of King's Lynn on B1454. Signed from A149 and A148

Fields of lavender resembling giant stripes of corduroy are a splendid sight from July to September on this northerly patch of the Norfolk countryside. Under new ownership, a National Collection of more than 120 varieties has been replanted here.

The surrounding gardens have been revitalised, too, with large raised beds near the Victorian watermill illustrating the use of this fragrant favourite in garden settings and in association with other plants. Although the lavender continues to dominate, these vibrant flowers are balanced by a host of other plants chosen for a long season of interest. This includes 50,000 bulbs, such as daffodils, tulips and erythroniums, 20,000 shrubs, herbaceous perennials and 40 different dahlias planted in a show area. A network of paths connects the planted borders and culminates in a bridged island.

Highland cattle cohabit a wetland habitat with quantities of birds and insects, while alpacas, Soay sheep, pygmy and golden Guernsey goats and rare breeds of pigs and poultry graze in the river meadow. One creature is unique to the garden – a 15m (50ft) long spider made of woven willow grown on site that allows children to run through its body and exit through its mouth.
▶ *Open all year – telephone or consult website for details*

6 Pensthorpe

The naturalistic garden uses grasses to great effect and a wildlife habitat demonstrates how to encourage butterflies.

Pensthorpe, Fakenham NR21 0LN

Tel: 01328 851465 | www.pensthorpe.com

LOCATION 1 mile E of Fakenham on A1067 Norwich-Fakenham road. Signposted

Although Pensthorpe's *raison d'être* is as a nature reserve for water birds and wildlife, it also includes three important gardens within its 250 acres of lakes and riverside walks. The millennium

garden, designed by Piet Oudolf in 1999, is a masterpiece of perennial planting (at its height from July to October). It is perhaps the best place in Britain to view his style of planting. Here he uses sedums, grasses, astrantias, eupatoriums and bronze fennel to form huge bold 'colonies' beside the water and winding gravel paths.

The smaller Wave Garden, designed by Julie Toll in 2005, combines wild and cultivated plants, and peaks earlier, in late spring and summer. Both gardens manage to merge gently into the natural landscape.

The third, a wildlife garden, designed and planted with the help of organisations such as Butterfly Conservation and the British Dragonfly Society, aims to help visitors attract wildlife into their own garden.

▶ *Open all year – telephone or consult website for details*

7 Hindringham Hall

Set around a Tudor house and moat, the garden was rescued from oblivion and is now a mix of traditional and modern styles.

Blacksmiths Lane, Hindringham NR21 0QA

Tel: 01328 878226

LOCATION 7 miles NE of Fakenham off A148 at Thursford. Passing village hall, turn left into Blacksmiths Lane before church

When the present owners arrived in 1993, the hall (not open) had almost lost its garden beneath a layer of grass and nettles. Now it has evolved into a delightful place, with a sloping walled vegetable garden and stream, and wild meadow areas.

Water features prominently – the stream is planted with primulas and yellow tree peonies, and the house is surrounded by a moat. It is an unexpected pleasure to see potatoes and asparagus growing near the water's edge.

In May and early June visitors can admire the view across to the west front of the house, where the moat is edged with bearded irises and the house approached along paths mown through cow parsley. But the garden looks good at many different times of year. Traditional roses mingle with pink-leafed actinidia on the old flint walls and the borders progress through the seasons to a hot crescendo in late summer. The Tudor flint house and medieval moat make an atmospheric backdrop to a garden that manages to integrate tradition with a number of modern twists.

▶ *Open for NGS, and for parties of 20-30 by appointment*

EAST ANGLIA

8 Kettle Hill

The garden has been cleverly developed to incorporate many romantic features, including a circular secret garden.

Blakeney NR25 7PN | Tel: 01263 741147

LOCATION 11 miles W of Cromer, just outside Blakeney on B1156 Langham road

With the help of designer Mark Rumary, the owners have transformed their 12 acre garden since 1991. A box-edged rectangular parterre has heart-shaped beds, heightened by topiary spirals and mop heads, influenced by the Romantic Garden Nursery at Swannington. A cleverly sited brick wall shelters a long mixed border packed with colour and unusual plants and leads to a secret garden.

A large lawn featuring a Gothic summerhouse extends from the house to mature woodland, where many ornamental trees have been added and bluebells and naturalised lilies carpet the ground in spring. Adjoining the house is a new rose garden, and the old one deep in the wood has been rejuvenated.

▶ *Open for parties by appointment*

9 Felbrigg Hall

This formal walled garden has a vine house, bee hives, octagonal dovecote and a National Collection of colchicums.

Felbrigg, Norwich NR11 8PR | Tel: 01263 837444

www.nationaltrust.org.uk

Historic Garden Grade II*/The National Trust

LOCATION 2 miles SW of Cromer off A148. Entrance on B1436

The Jacobean house faces south across the park, which is notable for its fine woods and lakeside walk. Designer Humphry Repton was probably employed here at the start of his career. It is, however, the 3½ acre walled garden, located at some distance to the east of the house and set on a south-facing slope, that is the real draw. It has been planted with a combination of fruit, vegetables, herbs and flowers in a formal design behind clipped hedges, and contains a vine house, beehives and a great octagonal brick dovecote with a flock of resident doves. In early autumn there is a display of more than 60 varieties of colchicums – a National Collection is kept here.

A ha-ha separates the park from the lawns of the house, where there is an orangery housing camellias. To the north on rising ground a collection of specimen trees and shrubs has been planted, including many of North American origin. This garden's 7½ acres are kept in good order, and restoration continues at a brisk pace.
▶ *Hall open. Garden and walled garden open main season. Park and woodland walks open all year – telephone or consult website for details*

10 Mannington Hall

An outstanding rose collection is divided into chronological sections, each reflecting the planting style of their date of origin.

Saxthorpe, Norwich NR11 7BB

Tel: 01263 584175

www.manningtongardens.co.uk

Historic Garden Grade II

LOCATION 5 miles SE of Holt off B1149

Lawns run down to a moat crossed by a drawbridge and herbaceous borders are backed by high walls of brick and flint in this charming garden. The moat also encloses a secret, scented garden in a design derived from one of the ceilings of the 15th-century house. Outside the moat are borders of flowering shrubs flanking a Doric temple, and woodlands beyond contain the ruins of a Saxon church and 19th-century follies.

Within the walls of the former kitchen garden, a series of rose gardens has been planted following the design of gardens from medieval

A BOX-EDGED PARTERRE HAS HEART-SHAPED BEDS AND TOPIARY SPIRALS

KETTLE HILL

to modern times and featuring roses that were popular in each period. A 20th-century rose garden incorporates a plant house, a vegetable plot and a children's garden. There are now more than 1,500 varieties of roses here.

A sensory garden has been created on the south lawn with a narrow channel of water and four large beds containing plants specially chosen to appeal to all the senses. A lake, woods and meadowland with extensive walks are other features in the garden.

▶ *Open main season – telephone or consult website for details*

11 Corpusty Mill Garden

Water predominates here and lush planting is combined with many formal structures, including follies, a Gothic arch and a grotto.

Corpusty, Norwich NR11 6QB

Tel: 01263 587223

www.corpustymillgarden.co.uk

LOCATION 6 miles S of Holt. Turn off B1149 at Corpusty; mill is in centre of village

This 5 acre garden gradually reveals itself as a complex series of interlinked spaces. The varied planting makes use of an enviable range of trees, shrubs, herbaceous and moisture-loving plants, and water is everywhere – in fountains, ponds, a stream, a small lake and a river.

Buildings and follies appear as the garden unfolds – a long, high flint wall inset with heads of Roman emperors, a Gothic arch with knapped flints, and a pitch-dark four-chambered grotto built of moss-covered ginger sandstone. Elsewhere, there is a Gothic ruin with a spiral staircase, a flint humpback bridge and a classical pavilion in the highly formal kitchen garden, with ornamental compost containers.

A separate area, rich in trees, has been developed as a landscaped meadow. Here a small lake with a raised bank and walkway on one side is dominated by a gunnera and a tall, slender stainless-steel cone, and a water-filled cave reveals a figure drowning or rising up from the mud. To the north, the River Bure forms a tranquil natural boundary.

By the house is a contemporary formal garden, with a stainless-steel water column and a central rill and pool. A further meadow with a stream, sculpture and a hidden viewing platform completes a well-judged sequence of different styles and moods.

▶ *Open for parties by appointment*

12 Blickling Hall

These glorious gardens in historic parkland include an orangery, woodland dell and fine parterre, providing year-round interest.

Aylsham, Norwich NR11 6NF

Tel: 01263 738030

www.nationaltrust.org.uk

Historic Garden Grade II*/The National Trust

LOCATION 15 miles N of Norwich, 1½ miles NW of Aylsham on N side of B1354

Although the gardens appear to be the perfect setting for the Jacobean house, they represent a panorama of garden history from the 17th to 20th centuries. The massive yew hedges flanking the entrance to the gardens date from the earliest period. To the east is the parterre with a central pool and four large corner beds planted by garden designer Norah Lindsay in the 1930s. These are surrounded by borders of roses edged with nepeta.

Flights of steps mount to the highest terrace, from which a vista cut through blocks of woodland leads to the 1730 Doric temple raised above parkland beyond. The two blocks are intersected by *allées* replanted in the 17th-century style with Turkey oak, lime and beech. To the south, the 1782 orangery houses half-hardy plants and a 1640s statue of Hercules by sculptor Nicholas Stone.

On the corner of the northern block is the Secret Garden, which was created in the 18th century and now consists of a lawn with a central sundial surrounded by high beech hedges. The shrub border through which the garden is approached was designed by Norah Lindsay, who was also responsible for the dry moat surrounding the house.

The gardens are filled with colour and interest right through from the spring flowering of more than 100,000 narcissi to the glorious display of autumn leaves. North of the parterre is a raised grassy area, possibly a remnant of the Jacobean mount, and an enormous, sprawling Oriental plane tree grows here.

Landscaped parkland to the northwest descends to the curving lake, formed before 1729 and later extended. The National Trust has now restored the park to its 1840 extent and replanted the Great Wood. West of the house stands a cedar of Lebanon and a collection of magnolias, and the park also features a 1773 Gothic tower and Bonomi's 1796 pyramidal mausoleum.

▶ *House open. Garden open all year – telephone or consult website for details*

EAST ANGLIA

13 Oulton Hall

A highlight here is the walled enclosure, where symmetrical block plantings and geometric ponds give a contemporary feel.

Oulton, Aylsham NR11 6NU

Email: clare@agnewdesign.com

LOCATION 4 miles NW of Aylsham off B1354. After 4 miles turn left for Oulton Chapel

THE EXOTIC GARDEN

Visitors approach by crossing a wooden bridge lined with petasites over the lakes and the lushly planted bog gardens that form the perimeter of the 7 acre garden. The inner core around the house takes on a more formal character and is separated into several distinct compartments that have been well thought out.

A walled enclosure at the heart of the garden is no longer given over to produce (although the old, gnarled fruit trees remain and new ones are being coaxed into espaliers) but has instead been redesigned with a distinctive new layout by the owner, a former Chelsea Flower Show medal-winner. It includes pleached hornbeams, bold, symmetrical blocks of grasses and white irises, shallow geometric pools and the repeated use of signature plants such as ferns, angelica and box.

While some parts are still being developed, others – such as the stone-supported pergola in the centre of the walled garden with its sumptuous white planting – appear to have been there for centuries. This is a place that challenges visitors to rethink the traditional country-house garden, and is a good example of what can happen when a designer has the courage to overlay a historical ground plan with new ideas.
▶ *Open for NGS, and by written appointment for large parties*

14 East Ruston Old Vicarage

A Mediterranean garden, box parterre and herbaceous borders display rare and unusual plants in this coastal garden.

East Ruston, Norwich NR12 9HN

Tel: 01692 650432 (daytime)

www.e-ruston-oldvicaragegardens.co.uk

LOCATION 15 miles NE of Norwich, 4 miles E of North Walsham. Turn off A149 onto B1159 signed to Walcot and Bacton, then left at T-junction. House is next to church after 2 miles

The twin strengths of this renowned garden are the architectural framework of walls and hedges and the profusion of plants. Two Norfolk churches and a lighthouse play a fundamental role as focal points at the end of skilfully crafted vistas. Tall dark hedges with openings beckon the visitor on towards a box parterre and sunken garden, herbaceous borders, a Mediterranean garden and – one of the most striking elements – a sizeable exotic garden. Rare plants are everywhere, set in gravel or in borders. Because of the garden's coastal setting, many are semi-hardy and shrubs from the Southern Hemisphere are well represented.

The 3 acre woodland garden, with its winding paths, feels connected to the garden as a whole. It has been enlarged, so there is scope for extensive plantings of *Hydrangea macrophylla*, flowering in autumn and complementing the trees and shrubs chosen for their autumn foliage.

In summer, the cornfield on the perimeter is a magnet for wildlife. An area of the garden called the Desert Wash has matured and its shapely exotics, sandbanks and boulders blend well, held together by rhythmical plantings of orange eschscholzias or Californian poppies.

The garden continues to provide interest throughout its 32 acres. The owners plan to transform the sunken garden into a rose garden, complemented by architectural plants and backed by a high trellis, and the trial work they conduct on garden and border pinks for the Royal Horticultural Society will be extended in 2010 to more than 100 varieties of border phlox.
▶ *Open main season – telephone or consult website for details – and by appointment for coach parties*

15 Hoveton Hall Gardens

Abutting Wroxham Broad, walkways wind down to an 18th-century lake, surrounded by azaleas and rhododendrons in spring.

Wroxham, Norwich NR12 8RJ

Tel: 01603 782558

www.hovetonhallgardens.co.uk

LOCATION 9 miles NE of Norwich, 1 mile N of Wroxham on A1151

It is impossible to separate this 15 acre garden from the wetlands of Wroxham Broad. Walkways winding between primulas and other bog plants lead to a long lake. In late spring and early summer this area is ablaze with mature azaleas and rhododendrons.

The garden splits neatly into three – a water garden, woodland planted with spring-flowering narcissi and featuring a kidney-shaped lake, and two formal walled gardens. One of these is the original 19th-century kitchen garden, where neatly labelled vegetables are still set out in the time-honoured way. In the other, enclosed in the 1930s, a spider's-web gate commissioned from wrought-iron artist Eric Stevenson in 1936 and a gardener's cottage covered with roses stand out. The borders encompass a wide range of traditional herbaceous and dry plantings. A new arboretum was planted in 2004.
▶ *Open main season – telephone or consult website for details*

16 The Exotic Garden

Tillandsias trail from the trees and other houseplants are found in the borders of this sheltered garden where exotics thrive.

6 Cotman Road, Thorpe, Norwich NR1 4AF

Tel: 01603 623167 | www.exoticgarden.com

LOCATION In E Norwich off A47 Thorpe road

Set on a south-facing hillside, tall trees and hedges create a sheltered microclimate for a rarified collection of exotic plants that includes gingers, bananas, aroids and succulents. The ½ acre garden reaches its peak in high to late summer, when cannas and brugmansias are in full bloom. It is renowned for its use of house plants as bedding plants – tillandsias may be spotted in the branches of trees that are underplanted with codiaeums, guzmanias and tradescantias. Philodendrons and *Monstera deliciosa* are also used in this way, flourishing during the summer months. A separate space is devoted to hardy exotics that need less maintenance and tolerate winter cold.
▶ *Open limited season – telephone or consult website for details – and for parties of ten or more by appointment*

17 The Bishop's Garden

A garden has existed on this site since 1100 and its hidden delights today include tree ferns and an intriguing grass labyrinth.

Bishop's House, St Martin's Palace Plain, Norwich NR3 1SB | Tel: 01603 629001

www.norwich.anglican.org/gardens

LOCATION In city centre opposite Law Courts

Tucked away behind Norwich Cathedral lies the private residence of Bishop Graham and his family. Open lawns protect archaeologically important areas of the historical site. Beyond, the visitor will find double herbaceous borders, a rose parterre, old fruit trees and an organic kitchen garden providing fruit and flowers for the ecclesiastical community.

There are collections of bamboos and Southern-Hemisphere plants, many rare, and the north border has been planted with an unusual concoction of old shrub roses, tree ferns and hostas. A new addition is a wild grass labyrinth with an ancient pear tree, 'Uvedale St Germain', at its heart.
▶ *Open for NGS and other charities – consult website for details*

EAST ANGLIA

18 Fairhaven Woodland and Water Garden

At the heart of the Norfolk Broads, ancient woodland is carpeted in spring with a mass of bluebells and candelabra primulas.

School Road, South Walsham, Norwich
NR13 6DZ | Tel: 01603 270449

www.fairhavengarden.co.uk

LOCATION 9 miles NE of Norwich. Signposted from A47 at junction with B1140

Three miles of wide, level pathways wind past ancient oaks and rhododendron groves, across bridges and manmade waterways to a small private inland broad with a thatched boathouse. The 130 acres here are the perfect place to escape to, particularly in spring when the foliage of oaks, willows and alders creates a light green canopy above honey-scented *Rhododendron luteum*, skunk cabbages and carpets of bluebells.

In a county well known for its dry climate, it is a treat to find a substantial collection of candelabra primulas growing in the organic, leafmould-rich soil built up from 1946 by the garden's creator, the second Lord Fairhaven. Regular signposting encourages children to stop and listen for woodpeckers and watch for tree creepers, and there are regular 20 and 50 minute boat trips along the garden's private broad.

▶ *Open all year – telephone or consult website for details. Guided walks for parties*

19 Bressingham Gardens

More than 4,500 varieties of perennials are on display alongside innovative new planting schemes in this inspiring garden.

Bressingham, Diss IP22 2AB

Tel: 01379 686900

www.bressinghamgardens.com plus visitor enquiries www.bressingham.co.uk

LOCATION 2½ miles W of Diss on A1066

Over the past few years, the two 6 acre gardens have undergone considerable change with imaginative planting and the creation of new areas.

The Dell Garden, with its signature island beds filled with more than 4,500 varieties of perennials and grasses, still retains its original 1960s design. Foggy Bottom, once the home of conifers and heathers, is now gradually being transformed as mature trees and conifers are thinned to make way for mixed plantings of shrubs, perennials and grasses. New vistas and woodland pathways create a sense of space, and strong architectural specimens are softened and brightened by flowers and foliage.

An old meadow has become the new winter and summer gardens, and *Geranium* 'Rozanne' and other species with a long season of interest are used to form rivers of colour between contrasting plants. The Fragrant Garden, characterised by open vistas and dense planting, adjoins the Dell, Adrian's Wood and Foggy Bottom, skirting by a National Collection of miscanthus next to a newly revealed pond.

Adrian's Wood, originally planted with trees in 1964 and devoted now to plants of North American origin, is filled in late summer with a mass of *Hydrangea arborescens* 'Annabelle', *Rudbeckia sullivantii* var. *deamii* and *Eupatorium maculatum* 'Gateway'.

▶ *Open most of year – telephone or consult website for details. Winter Garden open all year*

20 Besthorpe Hall

Tudor enclosures are a feature of this delightful formal garden where climbers and bearded irises proliferate.

Besthorpe, Attleborough NR17 2LJ

Tel: 01953 450300

LOCATION 14 miles SW of Norwich, 1 mile E of Attleborough on Bunwell Road. Entrance on right, past church

Since 1960, these expansive formal gardens with their raised, box-edged pools and fountains have been redesigned to enable the 5 acres to be run by a smaller number of gardeners – hence wall-to-wall cut flowers and vegetables in the kitchen garden have now been replaced with equally colourful but less demanding herbaceous borders and a nuttery.

The enclosures and much of the brickwork are Tudor in date and include a former tilt yard, now laid out with rows of yew topiary. What appears to be a ha-ha was in fact the ditch that was constructed to keep ordinary spectators away from the jousters.

Climbers are a special passion, and from late spring the walls are clothed with wisterias and many types of rose and clematis. A new collection of magnolias has joined the mature ones planted 30 years ago, and in May and June a collection of bearded irises saved from the garden of the artist Cedric Morris at Benton End is in full flower. Most groups visit Besthorpe in spring and

summer, however, the season is prolonged by buddlejas, a collection of colchicums from Felbrigg Hall and trees planted for their interesting winter bark.

▶ *Open by appointment only*

21 Bradenham Hall

Walled areas add character to the garden, which is renowned for its arboretum of 800 trees and a collection of narcissi.

Bradenham, Thetford IP25 7QP

Tel: 01362 687243/687279

www.bradenhamhall.co.uk

LOCATION 8 miles E of Swaffham, 5 miles W of East Dereham S off A47

Although lacking the history of some longer established Norfolk gardens, the 23 acres here comprise intimate spaces, well tended and clearly labelled plants, and many fun, experimental displays of plants.

The imposing 18th-century house, which is surrounded by extensive and finely kept lawns, was the birthplace of the boys'-own adventure novelist H. Rider Haggard, and his dog, Spice, was buried here.

The gardens are probably best known for the arboretum – a collection of some 800 varieties of trees and shrubs started by the current owner's late father – and for its extensive narcissus collection. It is, however, the walled gardens and barns that give the garden its charm. Around them a series of clearly defined outer rooms has been divided by yew hedges, providing shelter from the wind.

In spring, the pleached lime walk looks particularly fine. Later bearded irises flower against the courtyard walls and the kitchen garden with its quirky, eclectic borders flushes with colour. The small rose garden, with not an inch of bare space, has masses of old-fashioned varieties packed in.

▶ *Open for limited season, and for NGS – telephone or consult website for details. Coach parties are welcome on open days or at other times by written appointment*

SUFFOLK

The undulating rural landscape that inspired the painter John Constable has produced a range of gardens notable for their water features, herbaceous plants, wild-flower areas and woodland.

1 Bucklesham Hall

Water flows from a lake down a 16-step staircase to a stream in this terraced garden, designed as a series of interlocking areas.

Bucklesham, Ipswich IP10 0AY

Tel: 01473 659263

LOCATION 6 miles SE of Ipswich, ½ mile E of Bucklesham. Entrance opposite primary school

Made up of interlocking spaces, terraces and lakes, this inspiring 7½ acre garden has experienced two periods of creativity. It was started from scratch by the previous owners in 1973 and since 1994 it has been extended and improved by the present incumbents.

Surrounding the house are secret gardens packed with flowers. Beds of old-fashioned roses overflow their borders and a courtyard garden has been created using every kind of container. Spring and summer are spectacular, with displays of daffodils and tulips, rhododendrons, camellias and rare Japanese maples followed by an abundance of roses. A Monet-style bridge was built in 1999 with a waterfall between two lakes, and a 16-step water staircase has been constructed to allow the water to flow from an island lake into streams. These earth and water terraces descend to the woodland and beyond. New vistas appear around every corner.

▶ *Open for parties by appointment*

2 Blakenham Woodland Garden

Traditional English woodland blends with more exotic planting, with an intriguing grass landform at its core.

Little Blakenham, Ipswich IP8 4LZ

Tel: 07760 342131

LOCATION 4 miles NW of Ipswich, 1 mile off B1113

The 5 acre garden on a hill above the village was planted by Lord Blakenham between 1950 and 1982 as a rural retreat. This Conservative cabinet minister's passion for planting and the atmosphere he created have been intensified by the present generation of owners.

BUCKLESHAM HALL

Although the woodland is clearly managed, birds sing in the trees above a carpet of native primroses or bluebells in season. Other planting in the garden is more exotic. Rhododendrons, azaleas and magnolias now flower alongside bamboos and phormiums, interspersed with sculptures, belvederes and rustic huts.

At the heart of the wood is a surprise that never fails to enchant visiting children: a tilting, grass landform spirals down into a central chalk 'plughole', ringed by tall sycamores. There is also a dell reserved for the Blakenham badgers. The garden is at its best on a spring or early summer day.

▶ *Open limited season – telephone for details. Parties welcome by appointment*

3 The Priory

Lawns sweep down to lakes carpeted with water lilies and surrounded by a dazzling display of azaleas and rhododendrons.

Stoke by Nayland CO6 4RL

Tel: 01206 262216

LOCATION **8 miles SE of Sudbury on B1068**

Set on several levels with sweeping views over Constable country, this rewarding 10 acre garden has been in the care of one family for several generations. Linked manmade and spring-fed lakes nurture waterside and aquatic plants, including masses of water lilies. In spring, the water reflects the colour of early rhododendrons and azaleas. The focal point of one lake is a bright red oriental-style bridge leading to a pavilion, with views back towards the house. A terrace runs the full length of the house from a corner loggia and shelters blue and white agapanthus, *Amaryllis belladonna*, colchicums and nerines.

The walled garden, created in 1829 with a wood-framed conservatory for tender and scented plants along one wall, holds a colourful cottage-garden display of poppies, towering hollyhocks and other summer perennials. This follows on from the massed plantings of spring bulbs and forget-me-nots in neat, box-edged compartments in the former formal garden.

Running along the outside of the south-facing wall is a deep double border in which hyacinths and tulips flower in spring, followed by perennial geraniums, lilies and delphiniums, bulked out with tall plume poppies, stately perennials and with roses trained over an arching pergola. The kitchen garden has raised beds, a rose cutting garden and a stylish pigsty.

In 2008 another acre was added to the garden and planted up with small trees and shrubs. Around them spreads a flowery mead with mown paths winding through it.

▶ *Open for NGS and by appointment*

4 Smallwood Farmhouse

Imaginative combinations of plants, including 50 old-fashioned roses, can be enjoyed from specially postioned seats.

Smallwood Farmhouse, near Bradfield St George, Bury St Edmunds IP30 0AJ

Tel: 01449 736358

LOCATION **7 miles SE of Bury St Edmunds between A134 and A14. From the A134 at Sicklesmere turn to Bradfield St George, follow road towards Felsham. After Bradfield Woods sign take left turning towards Hessett, farmhouse is on left after Valley Farm sign**

The 2 acre garden surrounds the farmhouse like a tapestry, with jewel-like patterns of flowers and foliage. Close to the house are borders and terraces filled with more than 50 old-fashioned roses, clematis, herbs, shrubs and perennials, including alchemilla and phlox. Wooden posts and high rails hold climbers, such as the purple vine *Vitis vinifera*, away from the house walls, yet offer the impression that they are clothing the façades.

Water is an important element, with bridged stream channels bringing field water into a large pond at the front of the house. Paths lead into the far reaches of the garden, winding in summer through a waist-high meadow of grasses and oxeye daisies. At the end is a wrought-iron arbour encircled by *Rosa rugosa* 'Hansa'. There are plenty of places to sit and enjoy the fragrant climbing roses scaling trees and supports.

Vegetables flourish in raised beds, with horseradish a stately speciality. High-level wooden planters hold salads and herbs that enjoy the heat and enclosure of the gravelled Barn Garden.

All of the woodwork – on benches, bridges, seats, climbing plants supports and even the bird feeder – is painted an attractive grey-blue, providing a linking theme throughout the garden and a gentle but restraining element on the naturally exuberant plantings.

▶ *Open by appointment*

EAST ANGLIA

5 Euston Hall

Visitors can enjoy the landscape park – one of William Kent's greatest works – formal gardens, and a river walk to a watermill.

Thetford IP24 2QP | Tel: 01842 766366

www.eustonhall.co.uk

Historic Park Grade II*

LOCATION 11 miles NE of Bury St Edmunds, 3 miles S of Thetford on A1088

This is a fine example of an English landscape park. The 74 acre pleasure grounds laid out in the 17th century by diarist and garden designer John Evelyn have grown into a forest of yew, but straight rides trace out the original formal layout. Also from this period are the stone gate piers that, together with the remnants of a great avenue, mark the original approach to the house.

Fronted by terraces, the red-brick hall stands among extensive lawns and parkland along a winding river. The domed temple isolated on a hill to the east and the garden house in the formal garden by the hall were created by William Kent in the 1740s. The small lake was the work of 'Capability' Brown.

Today, the planting is restrained, with many fine specimen trees and a wealth of shrub roses, leaving the original designers' genius intact.
▶ *House open. Garden open for limited season – telephone or consult website for details*

6 Wyken Hall

A set of imaginative garden rooms designed to complement the Elizabethan house include a nuttery and copper beech maze.

Stanton, Bury St Edmunds IP31 2DW

Tel: 01359 250287

www.wykenvineyards.co.uk

LOCATION 9 miles NE of Bury St Edmunds on A143. Leave A143 between Ixworth and Stanton. Signed to Wyken Vineyards

The 4 acre garden surrounding this manor house is packed with inventive planting and is remarkable for its colours and scents, particularly in spring and early summer.

The beautifully maintained garden is divided into a series of rooms, starting with the wild garden and winter garden, which leads into the south and woodland garden, and then into the dell. Mown paths meander between shrubs and into a newly planted copper beech maze next to the nuttery and gazebo. Finally, they arrive

at a rose garden, enclosed on three sides by a hornbeam hedge and on the fourth side by a rose-laden pergola. Beyond the wall are knot and herb gardens, separated by yew hedges and designed by Chelsea Flower Show award-winner Arabella Lennox-Boyd.

An 'edible garden' and a English kitchen garden have been planted to the north of the house, and there is a pond just beyond the garden. Fields and orchards are inhabited by wandering hens, peacocks, guinea fowl and llamas, while the garden outbuildings are painted in American pioneering colours.
▶ *Open main season – telephone or consult website for details*

7 Haughley Park

A variety of distinctive gardens are reached via undulating parkland and mature woods, brought alive by acres of bluebells in spring.

Stowmarket IP14 3JY | Tel: 01359 240701

www.haughleyparkbarn.co.uk

LOCATION 4 miles NW of Stowmarket, signed to Haughley Park (not to Haughley) on A14

The 18th-century-style landscaped park and 19th-century planting of evergreens, rhododendrons and azaleas make an unusual combination in this huge garden. Unexpected secret gardens with clipped hedges or flint-and-brick walls hide pristine flowerbeds, climbers and flowering shrubs, each one with its own distinct character.

Herbaceous borders surround the main lawn, with a splendid lime avenue at the end drawing the eye across open countryside. Rhododendrons, azaleas and camellias grow on soil that is, unexpectedly for Suffolk, lime-free. The trees include a 12m (40ft) wide magnolia and an oak reputed to be 1,000 years old. Beyond are the walled kitchen garden, greenhouses and shrubbery.

In spring, the broad rides and walks through the ancient woodland reveal not only the newly planted trees, specimen rhododendrons and other ornamental shrubs but also 10 acres of bluebells, 2 acres of lilies-of-the-valley and half a mile of mauve ponticum rhododendrons.

In 2007 a number of large glass sculptures by Danny Lane were introduced into the gardens surrounding the barn, giving the place a contemporary edge.
▶ *House open by appointment. Garden open for bluebells and a limited season – telephone or consult website for details*

8 Columbine Hall

Formal grounds surrounding the medieval manor include a Mediterranean area with tropical planting and a bog garden.

Stowupland, Stowmarket IP14 4AT

Tel: 01449 612219

www.columbinehall.co.uk

LOCATION 1¼ miles NE of Stowmarket. Turn N off A1120 opposite Shell garage across village green, then right at T-junction into Gipping Road. Garden drive is on left

This charming 4 acre garden features well-structured plantings of great subtlety, with interest assured from April through to July. The lime-washed manor house, a fine example of medieval craftsmanship, stands in its rhomboidal moat like a ship in dock. The entrance courtyard is French in style. Clipped standards and box mounds, cardoons, a fig and a vine spring out of the gravel or hug the house. The architectural embellishments are also eye-catching.

The garden, much of it the work of eminent designer George Carter, has been developed since 1993. What is clever about the design is that it has a series of uncluttered spaces defined by hornbeam hedges. These are not outdoor rooms, for they allow movement through wide openings, glimpses into other parts of the garden and views out to the countryside. Flowers cluster at the base of pleached limes or in strips running parallel to grass paths.

Towards the perimeter, neat rides are mown through meadows beneath native trees. There is one surprise – a hidden, sinuous, carefully planted bog garden.

Leading on from the moist and shady conditions of the bog garden, a new garden is currently being developed where Mediterranean and sun-loving tropical plants bask in a sheltered spot on a west-facing terraced bank of the moat.

▶ *Open for NGS, and by appointment*

9 Bedfield Hall

The artistic, colourfully planted garden has at its heart a formal herb, vegetable and picking garden, hidden by yew hedges.

Bedfield, Woodbridge IP13 7JJ

Tel: 01728 628380

LOCATION 15 miles N of Ipswich off A140. Turn right onto A1120, and in Earl Soham turn left after church, signed to Bedfield. Take right turn into Church Road; house is just past church

The artistic bent of the owners is immediately obvious in this 2 acre garden, which surrounds the Gothic-style house that evolved between the 15th and 19th centuries.

One acre – the Platform – is girdled by a 13th-century moat, with a secondary moated area of nut trees and wild woodland; there is also an island. Central to the plan is a formal herb, vegetable and picking garden behind high yew hedges and arched wooden gates. It is ringed by calmer areas of varied greenery – yew and box topiary, grey-olive wooden arches and five bridges, also painted grey-olive and inspired by the Gothic finials on the house. The path through the garden leads over these bridges and across high walkways from one area to another, with elevated views over plantings of irises, roses, lavender, clematis, honeysuckles, grasses and much more.

Without ever retracing your steps, you then pass through a new orchard with a henhouse and along a topiaried yew walk beside the water lengthened by false perspectives, with vistas deliberately drawing in the surrounding arable fields.

The garden exhibits a strong structure and instinctive, well-informed planting. Church, tower and house make an interesting architectural group with the garden.

▶ *Open main season by appointment for parties of eight or more*

EAST ANGLIA

CLIPPED STANDARDS AND BOX MOUNDS, CARDOONS, A FIG AND A VINE SPRING OUT OF THE GRAVEL

COLUMBINE HALL

10 Helmingham Hall Gardens

Elegant gardens in an ancient deer park include a classic parterre, Elizabethan kitchen garden and intriguing knot garden.

Helmingham, Stowmarket IP14 6EF
Tel: 01473 890799 (Sarah Harris)
www.helmingham.com
Historic Garden Grade I
LOCATION 9 miles N of Ipswich on B1077

Nineteen generations of Tollemaches have lived at Helmingham, and although there have been many changes over the past five centuries there is still an Elizabethan atmosphere.

The double-moated Tudor mansion house, built of warm red brick, stands in a 400 acre deer park. A 19th-century parterre, edged with a spring border, leads to the Elizabethan kitchen garden, which is surrounded by a Saxon moat with banks covered in daffodils. Within the walls the kitchen garden has been transformed into a subtly planted potager. The herbaceous borders and old-fashioned roses surround beds of vegetables separated by arched tunnels of sweet peas and dangling gourds. Large beds along the walls have been split up by iron dividers and planted with geometrically arranged herb and box beds. Outside is a lushly planted south-facing spring border that includes many irises and peonies.

There are also wild-flower areas, fruit trees, a shady yew walk, knot and herb gardens. Lady Tollemache is a gifted plantswoman and designer, and her own garden owes much to her skills.

▶ *Open main season – telephone or consult website for details – and for parties by appointment*

11 Somerleyton Hall and Gardens

One of Britain's finest yew mazes can be found here alongside glasshouses, an aviary, a loggia and a wisteria-covered pergola.

Somerleyton, Lowestoft NR32 5QQ
Tel: 0871 222 4244
www.somerleyton.co.uk
Historic Garden Grade II*
LOCATION 5 miles NW of Lowestoft, 8 miles SW of Great Yarmouth on B1074. Signposted

Sir Morton Peto extensively rebuilt the Jacobean house in the mid 19th century as an Italianate palace, and the gardens reflect this. There are

12 acres of formal gardens, a walled garden, an aviary, a loggia and a winter garden surrounding a sunken garden displaying statues from the original 19th-century winter garden.

Of special note are the 1846 yew hedge maze by watercolour painter and landscape gardener William Nesfield, the 80m (260ft) long iron pergola covered in wisteria, vines and roses, and the peach cases and ridge-and-furrow greenhouses designed by architect and gardener Sir Joseph Paxton, which now contain peaches, grapes and a rich variety of tender plants. The Victorian kitchen garden has been redeveloped, and there is also a museum of bygone gardening equipment in the grounds.

▶ *Open main season – telephone or consult website for details*

12 Woottens of Wenhaston

Irises and hermerocallis are among the nursery's specialities, and the growing fields are opened so visitors can enjoy the blooms.

Blackheath, Wenhaston, Halesworth IP19 9HD

Tel: 01502 478258

www.woottensplants.co.uk

LOCATION 14 miles SW of Lowestoft, ½ mile S of Blythburgh off A12. Turn left in Wenhaston by marked sign

The 2 acre iris field and 1 acre hemerocallis field have special openings for their brief but fabulous flowering seasons. However, while excavating a car park for the iris field the owner found himself with enough extra topsoil to remove the lawn from his private garden and create a series of raised beds. These are now planted with attractive combinations of herbaceous plants, ranging in colour and content from shaded greens and whites to exuberant mixes of poppies, alliums, columbines and, of course, the ubiquitous irises.

Since most of the plants are clearly labelled and many are for sale in the nursery adjoining, inspired visitors can take the ideas home and easily re-create the effects in their own gardens.

▶ *Garden open main season. Iris field open end May to early June. Hemerocallis field open mid July – telephone or consult website for details*

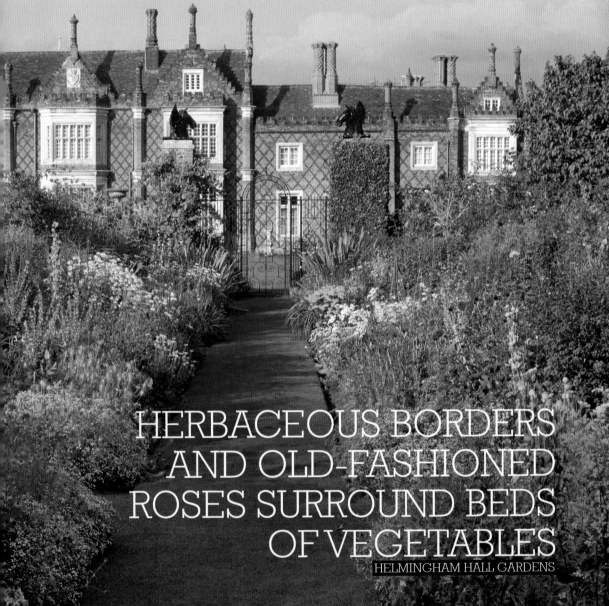

HERBACEOUS BORDERS AND OLD-FASHIONED ROSES SURROUND BEDS OF VEGETABLES
HELMINGHAM HALL GARDENS

Central England

The dramatic scenery of the Peak District, the flat Lincoln Wolds and golden Cotswold Hills reflect the diversity of England's heartland. The rewards of industry produced many great houses and paid for ornate gardens that reflected the wealth and status of their owners.

KEY

1 Garden location
— County boundary
Motorway
Principal A road

The Wolds

A16

A1028

11

10 9 Skegness

A52

Boston

A16 A17

Spalding

sby

DERBYSHIRE

Dominated by the magnificent Peak District, the county is a mix of unspoilt countryside and industrial scenery. Water features, mature trees and quirky topiary define the planting in its great gardens.

1 Calke Abbey

An auricula theatre is one of the highlights, as well as vibrant walled compartments, a productive kitchen garden and an orangery.

Ticknall DE73 7LE | Tel: 01332 863822

www.nationaltrust.org.uk

Historic Garden Grade II*/The National Trust

LOCATION 10 miles S of Derby, off A514 at Ticknall

Previously owned by the Harpur-Crewe family, who built the estate village, Calke has a long history punctuated by neglect. However, the National Trust has slowly and sensitively brought the 20 acre garden back from the brink of decay. The vinery in the physic garden has been restored, as have the tomato house, frames, pits, backsheds and the early 19th-century auricula theatre – an alcove with tiered shelving displaying auriculas – possibly the last surviving one in Britain. In summer, pelargoniums replace the auriculas on the shelves.

Flowers, fruit and old varieties of vegetables are grown in the two walled compartments formerly kept for flowers and herbs. The third compartment is the kitchen garden, which is overlooked by an orangery and a recently restored peach house, and it houses a head gardener's office of 1777. An orchard of old local apple varieties is of particular interest.
▶ *House and garden open main season – telephone or consult website for details. Park open all year*

2 Melbourne Hall Gardens

The gardens are a wonderful representation of the French style, featuring a birdcage arbour, yew tunnel and lead statuary.

Melbourne DE73 8EN | Tel: 01332 862502

www.melbournehall.com

Historic Garden Grade I

LOCATION 8 miles S of Derby between A514 and A453, off B587 in Melbourne

The gardens were laid out in the late 17th and early 18th centuries by design team London and Wise in the style of leading French garden and landscape designer Le Nôtre. Few alterations have been made to the original design. They are in immaculate condition and feature some unusual magnolias that flower in early April. Avenues culminate in statuary and fountains, including a lead urn of The Four Seasons by van Nost, whose other lead statuary stands in niches of yew.

A series of terraces runs down to a lake, the Great Basin, and a grotto is engraved with an inscription by 19th-century politician and writer George Lamb. The Birdcage, an exquisite iron arbour dating from 1706, can be seen from the house at the end of a long yew-hedged walk.
▶ *Open main season – telephone or consult website for details*

3 Elvaston Castle Country Park

Enclosed within 11 miles of evergreen hedges are Italian and Old English gardens, fine topiary and an ornamental lake.

Borrowash Road, Elvaston DE72 3EP

Tel: 01332 571342

www.derbyshire.gov.uk

Historic Garden Grade II*

LOCATION 2 miles SE of Derby on B5010 between Borrowash (A6005) and Thulston (A6). Signed from A6 and A52

The 200 acre gardens were designed by William Barron in the early 19th century for the 4th Earl of Harrington and include Italian, parterre and Old English gardens, all contained within 11 miles of hedges. It is probable that these were the first garden rooms, which influenced others when, 20 years after their establishment, they were opened to the public.

The features include extensive topiary, tree-lined avenues and a large ornamental lake, golden gates, a boat house and a Moorish temple, as well as distinctive cedars of Lebanon. Barron transplanted mature trees as high as 13m (40ft) from as early as 1831, using his unique transplanting machines, one of which is housed at the Royal Botanic Gardens, Kew.
▶ *Open all year – telephone or consult website for details*

MELBOURNE HALL GARDENS

4 Derby Arboretum

The country's first urban arboretum has 40 species from around the globe, including an Indian bear tree and silver pendant lime.

Arboretum Square, Derby DE23 8FN

Tel: 01332 716518

Historic Garden Grade II*

LOCATION Between Reginald Street and Arboretum Square

The first specifically designed urban arboretum in Britain – and the country's first public park – this was commissioned in 1839 from John Claudius Loudon, whose original plans involved the planting of 1,000 trees. It has recently benefited from a multi-million pound restoration project.

Today, this charming park is home to 40 varieties, many from around the world, all individually numbered, and there is also a tree trail. Notable trees include the red oak, the Indian bear tree and the silver pendant lime.

▶ *Open all year – telephone or consult website for details*

5 Kedleston Hall

Landscaped grounds blend into parkland and in early summer are ablaze with colour from a spectacular display of rhododendrons.

Kedleston, Derby DE22 5JH | Tel: 01332 842191

www.nationaltrust.org.uk

Historic Garden Grade I/The National Trust

LOCATION 4½ miles NW of Derby on Derby-Hulland road between A6 and A52. Signposted

Mature parkland draws the eye to a neoclassical Robert Adam palace. Its fine rhododendrons are worth seeing in their own right, but other notable attractions include the hexagonal-domed summerhouse, the Venetian-windowed fishing house, the orangery, the bridge across the lake, the aviary and slaughterhouse (now a loggia) and the main gateway.

The formal part has a sunken rose garden, and the Sulphur Bath House, one of the earliest 18th-century landscape park features, has been restored.

▶ *Hall open. Garden open main season – telephone or consult website for details. Park open all year*

6 Dam Farm House

Lavish plantings surrounded by high hedges, an arboretum and scree garden make this one of the county's best gardens.

Yeldersley Lane, Ednaston, Ashbourne DE6 3BA

Tel: 01335 360291

LOCATION 8 miles NW of Derby, 5 miles SE of Ashbourne on A52. Opposite Ednaston village turn, gate is ⅓ mile on right

Created from a field in 1980, this garden owes its existence to the inspiration of the owner, whose knowledgeable eye for good plants of all kinds – trees, perennials, shrubs and roses – is evident throughout.

Climbers are used abundantly for clothing walls and pergolas, even spilling down over high retaining walls. It is the quality of the planting that gives the garden its special character. Garden rooms span outwards from the house, mostly enclosed by high beech and yew hedges, while an evergreen tapestry hedge divides the arboretum from the main garden. The scree has a selection of choice alpines, and the stone troughs in the farmyard are also filled with plants.

One of the finest gardens in Derbyshire, this is still maturing after decades of intermittent planting. Many rare trees, shrubs and plants are propagated for sale.

▶ *Open limited season – telephone for details – and by appointment. Groups and coach parties welcome*

7 Chatsworth

This excellent example of a landscape garden boasts dramatic water features including a cascade and water-jet fountain.

Bakewell DE45 1PP | Tel: 01246 582204

www.chatsworth.org

Historic Garden Grade I

LOCATION 4 miles E of Bakewell, 10 miles W of Chesterfield on B6012, off A619 and A6

The 105 acres that make up one of Britain's greatest gardens have developed over four centuries and still reflect the fashions of succeeding generations of powerful landowners. The only remains of the 17th-century gardens of French-influenced design team London and Wise are the cascade, canal pond and copper 'willow tree' with water pouring from its branches.

During the 18th century 'Capability' Brown destroyed much of the formal gardens to create a landscaped woodland park. The vista he created from the Salisbury Lawn to the horizon remains unchanged, as does the lawn itself since no liming or fertilisers are used, allowing many varieties of wild flowers, grasses, moss and sedges to thrive.

Joseph Paxton's work still gives pleasure, including some rare conifers and the 84m (275ft) water jet from the Emperor Fountain. Although his Great Conservatory was a casualty of the First World War – 1m (3ft) wide stone walls in the old conservatory garden are all that remain to give an idea of its size – damaged areas of Paxton's giant rockeries were rebuilt in 2003.

From the 20th century come the orange and blue-and-white borders, the terrace, the display greenhouse, the rose garden, the old conservatory garden with its lupin, dahlia and Michaelmas daisy beds, and a yew maze planted in 1963. In the arboretum and pinetum the rhododendrons, laurels and sycamores have been removed and many new trees planted. The double rows of pleached red-twigged limes and serpentine beech hedge, both planted in the 1950s, are now rewarding features.

A classic cottage garden has two striking neighbours – a flight of yew stairs leading to a 'bedroom' where the four-poster is made of ivy and the dressing-table of privet, and a sensory garden. The 'indelibly British' kitchen garden has been re-sited and redesigned.

The first major piece of garden statuary to be placed in the garden for 150 years, 'War Horse' by Dame Elisabeth Frink, is sited at the south end of the canal, and her 'Walking Madonna' is a new and important presence.

▶ *House open. Garden open most of year – telephone or consult website for details*

8 Horsleygate Hall

Well-tended and planted with great care, this garden on a sloping site is dotted with quirky artefacts, pergolas and a gazebo.

Horsleygate Lane, Holmesfield S18 7WD

Tel: 0114 289 0333

LOCATION 8 miles SW of Sheffield, 8 miles NW of Chesterfield off B6051. Take B6051 to Millthorpe; Horsleygate Lane is 1 mile on right, with house at bottom of lane

When the present owners arrived in 1989, they set about transforming a 2 acre wilderness into an immaculately cared for garden that is as interesting for its plantsmanship as its design. There are few level areas – the garden works with the slope, with grass and bark paths winding around small lawns and shady corners.

Interesting and eccentric artefacts, furniture and structures abound, often made out of recycled materials and all in keeping with the part-Victorian, part-Georgian house. A wooden bridge and a small pool, pergolas, sculptures carved out of ash or Kilkenny limestone, lots of seats and tables, a gazebo and a couple of breeze houses beckon around corners or punctuate the view.

Unusual shrubs and trees are a particular passion, but there are perennials in variety, too. The contents of the large walled kitchen garden proclaim a keen interest in good food, destined for the family and B&B and holiday cottage guests, while guinea fowl and a Welsomer cockerel and his harem peck about the orchard.

▶ *Open for NGS, and by appointment*

9 Renishaw Hall

On an exposed hilltop site, ten gardens mix skilful plantsmanship, art and an Italianate atmosphere to great effect.

Renishaw, Sheffield S21 3WB
Tel: 01246 432310

www.sitwell.co.uk

Historic Garden Grade II

LOCATION 6 miles SE of Sheffield, 5 miles NE of Chesterfield on A6135. From M1 at junction 30, take A616 towards Sheffield for 3 miles through Renishaw

For nearly 20 years Renishaw had 'the most northerly vineyard in western Europe'. Also surprising at this northerly latitude and in an exposed location on top of a hill are enormous specimens of rare and slightly tender shrubs.

The owner in the 19th and early 20th centuries spent much of his life in Italy, and this is the style he re-created at Renishaw a century ago. Within a framework of vistas, walks and topiary, plants appear in ordered confusion in the sheltered gardens to the south of the house. Statues, terraces and the sound of splashing water enhance the Italianate atmosphere, and the recent addition of a water jet has added to the effect.

The present generation of owners increased the number of different gardens across the 8 acres (10 acres in all), divided and protected by yew hedges and columns. They also enlarged the borders, introduced innovative planting and linked the garden to the wood with new planting and paths.

At the end of a lime avenue on the top lawn stands sculptor Sir Hamo Thornycroft's statue of the Angel of Fame. Beyond the brick wall is a greenhouse that contains the National Collection of yuccas, and below that winds a spinney that badgers now share with a statue walk.

A nature trail leads to an avenue of camellias, on to a bluebell wood and on still further to the classic temple, Gothic lodge, old sawmill, cave and lakes. A fairytale children's garden has been added, with a living willow tunnel, a maze, carvings on the trees and silhouettes from story books.

▶ *Open main season – telephone or consult website for details*

10 Hardwick Hall

The tranquil walled courtyards of this spectacular mansion enclose an outstanding herb garden, orchards and shrub roses.

Doe Lea, Chesterfield S44 5QJ

Tel: 01246 850430

www.nationaltrust.org.uk

Historic Garden Grade I/The National Trust

LOCATION 9½ miles SE of Chesterfield, 6½ miles NW of Mansfield. From M1 junction 29 take A6175

The renowned Elizabethan mansion was built by Bess of Hardwick and designed by Robert Smythson in the late 16th century. Mature yew hedges and stone walls provide protection in what is an exposed 17½ acre escarpment site.

The borders of the south court have shrubs and herbaceous planting to give structure and extend the flowering period, while the west court's herbaceous borders are planted in strong, hot colours graduating to soft hues, with the peak flowering season in late summer and autumn. The east courtyard is planted with old varieties of shrub roses that have been underplanted with herbaceous perennials.

The herb garden is outstanding. In the southeast quarter is an orchard, with varieties of apples, pears, plums, gages and damsons, and the northeast orchard has been progressively replanted with old varieties such as crab apples, with the grass left long for naturalised daffodils and wild flowers.

▶ *Open main season – telephone or consult website for details. Country park open all year*

CENTRAL ENGLAND

10 ACRES INCLUDE RIOTOUS HERBACEOUS BORDERS AND A WOODLAND WALK

CERNEY HOUSE GARDENS

GLOUCESTERSHIRE

This county's gardens nestle into the Cotswolds' gentle landscape amid honey-stoned towns and villages. Many designs show the influence of the romantic English style and spring bulbs are a seasonal highlight.

1 Stowell Park

Terraced lawns, colourful borders and an impressive walled garden are enhanced by a picturesque Cotswold setting.

Northleach GL54 3LE

Tel: 01285 720610 (head gardener)

Historic Park Grade II

LOCATION 8 miles NE of Cirencester, 2 miles SW of Northleach off A429

This is a quintessential English country garden. The original Elizabethan house was enlarged in the 1880s and used as a shooting lodge, and it is thought that the original 8 acre garden was laid out in the 1870s.

Since 1981, new ideas and plantings have been introduced that are in harmony with the garden's traditional Cotswold character. A pleached lime approach leads to lawned terraces with herbaceous borders, old-fashioned roses and unspoilt views over the Coln Valley towards Chedworth Woods. The huge walled garden is divided into wide colour-themed borders, sections for cut flowers, fruit and vegetables, and a long rose pergola lined with box edging – an original touch.

A rose-circle centrepiece in the little orchard is balanced by a circular fruit cage beyond a hedge interwoven with climbing roses, honeysuckles and clematis. There are peach and vine houses, and a splendid array of pot plants in the greenhouse.
▶ *Open for NGS*

2 Eastleach House

Rill and walled gardens, perennial borders, a lime avenue and yew roundel echo the contours of the hillside setting perfectly.

Eastleach Martin, Cirencester GL7 3NW

www.eastleachhouse.com

LOCATION 6 miles SW of Burford off A361 Lechlade road or off A40 via Westwell and Eastleach Turville. House opposite church gates

Hidden away and relatively unknown, this 14 acre garden has been created since 1983. The owner has created a series of interlocking spaces and outdoor rooms, interweaving plants

and combining a wide range of colours and textures with great skill and sensitivity.

The fine Arts and Crafts house, sitting on the top of a hill, has become the reference point and fulcrum of the design. The rear façade looks out across lawn to the countryside through a pair of decorative wrought-iron gates. Beyond them, a lime avenue leads to a yew roundel encircling the statue of a stag. A meandering path through parkland filled with wild flowers and a miniature arboretum brings the visitor to the edge of the croquet lawn. Ascend the broad steps and opposite is an arbour and a tapestry shrub border.

Stand at the west end of the house, look down onto the rill and your eye is caught by the perfectly shaped balls of *Sorbus aria* 'Lutescens' beyond perennial borders that embrace the colour spectrum. Roses wind through clematis and around fastigiate Irish yews in the walled garden, and the only secret hidden from the house is the sunken wildlife pond beyond.
▶ *Open for NGS, and guided tours for parties of ten or more at other times. Requests in writing please*

3 Cerney House Gardens

The scent and colour of old-fashioned roses create a romantic atmosphere while snowdrops carpet the woods in spring.

North Cerney, Cirencester GL7 7BX

Tel: 01285 831300/831205

www.cerneygardens.com

LOCATION 3½ miles N of Cirencester off A435 Cheltenham road. Turn left opposite Bathurst Arms, signed to Bagendon; gates on right

Goats, sheep and horses graze around the house, which was remodelled in 1791, and wild flowers flourish in the meadow. The garden – in a sheltered hollow surrounded by beech woods – is full of colour and interest, with a relaxed and friendly atmosphere.

The 10 acres include riotous herbaceous borders and a woodland walk with more than 150 varieties of snowdrop among the hellebores in late January and February, followed by bluebells and other spring bulbs. There is a rockery, a geranium and thyme bank, a pink border, a richly stocked herb garden and a ▷

genera garden, where plants of the same family are grouped together. This area leads down to a pond and tree trail, as well as a National Collection of tradescantias and beds beside the house telling the stories of planthunters and renowned nurserymen.

The 3½ acre Victorian walled garden is filled with herbaceous borders, a knot garden, vegetables, climbing and old-fashioned roses and clematis. In April and May a kaleidoscopic display of tulips spreads throughout.

▶ *Open main season – telephone or consult website for details – and by appointment*

4 The Old Rectory, Duntisbourne Rouse

Created by one of Britain's leading garden designers, the garden includes an auricula house, sunken dell and wild-flower meadow.

Duntisbourne Rouse, Daglingworth, Cirencester GL7 7AP

LOCATION 3 miles NW of Cirencester off A417. From Daglingworth take narrow valley road for the Duntisbournes. After 1 mile house is on right

Since 1983 the garden writer and designer Mary Keen has created an intimate and inspiring 1½ acre garden, nestled among wooded Cotswold hills. It has been designed for atmosphere and to complement its setting.

It is topiary that gives the garden its bones, and the many different areas of changing level and mood are separated by yew or box hedges. The initial expanse of lawn at the front of the house gives way to areas of mass colour, an auricula house, a winter garden and a dark reflective pool.

There is interest and colour at every season. Winter brings snowdrops in variety, a crocus lawn and scented shrubs. Spring responds with an orchard of apple blossom and a sunken dell carpeted with *Anemone blanda*. Tulips are planted naturalistically and the collection of tall miniature bearded irises increases year on year. Drifting into summer the style becomes more exuberant, with plenty of roses and dahlias, and the gooseberry garden behind the house a gathering place for flowers in tones of orange and blue.

A meadow with wild flowers sprinkled like hundreds and thousands has now replaced the traditional herbaceous borders in the kitchen garden.

▶ *Open for NGS, and for parties of ten or more by written appointment*

5 Rodmarton Manor

Designed as a series of atmospheric outdoor rooms with year-round appeal, there is a wild garden, hornbeam tunnel and topiary.

Rodmarton, Cirencester GL7 6PF

Tel: 01285 841253

www.rodmarton-manor.co.uk

Historic Park Grade II*

LOCATION 6 miles SW of Cirencester, 4 miles NE of Tetbury off A433, halfway between Cirencester and Tetbury

Here is an opportunity to see an integrated Arts and Crafts design for house and garden by architect Ernest Barnsley. Entering up a holly-hedged drive, an overflowing cottage garden is glimpsed on the way through the stableyard. The house is spread informally on the other side of a large, plain, circular lawn.

Well-cut topiary and hedges of beech, box and yew are a particular feature of the 8 acre garden, which is divided into a series of compartments and retains its original layout despite certain modifications and improvements made over the years. The Leisure Garden on the other side of the house was redesigned in 1958 and is constantly evolving, while plantings in stone containers in an area known as The Troughery are refreshed every two or three years.

Interest is year-round – a small winter garden adjoins the house, snowdrops in variety mass in the cherry orchard and the fine terrace, with a topiary garden on one side, looks out to a distant view of the daffodil paddock.

Spoilt for choice, you might explore the sunken garden or the white border, then discover the tunnel of hornbeam in the wild garden, framing a distant vista. The kitchen garden retains some of its original purpose but also contains a collection of old roses and other decorative plants, together with amusing topiary in the shape of birds and a pig.

Four maturing herbaceous borders, replanted year by year since 2006, are focused on a stone summerhouse within a walled enclosure, and already make a fine sight in midsummer.

▶ *House open. Garden open for snowdrops, and for limited season – telephone or consult website for details*

6 The National Arboretum, Westonbirt

Home to a spectacular and diverse collection of trees, the arboretum also features a National Collection of Japanese maples.

Westonbirt, Tetbury GL8 8QS

Tel: 01666 880220

www.forestry.gov.uk/westonbirt

Historic Arboretum Grade I

LOCATION 3 miles SW of Tetbury on A433, 5 miles NE of A46 junction

This is perhaps the finest arboretum in Britain, noted especially for its vast range of stunning mature specimen trees. Started in 1829, it now covers 600 acres and there are in excess of 17,000 numbered trees – including an exceptional National Collection of Japanese maples – extended in 2006 by the newly planted Rotary Glade. Numerous grass rides divide the trees into glades used for special plantings.

A short walk from the original arboretum is Silk Wood, with collections of native, Asian and American species. In spring, it is carpeted with primroses, wood anemones and bluebells. Colour is best in May when the rhododendrons and magnolias are in flower and in October when Japanese maples, Persian ironwoods and katsuras take centre stage.

From early December until Christmas the Enchanted Wood is illuminated at weekends with a wonderful festive display, and many champion trees are floodlit. Although the plant centre does not keep large stocks of plants, it offers some rare and interesting shrubs and trees, especially Japanese maples, conifers and specimen trees.

▶ *Open all year – telephone or consult website for details*

7 Dyrham Park

This outstanding landscape garden has one of the earliest architectural glasshouses, which was part of the original design.

Chippenham SN14 8ER │ Tel: 0117 937 2501

www.nationaltrust.org.uk

Historic Garden Grade II*/The National Trust

LOCATION 8 miles N of Bath, 12 miles E of Bristol on A46. Take M4 junction 18 towards Bath

Only a tiny fragment of the extensive Baroque garden designed by London and Wise survives to the east of the house. The terraces were all smoothed out in the late 18th century to form an 'English' landscape with a sweeping drive bringing the visitor in from the new entrance. Avenues of elms survived until the mid 1970s but have since been replaced by limes. The cascade in the garden on the west side of the house is still working and it is possible to make out the form of the original garden.

The west garden is currently being redeveloped to combine the formal boundaries of the 18th century with Victorian planting and contemporary elements. Architect William Talman's great orangery rekindles the former sense of splendour that the water gardens must have achieved in their heyday. This glasshouse is now used for growing a variety of citrus plants.

The views towards Bristol and elegance of the 'natural' landscape with the house and church tucked into the hillside, make this a superb example of English landscape gardening.

▶ *House open. Garden open main season – telephone or consult website for details. Park open all year*

8 Special Plants Nursery

Plants from around the world can be admired in this modern garden, which reaches a dramatic climax in late summer.

Greenways Lane, Cold Ashton, Chippenham SN14 8LA │ Tel: 01225 891686

www.specialplants.net

LOCATION 7 miles N of Bath just S of junction A46 and A420. Turn into Greenways Lane

Set high on the Cotswold Way, this 1 acre garden has a modern design and an architectural structure. An eye for colour and knowledge of unusual perennials has produced a dramatic display, which reaches a climax in late summer. The steepness of the south-facing site, which is sheltered by mature willows, ash and horse chestnut, enables many borderline tender plants and shrubs to flourish in deep gravel terraces and richly planted borders.

A modern pergola over the terrace is clothed with climbers. Bold shapes in gravel, water and grass echo the outlines of the surrounding scenery, and the colour associations include the deep crimson, almost black, border and the shades of apricot edging the new gravel garden.

There is a productive vegetable garden and the nursery is outstanding, selling a wide range of professionally grown and well-displayed perennials, both hardy and tender.

▶ *Open main season – telephone or consult website for details – and for NGS and parties by appointment*

CENTRAL ENGLAND

9 Badminton House

Rarely open to the public, these private gardens include elegant parterres, fountains and topiary, as well as 50 varieties of rose.

Badminton GL9 1DB | Historic Park Grade I

www.badmintonestate.co.uk

LOCATION 5 miles E of Chipping Sodbury, N of M4 junction 18, off B4040

It is the private gardens to the south and east of the house and the huge walled kitchen garden, placed out of sight of the park, that are the focus of interest for today's visitors. On the east side are two conservatories and a formal garden designed by landscape architect Russell Page shortly before his death. The private gardens, entered through an unobtrusive passageway off the west side of the house, are laid out in an asymmetrically formal quartet of rooms that complement the architectural *mélange* of this side of the house, with a herbaceous border and a hornbeam hedge running the full length.

Box-edged and yew-backed gardens encompass a central lawn facing the 1785 church opposite the entrance to the garden, and the quarters that form the rest of the rectangle are filled with parterres, fountains, topiary, lollipop trees and a controlled explosion of flowers.

In the 16 beds that make up the rose garden alone there are 50 different varieties, with the lemon-yellow 'Windrush' used as a linking thread. All are underplanted with an attractive combination of alliums, geraniums and violas. In the walled garden, the flowers that grow alongside the vegetables and herbs are mainly for cutting – six dozen roses, a dozen dianthus, hydrangeas, clematis, geraniums and more.

The elaborate formal gardens and avenues devised by design team London and Wise and landscape gardener Charles Bridgeman in the late 17th and 18th centuries may have been swept away, but the grandeur that is Badminton is still summed up in garden pioneer William Kent's masterpiece Worcester Lodge, a two-storey domed banqueting house that gives views of the ducal residence 2¾ miles away.

The gardens of Essex House, the dower house within the grounds, can sometimes be visited by appointment on the Badminton open days (tel: 01454 218203). Originally laid out and planted by the late writer and garden historian Alvilde Lees-Milne, they are a wonderfully romantic foil to the great park.

▶ *Open for two days in June – application form for tickets available from the website – for charity, and for private parties by prior arrangement*

10 Hanham Court Garden

Borders filled with old roses, peonies and lilies produce a wonderful scent in this garden that surrounds a manor house.

Ferry Road, Hanham Abbots, Bristol BS15 3NT

Tel: 0117 961 0593/1202

www.hanhamcourt.co.uk

LOCATION 5 miles E of Bristol city centre off A431 Bristol-Bath road. In Hanham follow A431; after second roundabout turn right onto Ellacombe Road, right onto Court Farm Road for 1 mile, then left onto Ferry Road at St Stephen's Green

Internationally acclaimed landscape gardeners Isabel and Julian Bannerman have created for their own enjoyment a garden in which they give free expression to the exuberant plantings and architectural statements that characterise much of their work. Their vision and sense of scale combine to make it a natural setting for the ancient manor house, church and tithe barn.

Passing through the Tudor gateway, visitors are drawn towards a gravel garden awash with

HANHAM COURT GARDEN

massive *Euphorbia wulfenii*, purple honesty, irises and clipped box, balanced by a long bed of massed head-high delphiniums. Beyond the tree house crouching in an ancient yew, a fine pattern-book gate leads to an orchard dominated by a vast walnut tree surrounded by fritillaries and later *Narcissus poeticus*.

The Bannermans' style of planting – highly selective with spectacular massed effects – comes into its own in the romantic long borders and surrounding enclosures. Early summer is distinguished by hundreds of peonies, *Lilium regale* and countless shrub roses – a breathtaking sight and unforgettable scent.

Below the level bastion of the main lawn with its yew obelisks lies the dell, where ancient medieval ponds have been cleared and tree ferns planted. Magnolias and giant white Himalayan lilies line many of the grass-mown paths leading to an architectural flourish in the shape of a Gothic stumpery reminiscent of the one they created for the Prince of Wales at Highgrove. Look out for the surprise water feature.

▶ *Open limited season – telephone or consult website for details*

11 Ozleworth Park

Twelve glorious acres have been divided into a variety of enclosures, including a water garden, stepped rill and wild area.

Ozleworth Park, Wotton-under-Edge GL12 7QA

Tel: 01453 845591

LOCATION 5 miles S of Dursley off A4135 Tetbury-Dursley road

This 12 acre garden, now restored to its original Victorian splendour by a series of distinguished designers, is magnificent in the scale and sophistication of its plantings and the artistry of its design. Multiple enclosures are laid out within yew hedges or beautiful old walls. A stepped rill with slabs of stone and square ponds rises up a steep hillside to a wild area at the top. An espaliered pear pergola underplanted with alliums and agapanthus is reached via a green yew corridor. An 1806 bath house is encircled by a walkway and deep borders are planted with a wide range of shrubs and perennials.

One of the most successful spaces is the water garden, tucked away at the perimeter, where two long rectangular pools studded with water lilies and separated by a bronze statue of Diana, the huntress, are flanked by a plump lavender hedge and a low yew hedge.

▶ *Open one day for charity – telephone for details*

12 Stancombe Park

A path descends through dark woodland and grottoes dripping with water to an atmospheric folly garden and a small lake.

Stancombe, Dursley GL11 6AU

Tel: 01453 542815

Historic Garden Grade I

LOCATION Between Wotton-under-Edge and Dursley on B4060

Set on the Cotswold escarpment, this site has all the ingredients of a Gothic bestselling novel. A narrow path drops into a dark glen, where the roots of huge oaks, copper beeches and chestnuts trip you, ferns brush your face, mossy walls drip with water and tunnels turn into grottoes. Even the plants live in wire cages. But this secret garden can be light and friendly when it is not raining. A millennium folly set at the head of a small pond has reused the façade of a ruined chapel found in the woods, and a bog garden has been planted behind.

▶ *Open for parties by appointment*

13 Througham Court

Science and landscape design unite to create a highly original garden with traditional and contemporary touches.

Througham GL6 7HG

www.christinefacer.com

LOCATION 8 miles W of Cirencester. From Birdlip, follow B4070 until left turn signed to The Camp; after The Camp take first left signed to Througham. Take second left turn down hill; house immediately on right

The intriguing house – a Grade II-listed Jacobean, 18th-century and Arts and Crafts hybrid – lies at the heart of this 55 acre estate, and the formal garden acts as a viewing platform for the landscape beyond. It is an amalgam of traditional elements, such as garden compartments, topiary, courtyards and terraces, and contemporary features – a wild grass meadow, a black bamboo maze, the zig-zag arboretum, a mound planted with late perennials and a new 'rusty border'.

Both the design and the details have been inspired by science. Reminders of the cosmos are expressed in stone and statuary, and in a host of allusive names, such as the Cosmic Evolution Garden, Fibonacci Jumps, Entry Into Chaos Gate, Molecule Seat, and a new Anatomy of the Black Swan gate. A viewing terrace near the house draws inspiration from chiral, or mirror-image, molecules.

The owner, a scientist turned landscape designer, works closely with landscape architect Charles Jencks. There are light-hearted touches, too – a photinia hedge as background to a series of sculptured slate shards cascading down a slope, steps covered with a red astroturf 'carpet' and shimmering silk banners.

The complex stainless-steel gates, engraved Ancaster stone balls and a slate starburst linked to a black reflective pool and a rill all demonstrate high-quality workmanship. The planting shows the same fine eye for colour and a talent for blending and juxtaposing plants in subtle or startling groups.
▶ *Open by appointment: parties of more than 20 welcome (with lecture tour – fee on application)*

14 Misarden Park Gardens

Set at the head of the Golden Valley, this stunning garden includes a spring walk, millennium rill and Lutyens loggia.

Miserden, Stroud GL6 7JA | Tel: 01285 821303

www.misardenpark.co.uk

Historic Garden Grade II*

LOCATION 6 miles NW of Cirencester, 3 miles off A417. Signposted

This timeless English garden, which commands spectacular views over the Golden Valley, has most of the features to be expected in a garden started in the 17th century. Notable are the extensive yew hedges and yew walk, the Yorkstone terrace, the loggia by Edwin Lutyens overhung with wisteria, and a good specimen of *Magnolia* x *soulangeana*. The south lawn supports splendid grass steps and a fine, ancient mulberry.

West of the house the ground ascends in a series of lawns, terraces and shrubberies. Within the walled garden the long double herbaceous borders have been reconstructed with mixed plantings and themed colours link the beds. The former rose walk has been replanted as a mixed border in shades of apricot and grey, echoing the neighbouring parterre that contains hebes, lavender, tulips, alliums and 'Chanelle' roses. A rill with a fountain and a summerhouse were added as a feature to mark the millennium.

Beneath the house, blue 'Rozanne' geraniums, asters and agapanthus, together with golden rubus, *Populus richardii* and gleditsia lead the eye to a venerable cedar in the park below. There are many fine specimen trees and the spring show of blossom and bulbs is spectacular. A good nursery, open daily (except Monday) ajoins.
▶ *Open main season – telephone or consult website for details – for NGS and for parties by appointment*

15 Painswick Rococo Garden

A wonderful reminder of a particular period in English planting, this gem of a garden is also renowned for its display of snowdrops.

Painswick GL6 6TH | Tel: 01452 813204

www.rococogarden.org.uk

Historic Garden Grade II*

LOCATION ½ mile from Painswick on B4073. Signposted

This rare Rococo survival is protected by a charitable trust, and a large amount of time and money has been spent on its sensitive and comprehensive restoration. Since work began in 1984, new plantings have matured alongside the beech woods and older specimen trees.

Rococo gardening was an 18th-century combination of formal geometric features with winding woodland paths, revealing sudden incidents and vistas – in essence a softening of the formal French style, apparent from about 1715 onwards in all forms of art. The basis for Painswick's present restoration is a painting of 1748 by Thomas Robins (1716-78) for Benjamin Hyett, who created the garden in the grounds of the house built by his father in 1735.

Eighteenth-century garden buildings stand next to winding paths or at the end of formal vistas with dramatic views of the surrounding countryside. An ornamental kitchen garden dominates the centre of the garden, and a snowdrop wood spans a stream that flows from a pond at the lower end. Elsewhere wild flowers are allowed freedom to roam, contrasting with the formal herbaceous borders that surround a white Gothic screen.

In celebration of the 10 acre garden's 250th anniversary, an intriguing maze designed by crossword compiler Angela Newing was created in the adjoining farmland.

▶ *Open most of year – telephone or consult website for details*

16 Sudeley Castle and Gardens

Set amid the ruins of the castle, the formal gardens are festooned with old roses and clematis, framed by blocks of topiary yews.

Winchcombe, Cheltenham GL54 5JD

Tel: 01242 602308 | www.sudeleycastle.co.uk

Historic Garden Grade II*

LOCATION 8 miles NE of Cheltenham off B4632 at Winchcombe

There has been a house on this magnificent site, with views of the surrounding Cotswold Hills at every turn, for more than 1,000 years. Although there are ten individual gardens, each one flows smoothly into the next, leading from the entrance via a wild-flower walk, a decorative Victorian kitchen garden, a canal and a pheasantry to the formal gardens and lawns surrounding the house and its church.

The Queen's Garden opposite the ruins of the banqueting hall is outstanding. Laid out in the 19th century on the site of the original Tudor parterre, it is entered between two huge topiary drums of yew and surrounded by clipped double yew hedges. A raised grass walk punctuated by large golden and green yew shapes runs along two sides, with a ha-ha marking the transition to parkland.

Old English roses, including the peachy-yellow 'Phyllis Bide', tumble in borders and over arbours, accompanied by clematis, alliums and herbs. Elsewhere a secluded garden, a white garden, a knot garden, a carp pond, collections of buddleias and tree peonies, and a staircase folly lodged in a tree await discovery. Ancient buildings and recent plantings coexist in perfect harmony.

▶ *Castle and gardens open main season – telephone or check website for details. Guided tours by arrangement*

17 Stanway

This terraced water garden is home to the world's tallest single-jet fountain as well as many pools and waterfalls.

Winchcombe, Cheltenham GL54 5PQ

Tel: 01386 584469

www.stanwayfountain.co.uk

Historic Garden Grade I

LOCATION 1 mile E of B4632 Cheltenham-Broadway road, 4 miles NE of Winchcombe

Stanway is a honey-coloured Cotswold village with a Jacobean house that has changed hands just once since AD 715. The garden rises in a series of dramatic terraced lawns and a rare, picturesque grasswork to the pyramid, which in the 18th century stood at the head of a 190m (620ft) long cascade descending to a formal canal on a terrace above the house. At 36m (120ft), it exceeded in length and height its famous rival at Chatsworth (see page 160).

Inside the house is a fascinating painting recording the cascade as it looked in the 18th century. The canal, the upper pond behind the pyramid, a short section of the cascade and the upper fall below the pyramid were restored in 1998, and a spectacular 100m (330ft) high single-jet fountain (the tallest garden fountain in the world) added.

The recently restored medieval pond in the Lower Garden has enhanced the beauty of the 14th-century tithe barn. On the hillside to the east of the pyramid is the upper cascade – a series of pools and waterfalls. From here there are magnificent views of the cascades, canal, fountain, house and Vale of the Severn. A high walk along the hillside above the cascade reveals the splendid park trees around the 23 acre site.

▶ *Open main season – telephone or consult website for details – and tours for parties by appointment*

CENTRAL ENGLAND

18 Colesbourne Park

Renowned for its snowdrop collection, many of which are rare varieties, the garden also has fine displays of daffodils and hellebores.

Near Cheltenham GL53 9NP | Tel: 01242 870264

www.colesbournegardens.org.uk

LOCATION 6 miles S of Cheltenham on A435

One of the joys of late winter and early spring in the Cotswolds is a visit to the famous snowdrop collection at Colesbourne Park, and the season has now been extended by a restoration project to celebrate the great days of Victorian plantsman and collector Henry John Elwes, who owned the 2,500 acre estate. Then the garden was celebrated for its trees as well as its bulbs, and today many early flowering scented shrubs and thousands of small-flowered daffodils have been planted in the meadow and around the lake, and a collection of hellebores is flourishing among other bulbs in the woodland.

But the glory of the garden is still the snowdrops – great swathes of many different varieties spreading through the woods and beside the lake, and some 250 rare and beautiful cultivars displayed in the Spring Garden and in raised beds near the house. Formal beds next to the house open onto wide lawns giving fine views across the surrounding parkland.

▶ *Open Feb weekends for snowdrops, and for parties by appointment*

19 Kiftsgate Court

A water garden showcasing a fountain with foliage sculpture makes an unusual feature in this imaginative, colourful garden.

Chipping Campden GL55 6LN

Tel: 01386 438777 | www.kiftsgate.co.uk

Historic Garden Grade II*

LOCATION 3 miles NE of Chipping Campden and near Mickleton, close to Hidcote

The house was built in the late 19th century on a 6 acre site surrounded by three steep banks, and the 4 acre garden is the creation of three generations of women gardeners. Much of the work was done after the First World War by the present owner's grandmother and her original colour schemes in the borders have been maintained with few alterations.

In spring, the white sunken garden is covered with bulbs and there is a fine show of daffodils along the drive. June and July are the peak months for colour and scent, but the old and species roses are the highlight of this garden, home of *Rosa filipes* 'Kiftsgate'. Notable too are perennial geraniums, a mighty wisteria and many species of hydrangea, some very large. In autumn, Japanese maples glow in the bluebell wood. Unusual plants are sometimes among those available for sale.

The owners have added a modern touch – a simple flower-free water garden, with a foliage sculpture designed by fountain creator Simon Allison reflected in the black water of the pool.

▶ *Open main season – telephone or consult website for details*

20 Hidcote Manor Garden

This Arts and Crafts masterpiece was specially designed in the 20th century to be a 'wild garden in a formal setting'.

Hidcote Bartrim, Chipping Campden GL55 6LR

Tel: 01386 438333

www.nationaltrust.org.uk/hidcote

Historic Garden Grade I/The National Trust

LOCATION 3 miles NE of Chipping Campden

One of Britain's most celebrated gardens, it combines a strongly architectural framework with miles of sculptured hedges delineating a large number of formal outdoor rooms. Some of these – the Pillar Garden, the Long Walk and Bathing Pool Garden – are Italianate in feeling, and many are filled with dramatic and diverse plantings.

This Arts and Crafts *tour de force* was created in the early years of the 20th century, demonstrating the former American owner's strong sense of design, great planting skills and his idiosyncratic way of combining plants. He made many new introductions and rediscovered many forgotten species, some of which he collected himself – several varieties now bear the Hidcote name.

Since acquiring the 10½ acre garden in 1948, the National Trust has done its best to retain the spirit of the original, however, recently uncovered evidence confirmed that the planting legacy had been steadily eroded over the years. Thanks to a £1.6 million grant in 2006, the 12 year plan is focused on making a gradual return to the original owner's vision of 'a wild garden in a formal setting'. His plant house has been re-created and the East Court Gardens and Rock Bank restored.

▶ *Open main season – telephone or consult website for details – and for parties by written appointment*

HIDCOTE MANOR GARDEN

21 Upton Wold

A network of hedges defines a series of beautifully constructed garden rooms – including rose and pond gardens.

Northwick Estate, Moreton-in-Marsh GL56 9TR

Tel: 01386 700667

LOCATION 5 miles NW of Moreton-in-Marsh on A44. Pass Batsford, Sezincote and Bourton House, continue up Bourton hill, pass Troopers Lodge Garage at A424 junction, and drive is 1 mile further on right

Hidden away in a hollow, two elements have combined to make this an intriguing and rewarding garden – the rolling lie of the land and the intellectual creativity of the present owners. Starting in 1976 with a barren and neglected estate, they called in landscape architects Brenda Colvin and Hal Moggridge to lay out a network of hedges sheltering various garden rooms, and water garden designer Anthony Archer-Wills to construct a canal and fountain garden at the rear of the early 17th-century house.

The fruit and vegetable gardens, rose gardens, hornbeam *allées*, wild-flower meadows and a pond garden are all expressive of a formal and quintessentially English style.

The 9 acres here, however, are imbued with an energy and unconventionality. A long and narrow herbaceous border is sandwiched between a wall and a tall yew hedge with elongated 'windows' cut through. The intimate Hidden Garden is a sloping, triangular wedge filled with unusual magnolias and other fine specimen trees, underplanted with herbaceous perennials and a froth of Queen Anne's Lace. A patterned pathway leads down to a sloping tunnel of *Malus* 'John Downie' flanked by a clipped 'cloud' hedge, and an arboretum contains a National Collection of 200 walnut trees in 14 different species.

Everywhere rare and unusual plants abound, with smaller-scale treasures woven into borders and important specimen trees placed at strategic points as eye-catchers. The garden reaches its peak from April to July – allow several hours to do it justice.

▶ *Open May to July by appointment*

22 Sezincote

An extraordinary Moghul-style house is surrounded by a romantic water garden with Indian-influenced features throughout.

Moreton-in-Marsh GL56 9AW

www.sezincote.co.uk

Historic Garden Grade I

LOCATION 1½ miles W of Moreton-in-Marsh on A44 just before Bourton-on-the-Hill

The entrance to Sezincote is up a long, dark avenue of holm oaks that opens into the most English of parks, landscaped by Humphry Repton. Turning the last corner there's a surprise – an English country house built in Moghul style.

The form of the garden has not changed since Repton's time, but the more recent planting was carried out by the current owner with help from garden designer Graham Stuart Thomas. On her return from India in 1968 they laid out the Persian Paradise Garden in the south garden with canals and Irish yews. Behind this is the great curved orangery, now home to many tender climbing plants.

The house is sheltered by copper beeches, cedars, yews and limes, which provide a fine backdrop for the exotic shrubs. Streams and pools are lined with clumps of bog-loving plants, and a stream is crossed by an Indian bridge adorned with Brahmin bulls. Planted for year-round interest, the garden is particularly striking in autumn.
▶ *House open. Garden open most of year – telephone or consult website for details – and for NGS*

23 Temple Guiting Manor

A modern garden, boldly designed and tastefully planted, it has three terraces – with an orchard and canal – at its heart.

Temple Guiting, nr Stow-on-the-Wold GL54 5RP

LOCATION 7 miles from Stow-on-the-Wold on B4077

A remarkable modern garden now defines the Tudor manor farm. Designer Jinny Blom has created a new linear flow, stretching out longitudinally from the side of the house. The Peacock Garden fans out into a number of beds filled with *Cirsium rivulare*, *Aquilegia* 'Ruby Port', grasses, towering white eremurus, *Veronicastrum album*, *Rosa chinensis mutabilis*, *Thalictrum* 'Thundercloud', alstroemerias, aconitums and feathery sanguisorbas.

The heart of the garden is terraced, with an orchard on the upper level surrounded by box squares and planted in a cool blue and white palette with irises, lavender, delphiniums and hydrangeas. A double screen of pleached hornbeams underplanted with cardoons, agapanthus, lilies and white delphiniums frames an elegant 30m (100ft) long canal on the lower level. This area also gives access to the Granary Walk, with a mass of perovskias and roses, and from here a gnarled ivy arch leads into a tennis court where clipped box plants serve as ball boys.

The terrace below the canal is subdivided into a yew and a box parterre filled with violas, dicentras, foxgloves and roses, opening up the view over an award-winning dry-stone retaining wall into the valley below. A wild grassy walk leads back to the Peacock Garden.

Blom's latest project is a courtyard garden linking the restored barns, with cut-leaf limes and curving box-edged beds holding salvias for intensity of colour and herbs for culinary use.
▶ *Open for NGS*

24 Abbotswood

Elegant gardens yield to the surrounding Cotswold landscape, with fritillaries and orchids cloaking the sides of the ravine.

Stow-on-the-Wold GL54 1EN

Tel: 01451 830173

Historic Garden Grade II*

LOCATION 1 mile W of Stow on B4077

This 20 acre Cotswold garden retains its Edwardian charm, merging into the landscape with descending streams, surrounding woodland. The elegant formal gardens around the house were originally designed by Edwin Lutyens with a fountain, terraced lawn, sunken garden, lily pond and rose garden, all planted in harmonious style. The box-edged blue garden, with its deep blue forget-me-nots and later *Salvia farinacea*, is particularly attractive.

Herbaceous borders are full of interest and colour, and there are extensive heather beds, flowering shrubs, specimen trees and rhododendrons in shades of pink. In spring fritillaries yield to spotted orchids in the wild garden beside the stream that meanders down into the ravine, its slopes massed with bulbs, and into the River Dikler, which has been widened to form a lake. The walled kitchen garden includes a small orchard and rose garden.
▶ *Open for NGS and other charities, and by appointment*

25 Rockcliffe

Geometric beds, beech obelisks and topiary doves leading to a stone dovecote are striking features in this varied garden.

Lower Swell, Stow-on-the-Wold GL54 2JW

LOCATION 3 miles W of Stow-on-the-Wold on B4068

The 7 acre garden looks due west towards a stretch of unspoilt country enclosed by a curving shelter belt of mature park trees. Two elegant pavilions added to the house pull the composition together and create a generous forecourt. On the stone slabs is a series of geometric beds planted with 'Sawyers' lavender, the centrepiece a box-edged spoked wheel with a stone wellhead in the centre; the paving is covered with lime-green *Alchemilla mollis*.

From the forecourt the view is of beech obelisks stalking up the broad grass ride towards the new ha-ha and beyond to open countryside. Between the terrace and the tree-lined boundary to the north is a shady enclosure where a stone-edged pool is overhung by six *Cornus controversa* 'Variegata'. This lower-level garden leads to another where two simple canals of reflective water are framed by Yorkstone paving.

Then come three flower-filled boîtes – two yew-edged rooms, richly planted in shades of white and purple-blue, and a scented swimming-pool garden with huge bay trees and a pool-house covered with 'Zéphirine Drouhin' roses.

The walled kitchen garden is productive and pretty, but on the other side of the kitchen garden comes a theatrical flourish – topiary yew birds perching in pairs on the slope leading through the orchard to an octagonal stone dovecote.

▶ *Open for NGS and other charities, and by appointment for parties of ten or more*

26 Daylesford

Formal and naturalised planting combine in this restored landscaped garden, whose highlights include lakes and an orangery.

Daylesford Estate Office, Moreton in Marsh GL56 0YH

Tel: 01608 658888

LOCATION Off A436 between Stow-on-the-Wold and Chipping Norton

In its striking setting, with sweeping lawns, lakes and woodland, every aspect of Daylesford is a delight. The house is in the Anglo-Indian style, a nod to its colonial connections, and the landscaped grounds include a Gothic orangery, walled garden and lakes. Since 1988 the present owners have gradually restored and re-created the original combination of semi-natural parkland, putting particular emphasis on naturalised plantings that contrast with the garden's more formal areas.

The orangery has an impressive display of blue *Salvia guarantica* along the south-facing wall, as well as a collection of citrus in large clay pots and in a central bed underplanted with box. Behind is the sheltered Secret Garden, designed by Chelsea Flower Show winner Rupert Golby, with tender exotics, a pavilion and a pool presided over by a 17th-century Neptune.

Above the orangery, shrubs and climbing roses have been planted in meadowland. From the top lake a waterfall cascades into the dell, the stream flowing over a series of falls before emptying into the bottom lake.

A scented walk and stumpery lead to the 2 acre walled garden, which is run organically, with peach and orchid houses, a potager and a series of yew-hedged areas. Beyond a cut-flower garden and quince lawn is the raised rose garden. Topiary echoes the Anglo-Indian theme.

▶ *Open for NGS, and occasional charity events*

27 Stone House

Planted with unusual bulbs, shrubs and perennials, the cottage garden also has a crab-apple walk and herb garden.

Wyck Rissington GL54 2PN | Tel: 01451 810337

LOCATION 1½ miles S of Stow-on-the-Wold off A429 just NE of Bourton-on-the-Water

This garden displays a stylish simplicity in both design and planting, while avoiding horticultural cliches. The 2½ acre site is filled with unusual bulbs, shrubs and herbaceous perennials, including an abundance of aquilegias and hostas. The garden also makes bold use of euphorbias.

There is a crab-apple walk, rose borders and a herb garden, and fritillaries are naturalising in the meadow walk. A spring-fed stream bubbles throughout the garden. The area of sloping, box-edged lawns leading down from a terrace via rounded brick steps to the water's edge is especially charming.

The design makes full and sensitive use of the sloping site and the views out across a ha-ha to unspoilt countryside, and cleverly conceals a swimming pool and tennis court.

▶ *Open for NGS, and by appointment*

CENTRAL ENGLAND

HEREFORDSHIRE

Imaginative gardens, set against the dramatic backdrop of the Malvern Hills or Wye Valley, make good use of the county's fine vistas and combine skilful planting with inventive features.

1 The Long Barn

Exuberant plantings selected for colour and texture are contained within a simple framework of nine enclosures.

Eastnor, Ledbury HR8 1EL

Tel: 01531 632718

LOCATION 8 miles SW of Great Malvern, 2 miles E of Ledbury on A438, approx ½ mile from junction with Ledbury-Malvern road

In 1995 the owners were faced with an empty plot on the edge of an orchard, its boundaries fixed by stone pigsties, a tall hedge, a brick barn and a green lane. Now the ¼ acre garden sits contentedly in the landscape, anchored by a strong design of nine enclosures and co-ordinated by a central path leading the eye to an orchard, where there is an obelisk 'borrowed' from the Eastnor Castle estate, and then to the Malvern Hills in the distance. They did not consult a rule book, relying instead on instinct, experiment and the plants' own inclinations.

THE LONG BARN

One enclosure includes a weeping pear, a group of perovskias, pale-flowered garlic chives and the sword-leaves of *Iris sibirica* 'Silver Edge'. In another, fountains of grasses create a calm and neutral backdrop. There is structure and formality here – six substantial *Viburnum tinus* 'Eve Price' form a pattern alongside the main gravel path, and rows of irises are tidily cut down and drawn up in lines – but the rhythm is easy.

In summer, the masses of old and scented roses are carefully segregated by colour and, in autumn, when many of the plants are dying a colourful death, the underlying structure of paths, walls, green lane and repeat shrubs makes itself felt.
▶ *Open main season – telephone or consult website for details – and by appointment*

2 Whitfield House

Two award-winning designers have created a garden of the highest standard, including a terrace with cube-shaped pleached limes.

Wormbridge HR2 9BA | Tel: 01981 570202

Historic Garden Grade II

LOCATION **8 miles SW of Hereford on A465 Abergavenny road**

This is a splendid example of creative continuity. The 15 acre landscape garden, created in 1750 in the Picturesque style, has been cultivated ever since and is still maintained and reinvented to a standard that will please the most discerning eye. A giant cedar of Lebanon stands near the 18th-century house in a wild-flower meadow bright with cowslips and orchids. Beyond lies a field of cattle and woodlands that are dominated by giant redwoods while other magnificent trees cover the hills above. A huge yew hedge, its crest sculpted into topiary shapes, surrounds the lawn at the back of the house.

On the terrace, pleached limes have been trained as cubes, and borders designed by Chelsea Flower Show Gold Medal winner Rupert Golby are patterned with ceanothus, cistus and teucriums. Large magnolias underplanted with narcissi and lily-flowered tulips stand against the walls surrounding the carriage-house yard, and in front of the house magnolias also command the bank and steps that fall away from an Italianate terrace formally planted by another Chelsea Flower Show winner – Arabella Lennox-Boyd. The eye is drawn to an enclosed view of lakes and thence to an island folly in the Castle Pool and a statue in the far distance. A fernery of matteucia with martagon lilies grows among stone masonry under the sheltering canopy of a copper beech. The walled vegetable and cutting garden is reached through a recently rebuilt camellia house with a classical portico. There is a ginkgo tree here, which has the largest girth in the country.
▶ *Open for NGS, and by appointment*

3 Brilley Court

A farmyard has been transformed into a beautifully manicured garden, with vibrant tulips, topiary and a display of orchids.

Whitney-on-Wye HR3 6JF | Tel: 01497 831467

LOCATION **6 miles NE of Hay-on-Wye, 5 miles SW of Kington, 1½ miles off A438 Hereford-Brecon road; signed to Brilley**

Located on the border between England and Wales, with wonderful views to the Black Mountains, the 3 acres set around the ancient farmhouse have been transformed by the present owners. A farmyard is now, after 30 years, a well-groomed garden with roses tumbling over the house and a dazzling tulip display in spring.

Sloping to the southwest, it is sheltered from the prevailing winds and surrounded by low walls to keep out livestock. A terrace has been created with overflowing pots, relaxed plantings in pastel colours and well-clipped topiary.

Herbaceous borders surround the lawns and a brick path with box hedging leads through the old, walled ornamental kitchen garden with its espaliered fruit trees and arches, vegetable beds and a cutting garden, part of which is being planted by the owner as a memorial garden to her late mother.

The owner is responsible for maintaining and planting the nearby Hay Festival site, and a large quantity of ornamental greenery is housed in the garden for the celebration. The area includes an ornamental greenhouse and trialling ground for tulips and English roses, and another greenhouse houses fine specimens of orchids.

Across the lane a deep valley with a stream running through it has become a 4 acre wild garden, filled with wild flowers and birdsong. In 1987 it was cleaned and planted with a collection of specimen trees, including many acers, *Magnolia wilsonii*, *Malus hupehensis*, *Tulipifera liriodendron*, a collection of Loderi rhododendrons and a magnificent *Metasequoia glyptostroboides*.
▶ *Open for NGS, and by appointment*

CENTRAL ENGLAND

4 Rhodds Farm

This stylish and imaginatively planted garden makes good use of the undulating landscape to display its many features.

Lyonshall HR5 3LW | www.rhoddsfarm.co.uk

LOCATION 1 mile E of Kington off A44. Take small turning S just E of Penrhos Hotel

The topography and natural features of the farmland are crucial to the success of landscape designer Cary Goode's plans for her own garden, with splendid views along the hills of the Marches. When work started, the site was prepared with new topsoil and the level of the ground raised around the house to create a box-hedged lawn and a sunny gravel garden with a water sculpture. Beside a new wavy-topped yew hedge on the front façade are parterres of irises and alchemilla, with a carpet of geraniums and lambs' ears spreading under dwarf box balls.

Pear trees line the path leading to a dovecote built of brick in traditional style to echo that of the converted barn, and an apple walk sparkles in spring with naturalised tulips and narcissi. There are also hot perennial borders blazing out in high summer in shades of red, orange, purple and white; a further border is planted with unusual varieties of shrubs, roses and herbaceous perennials.

Evergreen pines are used imaginatively, associated at one corner of the garden with hippophae and an exochorda, and elsewhere a boardwalk runs alongside a duck pond where mallards make inroads into ligularias, gunneras and *Helenium* 'Lemon Queen'.

Behind the house the land rises steeply, topped by mature oaks and planted with viburnums, roses and hydrangeas, with *Symphytum caucasium* adding a springtime injection of electric blue.
▶ *Open for NGS, and for parties by appointment*

5 Hergest Croft Gardens

A steep-sided valley reminiscent of a Himalayan hillside is surrounded by a superb collection of trees and shrubs.

Kington HR5 3EG | Tel: 01544 230160

www.hergest.co.uk

Historic Garden Grade II*

LOCATION 14 miles W of Leominster, ½ mile W of Kington off A44

The 50 acres of gardens and woodland, owned by three generations of a plant-collecting family, were laid out originally over a century ago, with the writings of Arts and Crafts advocate William Robinson influencing the design. Around the house is a collection of large, beautiful and often rare trees, including 20 champions. Exotic trees and shrubs were later added to the collection, and recent introductions include the Chinese plants in the maple grove.

From the house a sycamore walk leads via borders of early summer peonies to the maple grove and azalea garden, where rhododendrons, azaleas and hydrangeas in variety are underplanted with primulas, hellebores, foxgloves, ferns and meconopsis. A boundary path planted with colchicums in long grass runs outside a formal yew-hedged croquet lawn to a shrub border featuring unusual varieties of viburnums, deutzias and philadelphus of a size seldom seen (all clearly labelled with names and planting dates). On the other side a large rockery combining ferns, bulbs, trilliums and martagon lilies leads to a collection of exotic maples and a lily pond.

Past the orchard is a meticulously tended kitchen garden with wide double herbaceous borders and extensive rose beds alongside the vegetables. Further from the house, parkland to the south and west stretches out to meet the countryside. From here it is a10 minute walk to Park Wood, perhaps the greatest of Hergest's many treasures, where on the steep, moist, enclosed valley sides species of camellias, magnolias and rhododendrons grow in such profusion that the scene is truly Himalayan.
▶ *Open main season – telephone or consult website for details*

6 Westonbury Mill Water Gardens

Moisture-loving plants flourish in and around a network of streams and ponds, while follies add an element of surprise.

Pembridge HR6 9HZ | Tel: 01544 388650

www.westonburymillwatergardens.com

LOCATION Off A44 between Leominster and Kington. From Pembridge take Kington road for 1½ miles; garden is signed on left

Water tumbling, spouting and gently flowing is the soundtrack in this 3½ acre garden carved out of an overgrown water meadow in the late 1990s. The owner dug out the mill leat, excavated a large pond and created a series of boggy areas, channels and cuts, all fed from the brook that forms the northern boundary of the garden. He then embarked on an ambitious programme of planting, initially of water plants, which now form swathes of lush foliage and flowers from early spring to autumn. More recently he has extended the interest with a sloping bed of prairie-style perennials and grasses and two glades of mixed trees and shrubs in a wild-flower meadow at the bottom of the garden.

The whole place is criss-crossed by paths leading to a series of dells and walkways screened in high summer by trees, shrubs and towering stands of *Filipendula camtschatica*, *Rodgersia podophylla*, *Gunnera manicata* and other attention-grabbers, while mounds and banks formed from the excavated soil provide views to the meadows and hills beyond.

This is a tranquil, relaxed garden where self-seeded species are welcome. It is also a highly individual one where the owner's love of quirky constructions has resulted in a stone tower, home to a flock of white doves and embellished with gargoyles that spew water down onto unsuspecting passers-by, a Yemen-inspired thatched open hut and a domed fern grotto made from wine bottles that glow in the sun like cathedral windows.

▶ *Open main season – telephone or consult website for details*

7 Stockton Bury

An impressive range of species thrive in this garden, including several rare varieties of philadelphus, many orchids and peonies.

Kimbolton, Leominster HR6 0HB

Tel: 01568 613432 | www.stocktonbury.co.uk

LOCATION 1 mile NE of Leominster. From A49, turn right onto A4112 Kimbolton road

Thoughtfully laid out over a 4 acre site divided by stone-and-brick walls and yew hedges, this garden is a feast for the plant-lover's eye. In a virtuoso display, a variety of climbing and herbaceous clematis are grown through and under shrubs among an array of herbaceous plants of myriad shapes and colours. *Iris sibirica* surround the Dingle among hostas and primulas, producing clashes of orange, red and purple, and water lilies and zantedeschias are equally splendid.

There are orchids and martagons in profusion, peonies and tree peonies, deutzias, viburnums and lilacs, and several unusual varieties of philadelphus flowering alongside the beautiful *P.* 'Belle Etoile'. A charming rock garden planted with a choisya and daphnes provides a shaded seating area.

Other unusual features are the large medieval dovecote, left unoccupied so that the construction of the nesting boxes can be viewed from the inside – after negotiating the Lilliputian door – an apiary featuring traditional bee skeps and a subterranean hot tub that is positively Roman in feel. The lawns are weed-free and perfectly edged. Many unusual plants, including trilliums, are for sale and reasonably priced.

▶ *Open main season – telephone for details*

8 Brockhampton Cottage

Colour plays an vital part here, with a palette of colours specially chosen to complement the dusky-pink house.

Brockhampton, near Hereford HR1 4TQ

Tel: 01989 740386

LOCATION 8 miles SE of Hereford, 5 miles N of Ross-on-Wye off B4224. In Brockhampton take road signed to Brockhampton Church, continue up hill for ½ mile; after set of farm buildings driveway is on left over cattle grid

In this 3 acre garden, created since 2000, the founders of internet nursery Crocus have worked with garden designer Tom Stuart-Smith to anchor the plantings with dexterity within a stunning landscape. The strong but restricted planting palette of pinks – using such stalwarts as echinaceas, persicarias and dark-leaved sedums – blends well with the dusky-pink stone house, while a wide variety of grasses echo the crop plantings in the surrounding fields. Among the many eye-catching plants are dwarf narcissi, *Anemone nemorosa* 'Robinsoniana', black-flowered tulips and scillas for spring, perlargoniums in pots for summer scent.

On the west side eight topiaried beech trees stand sentinel between the raised Yorkstone terrace and the perry pear orchard below. On the main garden front the slope is cleverly dealt with by means of a series of shallow, stone-edged grass terraces flanked by a pair of generous herbaceous borders that give way to others sweeping outwards towards the view.

Beyond the garden, wild-flower meadows drop to a large serpentine lake fringed by gunneras, *Iris sibirica* and many bulbs (a swathe of land was scooped out to make the lake visible from the house) and a young arboretum planted largely with American species in a gesture of ancestral respect. Then the rolling panorama of woods and fields takes over.

▶ *Open for parties by appointment*

LOWER HOPTON FARM

9 Hampton Court Gardens

Magnificent gardens surround a medieval castle, and can be admired from a Gothic tower at the heart of a thousand yew maze.

Near Hope under Dinmore, Leominster HR6 0PN

Tel: 01568 797777

www.hamptoncourt.org.uk

LOCATION 5 miles S of Leominster, on A417 near junction with A49 between Leominster and Hereford

This garden's future is now guaranteed by the opening of the 15th-century Grade I-listed castle for tours and special events. Created in 1996 from a suitably grand plan, the garden has been laid out mainly in a pattern of squares and rectangles, in a style in keeping with the original building. Original Victorian brick walls separate the different parts of the garden, two of which are subdivided by substantial constructions – oak pergolas, woven birch and hazel supports, and railway sleepers defining parterre flower beds, borders and vegetable gardens.

In the main garden large herbaceous borders are loosely planted to soften the fairly strict plan, with the liberal use of big perennials like *Campanula lactiflora*, bronze fennel, echinops, delphiniums, macleayas, foxgloves and cardoons, and a backing of climbers and shrubs including *Sambucus nigra*, carpenteria and *Cotinus coggygria*. In the parterres alliums precede and then enhance the flowers of low-growing shrub roses. A decorative potager produces fruit, herbs and vegetables for use in the café, which is located in the Joseph Paxton conservatory.

Water is the one essential element. In the main garden a striking picture is made by canals and water steps dominated by twin pavilions, joined by pools of running water from (and returned to) the River Lugg. A further water feature lies in an enclosed garden with a stone summerhouse. Then, at the furthest extent of the garden (outside the rectilinear plan), is a naturalistic water garden with a waterfall and a hermitage. Finally, it is well worth negotiating the yew maze to reach the Gothic tower at its heart, at the top of which visitors can view the jigsaw below.

▶ *Telephone for details of opening times and prices*

10 Lower Hope

The garden has many points of interest, such as a white garden, woodland bog and glasshouse brimming with exotic species.

Ullingswick, Hereford HR1 3JF

Tel: 01432 820557

LOCATION 7 miles NE of Hereford. At roundabout on A465 near Burley Gate take A417 towards Leominster. After 2 miles turn right, signed to Pencombe and Lower Hope. Signposted

Visitors to this colourful and immaculately maintained 8 acre garden will marvel at its many features, including a woodland stream and bog gardens, a semi-circular lime walk and a small lake surrounded by wild flowers and young trees.

From the entrance a white garden leads away from a shady tree-fern stumpery opening onto lawns and colourfully planted island beds. Near-life-size sculptures of children are placed beside a pond overhung with Japanese maples of striking colour and texture. The woodland bog and water gardens boast impressive gunneras and swathes of candelabra primulas, and a laburnum walk in the wood near the old tennis court is equally magnificent in early summer.

Nearer the house a formal Mediterranean pool is convincing in style with its fountain, palms and quiet seclusion. Bananas, palms, melons, orchids and other exotic plants flourish in a fine glasshouse fronted by an enclosed garden of English roses and lavenders and a herb and vegetable garden. Prize-winning pedigree Hereford cattle and Suffolk sheep graze in the surrounding farmland.
▶ *Open for NGS, one day in August – telephone for details – and for parties by appointment*

11 Lower Hopton Farm

An Italianate design frames a wealth of hidden gardens and ornamental plantings, including a fine collection of peonies.

Stoke Lacy, Bromyard HR7 4HX

Tel: 01885 490294

LOCATION 10 miles NE of Hereford off A465 Bromyard-Hereford road

This is a gardener's garden in every sense. Created from a 5 acre field, the formal Italianate garden reflects the classic horticultural training of the owner. Since 1992 she has added a maze of secret places – an enclosure of topiary animals, a tangle of small, exquisite woodland areas planted with magnolias and shrub roses, and an impressive collection of peonies and tree peonies of rare colour and variety.

There are English borders, arbours dripping with laburnum, robinia, white wisteria and 'Debutante' roses, while trilliums, hellebores, smilacinas and other shade-lovers thrive on their moated island. Rare plants abound – more than 100 named cultivars of snowdrops, and species of roses, magnolias and other unusual shrubs, such as *Viburnum acerifolium* and the chestnut rose, *R. roxburghii*.

The canopy of some of the larger trees is being lifted and the smaller ones pruned to bring more transparency to the garden. A view across the lawn of a red Chinese bridge adds to these delights, and from the summerhouse the eye is led up the stream to a quiet copse where *Cardiocrinum giganteum* make a superb display each year.
▶ *Open for individuals and parties of 20 or more by written appointment*

12 The Picton Garden

A vibrant display of late-season perennials takes centre stage in this garden, with nearly 400 varieties of aster on show.

Old Court Nurseries, Colwall, Great Malvern WR13 6QE

Tel: 01684 540416

www.autumnasters.co.uk

LOCATION 3 miles SW of Great Malvern on B4218

The impressive plantsman's 1½ acre garden has developed as a setting for a display of asters (nearly 400 varieties) and other late-summer perennials. It owes much to the naturalistic prairie style of planting, mingling the great swathes of Michaelmas daisies with rudbeckias and echinaceas, heleniums and helianthus, together with seedheads of spent flowers and towering stands of bamboos. Trees and shrubs – including cornus, acers, hydrangeas and liquidambars – have been added to provide autumn interest and a new shrub bed was planted in 2006. Raised beds are surrounded by dry-stone walls, making an interesting feature.

The history of the garden goes back to 1906, when the original owner began selling asters, many of his own breeding, at Old Court Nurseries. His breeding programme has continued to the present day and the garden now boasts a National Collection.
▶ *Open limited season – telephone or consult website for details. Nurseries open main season*

CENTRAL ENGLAND

LEICESTERSHIRE

In a county renowned for its great estates, Leicestershire's gardens have a delightfully personal feel. Whether intimate or grand, the gardens' planting reflects the ideas and individuality of their creators.

1 Long Close

Hidden behind a high wall is a remarkable garden, its rhododendron-lined terraces reminiscent of a Cornish valley scene.

Main Street, Woodhouse Eaves, Loughborough LE12 8RZ | Tel: 01509 890376

www.longclose.org.uk

LOCATION 5 miles S of Loughborough between A6 and M1 junctions 22 and 23

This true plantsman's garden is approached without fanfare through a yard off the main street. Rounding the house there's a surprise – 20 acres with vistas stretching far into the distance over terraced lawns flanked by mature rhododendrons, azaleas, magnolias and tall specimen trees and evergreens. The formal terraces lead on to informal gardens coloured in spring by drifts of snowdrops, daffodils and bluebells and in summer by prolifically planted herbaceous borders, and paths wind towards pools and water gardens.

Now reaching maturity, the garden has been developed throughout the 20th century. The present owners have taken every advantage of the lime-free loam to grow plants not usually seen in this part of the world.

▶ *Open main season – telephone or consult website for details – for NGS, and for parties by appointment*

2 Goadby Hall

A line of ornamental lakes dating back to the 18th century makes an arresting backdrop in this beautifully planted garden.

Goadby Marwood, Melton Mowbray LE14 4LN

Tel: 01664 464202

LOCATION 4 miles NE of Melton Mowbray between A606 and A607

The approach to this 6 acre garden is at the head of a string of five ornamental lakes extending to over a mile. These have been dredged and restored to the beauty the Duke of Buckingham must have imagined when he created them in the 18th century. Surrounding the handsome manor house is a variety of separate gardens planted substantially in creams and greens and variegated plants to offset the dominance of the ironstone buildings and walls, with many varieties of daffodils and tulips for spring colour. A children's garden leads to the croquet lawn, then past the church to the secret rose and walled gardens. There is also a potager and stable garden, and a small orchard.

▶ *Open by appointment*

3 Belvoir Castle

On a hilltop overlooking the Vale of Belvoir, gardens are laid out in Italian-style terraces divided into smaller compartments.

Belvoir, Grantham NG32 1PD | Tel: 01476 871002

www.belvoircastle.com

Historic Garden Grade II

LOCATION 10 miles NE of Melton Mowbray off A607 by Belvoir. Signposted

The mock-Gothic castle straddling an isolated hill at the edge of the Vale of Belvoir occupies a natural belvedere, and its gardens are a fine foil for the drama of the site. On her return from the Grand Tour in 1819, the Duchess of Rutland redesigned the garden in the Renaissance manner. In the mid 19th century the terraces were planted and divided into smaller enclosures by topiary and hedging. During the 1870s spring bedding was introduced. Now various areas are devoted to roses and peonies, and snowdrops and daylilies are naturalised.

In the early 20th century yew hedges were laid around two sides of the garden and the rose garden was made. Some of the statues by Danish sculptor Caius Cibber that lined a curving terrace path are now in the Statue Garden. The private woodland garden, known as the Spring Garden, was laid out in 1810. It is set in a natural amphitheatre and contains statuary and a recently restored hexagonal root house dating from 1841.

The present Duchess is re-creating the brilliant colours of Victorian bedding with a tapestry of carefully chosen camellias, rhododenrons and azaleas, and the Duke has planted an avenue of *Quercus ruber* to reinforce the autumn colour.

▶ *Castle open; garden open main season – telephone or consult website for details. Spring Garden open all year for pre-booked parties*

4 Beeby Manor

A series of charming garden rooms have been designed for variety and interest, with tubs of tulips providing colour on the terrace.

Beeby LE7 3BL │ Tel: 01162 595238

LOCATION 5 miles E of Leicester. Turn off A47 in Thurnby and follow signs through Scraptoft

The atmospheric 4 acre garden runs uphill from the house to a series of lived-in outdoor rooms. The terrace near the house is laden with planters, with purple tulips in tubs producing a vibrant display in late April and *Rosa banksiae* going mad on the wall behind. Different species of narcissus also abound.

To the west of the front lawn a doorway beckons the visitor into a great hall of old clipped yew hedges with a formal lily pond in the centre. The exit leads to a modern sculpture in a bay of its own with a swimming-pool garden on one side and a wild garden on the other, and an arboretum beyond. A long and wide herbaceous border marks the return to the house.

▶ *Open by appointment*

5 Orchards

This idiosyncratic garden has an intriguing planting scheme – only species with plain green leaves have been selected.

Hall Lane, Walton, Lutterworth LE17 5RP

Tel: 01455 556958

LOCATION 4 miles E of M1 junction 20. From Lutterworth follow signs to Kimcote and Walton

This is an unusual garden, which is very much the personal creation of its owner. Vistas have been created throughout, and at one point the garden peers out over the surrounding countryside. There are a number of distinct areas, bounded by hornbeam hedges or upright shrubs such as hazel, some cool and green, others bright with flowers chosen to emphasise the passage of the seasons. Trees, shrubs and climbers are shaped to underline their natural form and this gives the garden a sculptural quality.

All the leaves are green – no variegated, gold or purple foliage here. Though not primarily a plantsman's garden, there are many interesting and unusual plants. Other features include an old orchard, an impressive wisteria draped over a large pergola, a circular reflective pool and a number of carvings and slate paving patterns.

▶ *Open for NGS, and by appointment*

CENTRAL ENGLAND

Playing with water

The play of light on a pool, the splashing of a rill or the thunder of a cascade – water provides both tranquillity and drama.

Water is a crucial element of every great garden, from the ancient gardens of Persia, Japan and China to those of the present day. How water is used is dictated in part by fashion but also by climate and landscape. In the medieval Moorish courtyards of the Alhambra and the Generalife in Granada in Spain, for instance, the sound of water is cooling. Likewise the water jumping down from watering can to watering can in the contemporary garden of Les Jardins des Paradis in Cordes in southwest France.

The needs of Britain's more northerly gardens are different. The still surface of the rectangular canal at Bodnant in North Wales reflects the 18th-century Pin Mill at one end, while the

waters tumbling over the boulders of William Armstrong's magnificent rock garden at Cragside in Northumberland are a reminder of the 19th-century industrialist's power and influence.

Contours of the land

Garden designers follow the contours of our rolling landscape, so that artificiality appears natural. Standing on the terrace of Bowood in Wiltshire, it is hard to detect that the lake below, its edges smudged by mist, was the creation of 'Capability' Brown in the 18th century.

Moats, once defensive, have become decorative. The moat at Hindringham Hall in Norfolk, for instance, is now part of a peaceful

which was built by the French designer Grillet for the 4th Duke of Devonshire – took two years to build and is fed from a 9 acre reservoir. Water dances down the hill, the sound varied by 24 steps, each of a different shape or height.

Fountains became fashionable again in the 1800s. Chatsworth's Emperor Fountain was constructed by Joseph Paxton in 1844 for the 6th Duke, who anticipated a visit from Tsar Nicholas I of Russia – hence its name. The Tsar, alas, never came, but the fountain was built with a jet that shoots water more than 80m (260ft) into the air.

Italianate gardens

An enthusiasm for Italianate gardens, inspired partly by Queen Victoria and Prince Albert's work at Osborne House on the Isle of Wight, reached perhaps its apogee at Witley Court, now a ghostly ruin in Worcestershire. The centrepiece of the grandiose parterre is the monumental fountain of Perseus and Andromeda, which cost the equivalent of £1 million to build in 1860. Likened to the sound of an on-coming steam train, the fountain has 120 jets of water hidden away among shells, sea nymphs, dolphins and a monstrous serpent. Restored by English Heritage in 2003, it is now fired daily between April and October.

The Italian style took a more tranquil turn at Buscot Park in Oxfordshire where, in 1904, Harold Peto created a series of canals and falls to take water down from the Neo-classical house to a lake. At Coleton Fishacre, an Arts and Crafts house built in the 1920s, a rill garden drops down the steep Devon hillside in gentle stages, flanked by tender exotics that flourish in the warm, damp climate.

One of the last works by garden designer Sir Geoffrey Jellicoe was the 1970s rill at Shute House in Dorset. Flanking landscape changes from formal to wild as the rill descends through the garden, passing through a series of atmospheric rooms before arriving at the beautiful Kashmiri bubble fountains.

Few gardens are grander – or indeed more costly – than the 21st-century garden at Alnwick, the vision of the current Duchess of Northumberland. Its Grand Cascade is built into earth banks that the Duchess discovered by chance while playing with her children. Computer-operated (unlike Chatsworth's Cascade, which is still turned on and off by hand), 33,000 litres (7,260 gallons) of water fall down every minute over a series of 21 weirs. Extra aquatic displays take place on the hour and half hour, splashing the unsuspecting on the terraces to the delighted squeals of visiting children. The desire to impress lives on.

scene, the manor house reflected in water that would formerly have protected it from assault. Far from being defensive in design, the extensive waterworks in the major 18th-century landscape parks – such as Stowe, Stourhead, Painshill and Blenheim – while apparently naturalistic, are in fact a testament to the wealth and influence of their aristocratic creators, who submerged villages, dammed streams and moved hills to form majestic lakes that snake out of view, connecting parkland with surrounding landscape.

Studley Royal Water Garden in Yorkshire is now part of a World Heritage Site. A Georgian masterpiece adorned with Classical statues and follies, this magical composition of canals, ponds, cascades, lawns and hedges was designed by John Aislabie between 1718 and 1742, and is one of the few formal early 18th-century landscape gardens to have survived in its original form.

Nothing impresses, however, like water falling from a great height, as it does down Chatsworth's Cascade, first completed in 1696. The Cascade –

LINCOLNSHIRE

Many fine English country gardens are located in this county, their walled expanses brimming with colourful herbaceous borders and set against the backdrop of the rolling Lincolnshire Wolds.

1 Aubourn Hall

Sweeping lawns, ponds and a woodland dell create a sense of space and tranquillity around the 17th-century manor.

Aubourn, Lincoln LN5 9DZ | Tel: 01522 788224

LOCATION 7 miles SW of Lincoln between A46 and A607

The 10 acres of gardens surrounding the fine red-brick hall include spacious undulating lawns and borders that sweep through rose arches or along grassy swathes to further lawns and gardens.

The diverse borders are carefully planted for maximum effect. There are also secluded areas in which to linger, including a formal rose garden with its central tiered copper planter, an area called the Golden Triangle edged with yew and planted with ornamental crab apple trees and spring bulbs, ponds and a woodland dell. A pool is surrounded by a pergola covered in roses and clematis, and a grass maze is a new attraction.

▶ *Open for NGS and charity, and for parties by appointment (tel: 07816 202353)*

2 Lincoln Contemporary Heritage Garden

The architecture of Lincoln Cathedral inspired the design of this garden, which has spectacular views over the Vale of Trent.

Medieval Bishops' Palace, Minster Yard, Lincoln LN2 1PU | Tel: 01522 527468

www.english-heritage.org.uk

English Heritage

LOCATION On S side of Lincoln Cathedral

An antique terrace, first recorded as a garden site in 1320, has been given a pure, uncluttered design. Deceptively simple, it makes clever allusion to the garden's history, linking it perfectly to the surrounding ruins and nearby cathedral.

Brick paths create a lattice pattern across a lawn, and fastigiate hornbeams have been planted within steel discs at the intersections. Like the ribs and bosses of Lincoln cathedral's vaulted ceilings, which inspired the design, the lattice succeeds in resolving the problem of asymmetry created by the irregular quadrilateral site. Clipped

lavender – a splendid sight in flower in summer – and the red 'Guinée' rose give localised colour. The garden may be enjoyed from seats set in yew niches, but the best views are from the East Hall terrace, where the full impact of what is in effect a contemporary knot garden can be appreciated.

▶ *Open all year – telephone or consult website for details*

3 Doddington Hall

Formal ornamental features lead to wilder stretches of the garden, one of which is renowned for its spring bulbs.

Doddington, Lincoln LN6 4RU

Tel: 01522 694308 | www.doddingtonhall.com

Historic Garden Grade II*

LOCATION 5 miles W of Lincoln on B1190

Grandeur and formality mix happily with relaxed plantings in this garden. Formality is represented by a gravel, box and lawn courtyard, with topiary unicorns from the family crest, beds of bearded irises, a yew *allée* and restored ha-ha, with an avenue of limes giving views to parkland beyond.

The wild gardens offer meandering walks through ancient trees, past a stream edged with flourishing *Lysichiton americanus*. From the Temple of the Winds, the landscape opens up.

Snowdrops and *Crocus tommasinianus* are followed by Lent lilies, fritillaries, cyclamen, narcissi and erythroniums, accompanied by rhododendrons.

In May and June there is a tapestry of colour in the walled garden. Box-edged parterres are filled with bearded irises and herbaceous borders are massed with towering echiums, syringas, peonies, alliums and phlox. The old walled kitchen garden, with an original pond and potting shed, has been restored. It includes many rare and heritage varieties of fruit and vegetables. Within the grounds is also a turf maze.

▶ *House open. Garden open most of year – telephone or consult website for details – and for parties by appointment*

4 Kexby House

While sympathetic to its Victorian heritage, more modern touches include colour-themed areas and a bog garden.

Kexby Lane, Kexby, Gainsborough DN21 5NE

Tel: 01427 788759

www.kexbyhousegardens.co.uk

LOCATION 12 miles NW of Lincoln, 6 miles E of Gainsborough on B1241, on outskirts of village

When care is lavished on a heavy clay soil for many years, the rewards are spectacular. The tall and bountiful plants growing in this 6 acre ▷

DODDINGTON HALL

garden – which does much to embellish the Victorian house – are testimony to this. By subdividing a large, decorative area with walls, pergola walks, hedges and paths, many intimate spaces have been created, with occasional long vistas through to the fields beyond.

Although the garden is Victorian in essence, there is an occasional nod in the direction of contemporary garden trends. Colour-themed areas include a gorgeous white garden and a hot border, a wild-flower meadow, perennial planting in swathes, screes, a bog garden and a carp pond.

What makes this garden special, however, is the informal planting of shrubs, herbaceous perennials and hundreds of roses in great deep borders in the English style, combined with the Italianate elegance of a long alley, lined with trees, sculptures, containers and box-edged paths and beds. The garden reaches its peak in midsummer, sandwiched between the flowering of thousands of spring bulbs and some splendid late-summer displays.

▶ *Open for NGS, and by appointment*

5 Hall Farm and Nursery

A plantsman's delight, six garden rooms – including a sunken garden and walled terrace – are filled with unusual perennials.

Harpswell, Gainsborough DN21 5UU

Tel: 01427 668412

www.hall-farm.co.uk

LOCATION 7 miles E of Gainsborough on A631

This 1½ acre garden combines the formal and informal in an imaginative way. The owners' delight in plants, satisfied by their adjoining nursery, is evident everywhere. There are hundreds of varieties of unusual herbaceous plants, roses and shrubs.

A rose pergola leads from a decorative paved terrace to the main area behind the farmhouse. Subdivided into six separate areas, each with at least two entry points, the whole becomes an intriguing maze of garden rooms linked by border-edged paths and pergolas. These areas include a walled top terrace, a formal double border walk, a sunken garden with seasonal planting, an orchard with a giant chessboard and a set of chessmen, and a newly restored wildlife pond and walkway. Here the borders have been planted with moisture-loving plants and grasses, providing a peaceful contrast to the other colourful flower-filled areas.

▶ *Open all year – telephone or consult website for details – and by appointment*

6 Normanby Hall

The Victorian kitchen garden has a potting shed, bothy and fern house, as well as a vinery displaying sub-tropical plants.

Normanby, Scunthorpe DN15 9HU

Tel: 01724 720588

www.northlincs.gov.uk/normanby

LOCATION 4 miles N of Scunthorpe on B1430

Built in the early 19th century, the house is set in 300 acres of historic parkland and mature gardens. Some fine mature trees survive, including a grand old holm oak, and avenues of copper beech and Wellingtonia. There are also stream walks, a bog garden, a Christmas garden, a newly planted woodland garden and a deer park. A Victorian woodland garden has been planted with Japanese maples, camellias and azaleas, and acid-loving woodland perennials such as the Himalayan blue poppy. The formal area south of the hall includes a 'boar's head' parterre and a sunken garden with a rectangular pond surrounded by herbaceous borders.

Farther away are two gardens enclosed by tall old walls and holly and conifer hedges. The first has good wall shrubs and climbers, and includes double herbaceous borders with colours progressing from hot to cool along its length. The second is a lavish reconstruction of the original Victorian kitchen garden, complete with a potting shed, bothy, vinery with a bed of sub-tropical plants, fern house and a display house. Fruit trees are trained against the walls and over arches, and those in the south-facing peach cases are under glass. There are decorative borders and four box-edged plots filled with organically grown fruit and vegetable varieties of the period.

▶ *Open main season – telephone or consult website for details – park open all year*

7 Elsham Hall

This imaginative garden combines art and nature with a sensory garden in a geometric design and a children's nursery garden.

Elsham, Brigg DN20 0QZ | Tel: 01652 688698

www.elshamhall.co.uk

LOCATION 2 miles from M180 junction 5/A180 interchange at Barnetby Top

This 4 acre walled garden is an exciting and stimulating space. From the medieval-influenced viewing mound, the visitor takes in a panorama that includes the One World Garden, where the planting is themed to represent the different continents. There is also a sensory garden, where salvias, lavenders and santolinas reflect the combination of geometrical angles and gyrations with which it is landscaped, and the imaginative Nursery Garden offers a combination of plants and animals to delight the young.

Modern aviaries, areas of grass and wild flowers and avenues of apple trees and hornbeams combine with boxed beech plantings to create a firm contemporary structure. There is also a lake, carp pond, arboretum and woodland walks.

▶ *Open main season – telephone or consult website for details – and by appointment*

8 The Old Rectory, Somerby

A real treat for hosta lovers, the garden boasts a vast range of American hybrids, two National Collections and a hosta walk.

Somerby, near Brigg DN38 6EX

Tel: 01652 628268 │ www.hostas.co.uk

LOCATION 4 miles E of Brigg off A1084

The preference in this 2½ acre garden is for shrubs and herbaceous plants with form and stature. Specimens are permitted space to develop in the borders that edge the sweeping lawns. The exotic hot border has excellent rheums and *Lobelia tupa*. There is also a well-planted pergola, raised display beds and a formal fish pond.

Hostas are a particular passion, displayed in a hosta walk, a large collection of unusual American hybrids (including National Collections of 'Mildred Seaver' and 'Lachman' hybrids), and the adjoining specialist nursery.

▶ *Open main season – telephone or consult website for details – and for parties by appointment*

9 Gunby Hall

These fine grounds – with extensive walled gardens, a wild-flower walk and classic borders – inspired a poem by Lord Tennyson.

Gunby, Spilsby PE23 5SS │ Tel: 07970 758876

www.gunbyhall.ic24.net

Historic Park and Garden Grade II/ The National Trust

LOCATION 7 miles NW of Skegness, 2½ miles NW of Burgh-le-Marsh on S of A158

This garden was described by Lord Alfred Tennyson as 'a haunt of ancient peace' in his poem *The Palace of Art*. The charming William

and Mary house, its walls smothered in fine plants, sits in 1,500 acres of parkland with avenues of lime and horse chestnut. The shrub borders, wild garden, lawns with old cedars and restrained formal front garden of nepeta and lavender beds backed by clipped yew provide a startling contrast to the main attraction of Gunby – its 8½ acres of walled gardens.

The pergola garden with an apple tree walkway has a maze of paths leading to beds of old roses, a herb garden and brimming herbaceous and annual borders. The second walled enclosure houses a kitchen garden reached after passing more borders of perfectly arranged herbaceous plants and hybrid musk roses. Backing onto its wall is another classic herbaceous border and, beyond that, an early 19th-century long fish pond flanked by the Ghost Walk, made eerie during autumn mists by the looming Irish junipers punctuating its length. There's also a wild-flower walk. Spring bulbs are at their best in April and May, roses in June and the herbaceous borders reach their peak from July to September.

▶ *House open. Garden open main season – telephone or consult website for details – and for NGS. Also open by written appointment to Mrs Claire Ayres*

10 The Old Rectory, East Keal

A fine example of an English country garden, this small site is packed with plants in its rambling beds, borders and rockeries.

Church Lane, East Keal, Spilsby PE23 4AT

Tel: 01790 752477

LOCATION 12 miles W of Skegness, 2 miles SW of Spilsby on A16

With its orchard, vegetable garden and lively planting, this is for many the perfect English country garden. Within the 1 acre site, 1,500 species and varieties tumble and jostle for space in and on the old walls, beds, borders, rockeries and ponds. Although the planting looks relaxed and informal, each part of the garden has been carefully planned to provide different habitats and ensure year-round interest.

Nestled on a hillside, the garden is criss-crossed by steps and paths passing through the different areas to seats positioned for peaceful contemplation or for views of the rolling Wolds. The conversion of a swimming pool into a pond and bog garden with a rose-laden pergola on one side has created an exotic new enclosure, and a dry garden has replaced part of the drive.

▶ *Open for NGS and other charities, and by appointment*

CENTRAL ENGLAND

HARRINGTON HALL

11 Harrington Hall

Grand lawns, raised red-brick terraces, colourful borders and a working kitchen garden surround the part-Tudor hall.

Harrington, Spilsby PE23 4NH

Tel: 01790 754570 (Gardener)

www.harringtonhallgardens.co.uk

Historic Garden Grade II

LOCATION 5 miles E of Horncastle, 2 miles N of A158

Idyllically sited in the Wolds, the red brick of the Tudor and 17th-century hall walled gardens and raised terraces provide the perfect backdrop for a variety of wall shrubs, climbers and colour-themed mixed and herbaceous borders set off by fine lawns. Referred to in Tennyson's *Maud*, it is hard to imagine that these romantic gardens and walks have ever changed, although they were replanted during the 1950s following wartime vegetable cultivation.

The 1 acre kitchen garden east of the house is a much more recent restoration. Formal in design and subdivided by a variety of hedges and paths,

it is a combination of the functional and purely decorative, featuring trained fruit trees, borders and a raised sitting area with a pond. Ornamental native trees link the formal pleasure gardens to the parkland beyond.

▶ *Open for NGS, other charities and by appointment*

12 Burghley House

Several centuries of horticultural fashion are on display here, with a Garden of Surprises adding contemporary appeal.

Stamford PE9 3JY │ Tel: 01780 752451

www.burghley.co.uk

LOCATION ½ mile E of Stamford on Barnack road, close to A1. Signposted

The Elizabethan house has survived the centuries intact. The park and gardens, however, were reinvented by each generation according to the horticultural fashion of the period, including a Baroque garden designed by George London in the 17th century and a 'Capability' Brown landscape with a superb bridge and serpentine lake. Several acres of garden were reclaimed from Brown's lost lower gardens in 1994 and turned into a sculpture garden that includes a permanent collection of more than 20 works.

A distinctive, contemporary statement has been added by designer George Carter in the 1 acre Garden of Surprises, which features a succession of enclosed garden rooms, buildings and vistas. He has drawn on watery jokes beloved of 16th and 17th-century European designers and given them a modern twist, including an artificial rain tree, jets, water 'furniture', a long black-lined rill and curtain-like fountains of water.

Topiary and sculpture, other Elizabethan hallmarks, are represented here by a maze, a parterre and bosquets, and clipped hedges of box yew, phillyrea and hornbeam. There are also busts of Roman emperors, mirrors and obelisks.
▶ *House open. Gardens and parkland open all year. Garden of Surprises open main season. South Garden open for spring bulbs – telephone or consult website for details*

13 Grimsthorpe Castle

Elegant flower and topiary gardens provide a foil for an ornamental kitchen garden that leads to tranquil woodland areas.

Grimsthorpe, near Bourne PE10 0LY

Tel: 01778 591205

www.grimsthorpe.co.uk

Historic Garden Grade I

LOCATION 4 miles NW of Bourne on A151 Colsterworth-Bourne road

The pleasure grounds that surround the castle on three sides display the formality demanded by a grand house with a pedigree stretching from the Middle Ages to the Age of Enlightenment. Some 17th-century traces remain in the parkland and deer park. Renowned architect Sir John Vanbrugh designed the north front and its dramatic courtyard in 1715 and 'Capability' Brown was called in to advise on the principal gardens in 1771.

Sweeping lawns, ornamental ponds, yew hedges, tightly clipped topiary, long herbaceous borders framing views across the lake and a formal rose parterre complete a picture of elegance. The formal gardens give way to a woodland garden and an unusual ornamental kitchen garden and orchard designed in the 1960s, before merging into the vast park. The gardens extend to 27 acres.
▶ *House open. Park and garden open main season – telephone or consult website for details*

14 Easton Walled Gardens

These 'lost' gardens have been restored to their former glory, with an acre of roses, seasonal meadow plantings and a turf maze.

Easton, Grantham NG33 5AP | Tel: 01476 530063

www.eastonwalledgardens.co.uk

LOCATION 7 miles S of Grantham, 1 mile E of A1 off B6403 N of Colsterworth

Abandoned in 1951 after the dismantling of the manor house, the revival of this 12 acre garden's fortunes began in 2002. As well as re-establishing the stonework, restoring the terraces and glasshouses and reclaiming the yew hedges – now a wonderful tunnel – the plantings have been enhanced by adding a 'pickery', a cottage garden, a turf maze, borders, walks and spring and summer meadows. Snowdrops, daffodils, sweet peas, irises and an acre of roses from renowned breeder David Austin are some of the highlights among the ever-changing display of bulbs, annuals, herbaceous perennials and vegetables.
▶ *Open for snowdrops. Main season – telephone or consult website for details – and for NGS*

15 Belton House

Stately grounds include formal Italian and Dutch gardens, a canal, lakeside walks and a richly planted orangery.

Belton, Grantham NG32 2LS

Tel: 01476 566116 | www.nationaltrust.org.uk

Historic Garden Grade I/The National Trust

LOCATION 3 miles N of Grantham off A607

The 33 acres of gardens are composed with perfect harmony and proportion. The extensive woodland has two lakes, a small canal and noble cedars, and a maze re-created from the 1890 original. The radiating avenues introduce drama into the landscape.

However, it is the formal area to the north of the house, beyond which the east avenue rises to the distant Bellmount Tower, that makes a visit memorable. The 1870s Dutch garden is a attractive composition with pillars of green yew and cushions of golden yew, pale gravel, formal beds cleverly planted and edged with lavender, and generously filled urns. The earlier sunken Italian garden has a large central pond with a fountain and, the high point, a restored and replanted orangery.
▶ *House open. Gardens open all year – telephone or consult website for details*

CENTRAL ENGLAND

NORTHAMPTONSHIRE

A farming county that is renowned for its 'squires and spires', Northamptonshire's gardens range from aristocratic deer parks and formal estates to beautifully planned and planted country gardens.

1 The Menagerie

A rococo folly provides a focal point in this surprising garden, which has hornbeam *allées*, a lion fountain and a shell grotto.

Newport Pagnell Road, Horton NN7 2BX
Tel: 01604 870957 (Administrator)
www.themenageriehorton.co.uk
Historic Park Grade II
LOCATION 6 miles SE of Northampton, on B526 turn left 1 mile S of Horton into field

The demolition of Horton House in 1936 left only three follies remaining in what was once a magnificent Georgian estate. The Menagerie was the 2nd Earl of Halifax's private zoo, built in the 1750s. It was rescued from ruin and in the 1980s a 'Georgian' garden full of wit and classical allusion was added.

The present owners have embellished the maturing grounds with a 'walled garden within a garden' dripping with roses and fruit, where narrow box-edged beds filled with vegetables and cut flowers are dominated by heraldic lions and a magnificent leonine fountain. In the formal gardens there are many statues, carefully positioned for effect, and even the informal railway cutting at the entrance – which visitors cross like a dry moat – sports handsome obelisks punctuating the views.

The design radiates from the house – hornbeam *allées* terminate in two round, reflecting pools, and each pool is also the focal view for a 'folly within the folly'. One is a miniature Palladian building that now serves as a chapel, the other a thatched cottage *ornée* made from knobbly knuckles of wood.

The central *allée* is a green space flanked by lime trees, and a quirky mound planted with acaenas affords an elevated view back to the south façade of the house, smothered in climbers, bamboos, lush mixed shrubs and herbaceous perennials. Below ground lies a mysterious shell grotto.

▶ *Open for NGS, and by appointment*

A THATCHED COTTAGE ORNÉE IS MADE FROM KNOBBLY KNUCKLES OF WOOD
THE MENAGERIE

2 Steane Park

A traditionally planted formal garden evokes the past with medieval fish ponds, historic buildings and a miniature castle.

Brackley NN13 6DP | Tel: 01280 705899

LOCATION On A422 between Brackley and Banbury, 1 mile E of Farthinghoe

Approaching the garden on a summer day through an old-established meadow filled with wild flowers, the visitor gains a sense of Steane's ancient roots. The areas around the 17th-century house are traditionally gardened with a mixture of shrubs and herbaceous planting, and tea may be taken on the north side under a spreading copper beech. The 1620 chapel in the grounds is an elegant building, dripping with wisteria and climbing roses, and with colourful herbaceous beds ranged beneath its walls.

Beyond the formal areas lie several medieval fish ponds and a canal lovingly dredged and restored, with simple planting and paths guiding the way through the garden. The whole place is full of the sounds of water and birdsong. A blue Monet bridge leads to a moon gate framing a landing stage with a view back up the canal.

Across the water, a miniature castle gives an overview of the garden from the battlements. The path then moves on beneath willow pergolas, a hornbeam arbour and a living tunnel of hazel, cotoneaster and white wisteria to a patch of ground dotted with informal wood 'sculptures'. A mighty bust of Bucephalus keeps watch as the visitor leaves.

▶ *Open for NGS, and for parties of ten or more by appointment*

3 Coton Manor Garden

Some 10 acres comprise a series of smaller gardens, including a rose garden and bluebell wood, that provide year-round interest.

Guilsborough, Northampton NN6 8RQ

Tel: 01604 740219 | www.cotonmanor.co.uk

LOCATION 10 miles NW of Northampton, 11 miles SE of Rugby near Ravensthorpe Reservoir, signed from A428 and A5199

Blessed with a south-facing slope, an abundance of springs and streams, and a predominantly neutral soil, the present owners have transformed this into one of the finest garden in the East Midlands. Most visitors enter beside the pergola clothed with clematis and *Rosa* 'Madame Alfred

Carrière'. Nestling below is the herb garden, on the site of a large shed formerly used to house waterfowl, which now roam freely in the lower garden, along with hens and flamingos.

The view across the Goose Park has been opened up and leads to a 3 acre meadow, filled with a wide range of species giving colour from late spring to August. Alongside this is a spectacular bluebell wood, the perfume of which permeates the air in May.

The more formal area near the house contains a new rose garden, each of its quadrant beds filled with the same plants. The abundant terrace pots are softened by valerian billowing from every cranny and pavement crack.

Massed hellebores and snowdrops start the year in the woodland walk, and the theme of seasonal areas continues down to the autumnal meadow border. The restraint of the formal rill is in restful contrast to the exuberantly planted Mediterranean bank and the stream garden leading down to a new bog garden.

The whole canvas is divided into different areas, each with its own mood and atmosphere but flowing from one into the next. Although the planting is thoughtfully composed, nowhere is there a slavish adherence to themed colours and the standard of maintenance and attention to detail is impeccable.

▶ *Open main season – telephone or consult website for details*

4 Cottesbrooke Hall

Within the 18th-century landscaped parkland are a collection of fine cedars, elegant formal gardens and wild areas.

Cottesbrooke, Northampton NN6 8PF

Tel: 01604 505808

www.cottesbrookehall.co.uk

Historic Garden Grade II

LOCATION 10 miles N of Northampton between A5199 and A508

The imposing house was built in 1702 and is thought to have inspired Jane Austen's novel *Mansfield Park* but in the surrounding gardens only the magnificent cedars to the west of the house remain from that period. The garden on view today was created between 1910 and 1930 and is the work of many renowned landscape designers. Geoffrey Jellicoe designed the entrance court with great restraint, enhancing the distant view of Brixworth's Saxon church. Edward Schultz was called in, as was Sylvia Crowe in the 1970s (her neat summerhouse in the pool ▷

garden provides a spot for restful contemplation) and, latterly, James Alexander-Sinclair advised on the replanting of the double herbaceous borders.

The formal area is divided into a series of individual spaces. Brick Court has a restrained style, surrounding a huge pine cloaked in a climbing hydrangea, and opposite is a Dutch garden of boxed beds richly planted for autumn colour. A new venture is the knot garden, where box patterns are clearly defined against the pebble floor. Beyond, more box surrounds massed *Rosa* 'Penelope' in the Philosopher's Walk. Throughout the garden, sumptuous pots provide colourful displays in summer.

Across the drive is a relaxed and informal wild garden on the banks of a tributary of the River Nene. Majestic cedars and vistas throughout the 18th-century parkland are a constant reminder of the garden's historic landscape setting.

▶ *House and garden open main season – telephone or consult website for details – and by appointment*

5 Kelmarsh Hall

Pleasure grounds surrounding an 18th-century house include a formal terrace, triangular walled garden and a turf maze.

Kelmarsh, Northampton NN6 9LY

Tel: 01604 686543 | www.kelmarsh.com

LOCATION 11 miles N of Northampton on A508 near A14 junction 2

Architect James Gibbs' 1730s Palladian house was originally surrounded by a contemporary 54 acre landscape with the obligatory lake and vistas, but during the 20th century a more intimate 14 acre garden was created. Huge, bulgy box hedges entice the visitor towards a carefully placed seat giving views across an old-fashioned rose garden and meadows grazed by British White cattle. The old drying-ground is enclosed by ancient yews, rather like a screens passage in a Tudor house, and planted with rich herbaceous borders. Another long border in brighter hues for late summer is maturing after restoration work.

The triangular walled garden, planted anew with vegetables, fruit and cut flowers, includes ornamental elements such as a simple turf maze and beautifully restored central glasshouse. Pots of tulips on steps and by doorways are replaced later in the season by dahlias and glowing annuals. A shaded white garden is laid out in an elegant design, while a rural lakeside ramble will appeal to the naturalist.

▶ *House open. Garden open main season – telephone or consult website for details*

6 Rockingham Castle Gardens

Situated on a dramatic escarpment, the imaginative new design retains an ancient topiary walk and 19th-century rose garden.

Market Harborough LE16 8TH

Tel: 01536 770240

www.rockinghamcastle.com

Historic Garden Grade II*

LOCATION 2 miles N of Corby on A6003. Signposted

The castle commands a magnificent position on a scarp with views northwards and an arboretum on the slope below. The most memorable feature in the 18 acre gardens is the Elephant Wall – huge, recumbent yew pachyderms that are a happy result of neglect two centuries ago.

The Cross Garden is planted with roses and lavender, and more roses are massed in the central roundel of the New Garden, which is surrounded by castellated yew. Extensions to this area, the site of the original motte and bailey, include yew hedges that will be accompanied in time by shrubs and herbaceous plants in mixed borders.

▶ *Castle open. Garden open main season – telephone or consult website for details*

7 Lyveden New Bield

Once an elaborate water garden, grass terraces, intriguing spiral mounds and a network of canals and moats still remain.

Oundle PE8 5AT | Tel: 01832 205358

www.nationaltrust.org.uk

Historic Garden Grade II*/The National Trust

LOCATION 4 miles SW of Oundle via A427, 3 miles E of Brigstock off A6116

Set in front of the roofless ruin of an Elizabethan banqueting house – the New Bield – are the fascinating remnants of an ornate water garden with truncated pyramids and spiral mounds, surrounded by canals, moats and raised terraces.

The New Bield was conceived by Sir Thomas Tresham and linked to the original manor house by a formal garden – the wider landscape was his deer park. Cruciform in shape, with a frieze decorated with emblems of the Passion, it proclaimed his Catholic faith at a time of systematic religious persecution. Both the man and his buildings paid the price. He ended his days in prison and the New Bield is now a roofless shell.

In spring and summer apple blossom and wild flowers fill and perfume the orchard, which has been replanted with hundreds of old fruit tree varieties. In winter, the stark geometry of the garden makes it an altogether more mysterious and ghostly place.

▶ *Open all year – telephone or consult website for details*

8 Deene Park

A box-edged parterre is an architectural addition to the garden, with well planted borders leading to an arboretum and lake.

Corby NN17 3EW | Tel: 01780 450278/450223

www.deenepark.com

Historic Garden Grade II

LOCATION 6 miles N of Corby off A43 Kettering-Stamford road

The 17 acre gardens enhance the noble house – the home of the Earl of Cardigan, who led the Charge of the Light Brigade in 1854. Running the whole length of the building is a box-edged parterre designed by the late interiors and gardens specialist David Hicks. It is now mature and redolent of summer scents.

To the west of the house is a long grass terrace beginning and ending with an octagonal folly. The upper side is clothed with a mixed border planted against a high brick wall. The effect of this great stretch is broken by hornbeam hedges and a central round garden enclosing a large and richly planted font.

To the other side the land slopes down to a canal-shaped lake, dominated by trees. Beyond the formal garden an arboretum leads to a large lake that feeds two other lower-lying stretches of water, the lowest spanned by an elegant stone carriage bridge. The garden offers areas of interest through the seasons – from the snowdrop days of February to the tail end of summer.

▶ *House open. Garden open main season – telephone or consult website for details – and for parties by appointment*

9 The Old Rectory, Sudborough

A decorative potager and rose garden are contained within clipped hedges in this garden, which has fine and varied plantings.

Sudborough, Kettering NN14 3BX

Tel: 01832 733247

www.oldrectorygardens.co.uk

LOCATION 7 miles SE of Corby off A6116 Corby-Thrapston road, A14 junction 12

'Garden open by appointment. However, as you're here, please come and enjoy it.' So reads the notice on the gate at the entrance to this garden, dignified by clipped panels of osmanthus and jasmine against the churchyard wall. Once you reach the intimate courtyard leading to the back door, with its huge pots of *Polygala x dalmaisiana* and aromatic geraniums, the high standards of design and detailing become apparent.

The garden proper lies to the south of the house and opens onto a broad lawn leading to a pond teaming with fish, and a brook marking the garden's boundary. The lawn is embraced by generous mixed borders planted with an eye for colour. To the west is a rose garden and peony border, and to the east a spring garden and hellebore collection.

Here, too, is the potager, with brick paths separating productive beds and apples appearing in many guises – hanging from step cordons and arches, trained into globes. Every possible attention is paid to detail (even the wall-trained peaches wear glass 'hats' to prevent leaf curl).

The neighbouring stable courtyard is richly planted in shades of peach and lemon, and near the house there is a hot, dry area for late colour with daphnes thriving in the cool shade beyond. Everywhere in the 2 acres the planting is held together by clipped box and holly, hebes and other formal elements.

▶ *Open main season – telephone or consult website for details – and by appointment*

IN SPRING AND SUMMER APPLE BLOSSOM AND WILD FLOWERS FILL AND PERFUME THE ORCHARD

LYVEDEN NEW BIELD

NOTTINGHAMSHIRE

The county has some unusual attractions, including one of England's most beautifully planted winter gardens and a contemplative Japanese garden complete with bridges, pagodas and ponds.

1 Felley Priory

Many rare and old-fashioned species thrive here and colourful herbaceous borders sweep down from the house.

Underwood NG16 5FJ

Tel: 01773 810230; 07763 189771

LOCATION 10 miles NW of Nottingham, ½ mile from M1 junction 27 off A608

The garden is full of rare delights, some of which are old-fashioned and many of them tender species. Grass banks step down to a large pond in the dip at the bottom and all around are fields.

The site feels open despite the original walls and interior dividing hedges planted to protect the house. The 2½ acre garden was established after 1976, with well planned colourful double herbaceous borders sweeping down from the house through stone-stepped terraces and between yew hedges. A deep border shelters a Jargonelle pear reputedly more than 400 years old, while an old mulberry is spectacular in fruit.

There are pergolas, knot gardens and tasteful topiary, a shrubbery that is almost a youthful arboretum, and a rose garden also planted with lavender and agapanthus. Spring brings an astonishing display of snowdrops, followed by hellebores and daffodils under orchard trees.
▶ *Garden and nursery open most of year – telephone for details – for NGS, and for parties by appointment*

2 Clumber Park

The park has Europe's longest double avenue of lime trees and the largest of all the glasshouses on National Trust properties.

Estate Office, Clumber Park, Worksop S80 3AZ

Tel: 01909 476592 | www.nationaltrust.org.uk

Historic Park and Garden Grade I/
The National Trust

LOCATION 4½ miles SE of Worksop off A1 and A57, 11 miles from M1 junction 30

The garden was largely the creation of the 9th Earl of Lincoln in the second half of the 18th century. He landscaped the 3,800 acre park, laid out the pleasure ground, serpentine walks and shrubberies, and commissioned two temples and a bridge for the mighty lake, which remain today. The Atlantic cedars and sweet chestnut trees in the pleasure ground are of breathtaking size.

Landscape designer William Sawrey Gilpin created an Italianate terrace to the south of the house during the 1820s and 1830s, laying out island beds and picturesque walks in the pleasure ground, and planting a 2 mile long lime avenue. The Lincoln Terrace was added in 1868. Also from the 19th century are the stable block and clock tower, and the ornate Gothic chapel built in the pleasure garden.

Since the demolition of the great house in 1938, the chapel has become the focus of the garden. The vinery and palm house have been restocked and the extensive glasshouses are the best and longest in the National Trust's portfolio.

The 4 acre walled kitchen garden contains a 110m (360ft) long double herbaceous border, now replanted using graduating colours, as well as cut-flower, fruit and vegetable and herb borders, a collection of regional (East Midlands) varieties of apple trees and a working Victorian apiary. During 2009 a soft fruit garden and a rose garden were planted.
▶ *Open all year – telephone or consult website for details*

3 Hodstock Priory

Masses of snowdrops, magenta cyclamen, golden aconites and hellebores make this garden a delight from December onwards.

Blyth, Worksop S81 0TY | Tel: 01909 591204

www.snowdrops.co.uk

LOCATION 5 miles NE of Worksop, 2 miles W of A1 at Blyth off B6045

This is one of the most beautiful winter gardens in England. Snowdrops, magenta cyclamen and golden aconites are everywhere, and there is an additional walk in the snowdrop wood from which to enjoy the astonishing display. Coloured stems of cornus and willow and the white trunks of *Betula jacquemontii* are reflected in the lake. There are two ferneries and banks of hellebores, and the hedges of sarcococca and avenues of winter honeysuckle add fragrance to the whole.

CLUMBER PARK

The working Victorian apiary is a great attraction, and the fan garden was re-created in 2002. Among the many old and interesting trees are *Cornus mas*, *Catalpa bignonioides*, a swamp cypress, tulip trees, acers and a paulownia.

▶ *Open for NGS*

4 'Pure Land' Japanese Garden

Carefully shaped trees combine with sculptures and water features to create a contemplative, oriental atmosphere.

North Clifton, near Newark NG23 7AT

Tel: 01777 228567

LOCATION 10 miles N of Newark on Trent on A1133. Signposted

The 1½ acre garden, created since 1980, is laid out in traditional Japanese style to provide a calm and contemplative setting for the relaxation and meditation centre based here. Ornaments and sculpture combine with neatly pruned and shaped trees and shrubs to create an oriental atmosphere that never descends into cliche.

Narrow paths, steps and stepping stones lead the visitor to a pagoda, a teahouse, a Zen gravel garden and a koi-filled pond, and the sound of running water is always present from the small waterfalls and streams that weave their way through the garden. The hardy herbaceous planting in the English style is informal and relaxed, contrasting successfully with the cloud pruning of many familiar conifers.

A new garden has been created using clear crystals, amethysts and semi-precious stones to represent hills, mountain, stream and sea, with rose quartz as the centrepiece of a glittering miniature landscape. The garden is lantern-lit every Friday, Saturday and Sunday during August and September (7-10pm).

▶ *Open most of year – telephone or consult website for details*

SHROPSHIRE

The rocky terrain has influenced garden design in Shropshire, resulting in many intimate plantsman's gardens overflowing with colour and texture. Unusual plant combinations produce some stylish displays.

1 Windy Ridge

A strong, geometric design and exuberant planting have transformed this compact site into an award-winning garden.

Church Lane, Little Wenlock, Telford TF6 5BB
Tel: 01952 507675
www.gardenschool.co.uk
LOCATION 2 miles S of Wellington off M54 junction 7; follow signs for Little Wenlock. Or 1 mile W of Telford bypass (A5223) via Horsehay

Halfway up Shropshire's landmark Wrekin, this award-winning garden of less than an acre has been created since 1990 from a paddock and a filled-in swimming pool. A strong, crisp, geometric design now anchors exuberant and skilled plantings of a standard rarely seen outside the marquees of national summer shows.

Paying careful attention to colour and texture, more than 1,000 species of plants, some of them rare, are combined harmoniously. Enthusiastic wielding of the pruning saw has turned trees – apple, *Parrotia persica*, amelanchier, *Arbutus unedo* and a frenzied *Corylus avellana* 'Contorta' – into sculptural features and created enticing views through their bare stems. Pools provide restful interludes and an excuse for experimentation with stunning bog and pool plantings.

▶ *Open for NGS, and by appointment*

2 Dower House

A sequence of thoughtfully planted gardens, each reflecting a different historical period, tells the story of British gardening.

Morville Hall, Morville, Bridgnorth WV16 5NB
Tel: 01746 714407
www.stmem.com/dower-house-garden
The National Trust
LOCATION 3 miles NW of Bridgnorth at A458/ B4368 junction, within Morville Hall grounds

This garden has been composed with great care and skill. Reflecting the history of the hall and the people who have lived there, the 1½ acre plot is laid out as a sequence of gardens within the garden, each one in the style of a different historical period. The design flows seamlessly between periods, from the austere simplicity of an ancient turf maze to the romanticism of a Victorian rose border.

The pace is well judged and planting is thoughtful, with particular attention paid to historical authenticity. The low-key signage is quirkily educational – who would have known that dwarf box was introduced in the 17th century but initially disliked for its 'naughty smell'? Old varieties of tulips and roses are a speciality and the formal vegetable garden with its apple and pear tunnel another highlight.

▶ *Open main season – telephone or consult website for details – and for parties by appointment*

3 Preen Manor

An imaginative series of cottage gardens and an ornamental potager have been created amid the ruins of an ancient priory.

Church Preen, Church Stretton SY6 7LQ

Tel: 01694 771207

LOCATION 5 miles W of Much Wenlock on B4371. After 3 miles turn right for Church Preen and Hughley; after 1½ miles turn left for Church Preen, over crossroads. Drive is ½ mile on right

Threaded between the ruins of a medieval Cluniac Priory and a great Victorian mansion is a succession of cottage gardens. To the north of the kitchen garden wall are small gardens billowing with the usual cottage garden regulars – roses, perennial sweet peas, irises and poppies, geraniums, Jacob's ladder, astrantias and aquilegias. Their combinations are well considered and sometimes unexpectedly lively for such an ancient site, such as a pathway lined with espaliered apples and enlivened with splashes of shocking pink columbines and orange Welsh poppies.

The ornamental kitchen garden, with its decorative vegetables and standard gooseberries trained into neat umbrellas, is a great success. In the Vestry Garden, the ivy-clad 'doughnut' of roses was inspired by a trip to Williamsburg.

To the south, overlooking the wooded scarp of Wenlock Edge, lie formal lawns with neat lines of box clipped to mimic the architectural detailing of the kitchen garden wall, avenues of trees, and a narrow canal pool. Beyond that, the 12 acre grounds dissolve into ancient woodland, where the monk's old bathing pools shelter skunk cabbage, primulas and the umbrella plant, *Darmera peltata*.

▶ *Open for NGS, and for parties of 15 or more in June and July by appointment*

4 Millichope Park

A dramatic entrance through a limestone tunnel leads to landscaped parkland punctuated by an obelisk and rotunda.

Munslow, Craven Arms SY7 9HA

Tel: 01584 841234

Historic Park Grade II*

LOCATION 8 miles NE of Craven Arms, 11 miles N of Ludlow on B4368

A conventional carriage drive across traditional parkland plunges abruptly into a deep, cool cutting and tunnel slashed through the Wenlock limestone to ensure a theatrical arrival. The glory of Millichope lies in its landscaping and fine specimen trees. The original 18th-century landscape of woodland, pools and cascades was embellished by a 10m (33ft) tall obelisk and an Ionic rotunda. Walks meander around this fine focal point, picturesquely perched on a clifftop above the lake, and through orchid-spiked hay meadows and rose-swagged woodland (carpeted earlier in the year with snowdrops, daffodils and bluebells).

The cutting is crossed by a steep Chinese-style bridge, commissioned in the 1970s. A series of charming small gardens designed to enclose a swimming pool have also been added. Framed by yew hedges and sculptural gates, these intimate spaces with rich herbaceous plantings provide a welcome contrast to the openness of the park.

The lake boasts islands, an arched Victorian boathouse and an echo chamber, an ingenious device to magnify the sound of a cascade.

▶ *Open in Feb for snowdrops, and May for bluebells – telephone for details*

PREEN MANOR

5 Cumberley

Designed with a strong Japanese influence, the tranquil garden includes a teahouse, a Zen garden and a white wisteria tunnel.

Cumberley Lane, Hope Bagot, Ludlow SY8 3LJ

Tel: 01584 891659

LOCATION 5 miles E of Ludlow off A4117. In Clee Hill turn right onto B4214, signed to Knowbury. After 1 mile, turn left into Hope Bagot Lane, then second right into Cumberley Lane

On the southern slopes of Titterstone Clee, this 2 acre plot has been created since 2001. Inspired by Japanese gardens and designed for meditation, contemplation, peace and movement, it takes the form of a journey. Beginning in the original farmyard, planted now with shallow-rooted sun-lovers such as lavender and hyssop, self-sown *Erigeron karvinskianus* and wild irises from Provence, it passes through a planked timber barn, and along an *allée* lined with olive-like *Pyrus kotschyana* 'Silver Sail', making a brief visit to a pair of 'his and hers' gardens. Hers is an old-fashioned rose garden, while his is an English interpretation of a Zen garden.

Moving on, a tunnel of pure white wisteria leads into an uneven and shady *roji* or tea path, coolly atmospheric with a limited evergreen planting palette of ferns, *Drimys lanceolata* and a bristly *Ophiopogon japonicus* 'Dragon's Beard'. This leads to the central feature of the garden – a teahouse settled under a mighty English oak.

From here, the path meanders through 6 acres of woodland walks and wild areas before returning to the main garden. Although primarily a green garden, there are hosts of unusual and rare plants, with clematis a speciality. White foxgloves abound and the garden's serene atmosphere is especially haunting at dusk and by moonlight.
► *Open for charity, and for parties by appointment*

6 Holly Grove

An extensive plant collection is contained in a series of garden rooms, including a box parterre and lavender and herb gardens.

Church Pulverbatch, Shrewsbury SY5 8DD

Tel: 01743 718221

LOCATION 6 miles S of Shrewsbury off A49

This is one of those rare gardens that seems to have it all. The setting is idyllic, deep in the countryside with views out over flower-studded pasture (grazed by rare White Park cattle) towards the south Shropshire hills. The timeless quality of the 3 acre formal gardens, with a box parterre to the front, herb garden to the rear and rose, pool, lavender and vegetable gardens to the side, complement the square formality of the handsome early Victorian house.

The neatly trimmed yew and beech hedges and the pleached lime *allées* on either side of the rose walk provide shelter for an extensive plant collection that will delight the connoisseur. Among the herbaceous rarities calling out to be spotted are *Astrantia major* 'Gill Richardson', *Carmichaelia odorata* 'Lakeside', many different trilliums and a notable collection of equally rare trees – *Fagus sylvatica* 'Brathay Purple', *Quercus dentata* 'Pinnatifida' and *Hepacodium jasminoides* – are to be found in the adjoining arboretum. A stroll down to the large pool surrounded by wild-flower meadows, traditionally managed by the resident Soay sheep that graze there in late summer, concludes a visit to this enchanting garden.
► *Open for NGS, and by appointment*

7 Wollerton Old Hall

Colour and form dominate in this beautifully planted garden, where a hot area contrasts with a scented white garden.

Wollerton, Hodnet, Market Drayton TF9 3NA

Tel: 01630 685760 (daytime)

www.wollertonoldhallgarden.com

LOCATION 12 miles NE of Shrewsbury off A53. Signed off A53 between Hodnet and Tern Hill

In design and layout this is a garden in the classic English style. Within a little over 4 acres is a series of beautifully planted garden rooms, each distinct in character yet very much part of the whole. This effect is achieved through the careful positioning of a number of principal and secondary axes upon which the overall plan of the garden depends, with yew hedging creating an all-embracing, green framework.

Within the different garden rooms, contrasts are much in evidence. Fiery borders in the hot garden, stunning in August, are tempered with cool whites in a scented garden. Openness, in the form of a broad expanse of lawn, contrasts with the intimacy of a pergola dripping with roses and clematis.

Artistry, vision and discipline combine here to create a garden of exceptional quality.
► *Open main season – telephone or consult website for details*

8 Hawkstone Park

Climb spiral steps to admire the view or cross a rustic bridge over a chasm in this adventureland of cliffs, crags and follies.

Weston-under-Redcastle, Shrewsbury SY4 5UY

Tel: 01939 200611 | www.hawkstone.co.uk

Historic Park Grade I

LOCATION 13 miles NE of Shrewsbury via A49, 6 miles SW of Market Drayton on A442. Signed from Hodnet

The rugged terrain here inspired Sir Rowland Hill (pioneer of the postage stamp) and his son to create an intricate network of paths – at times hugging the huge sandstone bluff, at others tunnelled through it – to link a series of follies that thrilled countless visitors between about 1750 and 1850. Reconstruction after years of neglect now allows today's visitors to tread in the footsteps of those intrepid adventurers. Climb 150 spiral steps to enjoy stunning panoramic views over 13 counties, cross an unnervingly narrow rustic bridge spanning a 26m (85ft) chasm or venture down a narrow cleft between towering moss-covered cliffs before exploring a vault-like grotto.

Rhododendrons have virtually engulfed the original arboretum and the deer park has been replaced by a golf course, but the 3½ mile route (allow 3 hours to enjoy it fully) affords the fit and able of all ages a better understanding of this historic 'naturalistic landscape' as well as being an immensely satisfying walk.

▶ *Open most of year – telephone or consult website for details*

9 Hodnet Hall

Sheltered by ancient woodland, a superb collection of semi-woodland plants overlook a string of pools and wild-flower meadows.

Hodnet, Market Drayton TF9 3NN

Tel: 01630 685786

www.hodnethallgardens.org

Historic Park Grade II

LOCATION 12 miles NE of Shrewsbury, 5½ miles SW of Market Drayton, at A53/A442 junction

Parts of the ancient oak and beech woodland still survive in this superb garden, sheltering a significant collection of semi-woodland plants that thrive in the moisture-retaining, lime-free soil. The 60 acre valley site was remodelled in the 1920s, the stream dammed to make a chain of pools that are still a delight to explore. Although a notable historic garden, it nevertheless feels in tune with today's tastes, with generous drifts of perennials anchoring the mature planting and mown grass paths cut through species-rich wild-flower meadows. Planned on a sweeping scale, there are also intimate corners to discover.

After climbing the imposing terrace steps, making the steep 30m (100ft) ascent through densely planted slopes, and turning to the right down the broadwalk past stately herbaceous borders, the eye is caught by the entrance to a narrow path flanked by two stone obelisks. Venturing down it, visitors enter a secluded garden dominated by a superb *Cornus florida*, with views out over the main pool to the 1656 dovecote silhouetted on the horizon. The path then passes a diminutive summerhouse before descending weathered sandstone steps beneath gnarled rhododendron trunks. Allow time to explore and don't miss the extended woodland walk and the well-tended kitchen garden.

▶ *Open for limited season – telephone or consult website for details – for NGS and for parties by appointment*

10 Lower Hall

Stylish combinations of different colours and species of plants are used to good effect in this contemporary garden.

Worfield, Bridgnorth WV15 5LH

Tel: 01746 716607

LOCATION 4 miles NE of Bridgnorth. Take A454 Wolverhampton-Bridgnorth road, turn right to Worfield and right again after village stores

This modern 4¼ acre plantsman's garden has been developed since 1964. The courtyard and fountain are featured in many design books. There is a good use of colour combinations and plant associations throughout the garden – from one red border to another of white and green, forming a cool contrast.

The walled garden has a magnificent display of roses, clematis and irises in season. The water garden, which is separated from the woodland garden by the River Worfe, has two bridges and two weirs, and a deck built over the pool exploits the view across to the colourful primula island. The woodland garden includes rare magnolias, a collection of birches with bark interest, acers, cornus, azaleas and amelanchiers. There is all-year variety and colour here.

▶ *Open April to July for parties by appointment*

CENTRAL ENGLAND

BIDDULPH GRANGE

STAFFORDSHIRE

Amid its old industrial and fine rural scenery, Staffordshire boasts a range of historic gardens and impressive landscape parks, some containing magnificent – and nationally important – garden buildings.

1 Biddulph Grange

Paths take visitors on a horticultural tour of the world, through Egyptian, Italian and Chinese designs, in this innovative garden.

Grange Road, Biddulph ST8 7SD

Tel: 01782 517999 (Garden Office)

www.nationaltrust.org.uk

Historic Garden Grade I/The National Trust

LOCATION 3½ miles SE of Congleton, 7 miles N of Stoke-on-Trent. Access from A527 Biddulph-Congleton road

One of the most remarkable gardens to be created in 19th-century Britain, the rediscovery and restoration of the 15 acres here is a great success story for the National Trust. In front of the house terraces descend to a lily pond. A pyramid and obelisks of clipped yew mark the Egyptian garden, while the Chinese garden has a joss house, a golden water buffalo overlooking a dragon parterre, a watch tower and a temple reflected in a calm pool.

The stumpery demonstrates an innovative Victorian method of displaying suitable plants. Verbena, araucaria and rose parterres and the Shelter House and dahlia walk (with more than 600 dahlias) have regained their mid 19th-century appearance. The long Wellingtonia avenue, felled and replanted in 1995, is beginning to make its presence felt again, and the arboretum pool and woodland terrace are being restored.

▶ *Open most of year – telephone or consult website for details*

2 Wilkins Pleck

A series of elegant garden rooms featuring a knot garden and rose arbour are contained within a framework of yews and hornbeams.

Off Three Mile Lane, Whitmore ST5 5HN

Tel: 01782 680351

LOCATION 5 miles SW of Newcastle-under-Lyme off A53

Set in rolling Staffordshire landscape, the 6 acre garden and its young arboretum is disturbed by little save the birdsong that echoes through the *allées* and borders, parterres and pools. Carved out of a soggy, clay field, it has been created by the present owners since the late 1990s. A framework of tall yew screens, brick walls and fastigiate hornbeams contains an elegantly proportioned series of rooms. At the heart lie four rectangular areas – a knot garden, a sinuous interweaving of box hedges leading to an arbour clothed in *Rosa* 'Paul's Himalayan Musk', two herbaceous enclosures filled with roses and perennials, and one planted mainly with clipped gold and white plants. Along one side two traditional herbaceous borders run towards a hot garden that peaks in late July, and from its fiery planting, visitors pass into the relative coolness of a leafy tunnel and a formal avenue of pleached limes focusing on a statue. Beyond lies a large pond spanned by two Monet-style bridges covered in a blanket of native water lilies.

▶ *Open for NGS, and for parties by written appointment*

3 Alton Towers

The grounds of the theme park contain a varied collection of features, including a pagoda fountain and Dutch garden.

Alton ST10 4DB | Tel: 08705 204060

www.altontowers.com

Historic Park Grade I

LOCATION From N take M6 junction 16 or M1 junction 28, from S take M6 junction 15 or M1 junction 23A. Signposted

This Elysium of ornamental garden buildings was created between 1814 and 1827 by the 15th Earl of Shrewsbury. The 500 acre grounds contain many unusual features, including the three-storey, cast-iron Chinese pagoda fountain – a copy of the To Ho pagoda in Canton.

Landscape architect W.A. Nesfield played a key role in the design (one of his parterres is still in situ). The enormous rock garden is planted with a range of conifers, acers and sedums. The fine domed conservatory houses pelargoniums and other colourful plants by season, and the terraces have rose and herbaceous borders.

There is also a Dutch garden, Her Ladyship's Garden featuring yew and rose beds, an Italian garden, a yew-arch walkway and woodland walks, while a canal adds further interest.

▶ *Theme park, ruins and grounds. Open main season – telephone or consult website for details*

4 Shugborough

The park has eight monuments of national importance – including one that is believed to be linked to the Holy Grail.

Milford, Stafford ST17 0XB

Tel: 01889 881388 | www.shugborough.org.uk

Historic Park Grade I

LOCATION 6 miles E of Stafford on A513

Shugborough is of major interest and importance for both its fine 18th-century house and historic 878 acre park. Many of the garden buildings are ascribed to architect James 'Athenian' Stuart and were built for Thomas Anson from 1740 onwards. The park is remarkable for containing eight monuments of national importance, including an early example of chinoiserie in the form of a teahouse, a Temple of the Winds, a Doric temple and the Shepherd's Monument, rumoured to have links to the Holy Grail.

A parterre with grand clipped yews is just one element in the 22 acre formal gardens, where the Victorian layout and terraces by landscape architect W.A. Nesfield were revitalised in the 1960s by Graham Stuart Thomas (moonlighting from his job as one of the National Trust's key horticultural advisers).

Seasonal attractions include massed plantings of daffodils along the riverbank, azaleas and rhododendrons, a fine and long-flowering herbaceous border and good autumn colour. Parts of the park have been restored to its 18th-century appearance by the planting of more than 1,000 trees, predominantly oak and sweet chestnut, while a 350-year-old yew tree with a crown circumference of 175m (574ft) has been recorded as the widest in Britain. Since 2007, the main activity has been the restoration of the walled garden. Derelict for nearly a century, it has been reincarnated as a working kitchen garden staffed by men and women in period costume.

▶ *Estate open main season – telephone or consult website for details – and for parties by appointment*

CENTRAL ENGLAND

201

5 Weston Park

'Capability' Brown created the historic park and pleasure grounds, which feature a rose walk, Italianate parterre and woodland.

Weston-under-Lizard, Shifnal TF11 8LE

Tel: 01952 852100

www.weston-park.com

Historic Park Grade II

LOCATION 6 miles E of Telford on A5, 7 miles W of A6 junction 12, 3 miles N of M54 junction 3

The handsome 1671 house was later anchored within sweeping parkland covering 1,000 acres by 'Capability' Brown, who also created pleasure grounds to the east and west of the building. Woodland is planted with spring bulbs, bluebells, rhododendrons and azaleas encircling pools, and magnificent trees form a majestic backcloth to the many shrubs. A rose walk leads to a deer park, and the rose garden and 19th-century Italianate parterre by the house have been restored.

The architectural features in the park – the Temple of Diana, Roman bridge and orangery – were all designed by James Paine. For children there is a railway, an adventure playground and a yew maze to get lost in.

▶ *House open. Park and gardens open main season – telephone or consult website for details*

6 The Dorothy Clive Garden

This intimate garden is split into two parts – one with a mass of rhododendrons and azaleas, the other featuring an alpine scree.

Willoughbridge, Market Drayton, Shropshire TF9 4EU

Tel: 01630 647237

www.dorothyclivegarden.co.uk

LOCATION 7 miles NE of Market Drayton, 1 mile E of Woore on A51 between Nantwich and Stone

Created by the late Colonel Clive in memory of his wife, the 12 acre gardens are divided into two main areas – the Quarry Garden, which is cut into a slope and filled with a fine collection of rhododendrons and azaleas, and the Hillside Garden, which incorporates an alpine scree garden, a pool and several colourful perennial borders.

Since 2003 great emphasis has been placed on creating more imaginative plantings, and the results can be seen in a succession of spectacular summer borders. There is also a gravel garden,

a laburnum arch and a waterfall that was constructed in 1990 to commemorate the 50th anniversary of the gardens.

In spring, rhododendrons, tulips and unusual bulbs, and an azalea and daffodil walk enliven the garden. In summer, colourful shrubs and perennials take over, followed in autumn by an extensive collection of trees providing good foliage colour.

▶ *Open main season – telephone or consult website for details*

7 Trentham Gardens

The restoration of the Italian gardens aims to return these grounds to the glory of their heyday, with a modern emphasis in parts.

Stone Road, Trentham, Stoke-on-Trent ST4 8AX

Tel: 01782 657341

www.trenthamgardens.co.uk

Historic Park Grade II*

LOCATION 2 miles S of Stoke-on-Trent on A34, 2 miles E of M6 junction 15

The progressive aggrandisement of Trentham Hall took place over several centuries, and if the current project to restore the gardens fulfils its ambitions it will be a worthy chapter in a fascinating story. In 1759 'Capability' Brown was brought in to re-landscape the 750 acre park and in 1833 architect Charles Barry was commissioned to lay out the Italian Flower Gardens – the two most important features remaining today.

When, in 1911, the 2nd Duke of Sutherland sold up, most of the hall was demolished and the grounds degenerated into a public amenity space, although some magnificent trees and decaying garden buildings remained as reminders of the glory days. Now garden and landscape designers Dominic Cole, Piet Oudolf and Tom Stuart-Smith, with garden manager Michael Walker, are masterminding its salvation.

The upper part of the Italian Gardens has been restored and the lower part reinterpreted in the modern perennial style. Following this, trees will be planted in perimeter woodlands and in the western pleasure ground to connect the formal gardens to the park, while wild-flower and perennials meadows will lead to a grass amphitheatre overlooking the lake. There is a delightful 2 mile walk around the lake, which has an avant-garde bridge.

▶ *Open all year – telephone or consult website for details*

TRENTHAM GARDENS

WARWICKSHIRE

Quintessentially English, this scenic county has a rich history that is reflected in its gardens, including a knot garden designed to impress a queen and a great landscaped park designed by 'Capability' Brown.

1 Garden Organic Ryton

Living in harmony with nature is the theme of these landscaped gardens, which include the world's first bio-dynamic garden.

Wolston Lane, Coventry CV8 3LG

Tel: 024 7630 3517

www.gardenorganic.org.uk

LOCATION 7 miles NE of Leamington Spa, 5 miles SE of Coventry. Turn off A45 onto Wolston Lane

Ryton was set up in 1985 to be a centre of excellence for organic horticulture. In a beautifully landscaped setting, it provides a wide range of inspirational and educational displays of herbs, roses, unusual vegetables, fruit, together with information on wildlife gardening, composting and disease control. The site also boasts the world's first bio-dynamic garden.

At the heart of the 10 acres is a vibrant and informal display of herbaceous perennials. The individual gardens include demonstrations of organic techniques. There are also gardens for the visually impaired and those with other special needs, a bee garden, one for the enthusiastic cook, a Paradise Garden and an apple and pear orchard.

The interactive visitor centre, known as the Vegetable Kingdom, houses the Heritage Seed Library, a collection of more than 800 endangered vegetable varieties. There is also plenty to amuse and interest children of all ages.

▶ *Open all year – telephone or consult website for details*

2 Farnborough Hall

This 18th-century garden has a broad ornamental terrace walk lined with trees and punctuated by two temples.

Farnborough, Banbury OX17 1DU

Tel: 01295 690002 | www.nationaltrust.org.uk

Historic Garden Grade I/The National Trust

LOCATION 6 miles N of Banbury, ½ mile W of A423 or 1½ miles E off B4100

This 18 acre site marks the movement towards the great landscaped parks at the end of the 18th century. Climbing gently along the ridge looking towards Edgehill is an S-shaped terrace walk built by landowner William Holbech in order to greet his brother on the adjoining property. Two temples and a game larder lie along the walk, with an obelisk at the end. The trees are beech, sycamore and lime.

The spectacular grounds were improved in the 1740s with the aid of Sanderson Miller, the architect, landscape gardener and dilettante, who lived at nearby Radway. Beyond a giant cedar is part of the site of the former orangery, a rose garden, and a yew walk with steps at the end, where there is a seat with a fine view over the river, the cascade and the countryside towards Edgehill. The beautiful honey-coloured house, which has belonged to the same family since 1684, was reconstructed in the 18th century and richly decorated with fine rococo plasterwork.

▶ *House and grounds open for limited season – telephone or consult website for details*

COUGHTON COURT

3 Upton House

Dramatic terraced gardens on a sloping site afford fine views across Edgehill, and include a National Collection of asters.

Banbury OX15 6HT | Tel: 01295 670266

www.nationaltrust.org.uk/uptonhouse

Historic Garden Grade II*/The National Trust

LOCATION 12 miles SE of Stratford-upon-Avon, 7 miles NW of Banbury on A422

This garden is memorable for the sheer drama of its setting. It swoops down from the house, which stands on ironstone over 210m (690ft) above sea level on Edgehill. Below a great lawn, the garden descends in a series of long terraces, with an impressive flight of stone steps leading down to a large lake. In the centre is a huge, sloping kitchen garden, and below this a mirror pool.

The sheer scale of the plan creates an immediate impression, but it is worth taking a closer look at the plantings. There are many unusual species, particularly perennials and bog plants, and a National Collection of asters spp. *amellus*, *cordifolius* and *ericoides*.

▶ *House open. Garden open most of year – telephone or consult website for details – and for parties of 15 or more by appointment*

4 Woodpeckers

A country garden that provides interest throughout the year, with a fern border, ivy arbour, wild-flower area and arboretum.

The Bank, Marlcliff, Bidford-on-Avon B50 4NT

Tel: 01789 773416

LOCATION 7 miles SW of Stratford-upon-Avon off B4085 between Bidford and Cleeve Prior

This 2 acre garden is a model example of a rural garden. It has been planned for year-round interest and contains a wide range of design and planting ideas that blend well with the surrounding countryside. A small arboretum with a wide selection of choice trees provides contrast in form and colour.

Moving around the garden, there are many surprises. There's a wooden figure of St Fiacre surrounded by old roses with clematis climbing through and an attractive small potager, as well as colourful and unusual herbs and vegetables. A knot garden has been created in box, and room has been found for topiary, an ivy arbour with statue, a fern border, several island beds with splendid ranges of plants, a Mediterranean garden, a cactus and succulent greenhouse and a round greenhouse for tender plants.

The terrace has a range of troughs and alpine plants, and there is a delightful pool and bog garden. A belvedere of framed English oak affords fine views of the garden, including a wild-flower area in spring. A two-storey oak building with a balcony overlooks the arboretum and rose garden.

It is also worth visiting in winter to see the trees and a border designed to look interesting at this neglected time of year, and in February for a mass of snowdrops in many different varieties.

▶ *Open for NGS, and by appointment*

5 Coughton Court

Behind a Tudor gatehouse, a colourful courtyard and intricate Elizabethan knot garden echo the design of the house.

Alcester B49 5JA

Tel: 01789 400777

www.coughtoncourt.co.uk

LOCATION 8 miles NW of Stratford-upon-Avon, 2 miles N of Alcester on A435

At the rear of the mainly 16th-century house, the formal U-shaped courtyard has beds planted with bulbs, roses and perennials, and a central quatrefoil pool with a fountain, which mirrors ▷

CENTRAL ENGLAND

the stone detailing on the house. Beyond, twin avenues of *Tilia platyphyllos* 'Rubra' end at blocks of yew enclosing a pair of urns, behind which are two little sunken gardens. The spacious lawn then tapers off to meet the river and the countryside. It is a bold design, well matched by simple plantings, and this is repeated throughout – roses, alliums, tulips, geraniums, violas and alchemilla are some of the signature plants to be seen in summer.

The gardens to the side of the house are varied and packed with interest. They include a white garden of clematis and perennials, an early summer garden in which standard wisterias are trained over hoops and underplanted with peonies supported by twigs, and an award-winning rose labyrinth. This boasts more than 200 different varieties including damasks, albas, teas and noisettes, floribundas and many old-fashioned English roses. The generous herbaceous borders, separated by a cool strip of lawn, display a sophisticated designer palette, with shades of mauves and blues opposing reds, dark purples and lime green.

In one enclosure a statue commemorates the Asian tsunami, while one of Rosamund Clifford, mistress of Henry II, graces another. A riverside walk through woodland that is covered with bluebells in May leads to a bog garden. A decorative orchard contains many traditional varieties of fruit, and there is also an organic vegetable garden.

In spring, the display of more than 400,000 daffodils is outstanding. This includes Europe's only collection of the rare and unusual late-flowering Throckmorton daffodils, named after the Throckmorton family, who have lived here for generations and still manage the main garden areas.

▶ *House and garden open – telephone or consult website for details – also open for parties by appointment*

6 Warwick Castle

For his first solo commission, 'Capability' Brown shaped the castle grounds using cedars of Lebanon to frame the views.

Warwick CV34 4QU | Tel: 0870 442 2000

www.warwick-castle.com

Historic Park Grade I

LOCATION In Warwick

The magnificent castle stands on the banks of the River Avon, surrounded by 60 acres of beautiful grounds landscaped by 'Capability' Brown. His work at Warwick Castle was one of his earliest independent commissions, for which he received much praise, encouragement and publicity. He removed the old formal garden outside the wall and shaped the grounds to frame a view using an array of magnificent trees, notably cedars of Lebanon.

In 1753 he began to landscape the courtyard, removing steps, filling in parts of the yard and making a coachway to surround the large level lawn. He then worked on the creation of a park on the other side of the 11th-century mound.

In 1779, when Brown's remodelling was barely 20 years old, a grandiose scheme of expansion was embarked upon that involved demolishing several streets in the town. In 1786, the conservatory at the top of Pageant Field was constructed, which today houses a replica of the famous Warwick Vase. From here visitors can view the panorama before them – the Peacock Garden and the tree-lined lawn of Pageant Field, which meanders down to the gently sloping banks of the River Avon. On the other side of the castle entrance is the Victorian rose garden, re-created in 1986 from Robert Marnock's designs of 1868.

▶ *Castle open. Grounds open all year – telephone or consult website for details*

DAFFODILS, ROSES, IRISES AND THE TURNING LEAVES OF TREES AND SHRUBS PROVIDE A CONSTANT PROCESSION OF COLOUR

ARBURY HALL

7 Kenilworth Castle

Built to impress Queen Elizabeth I, an elaborate design of eight knot gardens can be viewed from a raised walkway.

Kenilworth CV8 1NE | Tel: 001926 852078

www.english-heritage.org.uk

English Heritage

LOCATION 4 miles N of Warwick, 5 miles SW of Coventry off A46. Signed from Kenilworth

Historically fascinating, this is the most complete picture of a 16th-century garden to be found anywhere in the country. Built at huge expense by Robert Dudley, Earl of Leicester, for a visit by Elizabeth I in July 1575, it has been re-created by English Heritage at equally huge expense and to the highest standard. Parts of the castle have also been restored.

The design of eight knot gardens, filled with the scented plants of the period, was intended to be viewed primarily from the raised walkway running along one side of the castle. Box was not then in fashion, so the beds are surrounded either with thrift (*Armeria maritima*) or wild strawberries (*Fragaria vesca*). The layout was based upon a letter from Rogert Langham, Keeper of the Council Chamber Door. He describes the fountain, the birdcage and the mixed hedging around the outside of the different knots.

Meticulously researched and well presented, this privy garden will continue to develop as the shrubs and topiary mature. To one side of the gatehouse an attractive area has a knot garden, with large phillyreas as centrepieces and the box hedging clipped into gentle waves.
▶ *Open all year – telephone or consult website for details*

8 Packwood House

The well-preserved grounds feature striking topiary, with a collection of yews said to represent the Sermon on the Mount

Lapworth, Solihull, Birmingham B94 6AT

Tel: 01564 782024 | www.nationaltrust.org.uk

Historic Garden Grade II*/The National Trust

LOCATION 11 miles SE of central Birmingham, 2 miles E of Hockley Heath on A3400

Hidden away in a rather suburban part of Warwickshire, this 7 acre garden is notable for its intact layout of courtyards, terraces and brick gazebos, dating from the 16th and 17th centuries when the original house was built. Even more remarkable is the almost surreal yew garden that is traditionally believed to represent the Sermon on the Mount. In fact the 'Multitude' were planted in the 1850s as a four-square pattern round an orchard but the result is now homogenous. A spiral mount of yew and box is a delightful illusion – note also the clever use of brick.

A sunken garden was made in the 1930s and earlier design features restored. In spring, drifts of daffodils follow the snowdrops and bluebells carpet the copse, while shrubs flower on red brick walls. Herbaceous borders, the sunken garden, terrace beds and climbing roses and honeysuckles are a riot of summer colour, and autumn brings changes in foliage.

The walled kitchen garden has been improved after many years of neglect. Don't miss the attractive lakeside walk and wild-flower meadows.
▶ *House and garden open most of year – telephone or consult website for details. Park open all year*

9 Arbury Hall

In stark contrast to its urban surroundings, the hall's tranquil gardens are set in rolling parkland, with a fine rose garden.

Arbury, Nuneaton CV10 7PT

Tel: 024 7638 2804

www.arburyestate.co.uk

Historic Garden Grade I

LOCATION 10 miles N of Coventry, 3½ miles SW of Nuneaton off B4102

Although an array of factories surround the gate of the 50 acre park, a picturesque landscape has survived within, surrounding a Gothic Revival house with earlier stables by Christopher Wren, three rush-fringed lakes, a network of canals and many fine trees.

Daffodils, bluebells and rhododendrons, roses and irises, and turning leaves of trees and shrubs provide a constant procession of colour from spring to autumn. The formal rose garden is memorable for its tilting terrain enclosed by a venerable yew hedge and a mellow brick orangery.
▶ *House and garden open limited season – telephone or consult website for details*

CENTRAL ENGLAND

WORCESTERSHIRE

Acres of historic landscaped parkland overlook the Malvern Hills and Severn Valley, much of it recently restored, while many of the county's private gardens reflect modern planting tastes.

1 Overbury Court

Water is a dominant feature in this garden, which has a rill, cascades and a series of pools surrounded by naturalistic plantings.

Overbury, Tewkesbury GL20 7NP

Tel: 01386 725111

Historic Garden Grade II*

LOCATION 9 miles SW of Evesham, 5 miles NE of Tewkesbury (A46/A435) roundabout

Largely laid out in the late 19th and early 20th centuries, the superb 6 acre garden provides the setting for a fine early 18th-century house. It is bordered by lush parkland with unspoiled views. Everywhere there is water. Behind the house, a brook issues into a grotto, and rough steps wind between cascades and through naturalistic plantings of hostas, filipendulas, wild garlic and ferns, backed by mature box bushes. The brook, emerging along a broad rill bordered on one side by meadow and on the other by lawn, descends through gentle cascades and winds around a series of pools beyond a great lawn. Huge plane and lime trees overlook the grass and water.

Massive yew hedges separate this part of the garden from the more formal area to the south, where the centrepiece is an avenue of Irish yews flanked by a sunken bowling lawn and a formal

pool. Again, the planting is simple yet stunning – to the east a crinkle-crankle border of gold and silver foliage, to the west a sunken double mixed border displaying old-fashioned and species roses, underplanted with geraniums and *Alchemilla mollis*.

▶ *Open by appointment only*

2 Rose Villa

Here a traditional country garden with an orchard, roses and a wild-flower meadow has been given a contemporary feel.

Beckford, Tewkesbury GL20 7AD

Tel: 01789 404100/404166 (weekdays)

LOCATION Off A46 between Tewkesbury and Evesham, approx 5 miles from M5 junction 9

The strong design here, the work of the architect and landscape designer Charles Rutherfoord, lifts the 1½ acre garden out of the ordinary

CROOME PARK

and provides a splendid setting for the owner's luxurious plantings. He has divided the trapezoidal space into several distinct areas and created an undulating landscape that disguises nearby buildings and provides hidden corners. The brick-built garden room on the lower lawn and the canal that projects from its south wall are elegant centrepieces.

Created in 2000 in a wilderness behind an early 19th-century house, it shows how a traditional country garden – complete with neat lawns, an old ha-ha, an orchard, billowing plantings of perennials and roses, and a wild-flower meadow – can be transformed into one with a distinctly contemporary feel.

▶ *Open especially for The Most Amazing Gardens to Visit in Britain – telephone for details*

3 Croome Park

Visitors can enjoy miles of walks through the parkland and gardens, which are dotted with follies, listed buildings and a grotto.

Builders Yard, High Green, Severn Stoke WR8 9JS

Tel: 01905 371006

www.nationaltrust.org.uk/croomepark

Historic Park Grade I/The National Trust

LOCATION 8 miles S of Worcester off A38 and 6 miles W of Pershore off B4084

'Capability' Brown's career as an independent landscape designer and architect was effectively launched by his work at Croome Court, of which today's 670 acre park was once an integral part. He created a serpentine lake, complete with grotto, and a mile-long artificial river. Paths wind through shrubberies and past charming and ornate garden buildings, and the wider parkland contains follies by leading country house architects Robert Adam, James Wyatt and other designers.

The National Trust's ambitious restoration, completed in 2006, has involved dredging the lake and river, returning the park to grazed pasture, and restoring the bridges across the lake, the classical temples and grotto, and the listed park buildings. More than 45,000 trees and shrubs have been planted to replace those lost from the original scheme.

▶ *House open. Park open most of year – telephone or consult website for details*

4 Little Malvern Court

Spring blossom is a highlight in this romantic garden, while old-fashioned roses steal the glory in early summer.

Little Malvern, near Malvern WR14 4JN

Tel: 01684 892988

LOCATION 4 miles S of Great Malvern on A4104 S of junction with A449

On the edge of the Malvern Hills and spread out beside an ancient gabled manor house and priory church, this 10 acre garden has romantic charm. The medieval fish ponds, bulging yew hedges clipped into fantastic shapes and a venerable lime tree remain from earlier gardens. However, much dates from 1982 onwards.

Close to the house, clipped hedges and pergolas define formal areas and are filled with soft planting to create satisfying contrasts. Moving from area to area, themes develop and vistas are opened up. Pale colours and soft textures are used to great effect, and the garden gains a modern edge by the elegant simplicity of some of the planting. This includes a clipped box hedge set against a yew hedge and a billowing choisya in the entrance forecourt, or the simple horseshoe of pleached limes set around a small lawn.

Below the house, mown grass paths flanked by wild flowers and maturing trees wind round a series of small lakes connected by weirs. At the top of the first lake are a rock garden and a watery gravel bed where primulas and irises are naturalising. This imaginative garden is worth several visits, especially in spring for the blossom and early summer for the old-fashioned roses.

▶ *Open for limited season – telephone or consult website for details – for NGS and by appointment*

5 Witley Court

Surrounding atmospheric ruins, the gardens feature a restored Italianate fountain as well as woodland and wilderness walks.

Worcester Road, Great Witley WR6 6JT

Tel: 01299 896636

www.english-heritage.org.uk

Historic Garden Grade II/English Heritage

LOCATION 10 miles NW of Worcester on A443

The spectacular ruin of Witley Court – purchased by the 1st Earl of Dudley in 1837 and gutted by fire a century later – looks out now over ploughed farmland where once would have stretched acres of parkland. The gardens, however, have been brought to life by the restoration of the magnificent Italianate Perseus and Andromeda fountain that formed the centrepiece of a vast and elaborate scheme of parterres, pools and pavilions by landscape architect W.A. Nesfield, divided from the park by an impressive ha-ha. The planting is replicated in parts to give an impression of the fountain's original setting, and the imagination does the rest.

Elsewhere in the grounds are the 19th-century woodland and wilderness walks, also restored, and a picturesque lake with a cascade. The ruined mansion and the adjoining Baroque church can also be visited.

▶ *Open all year – telephone or consult website for details*

6 Stone House Cottage Gardens

Wisteria, clematis and other climbers scramble up towers and follies in this small garden, which is overflowing with plants.

Stone, Kidderminster DY10 4BG

Tel: 01562 69902

www.shcn.co.uk

LOCATION 2 miles SE of Kidderminster via A448

Created since 1975, it is difficult to believe that this area of just under an acre was once flat and bare. The owner has skilfully built towers and follies to create small intimate areas and at the same time provide homes for many unusual climbers and shrubs. Yew hedges break up the area to give a vista of a tower at the far end, covered with wisteria, roses and clematis. Hardly anywhere does a shrub grow in isolation – something will be scrambling up it, often small, late-flowering clematis.

Raised beds are full to overflowing while shrubs and unusual herbaceous plants mingle happily. The highly regarded adjacent nursery specialises in wall shrubs, climbers and unusual herbaceous plants.

▶ *Open main season – telephone or consult website for details – and by appointment*

7 Hanbury Hall

The restored formal gardens include a sunken parterre displaying 18th-century plants, and a working orangery and mushroom house.

School Road, Hanbury, Droitwich WR9 7EA

Tel: 01527 821214

www.nationaltrust.org.uk

Historic Garden Grade I/The National Trust

LOCATION 4½ miles E of Droitwich, off B4090 or B4091

Magnificent gardens and parkland, covering 20 acres in all, surround the hall, which dates from 1701. The restoration of the early 18th-century gardens on the west side is proving a triumph as they mature.

The sunken parterre, surrounded by yew hedges, and the adjoining fruit garden with its trellis pavilions, have been authentically planted. The pattern of clipped box is filled with individual specimens of choice small plants of the period – auriculas, tulips and marigolds – laid out in colourful regular patterns. Citrus and clipped box balls in pots are displayed on the surrounding gravel walks.

Beyond, in the Wilderness and especially in the Grove, junipers and low box in a calm green space backed by young trees give a sense of how these formal woodland gardens would have appeared to their creators. Shrubberies rejuvenated with box, laurel, phillyrea and philadelphus stand neatly on vast expanses of smooth lawn, contrasting with fine trees extending into the parkland.

The orangery has been brought back into use, with pots of tender plants lining its terrace in summer, as has the curious mushroom house attached to it. Behind the orangery a large orchard is home to more than 40 old varieties of apple. Walks through the 400 acre park allow visitors to explore the re-planted avenues and well-preserved ice house, as well as enjoying spectacular views of the rolling Worcestershire countryside.

▶ *House and garden open most of year – telephone or consult website for details*

8 Spetchley Park

Exuberant herbaceous borders reflect a relaxed attitude to planting, even within a formal framework of yew hedges and walls.

Spetchley, Worcester WR5 1RS

Tel: 01453 810303

www.spetchleygardens.co.uk

Historic Park Grade II*

LOCATION 3 miles E of Worcester on A44. Leave the M5 at junction 7

The grand Victorian gardens of 30 acres, surrounded by 17th-century parkland, were laid out and extended by successive generations of the Berkeley family. The Edwardian gardener Ellen Willmott was a relative and helped to fashion the planting. Evidence of her work can be seen today – *Eryngium* 'Miss Willmott's Ghost' is still self-seeding in the vast herbaceous borders.

The current owner, a plant collector, is expanding the area under cultivation, with a view to allowing the plants to grow freely, even in more formal parts within and around the old walled garden. Everywhere gravel or daisy-strewn grass walks lead you on between yew hedges or old shrubberies to discover further areas punctuated by statues and fountains, and a visit in June is rewarded by spectacular expanses of naturalised martagon lilies and the delicate delight of *Campanula lactiflora*.

The garden also promises a surprise around every corner. This includes the quirky root house, statues of Adam and Eve overlooking a Bath stone alcove, and the mighty Lucombe oak tree on the Cork Lawn.

In the woodland garden, the collection includes dogwoods, acers and hydrangeas, and recent planting has introduced an array of rare trees and shrubs beneath the mature canopy. Park Lake is fringed with water lilies and bulrushes, with views to the deer park beyond. There are also views to the Malvern Hills, and unexpected vistas throughout.

▶ *Open main season – telephone or consult website for details*

CENTRAL ENGLAND

A SIMPLE HORSESHOE OF PLEACHED LIMES IS SET AROUND A SMALL LAWN

LITTLE MALVERN COURT

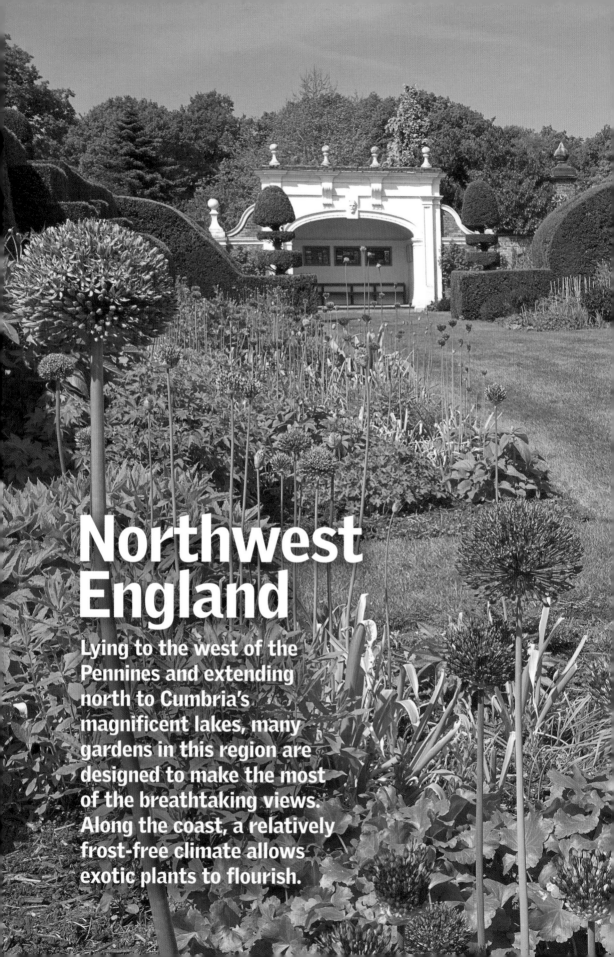

Northwest England

Lying to the west of the Pennines and extending north to Cumbria's magnificent lakes, many gardens in this region are designed to make the most of the breathtaking views. Along the coast, a relatively frost-free climate allows exotic plants to flourish.

CUMBRIA
222-225

CUMBRIA

Carlisle

A7
M6
A689
A69

A596

The
Pennines

9

Workington

A6

8 Penrith

Keswick

A66

A66

Whitehaven

Brough

**Lake District
National Park**

A6

A685

5
7 Windermere
6 A591
4 Kendal

A595

1
A65

A590

3 2

A683

4 Lancaster

5

M6

**LANCASHIRE
Liverpool and
Manchester**
226-229

Clitheroe

A585

Blackpool

M55

M65

A583

A677

Burnley

Preston

3 Blackburn

A59

A59

A666

M62

Southport

A570

Bury

Rochdale

M66

A565

M58

Wigan

M61

Bolton

M60

Oldham

A58

A580

St Helens

Salford

Manchester

M62

A56

6

Liverpool

2 1

4

Warrington

9 8

7

Stockport

A6

Birkenhead

5 Runcorn

M56

9

M53

A56

6

7

A523 10

Ellesmere
Port

5

Wilmslow

8

11

A537

3

12

CHESHIRE
214-219

Macclesfield

Chester

M6

A54

A41

A51

A534

A536

A530

Crewe

2

A49

1

KEY

1 **Garden location**
— **County boundary**
Motorway
Principal A road

Ramsey

A4

A1

Douglas

Castletown

CHESHIRE

Many remarkable gardens shelter in the valleys of the Pennines and Peak District, where soil that suits acid-loving plants, such as rhododendrons and azaleas, guarantees vibrant seasonal displays.

1 Bridgemere Garden World

Twenty inspirational display gardens in traditional and contemporary designs demonstrate different uses for plants.

Bridgemere, Nantwich CW5 7QB

Tel: 01270 521100 | www.bridgemere.co.uk

LOCATION On A51 7m SE of Nantwich. Signed from M6 junctions 15 and 16

Spread over 6 acres, this garden centre has 20 display gardens attached to it. Some are modern, others more traditional. They change with the seasons and are constantly being altered. One is Mediterranean in style with an area of terracotta, a fine stout pergola and many plants with striking foliage, while another has mock ruins overlooking a moat and an area devoted to moisture lovers.

A rockery and a pool filled with water lilies, surrounded by varieties of iris and astilbe, are backed by a collection of pines. Close to this is a superb bed of euphorbias, a reminder of just how many fine varieties of this plant there are. The displays of tulips are particularly impressive, and a good selection of azaleas and rhododendrons grows around the mound, which gives a fine view across the whole garden. Statuary, trellises, grottoes and garden ornaments are used to good effect throughout.

▶ *Open all year – telephone or consult website for details*

2 Cholmondeley Castle Gardens

The highlight of the landscaped castle grounds is a picturesque water garden laid out with temples to lend a classical feel.

Malpas SY14 8AH | Tel: 01829 720383

www.cholmondeleycastle.co.uk

Historic Garden Grade II

LOCATION 7 miles W of Nantwich, 6 miles N of Whitchurch on A49

Of the great formal garden laid out by nurseryman and garden designer George London in 1690, no trace remains. Instead, set in 40 acres

CHOLMONDELEY CASTLE GARDENS

of parkland and with an extensive range of mainly acid-loving trees and shrubs, the present gardens are designed to take advantage of spectacular views.

The early 19th-century castle perches majestically on a hill overlooking the estate, which includes two lakes and a well-sited cricket pitch. The lawns, which slope up to the castle, are covered with bulbs in spring.

The gardens to the west have some of the most interesting plants. In the glade, sheltered by large trees, are varieties of magnolia and cornus, an *Abutilon vitifolium*, a *Davidia involucrata*, species rhododendrons and a large liquidambar. On a lower level are primulas, narcissi and cyclamens.

The rose garden is one of the few formal areas. It consists of a pleasant layout of beds divided by stone-flagged paths, with a fine *Magnolia sieboldii* standing at the entrance. Most impressive of all is the temple garden, where the landscaping and architecture give a classical feel. Around a pool with its two grassed islands are some attractive combinations of shrubs and trees, and good use is made of purple, gold and blue foliage.

Tower Hill is a wilder area, where mature woodland of beech, oak and sweet chestnut is underplanted with camellias, more magnolias, azaleas, cornus and rhododendrons. Another water garden, known as the Duckery, has recently been restored and planted with rhododendrons, shrubs and trees, and a collection of ferns surrounds the two Victorian waterfalls.

▶ *Open main season – telephone or consult website for details – and for parties of 20 or more by appointment*

3 Ness Botanic Gardens

The clever positioning of trees for shelter enables a wide range of exotic plants, as well as azaleas and rhododendrons, to thrive.

Neston Road, Ness, Wirral CH64 4AY

Tel: 0151 353 0123

www.nessgardens.org.uk

Historic Garden Grade II

LOCATION 10 miles NW of Chester, 2 miles off A540 between Ness and Burton

Arthur Kilpin Bulley, a Liverpool cotton broker, began gardening on this site in 1898, using seeds from plants collected for him by George Forrest, the noted plant hunter. The gardens extend to 64 acres, and those who have experienced the northwest winds blowing off the Irish Sea will marvel at the variety and exotic nature of the plant life. The secret lies in the trees planted as shelter belts, and the aim has been to provide interest from spring onwards – through the herbaceous garden of summer to the heather and sorbus collections of autumn.

There are, in addition, areas of specialist interest, such as the Pinewood and adjacent areas, home to the best collection of rhododendrons and azaleas in the northwest of England. A National Collection of sorbus is held here.

▶ *Open all year – telephone or consult website for details*

4 Birkenhead Park

Joseph Paxton created the world's first civic park here, landscaped with curving lakes, a Swiss bridge and fine trees.

Birkenhead, Wirral CH41 4HY

Tel: 0151 652 5197

www.wirral.gov.uk

Historic Park Grade I

LOCATION 1 mile from centre of Birkenhead, S of A553

The world's first civic park and a milestone in garden history, this was designed by Joseph Paxton and opened in 1847. His aim was to create an idealised rural landscape of open meadows and naturalistic woodland. When garden designer Frederick Law Olmsted visited just three years later he wondered at 'the manner in which art had been employed to obtain from nature so much beauty'. Olmsted went on to incorporate much of what he had observed at Birkenhead into New York's Central Park.

Paxton's original vision is now re-emerging with an impressive restoration scheme in progress. The sinuous shapes of the lakes have been re-established, gates, iron railings and stonework refurnished or replaced, the Swiss bridge and the Roman boathouse on the lower lake restored, and an attractive new restaurant and gallery built. New plantings have been added, too. Although these are still immature, the many fine mature trees dominate the views as before.

▶ *Open all year – telephone or consult website for details*

5 Norton Priory Museum and Gardens

Set in the wooded grounds of a ruined Augustinian priory is a fine walled garden with a rose walk and ornamental borders.

Tudor Road, Manor Park, Runcorn WA7 1SX

Tel: 01928 569895

www.nortonpriory.org

LOCATION 2 miles E of Runcorn. From M56 junction 11 turn for Warrington and follow signs. From all other directions follow signs to Runcorn, then Norton Priory

The twin strengths of the gardens are a bold, coherent design and a great variety of plants. Both are to be found in the walled garden, located at some distance to the north of the property but clearly signposted.

Built in the mid 18th century, it has now been redesigned on more ornamental lines, with a rose walk running down the centre and two broad borders planted with a variety of shrub roses. It also contains an orchard of pears, plums, greengages and quinces (a National Collection of *Cydonia oblonga*, the tree quince, is held here), a vegetable garden and a distinctive herb garden. Along the south-facing wall a series of brick arches, covered with vines and honeysuckles and sheltering two large figs, is fronted by beds of perennials, planted with kniphofias, euphorbias, salvias and geums.

The woodland garden, covering 30 acres and containing many fine mature trees, surrounds the remains of the 12th-century Augustinian priory. The stream glade is the most attractive area, planted with azaleas and candelabra primulas, and a water-lily tank has a statue of Coventina (goddess of wells and streams) at its centre. There are many modern sculptures dotted around both parts of the garden.

▶ *Open all year. Walled garden open main season – telephone or consult website for details*

6 Arley Hall and Gardens

This charming garden is renowned for its herbaceous border, which is ablaze with colour from June to September.

Arley, Great Budworth, Northwich CW9 6NA

Tel: 01565 777353

www.arleyhallandgardens.com

Historic Garden Grade II*

LOCATION 5 miles W of Knutsford off A50, 7 miles SE of Warrington off A559. Signed from M6 junctions 19 and 20 and M56 junctions 9 and 10

Stretching over 23 acres, the gardens consist of many distinct areas, each with its own character, but it is for its superb herbaceous border that Arley is most famed. Dating from before 1846, it is reputed to be the earliest of its kind in England. At one end a classical pavilion provides a focal point framed by chess-piece topiary, there's a fine wrought-iron gate and a large range of perennials, includes some varieties used here a century ago.

Giving colour from June to September, the season begins with soft yellows, blues and silvers before the spires of delphiniums and aconitums make an impact along with the softer forms of gypsophila and achillea. Towards the end of the year the hotter colours of sedum, helianthus and crocosmias come to the fore.

There is plenty of interest elsewhere, too. The walled garden has perennials and shrubs grown in attractive combinations, and in the walled kitchen garden is a vinery with a good collection of tender plants and a fine border with climbing roses and clematis, irises and peonies. Topiary, mellow brickwork and stone ornaments add structure and character throughout.

Away from the more formal areas an extensive woodland garden has been created, where 300 varieties of rhododendron grow alongside rare trees and shrubs in a tranquil setting.

▶ *Hall open. Garden open main season – telephone or consult website for details*

A SERIES OF BRICK ARCHES IS COVERED WITH VINES AND HONEYSUCKLES, AND SHELTERS TWO LARGE FIGS

NORTON PRIORY MUSEUM AND GARDENS

TATTON PARK

7 Tatton Park

One of Britain's finest gardens, the park includes an elegant Italian garden, orangery and masses of rhododendrons and azaleas.

Knutsford WA16 6QN | Tel: 01625 374400

www.tattonpark.org.uk

Historic Garden Grade II*/The National Trust

LOCATION 3 miles N of Knutsford, signed from M6 and M56

Tatton Park was, for four centuries, the home of the Egertons, an immensely rich family who could indulge their every whim on their vast estate. The 50 acres of gardens here are among the finest in Britain and contain some unique features, created by the country's best designers.

Renowned designer Humphry Repton landscaped the grounds in 1791, and much of his work is still visible in the rolling parkland that surrounds the gardens. When Lewis Wyatt completed his work on the house in 1815 he designed the kidney-shaped flower garden and the elegant orangery. From 1859 Paxton was at work, and his fernery was built to take the collection of plants made by Lord Egerton's brother – it now houses New Zealand tree ferns. Also by Paxton is the Italian garden, the grandest and most formal part of the gardens. It is an arrangement of terraces spaciously laid out with an ornate design of clipped hedges and beds. They are overlooked by the south-facing portico of the house, which gives fine views across the acres of parkland.

A Japanese garden constructed in 1910 and recently restored has a wholly different feel. Set in a small valley, the contrasting textures of mounds of moss, delicate acer leaves, large stones and a gently flowing stream give it its particular charm, while large conifers provide a backdrop and lend it intimacy.

Tatton also has pools and lakes, huge numbers of rhododendrons and azaleas, a rose garden, a maze and an arboretum with some fine pines. With the help of Heritage Lottery Funding, a huge project is underway to restore the walled gardens to their former working glory, with areas of fruit and vegetables and large greenhouses, including a pinery for forcing pineapples.

▶ *Open all year – telephone or consult website for details*

8 Dial House

This sophisticated garden is based on the art of Piet Mondrian, with black-stained water, red-leaved acers and white cobbles.

62 Carwood Road, Wilmslow SK9 5DN
Tel: 01625 522098
LOCATION NE of Wilmslow off A538

Stunning in its simplicity, this modern garden is based on 1930s modernism and the paintings of Piet Mondrian. The atmosphere is cool and calm, and the planting is suitably restrained, allowing the garden's structure to play a dominant role.

The front garden focuses on a diagonal raised bed with yew hedges, water spouts and sharply constructed rectangular pools. At the rear a rectangular lawn is surrounded on two sides by canals filled with black-stained water. Stainless-steel water features are set in white cobbles to one side, interspersed with mature red-leaved acers – the main colour contribution to the garden. A gap in the shallow bank of azaleas leads to a bridge that crosses the canal to a lawn and bleached deck beyond. The whole garden is backed by spectacular trees in the adjacent wood.
▶ *Open on special charity days – telephone for details*

9 Lyme Park

A Palladian house dominates the gardens, which feature an orangery with an ancient fig and camellias, and a rose garden.

Disley, Stockport SK12 2NR	Tel: 01663 762023
www.nationaltrust.org.uk	
Historic Garden Grade II/ The National Trust	
LOCATION 6 miles SE of Stockport just W of Disley on A6	

The one lasting image you're likely to take home with you following a visit here is the view of the magnificent house in its landscaped setting seen from across the lake. Overlooking much of the garden is the south façade with its portico and fine statues of Pan and Neptune, designed in the 1720s by Giacomo Leoni in Palladian style.

But if the architecture has an Italian feel, the climate and surroundings do not. The estate stands high on the Pennines and is surrounded by moorland. To the east of the house, however, there are flowers to discover. The orangery, which is Victorian in feel, houses many ferns, an ancient fig and two camellias that are reckoned to be more than 180 years old. The Edwardian

rose garden, well protected by high hedges and walls, is laid out formally with a central pool and stone paths and ornaments. And in the generous double herbaceous border, designed originally by horticultural artist and garden designer Graham Stuart Thomas, a large collection of perennials changes from hot reds and yellows to cooler blues and pinks with the seasons.

Across the lake from the house is a wooded area with a rhododendron walk where new plantings are maturing well. To the west of the house, below the high stone terrace, lies the Italian garden, an ivy-edged parterre of 1860 that is planted with spring and summer bedding schemes.
▶ *House open. Garden open most of year – telephone or consult website for details*

10 Dunge Valley Rhododendron Gardens

These woodland gardens in a Pennine valley have outstanding collections of acers, azaleas, magnolias and rhododendrons.

Windgather Rocks, Kettleshulme, Whaley Bridge, High Peak SK23 7RF
Tel: 01663 733787
www.dungevalley.co.uk
LOCATION 6 miles NE of Macclesfield, 12 miles SE of Stockport in Kettleshulme. Signed from B5470 Macclesfield-Whaley Bridge road

Nestling in a small valley high in the Pennines, the location is so remote that often only the song of the lark or the cry of the curlew can be heard. Walks wind across and around the rocky valley, revealing wonderful views over the garden and into the rugged landscape beyond. It is a superb natural setting for many rhododendrons, camellias, acers and magnolias, with shrub and species roses providing interest later in the season.

When the garden was begun in 1983, pine, larch and hemlock were planted as shelter belts and now, even at an altitude of 300m (985ft), some surprisingly tender specimens survive. Rodgersias, rheums, primulas and other moisture-lovers cluster around the stream that runs through the valley, and close to the stone farmhouse are cultivated pockets of choice plants, including collections of meconopsis and peonies.

The expanding Hardy Plant Nursery now has one of the best collections of hybrid and species rhododendrons in the north of England, as well as meconopsis grown from seed collected by the owners in Nepal and Arunachal Pradesh (plants may be bought when the garden is closed – telephone for an appointment). The garden has increased to 8 acres with more than 600 new trees and shrubs added.

▶ *Open main season – telephone or consult website for details*

11 Mellors Gardens

In this allegorical garden, ornaments and small stone houses help to re-create John Bunyan's *The Pilgrim's Progress*.

Hough Hole House, Sugar Lane, Rainow, Macclesfield SK10 5UW │ Tel: 01625 573251

Historic Garden Grade II

LOCATION From Macclesfield take B5470 Whaley Bridge road. In Rainow turn off to N opposite church into Round Meadow, then turn first left into Sugar Lane and follow road down to garden

Where can you pass through the Valley of the Shadow of Death, climb Jacob's Ladder, see the Mouth of Hell and visit the Celestial City, all within 10 minutes? Here, at the heart of a valley in a rugged but attractive part of the Peak District, is an unusual 2 acre allegorical garden. Designed during the second half of the 19th century by James Mellor, much influenced by Swedish visionary Emanuel Swedenborg, it attempts to re-create the journey of Christian in John Bunyan's *The Pilgrim's Progress*.

There are many small stone houses and other ornaments to represent features of the journey. Most areas are grassed, with stone paths running throughout. At one end a large pond is overlooked by an octagonal summerhouse.

▶ *Open for limited season – telephone or consult website for details – and for parties of ten or more by appointment*

12 Henbury Hall

The landscaped grounds include a lake with a jet fountain, a laburnum tunnel, rare shrubs, and walled and sunken gardens.

Macclesfield SK11 9PJ

LOCATION 2 miles W of Macclesfield on A537

The classical house, modelled on the Villa Rotunda, a Renaissance villa outside Vicenza in northern Italy, sits confidently on a rising hill at the heart of the park. It has a remarkable 12 acre secret garden skilfully hidden by a backcloth of trees. The main garden to the northeast, centred around a lake with a high jet, has steep banks planted with rhododendrons, azaleas and small trees such as acers, laburnums and betula, which give it something of the aura of Stourhead (see page 105). Around the margins are beds of hostas, candelabra primulas, gunneras, irises and royal ferns.

There is a tunnel of *Laburnum x watereri* 'Vossii', and the garden includes many rare shrubs, including the blue-podded *Decaisnea fargesii*, the wedding-cake cornus (*C. alternifolia* 'Agentea') and *C.* 'Eddie's White Wonder', *Romneya coulteri*, *Embothrium coccineum lanceolatum*, *Rhamnus asplenifolia* and many magnolias.

The buildings here include a Chinese bridge, a small Chinese summerhouse and a Gothic folly. There is also a productive walled garden and a double herbaceous border. The tennis court is discreetly hidden and the swimming pool is sited within a conservatory.

At the entrance to the house is a small sunken garden with a round pool and fountain, and lawns divided into four and edged with miniature box. Three fine statues by master stone carver Simon Verity are placed around the garden.

▶ *Open for NGS*

WALKS WIND ACROSS AND AROUND THE ROCKY VALLEY, REVEALING WONDERFUL VIEWS OVER THE GARDEN

DUNGE VALLEY RHODODENDRON GARDENS

THE CELTIC CROSS
GARDEN IS ADORNED WITH
EYE-CATCHING TOPIARY
ABBEY HOUSE GARDENS

The art of clipping

Topiary has captured gardeners' imaginations through the ages, resulting in many different shapes in gardens all over Britain.

Gardens are as much about fashion as any other area of design, hence the importance of the 400-year-old garden at Levens Hall in Cumbria. Its 'Alice in Wonderland' topiary is a sole survivor of a gardening style that flourished in late 17th-century Britain, when the Grade I listed garden was created for Colonel James Grahme, a courtier of King James II.

Laid out in 1694 by Guillaume Beaumont, a pupil of Andre Le Notre, Louis XIV's gardener, the yew circles, cones, domes and spirals evoke a nation at play after the austerity of the Commonwealth. They also display French influence on the Stuart monarchs and their Tory supporters.

Most topiary was swept away in the 18th century as the political pendulum swung to the Hanoverians and the Whigs introduced naturalism into gardens. Levens survived, perhaps because of its remoteness from the political heart of the country.

Topiary is an ancient art. Evergreens such as yew, bay, holly, myrtle and phillyrea have all been shaped down the centuries, although it seems to have started with box. Evidence suggests that in 4000 BC, the Egyptians were clipping box hedges in their gardens, while Augustan Romans filled their gardens with box hedging and topiary.

Topiary was popular in medieval and 16th-century gardens, although the Tudors disliked the smell of box, preferring lavender, bay and holly. The recent reconstruction by English Heritage of the Earl of Leicester's lavish 1575 garden at Kenilworth Castle in Warwickshire (designed to win the hand of Elizabeth I), for instance, features mopheads of holly.

At Abbey House Gardens in Wiltshire, once the site of a Benedictine monastery, the crown of the Celtic cross garden is once again adorned with eye-catching topiary. Inspiration for its restoration came from 15th and 16th-century paintings.

Victorian fashions

Ostentatious Victorians displayed their wealth by laying out acres of carpet bedding. Also labour-intensive, topiary returned to fashion, as demonstrated by the magnificent Sermon on the Mount at Packwood House in Warwickshire. Bulging yews, leaning this way and that, some conical, others cylindrical, struggle up a slope towards the summit. There stands the Master, and below him, on a transverse walk, 12 mighty yews, known as the Apostles, with the four biggest specimens representing the Evangelists. With some as high as 14m (45ft), the bushes are a challenge for the gardeners, who work in places from a ladder set at 90 degrees, secured by ropes. A similar challenge is posed by the 12 razor-sharp yew pyramids, now nearly 9m (30ft) high, planted in the 1890s at Athelhampton in Dorset.

Early 20th-century topiary, inspired partly by the Arts and Crafts movement, caused flocks of clipped birds to alight on hedges across England. They can be seen among other strange topiary forms at Cliveden in Buckinghamshire, guarding the entrance to the Bathing Pool Garden at Hidcote in Gloucestershire and on plinths leading up to a stone dovecote at Rockcliffe in Gloucestershire.

Yew hunting parties

Fantasy is all part of topiary. At Mount Stewart in County Down, Lady Londonderry created a garden of many different rooms in the 1920s and 1930s. Clipped out of yew, an intricate family hunting party – including stags, the goddess Diana and two creatures from Celtic mythology – is depicted along the top of the hedge around the Shamrock Garden, while at its centre is a tabletop on which stands an Irish harp, both also in yew. At Knightshayes Court in Devon, too, lolloping topiary hounds pursue a fox along an immaculately clipped yew hedge that once enclosed the bowling green.

At Hinton Ampner in Hampshire, the garden writer and aesthete Ralph Dutton, the 8th Earl Sherborne, planted a yew avenue of pyramids and toadstools across the axis behind the house, while in front he enclosed a wild orchard within low box hedging and small pyramids. At the Manor House, Stevington in Bedfordshire, Judge Simon Brown and his wife, Kathy, have clipped 12 jurors from yew. Appropriately for a lawyer's garden, the *mise en scène* tells the story of the treason trial of finance minister Nicolas Fouquet in 1660s France.

Cloud pruning is now popular in Britain, working well with modern, minimal gardens. Introduced from Japan, it involves clearing leafy growth to reveal trees' branches and structure. In Japan, evergreen oaks, pines, hollies, yew – even azaleas – are clipped into cloud-like shapes, while landscape designer Tom Stuart-Smith dazzled at a recent Chelsea Flower Show with his cloud-pruned hornbeams. More extensive examples of cloud pruning on a wide range of trees, including horse chestnuts and leylandii, can be seen at the tranquil Pure Land Japanese Garden near Newark in Nottinghamshire.

LEVENS HALL

CUMBRIA

Exotic planting thrives in Cumbria, thanks to its virtually frost-free west coast climate. Great schemes set off the magnificence of the lakeland backdrop, while formal gardens balance colour with structured topiary.

1 Levens Hall

The historic topiary gardens that are part of the 17th-century formal grounds are renowned for their splendour and size.

Kendal LA8 0PD │ Tel: 01539 560321

www.levenshall.co.uk

Historic Garden Grade I

LOCATION 5 miles S of Kendal on A6
(M6 junction 36)

Designed in 1694 by James II's gardener, Guillaume Beaumont, this is a rare example of a historic formal garden that has survived intact and it also boasts some of the oldest topiary in the world. The garden has benefited from having only ten head gardeners in more than 300 years, providing continuity in the planting. But Levens

cannot be accused of sitting on its laurels and the influence of the current head gardener since the late 1980s has been truly innovative.

The garden is worth repeat visits to see the explosion of tulips in spring and sweeping carpets of yellow antirrhinums and *Verbena rigida* in summer. Spectacular at any time of year are the enormous topiary specimens that, having established their individual characters over the centuries, now lean and bend like giant chess pieces. Over the wall lies a 1994 tercentenary fountain, bordered with pleached limes.

Elsewhere paths lead through ancient and gnarled beech hedges, past beech roundels (at their best in spring when swathes of wild garlic flower at their feet), along herbaceous borders to imaginative vegetable gardens and a nuttery.
▶ *House open. Garden open main season – telephone or consult website for details*

2 Yewbarrow House

Magnolias and olive trees are among the many exotic plants that thrive in this garden with views over Morecambe Bay.

Hampsfell Road, Grange-over-Sands LA11 6BE

Tel: 01539 532469

www.yewbarrowhouse.co.uk

LOCATION 15 miles SW of Kendal off A590. Take B5277 to Grange-over-Sands, continue up main street past railway station to mini roundabout and turn right. At crossroads turn right, then left up Hampsfell Road

This fellside garden with a breathtaking view over Morecambe Bay lies on the site of a Victorian garden that, except for the kitchen garden, had mostly reverted to woodland. Boundary trees provide shelter from the prevailing wind and, together with an almost frost-free microclimate and well-drained soil, enable exotic plants from all over the world to flourish.

Some 4½ acres are divided into individual gardens by attractive limestone walls. There are Mediterranean and gravel gardens, ferns in woodland, a Japanese garden with a swimming pool disguised as a hot spring pool and a teahouse, flower terraces and a rhododendron area. Included in the mix are olive trees bearing flowers and some ripe fruit, phormiums, palms, yuccas, *Magnolia grandiflora*, *Paulownia tomentosa*, cannas and much more. Late summer and autumn are probably the best times to visit but the garden has been planned so there is always something in flower alongside evergreen plants providing colour and structure.
▶ *Open for NGS, and by appointment*

3 Holker Hall

The woodland gardens are at their best in spring and summer when magnolias and delicate shade-loving plants steal the show.

Cark-in-Cartmel, Grange-over-Sands LA11 7PL

Tel: 01539 558328 | www.holker-hall.co.uk

Historic Garden Grade II

LOCATION 4½ miles W of Grange-over-Sands, 4 miles S of Haverthwaite on B5278

Essentially a spring garden, Holker Hall has a welcoming and informal atmosphere and plantings that have developed over the years in a seemingly effortless way. It holds an annual festival, which has become a leading celebration of gardening and the countryside in the

northwest. The 25 acres of woodland walks and formal gardens, set in 125 acres of parkland, lie close to Morecambe Bay – of which there are glimpses from the woodland – and enjoy a mild west coast climate.

The garden has been cared for by its innovative and knowledgeable owners since the late 1970s. Some mighty rhododendrons survive from the original planting and dominate the garden in spring and early summer; the magnolias are also impressive. The range of shade-loving shrubs has been extended with a National Collection of styracaceae and massive eucryphias play a major role in the woodland from mid to late summer. The woods contain many rare and beautiful trees, most of them tagged and chronicled in the excellent guide to the garden walks.

There is another side to Holker – the varied formal gardens near the house, which have been created and developed to great effect. The cascade, echoing the more renowned falls at Chatsworth, is evocative of the Villa d'Este at Tivoli in Italy. The garden is also home to the huge Holker lime – one of the 50 trees selected as part of Her Majesty's Jubilee celebrations.
▶ *House and garden open most of year – telephone or consult website for details*

4 Windy Hall

Magnolias overhang an old quarry in this relaxed hillside garden, which has collections of aruncus and filipendulas.

Crook Road, Windermere LA23 3JA

Tel: 01539 446238

LOCATION 1 mile S of Bowness-on-Windermere, on B5284. Turn up Linthwaite Hotel driveway

Four acres around Windermere have been worked around a row of early 17th-century terraced cottages now converted into a single home, which is tucked beneath a stony hillside. To the front of the house a yew hedge and rose-covered pergola enclose the Best Garden, the most formal area in an informal garden.

The rear garden stretches up the steep slope, leading to woodland underplanted with species rhododendrons at the highest level. A deserted quarry area overhung by *Magnolia sinensis* and *M. wilsonii* and carpeted with moss has all the calm and simplicity of a Japanese garden. Other international influences crop up throughout the garden in the design and in the plants grown, some of which were raised from seed collected on expeditions to China.

The owners' scientific backgrounds have led to the cultivation of National Collections of aruncus and filipendulas – not just herded into trial ground beds, but integrated within the garden. They actively encourage all wildlife (except deer and rabbits) – one pond is a dedicated 'insect factory' and the original kitchen garden provides abundant fruit for both birds and owners.

Ornamental wildfowl, pheasant aviaries and a flock of Hebridean sheep enlivens the scene. There are 28 years of good gardening practice to be learned from a visit here.

▶ *Open for NGS, and by appointment*

5 High Cross Lodge

A cascading stream weaves its way through this sloping exotic garden, where tall tree ferns benefit from high rainfall.

Bridge Lane, Troutbeck LA23 1LA

Tel: 01539 488521

LOCATION 2½ miles N of Windemere off A591. From Windermere, turn right after Lakes School into Bridge Lane next to YHA

The present owner has created an exotic garden on a 1 acre slope that would be remarkable in Cornwall, never mind the Lake District. Fortunately it is protected to the north by columns of conifers 30m (100ft) tall.

Tree ferns, some 30 in all, are a highlight, thriving in the region's generous rainfall. Yuccas, phormiums and bamboos mingle with architectural plants such as euphorbias, *Melianthus major*, alliums, eucomis and the palms *Chamaerops humilis* and *Trachycarpus fortunei*, with *Cordyline australis* contributing to lend an evergreen structure.

This is an acid-soil area so rhododendrons, azaleas and acers also make an appearance and a delightful stream fed by a nearby pond on the fells weaves its way under various bridges before disappearing into the beck below the garden. The sound of trickling water adds to the peaceful atmosphere, which can be enjoyed from a charming summerhouse situated at the top of the garden.

▶ *Open for NGS, and by appointment*

6 Brantwood

Victorian visionary John Ruskin lived here and his intriguing garden includes a horticultural depiction of Purgatory.

Coniston LA21 8AD | Tel: 01539 441396

www.brantwood.org.uk

LOCATION On E side of Coniston Water off B5285, signposted. Regular boat services

This is a superb site with wonderful views, atmosphere and history. The rocky hillside behind the house is threaded with a wandering network of paths created by John Ruskin, the Victorian artist and visionary social reformer, to delight the eye and please the mind. A succession of eight small, individual gardens threads through the landscape, exploring themes that fascinated Ruskin. This 'living laboratory' of ideas is being revived, and Ruskin's Professor's Garden, the woodland pond and harbour walk are maturing.

An extensive collection of British native ferns surrounds an icehouse and several waterfalls. There is a British herb garden, and the allegorical Zig-Zaggy, a series of meandering paths winding up a mound, depict the levels of Purgatory found in Dante's *Divine Comedy*. The High Walk, actually a Victorian viewing platform, encourages contemplation of the magnificent lakeland scenery beyond the garden. The high points of the year here are spring and autumn.

▶ *House and garden open most of year – telephone or consult website for details*

7 Holehird

On a hillside overlooking Windermere, the garden has three alpine houses, a cascade garden and a Victorian terrace.

Patterdale Road, Windermere LA23 1NP

Tel: 015394 46008

www.holehirdgardens.org.uk

LOCATION 1 mile N of Windermere on A592 Patterdale road

Managed by a charity dedicated to promoting and developing the science, practice and art of horticulture with special reference to the conditions in the Lake District, this garden is maintained to a high standard by its members, who are all volunteers. It lies on a hillside site alongside the house with a natural watercourse and rocky banks looking over Windermere to the Langdale Pikes. There are 20 acres of attractive gardens and trial areas, and also alpine houses.

Much of the earlier planting has been preserved, including many fine specimen trees, together with acid-loving plants that do well in the free-draining soil. Highlights are the summer-autumn heathers, winter and spring-flowering shrubs, alpines, grasses and National Collections of astilbes, hydrangeas and polystichums. Fine herbaceous borders, herbs and climbers occupy the walled garden.

The site has expanded to encompass the lower Victorian terrace of the estate, linked by a beautiful cascade garden, and includes fountains, a pergola and other original period features. A woodland walk has been planted with specimen maples and drifts of snowdrops.

The views of the fells from the garden are breathtaking. The Lakeland Horticultural Society now also manages the Holehird Tarn with its many resident birds and fish; the aim here is to reinstate the overgrown paths and introduce sympathetic wild gardening schemes.

▶ *Open all year – telephone or consult website for details – for NGS, and for parties by appointment*

8 Dalemain Historic House and Gardens

The grounds include a Tudor knot garden, a Stuart terrace and an orchard with old-fashioned varieties of apple.

Dalemain Estate Office, Penrith CA11 0HB

Tel: 01768 486450

www.dalemain.com

Historic Garden Grade II*

LOCATION On A592 3 miles W of Penrith on Ullswater road

Dalemain, essentially a plantswoman's garden developed with an artist's appreciation for form, texture and colour, has evolved in the most natural way from a 12th-century defensive pele tower with its kitchen garden and herbs. The Tudor-walled knot garden remains, as do the Stuart terrace (1680s) and the walled orchard where apple trees like 'Nonsuch' and 'Keswick

Codling', planted in 1728, still bear fruit. The gardens were re-established during the 1960s and 1970s with shrubs, a collection of more than 100 old-fashioned roses and other rarities, together with richly planted herbaceous borders along the terraces and around the orchard.

A wild garden displays a fine collection of Himalayan blue poppies in early summer. From here, visitors can walk past the Tudor gazebo into woodland overlooking the Dacre Beck.

▶ *House open. Garden open most of year – telephone or consult website for details*

9 Hutton-in-the-Forest

Elaborate gardens near the house include terraces that date from the 17th century, an old walled garden and Victorian topiary.

Penrith CA11 9TH | Tel: 01768 484449

www.hutton-in-the-forest.co.uk

Historic Garden Grade II

LOCATION 6 miles NW of Penrith on B5305 (M6 junction 41)

The garden is a compelling setting for an intriguing house that ranges across the centuries – from a 13th-century pele tower to Victorian architect Anthony Salvin's handsome alterations. The garden is itself a mixture of features from the 17th to the 20th centuries. It has great visual appeal, with a magnificent view from the 17th-century terraces embellished with Victorian topiary. The walled garden, dating from the 1730s, is divided into compartments and contains excellent herbaceous borders, trained fruit trees and roses.

The backdrop of the house, the surrounding yew hedges and compartments and well-filled herbaceous borders combine to make a dramatic composition. Some of the mature woodland trees were planted in the early 18th century. Other features in the grounds include a 17th-century dovecote, an 18th-century lake and a cascade.

▶ *Open main season – telephone or consult website for details – and for parties by appointment*

NORTHWEST ENGLAND

A WILD GARDEN DISPLAYS A FINE COLLECTION OF HIMALAYAN BLUE POPPIES
DALEMAIN HISTORIC HOUSE AND GARDENS

LANCASHIRE, LIVERPOOL AND MANCHESTER

Glorious gardens, planted and tended with artistry and imagination, grace the region's urban spaces and rural surroundings. Unusual, often eccentric designs underlie many of the modern schemes.

1 National Wildflower Centre

Conservation is the focus of this urban garden, where native wild flowers such as harebells and marsh marigolds thrive.

Court Hey Park, Roby Road, Liverpool L16 3NA

Tel: 0151 738 1913 | www.nwc.org.uk

LOCATION 5 miles E of Liverpool city centre, just off M62 junction 5

Set in the 35 acre Victorian Court Hey Park, this tranquil haven is only 5 miles from Liverpool city centre. It was opened in 2001 thanks to funding from the Millennium Commission to promote the creation of new wild-flower habitats and the preservation of native species.

The former walled garden lies at its heart, housing a wild-flower nursery and demonstration areas interestingly planted with combinations of around 60 species of wild flowers. It is managed as a subtly tended wilderness, displaying the vibrant colours of native British wild flowers such as harebells, cowslips and marsh marigolds, sweet violets, oxeye daisies and yellow flag irises. There are also three natural ponds, which help to attract a wide variety of wildlife.

Old buildings have been refurbished and lie alongside a modern, award-winning building with a rooftop walkway and flower meadow, which gives an aerial view of the centre and park.

▶ *Open main season – telephone or consult website for details*

2 Liverpool Botanic Gardens

A greenhouse holds a collection of cacti and orchids while the Japanese garden features acers, bamboo and pines.

Calderstones Park, Liverpool L18 3JD

Tel: 0151 225 4877 | www.liverpool.gov.uk

LOCATION 4 miles SE of city centre, S of A562

One of the best 'free' gardens in the country, this 126 acre landscaped park has mature trees, a lake and a rhododendron walk. Close to the house, a series of gardens is set around the old walled garden. To the front of the house, a long herbaceous border, 6m (18ft) deep, has a range of colourful perennials. Beyond this, the flower garden features large clumps of grasses and daylilies as well as beds of annuals.

Overlooking the flower garden is a greenhouse containing a sample of National Collections of codiaeums, dracaenas and aechmeas, many fine orchids in season and an impressive collection of cacti. To the rear of the greenhouse the Old English flower garden has beds of perennials, bulbs and shrubs set within a formal layout of paths, with a circular lily pool and pergolas bearing clematis, vines, golden hops and honeysuckle at its centre.

In the Japanese garden, acers, pines and clumps of bamboo fringe a chain of rocky streams and pools. A recently restored rock garden, a large lake, a bog garden and a rose garden can be found on the outer edges of the park. Children will enjoy the 'text garden' maze and the millennium playground.

▶ *Park, Old English and Japanese gardens open all year – telephone or consult website for details*

3 Mill Barn

This imaginative riverside garden has follies, sculptures and a suspension bridge from which to view the many perennials below.

Goose Foot Close, Samlesbury Bottoms, Preston PR5 0SS

Tel: 01254 853300

LOCATION 6 miles E of Preston on A677 Blackburn road, turn S into Nabs Head Lane, then Goose Foot Lane

The sight and sounds of the River Darwen are ever-present in this tranquil garden. An elevated viewing platform extending from the conservatory provides an initial impression of the garden, and terraces near the house invite the visitor to discover follies, sculptures and semi-wild areas where nature is only just under control.

A wire and metal bridge leads to a folly (under construction), and walks up the bank through the woods give good views down to the river and glimpses back to the garden. On the riverbank are extensive plantings of perennials and further along a spectacular 'Paul's Himalayan Musk' rose climbs up a tall tree.

There is a sense of fun and adventure here. The owner is experimenting with vigorous perennials set among grassed areas and fruit trees. A lengthy herbaceous border sweeps along one boundary and is backed by a yew hedge cut in the form of a dragon. A heptagonal summerhouse nestles among tall plants, with a stone folly disguising a septic tank opposite and a temple of alchemy has been created from an old sluice gate.

An alien-looking sculpture by David Booth, which is set into the wall, overlooks a rectangular pool with a good variety of water plants. The artistic influences of the potter-owner combine with the beautiful setting to give this garden its special appeal.

▶ *Open for NGS and for individuals by appointment, and mid June to mid July for parties by appointment*

4 Gresgarth Hall

An exciting, multi-faceted garden, it has been developed as a testing-ground for a range of design styles and plantings.

Caton LA2 9NB │ Tel: 01524 771838

www.arabellalennoxboyd.com

LOCATION 4 miles NE of Lancaster. From M6 junction 34 take A683 towards Kirkby Lonsdale, then turn right in Caton village to Quernmore

The rare mix of plant artistry, natural elements and great maintenance sets Gresgarth, the garden of renowned designer Arabella Lennox-Boyd, apart from many others. The setting is a cold valley cut out of the surrounding fields over millennia by a tributary of the River Lune called Artle Beck. The sound of water is ever present, and water plants are the first to catch the eye. The terraces sweeping down from the house to the lake are romantically planted with roses, clematis and more tender plants in season, and the predominating pinks, purples and ▷

GRESGARTH HALL

silver-whites perfectly complement the rugged grey stone of the Gothic house.

One small garden consists of a superb pebble mosaic of swirling cloud forms by Maggy Howarth, with each corner featuring the zodiac sign of one of the four family members. There is also an olive tree for the Italian-born Lady Lennox-Boyd, a temple for architecture and the meteorological elements. The kitchen garden, a short walk away, displays the same qualities of innovation and order as can be found throughout the 12 acres.

The valley is planted on both sides with a collection of rare and interesting trees and shrubs, many of them grown from seed collected in Japan. There are new pathways on the southwest slope of the valley and a river viewing deck has been added on the house side. A Chinese-style bridge that crosses the fast-running beck entices the visitor to seek out the sculptures, classical and modern, including a folly and tufa obelisk set among feathered birch trees. A beech walk snakes to one side of the garden. The whole design is so seemingly effortless that the unfolding areas — colour-themed borders, a pleached lime walk and a circular lawn — appear as a continuous joyous indulgence for the senses.

▶ *Open for limited season — telephone or consult website for details*

5 Clearbeck Arts Garden

Run on organic principles, the garden makes innovative use of recycled materials in sculptures dotted throughout the site.

Higher Tatham, Lancaster LA2 8PJ

Tel: 01524 261029

www.clearbeckgarden.org.uk

LOCATION 10 miles E of Lancaster. From M6 junction 34 take A683 towards Kirkby Lonsdale, turn right on B6480 and follow signs from Wray

With fine views to the Three Peaks and the Lake District, the owners have created this unusual 5 acre garden since 1972. Surrounded on three sides by farmland, a sense of open countryside pervades and the relaxed planting around the lake and boundaries helps to encourage an enormous variety of wildlife into the garden.

Spaces are shaped to offer surprises around every corner, and eccentric buildings, some of them semi-buried, are part of the landscape. Allegorical themes inspire some parts, such as the Garden of Life and Death. This is entered through a large pyramid made from recycled materials,

and fits in perfectly with the organic nature of the garden. Dominating the upper part of the garden is a 2 acre lake spanned by a wooden bridge that twists and turns on its route over the water, and a convincing mock-classical temple stands to one side with views back into the garden and across the water. Among the clever lakeside sculptures is a striking fish made of recycled CDs, and other metal sculptures adorn the paths winding around the garden.

The generous planting includes large collections of shrub roses and beds of mixed perennials surrounding the stone house. With its grass maze, a folly called Rapunzel's Tower and little hiding places, the garden will also appeal to children.

▶ *Open for NGS and for parties by appointment*

6 Fletcher Moss Botanical Gardens

At the heart of Manchester, this botanical oasis includes a rockery, collections of alpines and Chusan palms, and a water garden.

Mill Gate Lane, Didsbury M20 2SW

Tel: 0161 445 4241

LOCATION 5 miles S of city centre on Mill Gate Lane, S of A5145, close to centre of Didsbury

Here, close to a busy part of south Manchester, is a tranquil green oasis of 21 acres, with a large range of plants, an historic rockery and a water garden — and it is free to enter.

The creation of the garden began in 1889 with the large rockery (in effect, a mountainside in miniature) on which a collection of alpines was grown. It is still impressive, with large stones embedded in the steep south-facing slope forming a series of terraces, paths for the visitor and pockets of soil for the plants — including massed alpines, bulbs and small shrubs, many conifers and the odd well-placed small tree. Japanese maples cast light shade in places, and there is a large tulip tree and a collection of Chusan palms.

A small stream cascades down the rocky terraces to the rich foliage of the water garden. A restful walled terrace gives views across the garden to the meadows and trees of the Mersey Valley. It was also here that the RSPB was founded in 1889.

▶ *Open all year — telephone or consult website for details*

7 Walkden Gardens

Known locally as the 'Secret Garden', this inspiring park has a Japanese stroll garden, cherry walk, fuchsia and scented gardens.

Derbyshire Road, Sale, Manchester M33 3EL

www.walkengardens.co.uk

LOCATION 6 miles S of Manchester, ½ mile E of Sale town centre, at junction of Marsland Road (A6144) and Derbyshire Road

This is a gem of a park, transformed in recent years from a rather forlorn area into a modern showpiece. Supported and partially maintained by a strong 'Friends' group, it is an inspiring example of how urban public spaces may not only be regenerated but can continue to develop. Gates decorated with silhouettes of birds hint at what lies behind, giving a glimpse through to a circular dovecote, planted with roses, clematis and cistus.

Distinguished by a series of beech-hedged outdoor rooms, there's a ceramic and pebble mosaic 'compass point' at its heart. Beside the dovecote, the sinuous dry-stone wall seat snakes its way down one side of the entrance lawn, holding back a forest of *Rosa rubrifolia*. An authentic Japanese stroll garden leads on through a cherry tree walk to the newest project, Miss Cordingley's Garden, where a spiral of mown grass and low yew hedges (interrupted by substantial charred oak seats) appear through taller grasses with a copper beech at the centre.

The main borders of mixed planting dissect the gardens and lead on to other intimate areas. There's a wisteria arch, fuchsia, scented and conservation gardens and in the Field of Hope, planted by Marie Curie Cancer Care, a blaze of daffodils in spring spread beneath young maples.
▶ *Open all year – consult website for details*

8 17 Poplar Grove

Many plants have been selected for their foliage in this distinctive garden, which features a 'living' roof and unusual grotto.

Sale M33 3AX | Tel: 0161 969 9816

www.gordoncooke.co.uk

LOCATION SW of city centre off M60 junction 6. From A6144 at Brooklands Station turn into Hope Road; Poplar Grove is 3rd turning on right

That the owner is a landscape gardener and potter is soon evident, for in a small space and suburban setting he has created a most distinctive garden. It was a masterstroke to set the paths at diagonals to the main axis and this, together with the changes in level and varied use of building materials, creates interest throughout.

Many of the plants are chosen for their foliage shape and colour – phormiums, thistles, alliums, euphorbias, cordylines, grasses and ferns all contribute to the variety. A 'living' roof has been added to a porch and an unusual grotto sunk into the ground with plants growing over the top. This overlooks a long rectangular pool surrounded by pieces of modern sculpture. Other water features and fine ceramics are spread around the garden and within a new exhibition space.
▶ *Open June by appointment*

9 Dunham Massey

Set in an ancient deer park, the grounds include Britain's largest winter garden with a camellia walk and more than 170,000 bulbs.

Altrincham, Cheshire WA14 4SJ

Tel: 0161 941 1025

www.nationaltrust.org.uk

Historic Garden Grade II*/The National Trust

LOCATION 3 miles SW of Altrincham off A56

Fallow deer still roam freely in the park of this 3,000 acre estate. The house dates from the 18th century, but the broad stretch of water around its north and west sides is the original Elizabethan moat. Five avenues – which predate the English Landscape School of the 18th century – radiate out from a *patte d'oie* in front of a triple row of lime trees each side of the southern forecourt.

The 29 acres of gardens seem to improve every year, with some excellent new planting. Close to the entrance, bordering a small stream, are huge drifts of moisture-loving perennials and, further along beside a rustic bridge are *Meconopsis* x *sheldonii*, damp-loving ferns and a collection of acers. Fine specimen trees, including a *Quercus suber*, are to be found on the expansive lawn, which is overlooked by an 18th-century orangery and surrounded by banks of shrubs.

The Garden Wood shelters a large collection of azaleas and hydrangeas, and a new 7 acre winter garden – the largest in Britain – opened in 2009. More than 170,000 bulbs have been planted, together with a triangle of some 50 white-stemmed birches underplanted with black-stemmed cornus and snowdrops, a 50-strong camellia walk and hundreds of trees and shrubs chosen for their winter bark, scent or flower.
▶ *House and park open. Garden open most of year – telephone or consult website for details*

NORTH WEST ENGLAND

Northeast England

Spanning the rolling Dales as well as the heather-clad moors of Yorkshire and Northumberland, the varied landscapes contain a wealth of geological and natural riches. These have inspired the region's gardeners and resulted in a number of spectacular designs.

Berwick-
upon-Tweed

A1

A697

Bamburgh

⑫

⑩ ⑪
Alnwick

Northumberland
National
Park

⑨

A68

• Otterburn

A1068

A696

① Morpeth
②
⑧ ③
④

A189

Newcastle-
upon-Tyne
Gateshead

A69 Hexham

A692 Sunderland

⑦

⑥ ⑤

Consett

A167

Durham ⑬

A1(M)

DURHAM and
NORTHUMBERLAND
232-237

Hartlepool
Bishop
Auckland A689

⑭
Barnard
Castle A688

A66 Middlesbrough

Darlington

A66 Whitby

Richmond
⑳

North York Moors
National Park

A171

Hawes •

A1

A19

Scarborough

A170 Pickering

Thirsk

⑦

A165

Yorkshire Dales
National Park

㉑

① ②
③

A64 ⑥

Ripon
⑱ ⑳

⑤

YORKSHIRE
240-249

④

Bridlington

A65

⑲

A61

A166

Settle •

A59

Harrogate

A1237

⑰

⑯

York

A64

⑫ ⑭ ⑮

A658

⑬
Leeds

Bradford M621

A646
Halifax ⑪

Selby

⑧

A63

A1079 A165

Kingston-
upon-Hull

A58

M62

Wakefield

M62

A614

A63

A638

A19

M18

A635

M1

Doncaster

A628

⑩

A1(M)

A631

Sheffield

⑨

A57

KEY

① Garden location

County boundary

Motorway

Principal A road

Huddersfield

A629

Rotherham

DURHAM AND NORTHUMBERLAND

A variety of visionary gardens have been created in these northeast counties. Topiary, medicinal herbs, winter planting and the largest sandstone rock garden in Europe are among the highlights.

1 Bide-a-Wee Cottage

A disused quarry has been transformed into a dramatic garden, making full use of its setting to display a wide range of plants.

Stanton, Netherwitton, Morpeth NE65 8PR

Tel: 01670 772238 | www.bide-a-wee.co.uk

LOCATION 7 miles NW of Morpeth, 3 miles SW of Longhorsley, off A697 Morpeth-Coldstream road

One of the most enchanting and richly planted gardens in the northeast, its 2½ acres occupy a long-abandoned stone quarry and some of the higher surrounding land, combining formal, informal and wild features. The varied topography, soil and climate allow for a diversity of plants to be grown, from marsh-loving to drought-tolerant species, and the natural rock-faces have been exploited to maximum effect and enriched by sympathetic planting.

As well as being a skilled plantsman, the owner is a splendid mason whose stonework has done much to embellish the garden. There is also a timber summerhouse with an adjacent planting of arisaemas in a shady corner. Many of the plants are well labelled, and a National Collection of centaureas is held here. An excellent plant sales area offers unusual species (catalogue available).

▶ *Open main season – telephone or consult website for details – and for parties of 20 or more by appointment*

2 Herterton House

This 1 acre plot is cleverly divided into five areas, including a winter topiary garden and a knot garden planted with medicinal herbs.

Hartington, Cambo, Morpeth NE61 4BN

Tel: 01670 774278

LOCATION 11 miles W of Morpeth, 2 miles N of Cambo off B6342, signed to Hartington

The present owners took over the land and near-derelict Elizabethan building – with commanding views over picturesque upland Northumberland – in 1976. With vision and skill they have divided

their 1 acre plot into five distinct areas. In front, is a formal winter topiary garden. Alongside this is a cloistered 'monastic' knot garden planted mainly with medicinal, occult and dye-producing herbs.

To the rear, a flower garden with hardy flowers chosen with an artist's eye is their most striking achievement. This part of the garden contains more impressive topiary, which is appropriate to the formal setting in front of a period house. Many unusual varieties of traditional plants, including species from the wild, flourish here. The fourth area, the Fancy Garden, has a parterre and a gazebo raised on a terrace.

▶ *Open main season – telephone or consult website for details*

3 The Garden Cottage

An artistic garden is filled with unusual plants and imaginative plantings including a large bed modelled on a dry river course.

Bolam Hall, Bolam, Morpeth NE61 3UA

Tel: 01661 881660

www.gardencottagebolam.com

LOCATION 15 miles NW of Newcastle. Turn off A696 after turn to Belsay Hall, follow sign to Bolam – telephone in advance for directions

Protected by a long south-facing wall, the present owners have created a 1½ acre garden of great artistry and imagination. The centrepiece is a large bed modelled on a dry graveled river course and surrounded by a terrace with beds built up to suggest riverbanks, creating the impression of a sunken garden. A recent addition is the Contemplation Garden with low-maintenance, naturalistic plantings.

Everywhere the colours are exuberant, both warm and cool, and the planting is inspirational, with new and unusual plants introduced regularly. Structural planting is well conceived – a beech arch, buttressed by a pair of cone-shaped yews, finds an echo in a single beech near the southern boundary – and winter interest is sustained by the coloured stems of cornus and willow.

Abstract and animal sculptures enliven the main garden, where there are also secluded areas with seats for relaxation. North of the protective wall a large meadow garden is maturing.

▶ *Open for NGS and other charities, and by appointment*

4 Belsay Hall, Castle and Gardens

Snowdrops and lilies attract visitors to these plant-rich gardens in spring, while a quarry garden provides year-round interest.

Belsay, Newcastle-upon-Tyne NE20 0DX

Tel: 01661 881636

www.english-heritage.org.uk

Historic Garden Grade I/English Heritage

LOCATION 14 miles NW of Newcastle on A696

With rare, mature and exotic specimens spread throughout the 30 acre site, this beautifully tended garden is well worth repeated visits. Of particular note are the snowdrop and lily collections.

The gardens were created between 1795 and 1933. Formal terraces were built around the austere neo-classical hall, leading through woods to a unusual 'garden' fashioned inside a quarry, which provided the building with its stone. The Victorian features were added later.

The hall terrace looks across to massed rhododendrons, and a path from the 18th-century hall leads through formal areas – a flower garden, a magnolia terrace and a winter garden – to the quarry garden and from there to the 14th-century castle, about half a mile away on fairly level ground.

The winter garden featuring many heathers also has rhododendrons and a 28m (92ft) high Douglas fir planted in 1839. An unexpected pleasure is the croquet lawn, which is in ▷

HERTERTON HOUSE

regular use. The quarry garden was carefully contrived, dominated by massive hewn slabs covered in lichen to achieve a wild romantic effect. The sheltered microclimate has resulted in the luxuriant growth of some remarkable and exotic trees and shrubs, which look dramatic in the light and shade of the sandstone gorge.

The 1½ mile Crag Wood walk is a stepped, serpentine path that passes by the lake and through the hanging woods opposite the hall to the south.

▶ *Hall and castle open. Gardens open all year – telephone or consult website for details*

5 Mowbray Winter Gardens

A striking glass-and-steel structure houses tree ferns, banana plants and citrus trees, which can be viewed from a treetop walk.

Burden Road, Sunderland SR1 1PP

Tel: 0191 553 2323

Historic Park Grade II

LOCATION In city centre

The Winter Gardens within the 24 acre Mowbray Park are not to be missed. A remarkable construction of glass and steel houses a variety of exotic plants. Tree ferns, banana plants, citrus trees and scented flowering shrubs create a lush canopy, which can be viewed from a treetop walk. A specially commissioned water sculpture by William Pye – whose work is also displayed at Gatwick airport – cascades in torrents, adding to the exotic atmosphere.

On the south side the habitat and atmosphere of a Mediterranean hillside is evoked by olive and citrus groves, a little stream and dry-stone terracing. The cracks in the wall are filled with colourful spring-flowering plants such as *Aristolochia sempervirens*, *Clematis cirrhosa balearica*, cyclamen and the sea squill, *Urginea maritima*.

The park itself, now restored to its Victorian splendour, is awash with colour in rose arbours, shrub borders and formal bedding displays. Winding paths lead to a quarry garden and a lime-stone crag at the more naturalistic southern end of the park.

▶ *Open all year – telephone for details*

6 Gibside

Restored decorative buildings are sited at key points in the landscaped grounds and fine vistas can be enjoyed.

Burnopfield, Gateshead NE16 6BG

Tel: 01207 541820

www.nationaltrust.org.uk

Historic Garden Grade I/The National Trust

LOCATION 6 miles SW of Gateshead, 20 miles NW of Durham from B6314, off A694 at Rowlands Gill. Signed from A1(M)

Gibside was once one of the finest 18th-century designed landscapes in England. In 1729, among wooded slopes cut through with radiating avenues, a series of buildings was commissioned. Each one was carefully sited, and all were constituents of a harmonious plan. They included a Gothic banqueting house, a Palladian chapel and stables. The landscape *pièce de résistance* was a grand terrace with a statue to British Liberty – on a column taller than Nelson's in London – at one end and James Paine's stately Palladian chapel, an architectural masterpiece, at the other.

The National Trust, assisted by the National Heritage Memorial Fund, has acquired 354 acres to secure the future of this great landscape garden and to protect the chapel's setting. Well-marked walks have been opened up with views to the ruined hall, orangery and other estate buildings in the grounds. Restoration of the ruined buildings and removal of the Forestry Commission's intrusive tree planting is ongoing.

▶ *Open all year – telephone or consult website for details*

7 The Garden Station

Once a country railway station, this garden has been designed on three levels and makes good use of its unusual setting.

Langley on Tyne, Hexham NE47 5LA

Tel: 01434 684391

www.thegardenstation.co.uk

LOCATION 9 miles W of Hexham off A69 Newcastle-Carlisle road. Turn onto A686 near Haydon Bridge. Continue past Langley Castle Hotel for 2 miles, then follow signs

Surrounding the restored Victorian railway station on the former Hexham to Allendale line running through Langley Woods, this is a tranquil and most unusual garden. Set out on three levels, there's a heavily wooded bank on one side that drops down to the old station and its platform, now planted with cottage-garden borders, tubs and a collection of scented plants. The lowest level, the railway track, is occupied by a lawn bordered by an attractive mixture of bulbs and perennials, ferns, shrubs and trees.

A richly planted woodland walk extends the garden eastwards along the route of the old railway line, passing under the arches of two magnificent Victorian railway bridges, which frame a long vista. The garden is an imaginative tapestry of foliage and texture, created in harmony with the landscape, and includes a gentle water cascade and several sculptures.

▶ *Open most of year – telephone or consult website for details – and for parties by appointment*

8 Wallington

An attractive woodland walk leads to a walled garden with a well-stocked conservatory and restored peach house.

Cambo, Morpeth NE61 4AR

Tel: 01670 773600

www.nationaltrust.org.uk

Historic Garden Grade II*/The National Trust

LOCATION **20 miles NW of Newcastle off A696 (signed on B6342)**

The handsome 18th-century house is set within 65 acres of lawns, terraces with fine views and flowerbeds. It is serene and quintessentially English. However, it is the walled garden across the entry road, accessed via an attractive woodland walk, that has the most appeal.

A rill runs from the pond to narrow lawns fringed with beds on two levels, and climbers cluster on the old walls. The sloping site reveals the layout of the garden, drawing attention to the harmonious and generously filled herbaceous border, and a rich tapestry of colour is revealed at every turn. There is an 18th-century garden house designed in Tuscan style, a Victorian peach house that has been restored and a spectacular Edwardian conservatory, which holds a diverse range of plants and a fountain of peace.

Outside, the walks step down from a classical fountain past beds redesigned in the 1930s, including notable heathers and many herbaceous perennials. Trees planted in 1738 include a great larch, the sole survivor of three original larches, by the China Pond.

▶ *House open. Walled garden and grounds open all year – telephone or consult website for details*

9 Cragside House

Europe's largest sandstone rock garden can be found here, alongside towering trees and vibrant displays of seasonal bedding.

Rothbury, Morpeth NE65 7PX

Tel: 01669 620333

www.nationaltrust.org.uk

Historic Garden Grade I/The National Trust

LOCATION **13 miles SW of Alnwick off A697 between B6341 and B6344**

In the 19th century Lord Armstrong, one of the greatest of Victorian engineers, clothed this hillside above the Coquet Valley with millions of trees and shrubs as the setting for a house designed by R. Norman Shaw that was, at the time, the wonder of the world. Below the house, the rock garden – the largest sandstone rock garden in Europe – is planted with an impressive display of heathers, shrubs, alpines and dwarf rhododendrons, which are spectacular in spring.

The path then descends towards the Debdon valley, crossing the river by an iron bridge from which there are views of the majestic conifers. It then continues to the 1864 clock tower overlooking a high-Victorian formal garden, which is set on three terraces with a quatrefoil pool as its centrepiece. The middle terrace contains an imposing orchard house with rotating fruit pots of 16 types of fruit, to one side of which is a bed planted with small foliage plants in formal patterns typical of the 1870s.

Carpet bedding is taken literally at Cragside – the two beds here are planted with a different design each year, often inspired by the patterns of carpets in the house. In the formal beds, some 6,000 tulips are planted for spring colour.

Between the middle and lower terraces is the dahlia walk, filled annually with 650 to 700 mixed cultivars and at its best in September and October. On the lower Italian terrace a loggia made of bold, pierced cast iron is a remnant of the extensive range of glass structures once found here.

The walk back through the valley impresses on the visitor the contrasting forces of wild romanticism and industrial technology, which influenced this estate in equal measure. A number of rare North American coniferous species, given to the National Trust by the Royal Botanic Gardens in Edinburgh, have been planted on the estate, which covers 1,000 acres in total.

▶ *House and garden open most of year – telephone or consult website for details*

NORTH-EAST ENGLAND

10 The Alnwick Garden

A grand cascade forms the centerpiece of this garden whose other highlights include a poison garden and an enormous treehouse.

Denwick Lane, Alnwick NE66 1YU

Tel: 01665 511350 | www.alnwickgarden.com

Historic Park and Garden Grade I

LOCATION 35 miles N of Newcastle upon Tyne. Take A1 and turn W at Alnwick

This contemporary garden has been created since 2001 within a walled garden that had been derelict since the 1950s. A grand cascade forms the spine of this contemporary garden. Enclosed by lines of arched hornbeam pergolas, the cascade sends water tumbling down a series of 27 weirs. The pattern of the fountains changes every half hour.

The path then leads to a formal ornamental garden, entered through three interlinked stone arches. This walled enclosure contains 16,500 European plants, the largest collection in Britain. Pergolas and arbours are covered in ramblers and vines, and rills lead to secret enclosed gardens with yew hedges. To the right of the entrance is a pretty rose garden. There is also one of the largest treehouses in the world, a poison garden featuring some of the world's deadliest plants, a bamboo labyrinth and the Serpent Garden, where William Pye water sculptures rise above a holly hedge.

The pavilion terrace looks south over the Grand Cascade and is linked to the rest of the garden by east and west terraces planted with specimen trees and topiary. The newest addition is an orchard with more than 300 Prunus 'Taihaku'.

▶ *Open all year – telephone or consult website for details*

11 Howick Hall

Best known for its woodland garden and spring bulbs, there is also a wild bog garden and an extensive arboretum.

Howick Estate Office, Alnwick NE66 3LB

Tel: 01665 577285

www.howickhallgardens.org

Historic Garden Grade II

LOCATION 6 miles NE of Alnwick, 2 miles N of Longhoughton, off B1339

Surrounding the imposing Georgian house are gardens created largely between 1920 and 2001. The tradition of plantsmanship and dendrology on a grand scale has continued, executed with appealing informality. The garden is worth visiting at every season, starting with drifts of snowdrops that are followed by a spectacular display of old daffodil varieties, with fritillaries to follow and tulips mingling with wild flowers in a Botticelli-like meadow. The borders around the hall then burst into life, and the woodland garden flowers with a rich variety of rhododendrons, camellias and magnolias, including two magnificent *M. campbellii*, all underplanted with drifts of shade-loving species.

The bog garden surrounding a pond has an interesting range of late summer-flowering plants grown from seed collected from the wild. Woodland walks to the west and east take in an arboretum planted with more than 12,000 trees and shrubs grown from seed collected in all parts of the temperate world, particularly China and Japan.

▶ *Open most of year – telephone or consult website for details*

12 Chillingham Castle

An original parterre of clipped box and yew in the castle's Elizabethan walled garden has been restored to its former glory.

Chillingham NE66 5NJ

Tel: 01668 215359/215390

www.chillingham-castle.com

Historic Park and Garden Grade II

LOCATION 12 miles NW of Alnwick between A1 (signposted), A697, B6346 and B6348

Since the 1200s, this has been and continues to be the family home of the Earls Grey and their kinsmen, and the medieval castle provides a spectacular backdrop to a remarkable garden. The original garden was laid out in 1684, removed by 'Capability' Brown in 1752, then replaced and landscaped in 1828 by Sir Jeffry Wyatville (who redesigned Windsor Castle).

The Elizabethan-style walled garden has been virtually excavated to rediscover its intricate pattern of clipped box and yew (enlivened by scarlet tropaeolum), with rose beds, fountains, a central avenue and a spectacular herbaceous border running the whole length. Outside the walled garden are lawns and a rock garden, delightful woodland and lakeside walks beside seasonal drifts of snowdrops, daffodils, bluebells and rhododendrons.

▶ *Castle open. Gardens open main season – telephone or consult website for details – and by appointment*

CROOK HALL AND GARDENS

13 Crook Hall and Gardens

Flower beds imitate the stained-glass windows in Durham Cathedral in this romantic garden with a moat and maze.

Sidegate, Durham City DH1 5SZ

Tel: 0191 384 8028

www.crookhallgardens.co.uk

LOCATION In centre of Durham, near Millburn Gate

The Grade I listed medieval manor house is surrounded by 6 acres of romantic themed gardens. These include secret walled enclosures where venerable fruit trees are clothed with 'Rambling Rector' and 'Wedding Day' roses, a garden planted with Elizabethan favourites and aromatic herbs, and one in which the flowerbeds have been designed to represent the stained-glass windows of the cathedral. There is also a moat pool, a wild-flower meadow and a maze.

Magnificent views of both cathedral and castle may be enjoyed from many parts of this attractive, peaceful place. It is a must on the itinerary for visitors to Durham, especially in June.

▶ *House and gardens open main season – telephone or consult website for details – and for NGS*

14 Eggleston Hall Gardens

Winding paths take the visitor past rare perennials and through a lovingly restored churchyard with Victorian greenhouses.

Eggleston, Barnard Castle DL12 0AG

Tel: 01833 650115

www.egglestonhall.co.uk

LOCATION 5 miles NW of Barnard Castle on B6278

The 4 acres of walled gardens accompanying the 19th-century house and its lodge include many plants of note – *Syringa emodi*, veratrums, epimediums, fritillaries, meconopsis and a host of rare perennials. The signature plant is *Celmisia spectabilis* 'Eggleston Silver' from New Zealand.

The winding paths within the main garden offer much excitement, rounding corners to reveal colourful vistas that change with the seasons. The old churchyard has been lovingly restored, with interesting plantings among the gravestones and within the sheltered, roofless area inside the church walls. Three Victorian greenhouses are still in everyday use, and a good range of plants is for sale in the nursery.

▶ *Open all year – telephone or consult website for details*

Architects of the land

The theatrical visions of a small group of designers has resulted in an abundance of fine landscaped grounds and enchanting vistas.

Lying far away from the social and political hub of London, the great estates of Yorkshire and the north counted originally almost as personal fiefdoms. During the 18th and 19th centuries, the Industrial Revolution increased the wealth of their owners who, in turn, made stars of the fashionable garden designers of the day.

Lancelot 'Capability' Brown, who started life as a garden boy and ended up Mayor of Huntingdon and a wealthy man, was at work at Scampston Hall in 1772 and 1773. His style of grouping parkland trees may have been dismissed later by the Picturesque school as 'belting, clumping and dotting', but the hall's owner, Sir William St Quintin, followed the designer's instructions, building a ha-ha, reshaping the lake and creating an island in it. Brown went on to add other ornamental touches, including a decorative bridge and a cascade.

Scampston was just one of many commissions that Brown was involved with during his long working life. Like the great designers and plantsmen of every generation – William Kent, Charles Bridgeman and Humphry Repton,

Joseph Paxton and William Robinson, Geoffrey Jellicoe and Harold Peto, Brenda Colvin and Hal Moggridge, Kim Wilkie and Christopher Bradley-Hole – he was a consummate professional, hardworking, confident of his skills and at ease with his rich and noble clients.

Many landscape designers are noted for their versatility and sense of theatre. Commissioned to improve the park and woods at Longleat in the 1960s, Russell Page found himself working on one of Lord Bath's pet projects – Cheddar Gorge. He was not only called upon to build a restaurant and museum but to work out every last detail, from the ashtrays to the waitresses' uniforms.

Life on the road

Joseph Paxton designed an airy glasshouse for the Duke of Devonshire at Chatsworth in 1836 to house the immensely rare Amazonian waterlily (diplomatically named *Victoria regia* by its finder, Robert Schomburgk) and then invited the press corps of the day to view the trophy, posing his daughter Annie on a tin tray on one of its vast saucer-shaped leaves. Paxton was able to

pass much of his year at Chatsworth, but other landscape designers had to spend long days on the road – the engineer Thomas Telford once compared himself to Napoleon on his Italian campaign, 'fighting battles at fifty or a hundred miles distance every other day'.

A sublime place

Scampston is one of a trio of grand houses, grouped with near-neighbour Castle Howard and Harewood House further to the south. At Castle Howard, the Earl of Carlisle chose John Vanbrugh and Nicholas Hawksmoor as his architects. But although he employed them to design follies and temples for the grounds he seems, like others of his generation, to have acted as his own landscaper. The waspish essayist Horace Walpole marvelled at his achievement: 'Nobody has told me that I should at one view see a palace, a town, a fortified city, temples on high places, woods worthy of being each a metropolis of the Druids, the noblest lawn in the world fenced by half the horizon, and a mausoleum that would tempt one to be buried alive.' The creation of this 'sublime' place involved the moving of an entire village that interrupted the earl's view.

Brown was also busy at Harewood, where his landscaped park was rivalled in Victorian times by the grandiose parterre laid out by Charles Barry.

Barry had refashioned a broad terrace in front of the house in Italian style in 1843. The 20th-century designer Sylvia Crowe mourned the 'gradual disintegration of the landscape tradition' as estates were transferred from gifted and enlightened amateurs to 'wealthy manufacturers, to whom Elysiums meant less than nothing'. At Harewood, however, the commissioner was a belted earl, and he and his successors spared the 18th-century parkland. Brown and Barry's designs continue to coexist, alongside some decorative modern flourishes. Castle Howard remains essentially the place admired by Walpole, and Scampston too has kept its rolling parkland.

Today, however, along with other grand gardens such as Broughton Grange in Oxfordshire, Scampston is memorable for spearheading a recent gardening trend – the revival of the 18th-century walled kitchen garden. Scampston's walled garden now has an unashamedly modern feel to it but other ancient walled gardens retain their original designs. Some are used to demonstrate organic methods or showcase traditional varieties of fruit and vegetables, while others have been turned into decorative potagers – an attractive kitchen garden radiating out from a centrepiece, in which fruit, vegetables, herbs and cutting flowers are combined to form a beautiful display.

TEMPLES ON HIGH PLACES AND WOODS WORTHY OF BEING EACH A METROPOLIS OF THE DRUIDS
CASTLE HOWARD

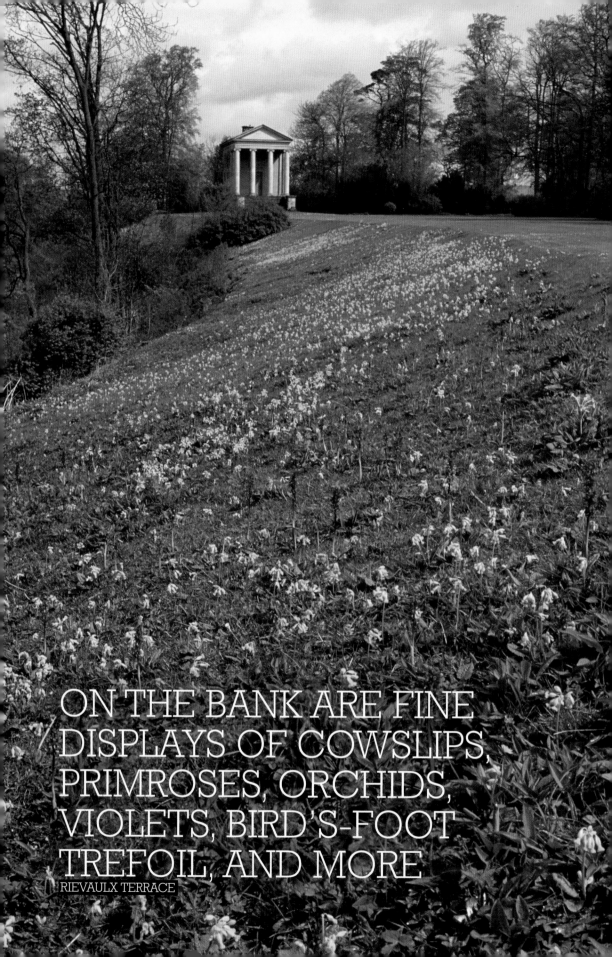

ON THE BANK ARE FINE DISPLAYS OF COWSLIPS, PRIMROSES, ORCHIDS, VIOLETS, BIRD'S-FOOT TREFOIL, AND MORE

RIEVAULX TERRACE

YORKSHIRE

Set amid the striking scenery of the Dales and moors, Yorkshire's gardens offer infinite variety – from remarkable terraces and historic landscapes to serene water gardens and naturalistic planting schemes.

1 Rievaulx Terrace

Vibrant spring flowers decorate the banks of the serpentine grass terrace, from which there are fine views to the Rye valley.

Rievaulx, Helmsley YO6 5LJ

Tel: 01439 798340 | www.nationaltrust.org.uk

Historic Park Grade I/The National Trust

LOCATION 10 miles E of Thirsk, 2½ miles NW of Helmsley on B1257

This is a wonderful example of the 18th-century passion for the romantic and picturesque. Here, the concept is achieved perfectly. The work was carried out around 1754 and consists of a half mile long serpentine grass terrace high above Ryedale, with views of the great ruins of Rievaulx, one of Britain's finest Cistercian abbeys. At one end is a Palladian Ionic temple-cum-banqueting house, at the other a Tuscan temple with a raised platform.

Visitors who want to see flowers should focus their attention on the grass bank below the terrace, where a mass of wild flowers can be found, including cowslips, primroses, orchids, violets, bird's-foot trefoil and ladies' bedstraw. Blossom throughout the spring season comes from cherries, blackthorns, rowans, whitebeams, elders and lilacs.

▶ *Open main season – telephone or consult website for details*

2 Nawton Tower

Formal, grassy paths thread through a series of carefully composed 'plant tapestries', with a surprise at every junction.

Highfield Lane, Nawton, York YO62 7TU

Tel: 01439 771218

LOCATION 14½ miles E of Thirsk, 2½ miles NE of Helmsley, off A170. In Nawton and Beadlam, turn left up Highfield Lane for 2 miles

The atmospheric 12 acre garden on the edge of the North York Moors was created during the 1930s. It consists of a series of formal grassy walks between living tapestries woven from a masterly selection of trees, rhododendrons, azaleas and old shrub roses, underplanted by drifts of bluebells and other spring bulbs. Every junction from the central walk leads to a fresh surprise, including a statue on a pedimented gazebo as the focal point of another pathway, a yew-hedged topiary garden, and a quiet clearing with a silent stone fountain at its centre.

▶ *Open limited season – telephone for details – and by appointment in spring*

3 Duncombe Park

The crescent-shaped half mile grass terrace has a temple at either end, while near the house is an elegant classical garden.

Helmsley YO62 5EB

Tel: 01439 772625/771115 (during open hours)

www.duncombepark.com

Historic Park Grade I

LOCATION 12 miles E of Thirsk, 1 mile SW of Helmsley off A170

Built in 1713, it is the grass terrace, similar to that at nearby Rievaulx (see left), for which the 35 acre garden is justly renowned. From the Ionic rotunda, a broad, sweeping terrace stretches half a mile in extent, resembling a wonderful green crescent moon. It leads to another grander temple in the Doric order, where the river in the valley below turns 300 degrees, giving the impression that the temple is set upon a promontory. Farther back towards the house, partly hidden in woodland, is a conservatory built in 1851, of which only the central orangery remains intact.

On either side of the house are sunken parterres (one white and grey, another red and purple) originally laid out in 1846 and recently restored. They contrast well with the huge yews partially encircling the perimeter, which in spring are bedecked with *Clematis montana*.

The house dominates the great square lawn with its large figure of Father Time sitting at the junction of grass and terrace. As a landscape it is a wonderfully simple composition – an essay in tones of green broken only by the extravagant display of a roaming peacock.

▶ *House open. Garden open main season – telephone or consult website for details*

NORTHEAST ENGLAND

4 Sutton Park

The terraced garden is a mix of casual and formal styles, including a parterre with pruned pear trees and a semi-wild glade.

Sutton-in-the-Forest, York YO61 1DP

Tel: 01347 810249/811239

www.statelyhome.co.uk

LOCATION 8 miles N of York on B1363

Part of the 72 acre park – laid out in the 1750s by designer Adam Meikle, a follower of 'Capability' Brown – was enclosed in the early 1960s and three terraces were planted, each with a distinct character. Large panels of lawn and crisp paving characterise the topmost terrace, which is flanked by borders filled with shrubs, old roses and herbaceous perennials. A wisteria tumbles out of a large old conifer. Broad steps lead on down past a fine Judas tree to a narrower terrace with a double parterre punctuated by eight weeping pears clipped to resemble silvery green umbrellas.

On the lowest terrace, a beech hedge marks the boundary while a magnificent cedar of Lebanon lends an air of maturity. This terrace has been transformed into a water garden, with a stone-edged canal pool. A pair of white-painted wirework gazebos festooned with roses stand at either end of the terrace.

To the west the garden becomes more natural with a semi-wild glade, which is enchanting in spring. An old Edwardian rock garden is being developed as a fernery, and beyond some fine old trees stretches a long, low laburnum walk.

▶ *House open. Gardens open main season – telephone or consult website for details*

5 Castle Howard

The impressive landscaped grounds are the work of Vanbrugh and Hawksmoor, designed in classical style with temples and fountains.

York YO60 7DA | Tel: 01653 648333

www.castlehoward.co.uk

Historic Park Grade I

LOCATION 15 miles NE of York, 5 miles SW of Malton off A64

Sir John Vanbrugh and Nicholas Hawksmoor, the two foremost architects of the early 18th century, pressed every one of the 1,000 acres of parkland and garden here into service to do justice to the scale and grandeur of the house, which was designed for the 3rd Earl of Carlisle in the first quarter of the 17th century.

Vanbrugh and Hawksmoor created a 3 mile long beech and lime avenue punctuated by eye-catching features leading up to the house. Other garden buildings were erected at key points, the most well known being Hawksmoor's mausoleum in the park and Vanbrugh's Temple of the Four Winds at the extremity of the garden. William Nesfield redesigned the formal gardens around the house, adding the Atlas Fountain in 1853 as the centrepiece of an elaborate south parterre but this was demolished barely 50 years later.

The 18th-century walled garden has been comprehensively redeveloped since 1975, when a rose garden was created to enrich the air and delight the eye. The plantings here and elsewhere in the grounds make up one of the most extensive collections of old-fashioned and species roses in the country. Delphinium borders add further interest and the old sundial garden has been transformed into an elegant potager.

The large early 18th-century woodland garden known as Ray Wood has been replanted with a wonderful collection of trees and shrubs, including species and hybrid rhododendrons, magnolias, acers and vacciniums. A separate 127 acre arboretum has been developed in conjunction with the Royal Botanic Gardens at Kew since 1975.

▶ *House open. Garden open all year – telephone or consult website for details*

6 Scampston Hall

A neglected walled garden has been transformed by a contemporary design that features grasses and meadow planting.

Malton YO17 8NG | Tel: 01944 759111

www.scampston.co.uk

Historic Park and Garden Grade II

LOCATION 5 miles E of Malton off A64

In 1998 the Dutch landscape designer Piet Oudolf, a leading figure in the 'New Wave Planting' movement of naturalistic garden design, was commissioned to produce a scheme for the almost derelict 4½ acre walled garden at Scampston. He came up with an imaginative take on a traditional garden feature – a series of garden rooms, each with its own distinct character.

Running the length of the perimeter wall is a border planted with spring-flowering shrubs and perennials underplanted by bulbs and autumn-flowering hydrangeas. The first space encountered is called Drifts of Grasses, with swathes of molinia – more than 6,000 plants – alternating with mown turf to create waves of purple spikelets in

August. To the north, lies a cut-flower garden laid out as a series of circular beds. To the south is the Silent Garden, where an army of yew pillars 3m (9ft) tall guards a large square reflecting pool.

Around the old dipping pool and conservatory, a perennial meadow demonstrates Oudolf's skill at naturalised planting, using colour, texture and form to give a long season of interest. A grove of katsuras (*Cercidiphyllum japonicum*) underplanted with woodland species acts as a backdrop and foil to the meadow plantings.

Beyond a garden inhabited by huge 3m (9ft) cubes of box lies the Serpentine Garden, which echoes the waves in the Drifts of Grasses area but instead uses undulating 2m (6ft) high walls of yew backed by broad shrub borders. Across a beech *allée* set in a cherry orchard and surrounded by wild flowers, the Mount, resembling an Aztec pyramid, provides a superb vantage point.

The 70 acres of gardens and park were originally laid out by Charles Bridgeman, although they were much altered later in the 18th century by 'Capability' Brown, who built the unusual Ionic 'bridge building' in 1772 to terminate a vista at the end of the lake. The large rock garden, built in 1890 and recently restored, looks at its best in May and June.

▶ *House and surrounding gardens open for limited period. Walled garden open main season, for parties of 20 or more, and for garden tours by appointment. Telephone or consult website for details*

7 Jackson's Wold

A formal potager, wild-flower meadow and a walled garden created from a cattle yard are just some of the attractions.

Sherburn, Malton YO17 8QJ

Tel: 01944 710335

www.jacksonswoldgarden.com

LOCATION 11 miles E of Malton, 10 miles SW of Scarborough off A64. In Sherburn take Weaverthorpe Road at traffic lights, then fork right to Helperthorpe Wold

The 3 acres of garden here have been carved from meadowland and a former farmyard, with a spacious lawn flanked by borders and rough grass as the introduction. Circular steps lead into the walled garden, divided by rose screens with the borders imaginatively planted in cool white and pale yellow on one side and hot red, pink and purple on the other.

Hostas abound around the entrance courtyard, where a sunny box-encircled pool is cooled by masses of purple salvias and more blue hostas,

and groups of cistus and potentillas anchor the house into the broad house lawn surrounded by elegantly sculptured borders planted with a backbone of shrubs and masses of perennials.

To the side of the house is a long, neatly laid out kitchen garden. Box-edged beds contain regiments of vegetables, while in the lower section a true-lovers' knot emphasises the formality and directs the eye to a Victorian-style greenhouse. A walk of limes, cut through a meadow white with cow parsley, leads towards a view over the Vale of Pickering. There is also a small nursery.

▶ *Open limited season – telephone or consult website for details – for NGS and by appointment*

8 Stillingfleet Lodge

Once run as a smallholding, the gardens have developed to create intimate spaces, with plants chosen for texture and colour.

Stillingfleet, York YO19 6HP

Tel: 01904 728506

www.stillingfleetlodgenurseries.co.uk

LOCATION 6 miles S of York. From A19 York-Selby road take B1222 signed to Sherburn in Elmet. In Stillingfleet turn opposite church

This charming and imaginative 2 acre garden has developed gradually since 1974 on a windswept plot sloping down to the River Fleet. The 18th-century farmhouse is surrounded by small, intimate spaces planted with great skill, each based upon a colour theme but with an emphasis on foliage and form. It is also a garden full of surprises.

Beyond a simple country hedge the scale is larger and bolder with an avenue of *Fagus sylvatica* 'Dawyck Gold' flanked on either side by long double borders – one part in shade, the other in full sun. A few carefully selected shrubs provide structure, but it is the herbaceous perennials, grouped together, that make the most impact.

Farther on is a meadow planted with specimen trees and species roses chosen both for their flowers and hips. Enveloped by naturalistic plantings, the pond sits comfortably with the meadow and leads into a play area.

More recently, a modern interpretation of a rill garden has been created, its simplicity in marked contrast to the luxuriant planting all around. The whole garden is rich in unusual herbaceous plants and has a particularly fine collection of hardy geraniums and pulmonarias.

▶ *Open main season – telephone or consult website for details – and for NGS*

9 Sheffield Botanic Garden

Some of the country's oldest glasshouses hold 15 collections of plants, organised by habitat or botanical theme.

Sheffield S10 2LN | Tel: 0114 268 6001

www.sbg.org.uk

Historic Public Park Grade II

LOCATION ½ mile from A625, 1 mile SW of city centre. Follow signs for University of Sheffield

First established on a 19 acre site in 1836, major works completed in 2005 have largely restored the original Gardenesque layout. The chief glory of the garden is the magnificent 90m (295ft) long pavilions that are among the earliest curvilinear glasshouses in the country.

The collections stand at the head of a broadwalk, flanked by herbaceous borders, that leads to a fountain. Paths radiate out into 15 different themed areas, including Mediterranean, American and woodland plantings. The rose garden has been restored to its original design and replanted with many old species and hybrids, however, the prairie garden is a modern concept, established from seed in 2004 and now dominated by plants ranging from spring-flowering *Baptisia australis* and *Phlox pilosa* to autumn-flowering *Aster gubinellus* and Rudbeckia fulgida. The National Collections of weigelas and diervillas are also exceptional.

▶ *Open all year – telephone or consult website for details*

10 Wentworth Castle Gardens

Extensive restored formal gardens include a garden planted in the shape of the Union Jack flag and a Victorian secret garden.

Lowe Lane, Stainborough, Barnsley S75 3ET

Tel: 01226 776040 | www.wentworthcastle.org

Historic Park Grade I

LOCATION 3 miles SW of Barnsley off M1 junction 37, 2 miles along minor roads between Stainborough and Hood Green. Follow signs for Northern College

This is one of the most exciting gardens in Yorkshire – 500 acres of parkland, 60 acres of pleasure gardens, a walled garden and a ¾ mile long serpentine lake, laid out between 1708 and 1791. A £15 million project is nearing completion, and visitors are encouraged to tour the garden and parkland to see this ambitious work in progress. It includes the restoration of the gardens, including the Union Jack Garden, the Victorian secret garden, Stainborough Castle and the park and woodland. The home farm has been transformed into a visitor centre and café.

▶ *Open all year – telephone or consult website for details – and for parties by appointment*

11 Dove Cottage Nursery and Garden

Relaxed in feel, yet carefully planned, this garden is packed with plants, with grasses adding movement and structure.

Shibden Hall Road, Halifax HX3 9XA

Tel: 01422 203553

www.dovecottagenursery.co.uk

LOCATION 4½ miles W of M62 off A58. From junction 26, follow sign for Halifax (A58); at junction with A644 cross traffic lights and turn left after 180m (600ft) down Tan House Hill

Although under half an acre in size, the garden is densely planted with not even a square inch of lawn to be seen. Created from a field since 1997,

DOVE COTTAGE NURSERY AND GARDEN

it is set between maturing yew hedges. Aside from a spine of low box hedging, it is composed entirely of herbaceous perennials put together in a similar style to that of Dutch garden designer Piet Oudolf.

The owners make frequent trips to the Netherlands and Germany, so the garden is rich in new cultivars, blended together with skill and imagination. Colour is a major consideration, with strong yellows, oranges and scarlet-reds kept to the bottom of the garden – the combinations reflect the influence of renowned designer Gertrude Jekyll. Grasses are also imaginatively used as structural plants, rather like shrubs but providing grace and movement that few shrubs can achieve.

A gravel terrace affords a wonderful view over this glorious tapestry with slender spires of veronicastrums threading their way down the slope. A seat is thoughtfully placed half way up.

The garden reaches its peak in late July, August and September, when the owners are able to take a break from their thriving nursery business and enjoy it.

▶ *Open main season – telephone or consult website for details*

12 Golden Acre Park

Mature woodland and gardens surround a lake in this park, which has trial beds for chrysanthemums and dahlias.

Otley Road, Leeds | Tel: 0113 2610374

LOCATION **NW of Leeds off A660 Leeds-Otley road at approach to Bramhope**

This municipal park holds National Collections of syringas, hemerocallis and large-leaved hostas. In addition, the northern groups of both the National Chrysanthemum Society and the National Dahlia Society hold trial beds in the demonstration gardens. There is also a lake, set back from which is a fine collection of azaleas, mostly old Ghent hybrids, flourishing in gentle shade with a backdrop of denser woodland.

A large cherry meadow leads on to a huge heather garden studded with pines and silver birch. The park also features a cottage garden, a courtyard with tender plants and a collection suitable for pots, a scree garden, an ornamental pond and fountain, and a miniature railway.

▶ *Open all year – telephone or consult website for details*

13 Tropical World

Birds and butterflies flutter among tropical plants in the exotic houses, which include a rainforest area and an arid house for cacti.

Roundhay Park, Roundhay, Leeds LS8 2ER

Tel: 0113 266 1850 | www.leeds.gov.uk

Historic Park Grade II

LOCATION **S of A6120 northern ring, off A58 Roundhay Road from city centre**

The 700 acre parkland with its fine trees and wild-flower meadows is a wonderful setting for the canal gardens, with their formal bedding and generous collections. Nearby are the Monet and the Alhambra gardens, and there is also a ravine, landscape gardens, woodland, a lake, waterfalls and a sham castle.

The exotic houses, inhabited by butterflies and birds, hold the largest collection of exotics outside Kew. Tropical plants surround waterfalls and pools, and an arid house holds a large number of cacti and succulents. There is an underwater world of plants and fish, a re-created rainforest environment and a nocturnal house where bush babies, monkeys and other animals can be seen.

▶ *Open all year – telephone or consult website for details*

14 York Gate

An imaginative use of local stone and architectural features enhances the collections of rare and unusual plants.

Back Church Lane, Adel, Leeds LS16 8DW

Tel: 0113 267 8240 | www.yorkgate.org.uk

LOCATION 2¼ miles SE of Bramhope, off A660

Local stone, cobblestones and gravel have been used alongside exceptional plantings to create this 1 acre garden of impeccable taste and style. Clever use has been made of architectural features and topiary, too.

It is also a plantsman's garden, with rare and unusual plants displayed in a sequence of different settings. These include a miniature pinetum, a dell with a stream, a canal garden, fern and peony borders, a herb garden with a summerhouse, a kitchen garden and white borders. An area known as Sybil's Garden has recently been redesigned in a more contemporary style, using grasses and summer-flowering perennials in pinks and blues.
▶ *Open main season – telephone or consult website for details*

15 Bramham Park

This rare example of a surviving early formal landscape garden has wide avenues, ornamental ponds and cascades.

Wetherby LS23 6ND | Tel: 01937 846000

www.bramhampark.co.uk

Historic Park Grade I

LOCATION 10 miles NE of Leeds, 15 miles SW of York, 5 miles S of Wetherby, off northbound A1

Bramham is one of only a very few early formal landscape gardens to survive virtually untouched – a plan of the garden made in 1728 reveals just how little has changed. The house and its 70 acres of formal gardens were created for the owner Robert Benson (later Lord Bingley) and completed by 1710. Near the house is a formal parterre and dry cascade – currently a rose garden, it is in the process of being restored to its original appearance – with a broad herbaceous border flanking one of the avenues leading down to the obelisk ponds and cascades. These distinctive water features and broad avenues are what makes Bramham so unusual.

The formal grounds are bounded by a ha-ha, with viewpoints into the surrounding 900 acre park provided at the end of avenues cut through the woodland or hedge-lined *allée*, in the French formal style championed by the eminent designer André Le Nôtre. Many of the buildings that adorn this remarkable landscape are the work of James Paine and date from the 1740s and 1750s.
▶ *House open for parties of ten or more by written appointment. Garden open main season – telephone or consult website for details*

16 Harewood House

Designed by 'Capability' Brown and Charles Barry, the grounds include an Italianate terrace, a lakeside garden and an aviary.

Harewood, Leeds LS17 9LG | Tel: 0113 218 1010

www.harewood.org

Historic Park and Garden Grade I

LOCATION 7 miles N of Leeds on A61

In 1772 'Capability' Brown was commissioned to improve the park surrounding a new mansion. The natural terrain was much in his favour and his refashioned landscape was painted by JMW Turner. Brown would still recognise the park, but Sir Charles Barry added a broad Italianate terrace to the house in 1843. Barry's elaborate box parterre with its mile of hedging has been restored and planted with blue hyacinths in spring and heliotropes in summer – the effect against the yellow-tinged stone of the house and walls is quite stunning. A broad herbaceous border, mixing perennial and tender plants as in Victorian days, continues the soft pastel colour scheme.

On the upper west terrace a simple and sophisticated modern garden was laid out in 1993, with hornbeam hedging reflecting the massive bulk of the house and centred around a terracotta dolphin fountain. Beneath the bastion wall, in contrast to the cool, subtle shades directly round the house, lies another border planted with hot colours, using many tender species not readily associated with Yorkshire gardens. Behind Carr's stable block is the Bird Garden, where plants are themed by geographical zone. This leads on to a woodland garden densely planted in the 19th century with a fine collection of rhododendrons.

At the head of the lake is a Himalayan garden, a sunken glade originally laid out in the 1770s and now graced by a stupa – a Buddhist memorial shrine built of local stone under the supervision of a Bhutanese lama. In 1999 of a spiral labyrinth was added in the old walled garden.
▶ *House open. Grounds open most of year – telephone or consult website for details*

RHS HARLOW CARR

17 RHS Harlow Carr

The RHS's northern show garden has a range of display gardens, in which innovative planting and creative designs are a hallmark.

Crag Lane, Harrogate HG3 1QB

Tel: 01423 565418

www.rhs.org.uk/harlowcarr

LOCATION 1½ miles W of Harrogate on B6162

Harlow Carr's beautifully planted streamside garden, criss-crossed by numerous packhorse bridges, shows how the boundaries of design and planting styles can be extended. It is also renowned for its variety of candelabra primulas.

From the lake a magnificent avenue sweeps through woodland and into an arboretum, passing a broad wild-flower meadow and bird hide. Elsewhere are display gardens, including a large herb garden, a shrub-rose walk, a scented garden and a border of ornamental grasses. A kitchen garden has been created using the raised-bed system and is separated from the neighbouring winter walk by modern herbaceous borders. In 2005, the old long walk, leading from the former entrance gates to the streamside, was replanted with perennials in the fashionable prairie style.

To celebrate the Royal Horticultural Society's bicentenary in 2004, the BBC commissioned a landmark gardening series, *Gardens through Time*, for which seven gardens were created here exploring fashions and tastes from the Regency period through to the present day.

Spanning 58 acres, Harlow Carr may not be as extensive as its southern sister, Wisley, but in its setting and diversity of plantings it more than holds its own. It also has the benefit of a plant centre stocking a wide range of plants that are found in the garden.

▶ *Open all year – telephone or consult website for details*

18 Studley Royal and Fountains Abbey

This World Heritage Site has a Georgian water garden with lakes, formal canals, follies and views of the abbey ruins.

Ripon HG4 3DY

Tel: 01765 608888

www.fountainsabbey.org.uk

Historic Park Grade I/The National Trust

LOCATION 4 miles SW of Ripon, 9 miles N of Harrogate. Follow Fountains Abbey sign off B6265 Ripon-Pateley Bridge road

The 880 acres of Studley Royal, deservedly a World Heritage Site, were created by John Aislabie. Formerly Chancellor of the Exchequer, his career ended in 1720 as a result of his part in the stockmarket crash that became known as the South Sea Bubble. He retreated to his estate in 1722 and worked until his death in 1742 to make the finest water garden in the country.

The lakes, formal canals and water features, with buildings such as the Temple of Piety, turned what is essentially a landscape with large trees and sweeping lawns into one of the most beautiful landscaped gardens in the world. The Banqueting House, which is believed to have been designed by Palladian architect Colen Campbell, gives fine views of the grounds, while the Surprise View, a door in a small building, allows a first glimpse of the distant ruins of Fountains Abbey.

▶ *Abbey, garden and deer park open all year – telephone or consult website for details*

19 Parcevall Hall Gardens

Set on a steep hillside in the scenic Dales, bedrock above the house has been exposed to create an impressive rock garden.

Skyreholme, Skipton BD23 6DE

Tel: 01756 720311

www.parcevallhallgardens.co.uk

Historic Garden Grade II

LOCATION 10 miles NE of Skipton, 1 mile NE of Appletreewick off B6265 Pateley Bridge-Skipton road

Perched on the side of a steep hill, this ¼ acre garden gives glorious views to a craggy distant peak known as 'Simon's Seat'. Broad graceful terraces follow the slope, and the whole garden is designed in the Arts and Crafts tradition. The planting has been sympathetically renovated

and includes a border of hardy fuchsias, a white border and two fine *Prunus* x *yedoensis*. A newly planted orchard containing old late-flowering apple varieties flanks the red borders, which provide the finale.

The garden and its environs lie on the South Craven Fault, enabling the owners to exploit the rock. Above the house a magnificent rock garden has been created by stripping away the thin soil to expose the bedrock – the result is spectacular. Set in light woodland crossed by small streams, masses of Himalayan poppies enjoy the dappled shade, while in summer the air is rich with the scent of the *Primula florindae* naturalised among the rocks and little rills.

Below, a rose garden that is said to be based on a traditional Mogul design has been replanted with modern English varieties. A camellia walk leads back down the hill towards the beck, where the acid soil is ideal for rhododendrons, many of which are unique to the garden.

▶ *Open most of year – telephone or consult website for details*

20 Newby Hall and Gardens

Grand herbaceous borders flanked by yew hedges are surrounded by formal garden rooms planted for year-round interest.

Ripon HG4 5AE

Tel: 0845 450 4068

www.newbyhall.com

Historic Garden Grade II*

LOCATION 4 miles SE of Ripon on B6265, 3 miles W of A1

The 25 acre garden as it appears today is mostly the work of Major Edward Compton, who in 1921 had the good fortune to inherit the house described by Celia Fiennes – author of *Through England on a Side Saddle in the Time of William and Mary* – in 1697 as 'the finest... I saw in Yorkshire'. The house was greatly enriched after 1766 by architect Robert Adam and furniture designer Thomas Chippendale. Compton swept away most of the Victorian features, but his alterations reveal a fine eye for proportion and perspective.

Compton also planted hedges and trees to provide shelter in the garden. Grassing over some Victorian parterres on the south front, he created a pair of herbaceous borders more than 200m (650ft) long, backed by yew hedges and leading down towards the River Ure. They remain Newby's most well-known feature and are a magnificent sight at the height of the season.

On either side of a broad cross-axis known as the Statue Walk is a series of enclosed gardens, each with a different theme and planting style. A formal rose garden, filled with old-fashioned roses and herbaceous plantings, is flanked by an autumn garden that brings the gardening year to a rich and fiery finale. Nearer to the house, the large enclosed garden known as Sylvia's Garden was formerly brought to a peak in time for the York races in May, but it has a longer season now.

Elsewhere, a curving pergola festooned with laburnum leads down to an enormous rock garden resplendent with an aqueduct and waterfall. In the more naturalistic areas off the two axis walks are extensive plantings of trees and shrubs. The garden contains a National Collection of cornus and is rich in rhododendrons and magnolias. There is also a well-stocked plant centre.

▶ *Open main season – telephone or consult website for details*

21 Thorp Perrow

Many rare trees and shrubs are found here, as well as a mass of spring bulbs, blossom and autumn leaves for year-round colour.

Bedale DL8 2PR

Tel: 01677 425323

www.thorpperrow.com

Historic Arboretum Grade II

LOCATION 10 miles N of Ripon, 2 miles W of Bedale, signed off B6268 Masham Road

With more than 2,000 species, the old-established arboretum boasts one of the finest collections of trees in England. To explore the 100 acres visitors can follow the tree trail, the nature trail or amble at their own leisure, passing the Victorian pinetum, a beautiful 16th-century woodland underplanted with shade-lovers, a 1 acre bog garden viewable from a raised walkway, an area planted specifically for bees and butterflies, and streamsides fringed by hostas and ferns. The year starts with a mass flowering of snowdrops, followed by thousands of naturalised daffodils, crocuses, chionodoxas, muscaris and scillas. Next come the bluebells, camassias and alliums. Wild flowers appear in summer, and the autumn colour provided by trees and shrubs is stunning.

National Collections of ash, cotinus, limes, laburnums and walnuts are planted here, and there are 62 champion trees. Plantings are continually being refreshed or reinvented, while falconry demonstrations, a collection of rare breeds and a children's play area extend the appeal.

▶ *Open all year – telephone or consult website for details*

22 Millgate House

This town garden makes good use of a small space, with more than 40 old-fashioned roses and many variegated evergreens.

Richmond DL10 4JN

Tel: 01748 823571

www.millgatehouse.com

LOCATION In Richmond, in corner of Market Square opposite Barclays Bank

From the Market Square a green door opens onto a corridor leading to a narrow stepped lane (known as a 'snicket' in Yorkshire) set between house and boundary wall. Pots filled with bold foliage line the path, while a golden hop and a *Clematis montana* festoon the walls.

The garden, just a third of an acre in size, is especially delightful in June and July. Opening off to the right, it is laid out before the charming Regency-fronted house and comprises two small rectangles set on two different levels linked by broad rustic steps. The top area has a small, naturalistic lawn, but the space is dominated by a large *Rosa helenae* trained over an iron support in the shape of a medieval tent – an appropriate nod at Richmond's long military history. This is balanced near the house by a fine *Magnolia* x *kewensis* casting its shade over a small tank with a lion mask. The sound of water echoes that of the waterfalls on the River Swale in the valley below.

The garden is rich in old roses and there are more than 40 different varieties scattered throughout with evergreen shrubs, including many specimens of variegated holly, yew and box, to give winter interest. The skilful underplanting never feels contrived, just natural and generous. This delightful garden is a wonderful education in the art of handling a restricted space.

▶ *Open main season – telephone or consult website for details – for NGS and by appointment*

Holyhead

Anglesey

Llandudno
6

Rhyl

A55

7 Bangor

8

Caernarfon

Mold

A470

Betws-y-coed

A5

A494

Wrexham

A487

5

Porthmadog

4

Snowdonia
National
Park

Bala

Llangollen

9

10

12

A499

3

Dolgellau

A494

A458

Welshpool

11

13

Machynlleth

NORTH and MID WALES
252-257

A483

Newtown

Aberystwyth

A44

LLangurig

A470

Cambrian
Mountains

Llandrindod
Wells

A44

1

A487

A485

2

Builth
Wells

A483

Cardigan

A470

A438

10

Fishguard

Llandovery

A40

Brecon

Black
Mountains

Pembrokeshire Coast
National Park

SOUTH WALES
260-263

7

Llandeilo

Brecon
Beacons
National Park

A479

Carmarthen

8

A48

Abergavenny

Monmouth

Haverfordwest

A40

9

Milford
Haven

A4076

A477

A465

Merthyr
Tydfil

A4042

A449

1

Tenby

Llanelli

A470

2

Chepstow

6

Swansea

Neath

3

Port
Talbot

Newport

M4

Bridgend

4

Cardiff

5

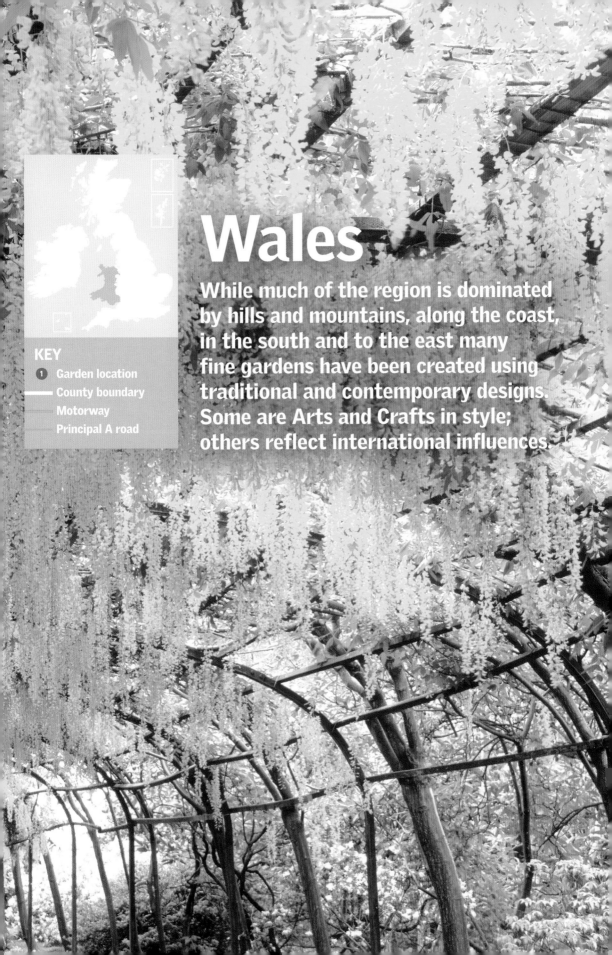

Wales

While much of the region is dominated by hills and mountains, along the coast, in the south and to the east many fine gardens have been created using traditional and contemporary designs. Some are Arts and Crafts in style; others reflect international influences.

KEY

1 Garden location
— County boundary
Motorway
Principal A road

NORTH AND MID WALES

Tradition and drama combine in many of these Welsh gardens. Some are superb period restorations while others display intriguing modern features and innovative planting schemes.

1 Llanllyr

Quirky features, including an ancient inscribed column, embellish the garden, which also has a colour-themed rose garden.

Talsarn, Lampeter, Ceredigion SA48 8QB

Tel: 01570 470900

Welsh Historic Garden Grade II

LOCATION 6 miles NW of Lampeter on B4337 Temple Bar-Llanrhystud road

This ancient site, home to Cistercian nuns in the 12th century, has a long and interesting history. Since 1989 the present owners have added their own imprint to the 4 acre garden, which was laid out in the 1830s around a 19th-century house. They have restored and developed the basic structure, creating wide borders on the north and east sides and an attractive box parterre on the south.

A densely planted shrubbery leads to a long colour-themed rose border, an inscribed Celtic Christian pillar and a summerhouse. Running parallel to the rose border is a striking formal pool crossed by a little stone bridge. An Italianate water garden includes a large fishpond and bog garden.

There is also an unusual cob-walled kitchen garden. Other interesting features are a labyrinth loosely based on the dreamer's journey in William Langland's poem *Piers the Plowman*, and a gravel garden with a carved oak column that measures the shadow cast by the sun throughout the year.
▶ *Open for NGS, and by appointment*

2 Cae Hir

A series of garden rooms, many of them themed by colour, a bog garden and a bonsai collection are highlights here.

Cribyn, Lampeter, Ceredigion SA48 7NG

Tel: 01570 470839 | www.caehirgardens.com

LOCATION 5 miles NW of Lampeter off A482. Turn left onto B4337 at Temple Bar

Begun in 1984, this idiosyncratic garden was made and is still managed by just one man. Its 6 acres – four on one side of the road where the house is situated and two on the other – rise gently at first, then more steeply from a natural stream and informal wildlife pools at the bottom of the garden to a summerhouse at the top. This gives fine views of the surrounding countryside.

Near the top of the garden, an 18m (60ft) long laburnum crescent is edged with *Geranium macrorrhizum* and underplanted with yellow and orange herbaceous plants to give a late summer show. A clipped yew hedge immediately below echoes the crescent shape. Despite the formality of the design, the garden does not have a formal feel and instead an element of wildness has been encouraged to settle it into the landscape.

The discreet rooms, several themed by colour, are separated by large swathes of grass, punctuated by standard trees. The owner's choice of hardy plants that don't require much maintenance has been turned to good effect, as they are often massed together for dramatic effect.

Trees are a passion here, some of which have been trimmed into unusual shapes. There is also a separate bonsai area.
▶ *Open main season – telephone or consult website for details*

3 Aber Artro Hall

An intriguing garden in tune with its Arts and Crafts house, it has an old tennis court planted in a William Morris wallpaper design.

Llanbedr, Gwynedd LL45 2PA

Tel: 01341 241777

LOCATION From N turn right off A496 in front of Victoria Inn in Llanbedr. After 1 mile turn right signed Cwm Nantcol

Situated in an elevated position a few miles from the coast, the 5 acre garden benefits from the protection of a steep hillside to the west and south but has fine views over woodland to Rhinog Farw to the east. The Arts and Crafts-style house sits perfectly in this landscape and the garden is carefully designed around it.

The back garden has a wide lawn leading to a steep rockery made in the 1950s. It is colourful in spring and early summer when the many rhododendrons flower, extending into the woodland garden above. Below the lawn, two

CAE HIR

terraced shrub borders look out over a formal vegetable garden, a fruit arbour and a laburnum arch. There's a tongue-in-cheek walled Italian garden, and an old tennis court has been laid out like a sheet of William Morris wallpaper, with flower shapes cut into it and planted up.

▶ *Open for NGS, and main season by appointment*

4 Portmeirion

Italianate-style gardens filled with exotic plants are in keeping with the extravagant architecture in this fantasy village.

Penrhyndeudraeth, Gwynedd LL48 6ET

Tel: 01766 770000 (Hotel Reception)

www.portmeirion-village.com

Welsh Historic Garden Grade II*

LOCATION 2 miles SE of Porthmadog near A487

Portmeirion is best known for the extraordinary collection of buildings (now holiday lets) that the architect Clough Williams-Ellis assembled between 1925 and 1972 to create a *faux* Italian village on a private peninsula on the coast of Snowdonia. There are some fine trees here – coast redwoods, Wellingtonia, Himalayan firs and a deodar cypress. Many were planted in Victorian times and therefore reflect the predilection for evergreens. Williams-Ellis added clipped Irish yews and exotic plants such as cordylines.

The mild climate on the peninsula, where winter frosts are rare, has made it possible to plant a good collection of rare and tender exotics. Many of these would not look out of place in a Cornish garden.

The herbaceous plantings within the village are formal and quite municipal. Beyond them lie 70 acres of woodland (which also predate Williams-Ellis), densely planted with rhododendrons and camellias that produce a fine display in May, together with an assortment of structures including a striking red-painted Japanese-style bridge.

Another example of Williams-Ellis' fine design skills is his own private garden at Plas Brondanw (see page 254), which is just 3 miles away.

▶ *Open all year, except Christmas Day*

wales

5 Plas Brondanw

The designer of Portmeirion has captured the drama of the great Italian gardens and added romantic architectural features here.

Llanfrothen, Penrhyndeudraeth, Gwynedd LL48 6SW | Tel: 07880 766741

Welsh Historic Garden Grade I

LOCATION 5 miles NE of Porthmadog between Llanfrothen and Croesor

The 17th-century house was handed over to the architect Sir Clough Williams-Ellis by his father when he was just 19, and he spent the next 70 years turning the 4 acre garden into a triumph of formal design. His main objective was to provide a series of dramatic and romantic prospects inspired by the great gardens of Italy and imprinted with architectural features including an orangery, a belvedere and a handsome balustrade. He also made a huge investment in paving, hedging and topiary (mostly yew) – if laid flat, the compartment hedging would cover 4 acres.

Hydrangeas and ferns flourish in the damp climate. Beyond the formal garden a chestnut avenue leads past a chasm to the pavilion folly and a superlative view of Snowdonia's mountains, visible from the end of every vista. Since this Williams-Ellis garden is quite different from Portmeirion (see page 253), visit both to experience the multi-faceted nature of his talent.
▶ *Open all year – telephone or consult website for details*

6 Bodysgallen Hall

Old blends with new in this varied garden, which has Edwardian roses and a striking circular parterre planted with herbs.

Llandudno, Gwynedd LL30 1RS

Tel: 01492 584466 | www.bodysgallen.com

Welsh Historic Garden Grade I / The National Trust

LOCATION 2 miles S of Llandudno. At A55/A470 junction turn onto A470 towards Llandudno. Hall is 1 mile on right

Like the imposing house, which was once a watch tower, the garden is a mixture of ancient and modern elements. The remains of a 17th-century grass terrace – now concealed in woodland overlooking Conwy Castle – is its oldest feature. But the focus today is a walled Edwardian rose garden far below the house, which is simple and very attractive. Other features include a raised terrace with a formal pool and another walled garden given over to a circular, radially arranged parterre planted with herbs.

The house and parkland were in a state of decay until they were turned into a commercial enterprise in 1980. Although still functioning as a high-class hotel, the building, its garden and 200 acres of parkland and woods have now been gifted to the National Trust. Major repairs and new projects have been undertaken, most remarkably the building of a sham castle and 19.5m (64ft) obelisk in the Picturesque style – once such a part of the Welsh garden tradition.
▶ *Open all year, daily*

7 Plas Newydd

Bordering the Menai Strait, this garden includes formal terraces and informal areas loosely planted with shrubs.

Llanfairpwll, Anglesey LL61 6DQ

Tel: 01248 714795 | www.nationaltrust.org.uk

Welsh Historic Garden Grade I/ The National Trust

LOCATION 4 miles SW of Menai Bridge, 2 miles S of Llanfairpwll via A5

Landscape designer Humphry Repton's suggestion of 'plantations ... to soften a bleak country and shelter the ground from violent winds' has resulted in an informal, open-plan garden, with shrub plantings in the lawns and parkland, and pleasant waterside and woodland walks. The ground slopes down to the Menai Strait, and there are wonderful views of the Snowdonia peaks.

There is formality here, too, such as a Mediterranean-style garden set out in terraces at the front of the house. An arbour has replaced a conservatory on the top level, and water falls from a rocky mound to a pool with an Italianate fountain on the bottom terrace.

Major restoration continues with the building of a deep grotto and the replanting of the mixed borders. The influence of the Gulf Stream enables many frost-tender shrubs to thrive, and a rhododendron garden is open in spring. Wild flowers appear in their season, summer brings displays of hydrangeas, and autumn colours the Southern-Hemisphere trees and shrubs in the arboretum. Admirers of Rex Whistler should visit the 18th-century house, designed by James Wyatt, to see the painter's largest work.
▶ *House open. Garden open main season – telephone or consult website for details. Rhododendron garden open May and June. Guided tours by arrangement*

8 Bodnant

The 80 acre garden, ablaze with colour in spring and autumn, comprises a series of terraces above a woodland area.

Tal-y-Cafn, Colwyn Bay, Conwy LL28 5RE

Tel: 01492 650460

www.bodnantgarden.co.uk

Welsh Historic Garden Grade I/
The National Trust

LOCATION 8 miles S of Llandudno, just off A470

Exploring the 80 acres of this fine, much-loved garden is a delight at any time of the year, although spring is the best time to appreciate the wonderful collection of camellias, rhododendrons and magnolias, and the autumn colour is stunning. The garden is more subdued in summer.

The sombre hall sits at the top of a series of large terraces that look across the River Conwy towards Snowdonia. On the lowest terrace, the Pin Mill commands the end of a rectangular canal. From here steep paths descend to the Dell, where majestic trees are underplanted with spring-flowering shrubs and streamside plants.

The garden is currently undergoing a revival. Trees that had become too large have been pruned or felled, tired borders replanted and overgrown areas cut back to reveal the original garden structure. The rose terrace below the house has been replaced and there has been some new herbaceous planting. There is a new £2 million visitor centre, and the walled plant centre (not National Trust) offers a good range of tender climbers and other plants seen growing in the garden.
▶ *Garden open main season – telephone or consult website for details*

9 Erddig

This 18th-century formal garden has been sensitively restored and includes fruit trees underplanted with bulbs from that period.

Wrexham LL13 0YT | Tel: 01978 355314

www.nationaltrust.org.uk

Welsh Historic Garden Grade I/
The National Trust

LOCATION 2 miles S of Wrexham off A525 or A483

When the National Trust acquired the estate in 1973 the house and its garden – a rare example of early 18th-century formal design influenced by the Dutch model – were almost beyond salvation. Both have now been carefully restored and, thanks to a bird's-eye view plan created by surveyor Thomas Badeslade in 1739, it has been possible to reconstruct the original garden.

Varieties of apple, pear and plum trees known to have been grown here in the 18th century are underplanted with narcissus and other bulbs from the period, and the formality is emphasised by a canal garden and fish pool. South of the canal walk is a Victorian flower garden, and other Victorian additions include a parterre and a yew walk.

To the west of the house are woods and parkland, in which landscape designer William Emes had a hand, and to the northwest lies an astonishing circular weir known as the Cup and Saucer. A National Collection of ivies is also held here. Apple Day is celebrated in October and the gardens are illuminated in December.
▶ *House open most of year – telephone or consult website for details*

10 The Garden House

A colour wheel by designer Gertrude Jekyll and a rippling privet hedge are just two of the bold designs in this modern garden.

Erbistock, Wrexham LL13 0DL

Tel: 01978 781149

www.simonwingett.com

LOCATION 5 miles S of Wrexham off A539. Signed in village

Overlooking the River Dee, this 5 acre garden comprises ten main areas planted round the modern house in an imaginative design.

Shrub and herbaceous borders are planted in monochromatic and complementary colour schemes, based on a colour wheel designed by renowned designer Gertrude Jekyll, and a golden privet hedge is clipped into waves with a circle of densely planted bergenias in the centre. Long paths are lined with some of the hydrangeas that are held here in a National Collection (there are more than 300 species and cultivars). Other features include a striking collection of conifers and a box-edged circular bed with a weeping pear underplanted with blue irises. A contemporary sculpture garden displays huge flower spikes fashioned out of steel.
▶ *Open main season – telephone or consult website for details*

wales

11 The Dingle Nurseries and Garden

Trees and shrubs planted in colour-themed groups create a striking effect in this garden that adjoins an excellent nursery.

Welshpool, Powys SY21 9JD

Tel: 01938 555145

www.dinglenurseryandgarden.co.uk

LOCATION 3 miles NW of Welshpool. Take A490 for 1 mile to Llanfyllin then turn left

The 4 acres of this informal garden are packed with trees and shrubs, all planted since 1968. The lawn in front of the house, bounded by borders of silvery shrubs and perennials, soon gives way to a bank running down to a lake, where narrow paths zigzag down the slope through a huge collection of trees and shrubs, including many maples, conifers and pittosporums. They are grouped into two main areas – one of silver and gold foliage, another of purple and gold – creating a dazzling effect when viewed from across the lake.

The only open spaces are the lawn and the lake itself, which carries reflections of the surrounding trees, especially eucalyptus. The woodland garden beyond is a mass of colourful ornamental trees of every kind, with woodland underplanting here and there. Right next door is one of the best retail nurseries in Wales, which holds an extensive list of species.
▶ *Open all year – telephone or consult website for details*

12 Chirk Castle

Climbers festoon the ancient castle walls while the surrounding formal gardens include topiary, a rockery and a hawk house.

Chirk, Wrexham LL14 5AF | Tel: 01691 777701

www.nationaltrust.org.uk

Welsh Historic Garden Grade I/ The National Trust

LOCATION 10 miles SW of Wrexham, 2 miles W of Chirk off A5, 1½ miles up private drive

The hulking medieval castle, its fortress walls now draped with a curtain of climbing plants, stands serenely in an 18th-century landscaped park of 12 acres. The trees and flowering shrubs, including rhododendrons and azaleas, contrast with the yews in the formal garden, which were planted in the 1870s. The long shrub border has been replanted in four sections, each flowering at a different season. The addition of many herbaceous plants gives it a more open feel and makes a good link with the 1920s border.

The rose garden contains mainly old cluster-flowered (floribunda) roses. From the terrace, with its stunning views over Shropshire and Cheshire, the visitor passes to the classical pavilion, then along a lime tree avenue to a statue of Hercules. There is also 19th-century topiary, a rockery and an old hawk house, and a pleasure-ground wood in which to stroll.
▶ *Castle open. Garden open – telephone or consult website for details*

13 Powis Castle

Enormous topiary yews overhang the celebrated and sumptuously planted terraces, with views over a wooded wilderness below.

Welshpool, Powys SY21 8RF

Tel: 01938 551929 | www.nationaltrust.org.uk

Welsh Historic Garden Grade I/ The National Trust

LOCATION ¾ mile S of Welshpool on A483

One of Wales' great gardens, it is admired principally for its hanging gardens – a series of 17th-century terraces filled with extravagant late 20th-century planting and punctuated by huge clipped yew trees and hedges. The terraces were part of a grand design, although the formal water garden below was abandoned in the 19th century and is now laid to lawn.

The remaining upper terraces contain 17th-century statues and a fine orangery housing conservatory plants and an aviary, but what draws people today is the extraordinary topiary and colourful deep borders, some mixed, some purely herbaceous, and others planted with exotics. The container planting is excellent, too.

The lower terraces survive as a rough grass bank dotted with flowering trees and shrubs. They look outwards to a wooded wilderness ridge. Down below can be seen the remains of a walled kitchen garden once hidden by tall trees but converted in Edwardian times into a colourful, formal flower garden with open lawns, borders, pergolas and closely managed fruit trees. The delphiniums and hollyhocks are a delight and there is also an informal pool and wild-flower meadow.
▶ *Castle open. Garden open most of year – telephone or consult website for details*

EXTRAVAGANT
PLANTING
PUNCTUATED BY
HUGE CLIPPED
YEW TREES
AND HEDGES
POWIS CASTLE

In praise of follies

Decorative, eccentric and often functionless, follies are designed to catch the eye and beguile the garden visitor.

The term 'folly' suggests something small and quaint but it can be used to describe anything from a tiny gazebo to the façade of a ruined castle. These buildings can be used to punch home a political message, as a focal point or just for the sheer enjoyment of their owners.

There is often an element of fakery, with follies constructed to look like ruins, such as William Chambers' Ruined Arch in the Royal Botanical Gardens at Kew. The taste for ruins may have originated after the Dissolution of the Monasteries in the 16th century led to their lands passing into private hands. Picturesque ruins of former monastic buildings were scattered about estates, and landowners lacking them would simply build their own.

Religious symbolism

Follies often featured religious symbolism. The engaging Rushton Triangular Lodge in Northamptonshire was designed in the 1590s by Sir Thomas Tresham, father of a Gunpowder Plotter. It displays its creator's Roman Catholicism with the number three, symbolising the Holy Trinity, a recurring theme – three floors, trefoil windows and three triangular gables on each side.

In the 18th century, this symbolism became political. The powerful Whig barons, who invited George I to become in effect constitutional monarch in 1714, espoused the ideals of republican Greece and Rome. With his temples at Stowe, Lord Cobham evoked a classical Arcadian idyll on an English estate. Ornament is used more sparingly at Stourhead in Wiltshire, home of the banker Henry Hoare, but the vision is similar. The three temples (to Flora and Apollo and the Pantheon) are glimpsed at intervals, disappearing from view, suddenly to re-emerge across the lake or between trees.

Follies were a form of self-advertisement, drawing attention to a landowner's wealth. And some have successfully outlived their houses. The Menagerie in Northamptonshire was built on the site of a private zoo, and was the focal point for Lord Halifax's vanished home, Horton House. The 1750s rococo building was restored in the 1970s

THE ANTE-ROOMS ARE LINED WITH FLINT, PEBBLES AND TUFA
STOURHEAD

by the architectural historian Gervase Jackson-Stops, and now has its own garden of herbaceous borders, avenues and pools.

Later in the 18th century, a fashion for the Gothic superseded the dominance of classicism, and landscapes became more naturalistic and less formal. Painshill Park in Surrey, created by the Hon Charles Hamilton between 1738 and 1773, has a dazzling array of follies, including a Gothic temple, a ruined abbey, a Turkish tent, a Chinese bridge and a hermitage. Hamilton paid a vagrant to act as the hermit, but the man didn't take to the solitary life and was sacked for drinking in local pubs. The grotto, with its glittering shells and stalactites (actually painted wood), was the work of Joseph Lane, the master grotto-maker of the 18th century.

Painshill bankrupted Hamilton, who retired to Bath. Hamilton shared a passion for *folies de grandeur* with his great-nephew, William Beckford, who built the 120ft, Neo-classical Beckford's Tower on Lansdowne Hill in Bath in 1827.

Atmospheric grottoes

The enchanting grotto at Stourhead was designed by Henry Flitcroft in 1748. The anterooms of the large, domed chamber are lined with flint, pebbles and tufa, with stones brought from Italy. Daylight filters into the grotto, striking the cleverly positioned statues.

Dewstow in Gwent is a very different grotto. Here an underground labyrinth beneath herbaceous borders unites the 18th-century love of grottoes with the Victorian passion for ferns and tropical plants. Constructed about 1895, the network was rediscovered after 50 years in 2000. Now restored, stone tunnels wind between the Tufa Grotto filled with ferns and the Lion Grotto planted with succulents and spiky tropical plants. There is a characteristic mixture of artifice and reality, with arches made of real and faced stone and natural rocks piled beside underground pools.

In the 20th century, the mantle of Joseph Lane and his son, Josiah, has descended on the shoulders of stone carver Simon Verity and shell artist Diana Reynell. They have been responsible for work on the grotto at Leeds Castle in Kent. Visitors to the maze there re-emerge through the underground cavern decorated with mythical beasts, created from shells, minerals and wood.

Above ground, the continuing appeal of follies is demonstrated by the many brick towers built over the past two decades at Stone House Cottage in Worcestershire. The owners added one year after year until the walled garden came to be known as the San Gimignano of Britain. They are tucked into the walls, or glimpsed at the end of corridors of hedging. Covered with climbing ramblers, the towers add charm to the exuberant planting.

SOUTH WALES

The National Botanic Garden of Wales stands at the forefront of a range of gardens that are highly individual in character, including bog gardens, hothouses and even a Victorian subterranean fantasy.

1 High Glanau Manor

An elegant Arts and Crafts garden, planted using a subtle palette of colours, enjoys far-reaching views over the Wye Valley.

Lydart, Monmouth NP25 4AD

Tel: 01600 860005

LOCATION 4 miles SW of Monmouth on B4293 between Monmouth and Chepstow

Situated high in the woods of the Wye Valley, this is one of the best examples of an Arts and Crafts garden in Wales. The house was built in 1923, and the current owners have been using the original plans for their restoration of the 12 acre garden. A swimming pool has been replaced with a 30m (100ft) double herbaceous border – an elegant and restrained planting in whites, blues, purples and greens, inspired by renowned designer Gertrude Jekyll. Alongside is a long path lined with lavender. Two terraces by the west of the house are similarly planted. Steps then descend to a charming octagonal lily pool and little fountain with narrow borders planted with roses. There is a woodland garden surrounding the house.
▶ *Open for NGS, and by appointment*

2 Veddw House

Unusual features here include a winding wave-shaped yew hedge, a black reflecting pool and a parterre filled with grasses.

Devauden, Monmouthshire NP16 6PH

Tel: 01291 650836 | www.veddw.co.uk

LOCATION 5 miles NW of Chepstow off B4293

On a sheltered slope near the Wye Valley, framed by old beech woods and with views in all directions, this complex and highly individual

VEDDW HOUSE

garden has been created since 1987 by the present owners. They are fuelled by instinct and imagination, and experimentation is key to their design philosophy.

There are 2 acres of flower garden and meadow, where the generously planted borders include repeat plantings of many unusual varieties. Around every corner is something of interest – a philadelphus border, a purple and grey border, a bed filled with striking grey elymus grasses, a hazel coppice and a magnolia walk.

The formal and colourful vegetable garden has standard hollies, clematis and cardoons growing amid the produce. From here an arch leads into the orchard and meadow, which is full of bulbs in spring, and grasses and wild flowers in summer.

Behind the house the ground rises steeply, with paths and steps leading to viewpoints. Yew hedges enclose a formal garden of clipped hedges and brick-paved paths, and a dramatic enclosure has a black reflecting pool and a seat with an arching back that echoes a sinuous hedge, clipped in the shape of a wave, in another part of the garden.

Overlooking these spaces is a parterre where box hedges form compartments replicating the 1824 tithe map of the area. The spaces between are filled with a variety of grasses. Farther up still is a hazel coppice and a 2 acre wood where old beeches, sorbus and hornbeams grow.

▶ *Open for limited season – telephone or consult website for details – and for parties of ten or more by appointment*

3 Dewstow Grottoes

A Victorian fantasy world of tunnels and grottoes has been restored and is now home to a large variety of ferns and spider plants.

Dewstow House, Caerwent, Monmouthshire NP26 5AH

Tel: 01291 430444

www.dewstow.com/gardens

Welsh Historic Garden Grade I

LOCATION 5 miles SW of Chepstow off A48

The 6 acres of gardens and grottoes were renowned in the lifetime of their Victorian creator as a remarkable local landmark. Above ground were rock gardens, ponds, ornamental areas, tropical glasshouses and a variety of plants from around the world. Below ground sprawled a labyrinth of man-made tunnels, carved out of Pulhamite rock – one of the most extensive and best-preserved examples of its kind in

the country. This extraordinary subterranean landscape has been restored by the present owner.

The network of tunnels, fern-filled caverns and artificial grottoes winds its way under the house and past small pools and fountains. Parts are illuminated by natural light while in others artificial light is required to negotiate them. Ferns, spider plants and *Ficus pumila* thrive in the moist, frost-free conditions.

This fantasy world is entered through a shady stumpery and emerges into a brightly planted bog garden ravine with a string of interconnecting lakes and small waterfalls. Next to the house a lively herbaceous border has been created below a high wall as a colourful backdrop to the lawn.

▶ *Open main season – telephone or consult website for details – for NGS, and for parties by appointment*

4 St Fagans

The extensive grounds of this open-air museum of Welsh life feature fish ponds, a rose garden and Italianate terraces.

St Fagans, Cardiff CF5 6XB

Tel: 029 2057 3500

www.museumwales.ac.uk

Welsh Historic Garden Grade I/ National Museum of Wales

LOCATION Near M4 junction 33. Signposted

The museum and castle are situated within 100 acres of grounds, which are now largely devoted to re-erected buildings from all over Wales. It is one of Europe's leading open-air museums. The garden has an Edwardian feel and is approached by crossing several large fish ponds and walking up the elegant terraces, designed in Italianate style.

Beyond a grove of old mulberries, the garden is divided into distinct formal enclosures hedged by yew and box, including a thyme garden planted with annuals. An attractive avenue of pleached limes leads to the front of the impressive house and a small courtyard containing a massive, elaborately decorated lead cistern with a skirt of box. Nearby, a rose garden has been filled with fragrant varieties from around 1900 in beds and on trellises. A central circular canal surrounds a bay arbour.

A separate Italian garden is a simple and pleasing space with 19th-century roses climbing its high walls. From one of these water pours out of spouts into a formal pool.

▶ *Open all year – telephone or consult website for details*

wales

5 Dyffryn Gardens

More than 30 themed garden rooms are enclosed by clipped yew hedges, including Italian, rose and lavender gardens.

St Nicholas, Cardiff, Vale of Glamorgan CF5 6SU

Tel: 029 2059 3328

www.dyffryngardens.org.uk

Welsh Historic Garden Grade I

LOCATION 4 miles SW of Cardiff on A4232 turn S on A4050 and W to A48

Dyffryn is perhaps Wales' most grandiose Edwardian house and garden, and has been designed in the Arts and Crafts style. The house is approached through open pleasure grounds bordered by heather banks and rockeries. Beyond, fringed by urns and bedding, are huge formal lawns, one for croquet, another bisected by a long lily pool and fountain. To their left, grass paths snake through an arboretum and to the right is a series of more than 30 garden rooms with themes including Pompeian, Italian, rose, theatre, lavender, swimming pool and paved court.

A recent lottery grant has been spent most conspicuously so far on the garden's buildings. However, the walled kitchen garden is also being restored as well as the Victorian fernery and alpine and heather collections. The planting and maintenance are also improving in stages.

▶ *Open all year – telephone or consult website for details*

6 Singleton Park and Botanic Gardens

The star attractions are four greenhouses displaying temperate, tropical and desert species as well as cash-crop plants.

Singleton Park, Swansea, West Glamorgan SA2 9DU | Tel: 01792 298637

www.swansea.gov.uk

LOCATION In Swansea. Entrance in Gower Road

Situated on the north side of the 110 acre park is a charming botanic garden. In just 4½ acres there is a wide range of plants, all well labelled and attractively displayed.

A double, mostly herbaceous border leads to a wide formal space bordered on one side by four linked greenhouses. Here plants from temperate, tropical and desert climates are displayed, as well as a collection of plants of economic importance, such as sugar cane, olives and coffee. In front of the greenhouses are display beds of asters, delphiniums, penstemons and irises, together with formal bedding displays. A terrace is flanked by *Wisteria sinensis* on one side and bordered by roses on the other, and special trees and shrubs are scattered throughout the gardens.

Singleton Park has several areas of interest including ornamental gardens containing rhododendrons and a bog garden, and an Italian garden.

▶ *Open all year – telephone or consult website for details*

7 Aberglasney Gardens

A huge atrium covering part of the ruined mansion is a highlight here, along with a striking cloister garden and yew tunnel.

Llangathen, Llandeilo, Carmarthenshire SA32 8QH | Tel: 01558 668998

www.aberglasney.org

Welsh Historic Garden Grade II*

LOCATION 3 miles W of Llandeilo on A40. Turn S at Broad Oak junction

Visitors flock to Aberglasney and it certainly has much to recommend it. Records go back to the mid 15th century, when mention was made of nine gardens, orchards and vineyards. Around 1600 the Bishop of St David's bought the estate, and it was probably he who built the gatehouse and cloister garden, surrounded on three sides by an arcaded stone structure supporting a broad parapet.

The estate was in a ruinous state until the Aberglasney Restoration Trust was created in 1995 and began the task of bringing the garden back to life. The cloister garden is now elegantly planted around a simple geometric design in grass, freckled with bulbs in spring. Below are the upper walled garden and a large rectangular pool. The lower walled garden is given over to vegetables and flowers for cutting. Within the walls of the ruined mansion the Ninfarium Garden has been created. A huge glass atrium covers the entire area, which has been paved and planted with warm temperate and sub-tropical plants.

To one side of the house is a rare example of a yew tunnel, impressively gnarled and twisted in its old age. Above and below the ancient walls woodland and streamside gardens have been created with dense colourful plantings of herbaceous plants and shrubs.

▶ *Open all year – telephone or consult website for details*

8 National Botanic Garden of Wales

A spectacular dome, the largest single-span glasshouse in the world, houses rare and endangered Mediterranean species.

Middleton Hall, Llanarthne, Carmarthenshire SA32 8HG

Tel: 01558 667132/667134

www.gardenofwales.org.uk

Welsh Historic Garden Grade II

LOCATION 8 miles E of Carmarthen, 7 miles W of Llandeilo off A48(M)

This is Wales' first national botanic garden, opened in 2000 with lottery funding and an agenda both botanical and educational. It stands in the grounds of the Middleton Hall estate, a remarkable 18th-century landscape park with a string of lakes. The house is gone, but the repair of the park and its species-rich grasslands is ongoing. The farm estate, centred in the working organic farm, has been designated a national nature reserve.

The garden is full of dramatic features of interest to gardeners. Most memorable is Lord Foster's domed Great Glasshouse, which is the largest of its kind in the world. Inside, set in a sunken landscape of rocky terraces, sandstone cliffs and gravelled slopes, endangered plants from six regions of the world with a Mediterranean climate burst into colour in spring. The great crescent of grassland that surrounds the glasshouse is spangled with daffodils and later with garden perennials in a colourful display.

The old walled garden is arranged ornamentally but demonstrates the genetic relationships between plants and contains a fine tropical house. A 220m (722ft) herbaceous border, the Broad Walk, includes colourful plants such as geraniums, penstemons and salvias. It runs from the garden entrance past a prolific bog garden and waterside education buildings to the old stables, where there is an apothecary's garden and a clutch of good-quality attractions. These include a restaurant, film theatre, shop, and a venue for exhibitions and classes.

In the parkland 'Woods of the World' – a collection of trees from parts of the world with a similar climate to Wales – is being created. The fine surrounding landscape and pollution-free location look set to make this an important garden for the future.

▶ *Open all year – telephone or consult website for details*

9 Picton Castle

Woodland gardens surround the castle, featuring giant redwoods and rare species of conifers and rhododendrons.

Haverfordwest, Pembrokeshire SA62 4AS

Tel: 01437 751326 | www.pictoncastle.co.uk

Welsh Historic Garden Grade II*

LOCATION 4 miles SE of Haverfordwest off A40

The castle is late 13th century in origin, later remodelled, and the nearly 40 acres of grounds match it for grandeur and historic interest. Woodland walks wind among massive oaks and giant redwoods, past rarities that include the biggest *Rhododendron* 'Old Port' in existence and a mighty metasequoia, a deciduous conifer presumed extinct but rediscovered in China in 1941.

In May and June many exotic shrubs reach their full splendour. By contrast, the walled garden features pretty herb borders, climbing roses and summer-flowering plants, with a pond and fountain creating a cool and calming atmosphere.

▶ *Castle open. Garden open most of the year – telephone or consult website for details*

10 Dyffryn Fernant Gardens

This garden makes the most of its terrain, with a lush bog garden and a jungle-like courtyard and wild-flower meadows.

Dyffryn Fernant, Llanychaer, Fishguard SA65 9SP | Tel: 01348 811282

www.genuslocus.net

LOCATION 2 miles E of Fishguard off A487 Cardigan road

Since 1995 this adventurous 6 acre garden has been created on an inauspicious site of boggy and stony ground. The courtyard garden and the house borders display a dizzy profusion of choice plants and shrubs.

The bog garden, formally laid out with slate paving, is dominated by a stainless steel obelisk – an inspired touch. The Rickyard has a formal layout and strong colour plantings. At the edges of the garden the planting is more subdued. Nicky's Tree stands at the centre of a grid of 50 beds with mown paths running between them, and each bed planted with a single variety of ornamental grass. New walks are currently being opened up in the garden and wild-flower meadows developed.

▶ *Open main season – telephone or consult website for details*

wales

Shetland
Islands

• Lerwick

Scotland

Nestled among the mighty peaks, remote lochs and deep glens, and often surrounding historic castles, many of the gardens in the north and centre make the most of their dramatic settings. Along the west coast and in the south, superb collections of exotic species flourish in the mild climate and remarkable formal designs abound.

KEY

① Garden location
— County boundary
— Motorway
— Principal A road

SOUTHWEST SCOTLAND

Classic gardens set around castles, contemporary plantings and exotic collections grace the landscape of southwest Scotland, many making use of mountain and lochside vistas in sophisticated designs.

1 Broughton House

Japanese elements mix with traditional cottage-garden plants in this unusual garden, designed by the artist E.A. Hornel.

12 High Street, Kirkcudbright, Dumfries and Galloway DG6 4JX | Tel: 01557 330437

www.nts.org.uk

Historic Scotland Inventory/
The National Trust for Scotland

LOCATION 28 miles SW of Dumfries. Take A75 from Dumfries past Castle Douglas, then 1 mile past Bridge of Dee take A711 to Kirkcudbright

This fascinating 1½ acre garden was created by landscape painter E.A. Hornel, who lived here from 1901 to 1933. It reflects the artist's interest in Oriental art following a visit to Japan, and incorporates both Japanese and Scottish features.

The garden starts with a sunken courtyard, where Japanese cherries blossom over low-level plantings. Beyond this is a cross between 'fantasy Japan' and 'fantasy cottage garden', with all the elements of a larger garden – a rose parterre, pergola, glasshouse, box hedges and herbaceous borders. Charming lily pools have flat stepping stones and dramatic boulders. At the end of the long central walk, beyond a hedge, is the River Dee, with its mudflats and saltings.
▶ *Garden open most of year – telephone or consult website for details*

2 Cally Gardens and Nursery

No fewer than 4,000 perennials and shrubs from around the world are on display here and sold in an adjoining nursery.

Gatehouse of Fleet, Castle Douglas, Dumfries and Galloway DG7 2DJ

Tel: 01557 815029 | www.callygardens.co.uk

Historic Scotland Inventory

LOCATION 30 miles SW of Dumfries via A75. Take Gatehouse turning. Signposted

This fine plantsman's garden and nursery, laid out within an 18th-century walled garden of slightly more than 2½ acres, is well worth a visit by plant lovers. The present owner started restoring the buildings in 1987, and there are now three dozen large borders filled with more than 4,000 varieties – the emphasis is on perennials and rare shrubs, with a number of unusual climbers trained against the mellow brick walls.

Many of these sought-after plants have been grown from seeds collected during the owner's numerous plant-hunting expeditions, and several hundred are available via a mail-order catalogue produced in November.

Outside the walled garden lies Cally Oak Woods which is threaded with nature trails. Recent plantings in the woodland include large areas of *meconopsis* (Himalayan blue poppies) which thrive in the mild climate here.
▶ *Open main season – telephone or consult website for details*

3 Glenwhan Gardens

A bog garden blends well with the moorland landscape and provides a tapestry of colour when the rhododendrons and primulas flower.

Dunragit, Stranraer, Dumfries and Galloway DG9 8PH | Tel: 01581 400222

www.glenwhangardens.co.uk

LOCATION 7 miles E of Stranraer, 1 mile off A75 at Dunragit

These 12 acre gardens, started in 1980, have spectacular views over Luce Bay and the Mull of Galloway, and are set in an area of natural beauty with many rocky outcrops. Because of the Gulf Stream and consequent mild climate, exotic plants thrive among the huge collections of trees, shrubs and plants from all over the world. In the maze of hilly plantings, seats and walkways overlook the central lakes and bog gardens, and sculptures are carefully positioned throughout the garden.

Collections are themed by genera or reflect the interests of the owners. There are enchanting woodland walks where rhododendrons flourish among many different kinds of primulas. A 17 acre moorland walk is sprinkled with native wild flowers. Most of the plants in the nursery are propagated on site.
▶ *Open main season – telephone or consult website for details – and by appointment*

LOGAN BOTANIC GARDEN

4 Logan Botanic Garden

A walled garden is filled with the brilliant blooms of exotic species while striking trees, bamboos and ferns flourish in woods.

Port Logan, Stranraer, Dumfries and Galloway DG9 9ND

Tel: 01776 860231

www.rbge.org.uk

Historic Scotland Inventory

LOCATION 14 miles S of Stranraer off B7065. Signposted

This 24 acre garden deserves far more acclaim than it receives and is well worth the extra effort required to journey to the remote southwest corner of Scotland. It is one of the most exotic gardens in Scotland – the balmy Gulf Stream climate is ideal not only for the tender, sweet-scented rhododendrons that are a speciality here, but it also allows a remarkable collection of exotic half-hardy plants to flourish. Logan Botanic holds many plants from the Southern Hemisphere (including 50 different species of eucalyptus), and about half of its holdings are plants that were originally collected in the wild in countries all around the world.

In the walled garden paths weave between colourful island beds, with scale and structure supplied by majestic tree ferns and *Cordyline australis*. Everywhere there are tender shrubs – leptospermums, embothriums, olearias, pittosporums, eucryphias.

The woodland area has a similarly large collection of trees, including magnolias, shrubs such as carpodetus, metrosideros (which is related to callistemon), elegant bamboos and tree ferns such as *Dicksonia fibrosa* and the striking silver *Cyathea dealbata*. Stroll to the highest point to enjoy the fine views over the Rhins to the Galloway Hills and beyond.

Wander through the Tasmanian Creek and admire the remarkable gunnera stand and Chilean collection. Then, since the rainfall here is 102cm (40in) a year, take shelter in the licensed salad bar that looks out onto an impressive group of Scottish native plants. Finally, venture out to see the rare and unusual plants in the nursery.

▶ *Open main season – telephone or consult website for details – and by appointment*

SCOTLAND

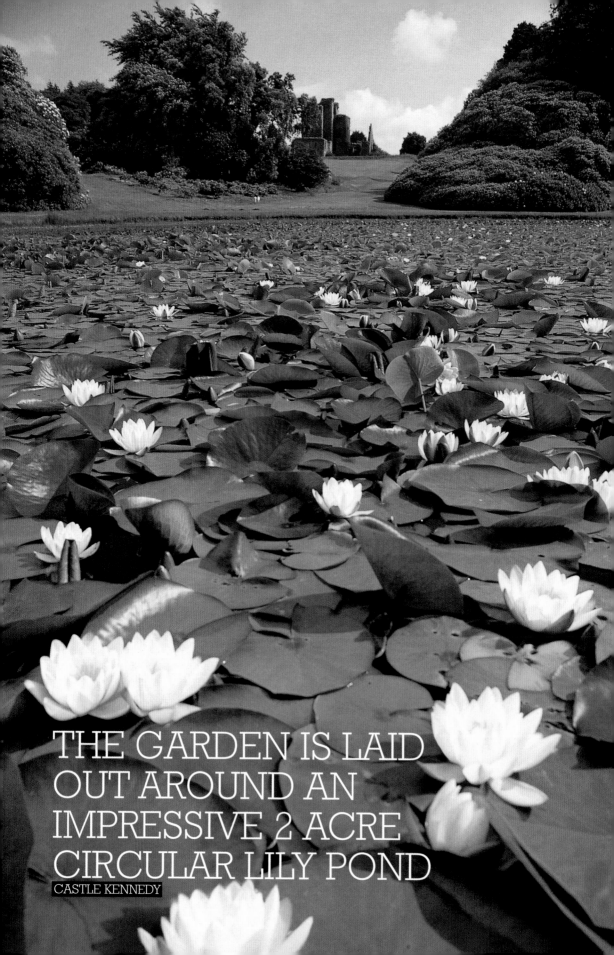

THE GARDEN IS LAID
OUT AROUND AN
IMPRESSIVE 2 ACRE
CIRCULAR LILY POND
CASTLE KENNEDY

5 Castle Kennedy

Highlights of the formal gardens surrounding the castle ruins include a huge lily pond, a fine pinetum and a monkey puzzle avenue.

Stair Estates, Rephad, Stranraer, Dumfries and Galloway DG9 8BX

Tel: 01776 702024/01581 400225

www.castlekennedygardens.co.uk

Historic Scotland Inventory

LOCATION 5 miles E of Stranraer on A75

These 75 acre gardens are set on a peninsula between two lochs and are spectacular in spring. Originally laid out in the late 17th century, they were later remodelled around the ruined castle, which burnt down in 1716. Large formal swathes of mown grassland were combined with massive formal gardens, crisscrossed by avenues and *allées* of large specimen trees.

The gardens are internationally renowned for its pinetum, good variety of tender trees and species rhododendrons, including many of renowned botanist Sir Joseph Hooker's original introductions from his Himalayan expeditions in the 19th century. There is a monkey-puzzle avenue and an avenue of firs underplanted with embothriums and eucryphias.

The garden is laid out around an impressive 2 acre circular lily pond, and a good walk from this brings the visitor back to the ruined castle and its walled garden, well planted with themed borders.
▶ *Open main season – telephone or consult website for details – and by appointment at other times*

6 Culzean Castle

Overlooked by a fortified mansion, the extensive grounds continue to benefit from a programme of restoration.

Maybole, South Ayrshire KA19 8LE

Tel: 01655 884400

www.culzeanexperience.org

Historic Scotland Inventory/
The National Trust for Scotland

LOCATION 12 miles S of Ayr on A719 coast road

Culzean is widely regarded as the National Trust for Scotland's flagship property. The country-park landscape covers 563 acres with a network of woodland and cliff-top paths. The gardens themselves occupy a spacious 40 acres. The castle, originally a medieval fortified house, was restructured by architect Robert Adam from 1777 in what has become known as his 'Culzean style'. This is reflected in the many fine architectural features throughout the grounds and the handsome home farm courtyard – now a visitor centre.

Restoration work continues, with a major undertaking being the consolidation and partial rebuilding of Adam's viaduct. The camellia house, a picturesque 1818 glasshouse, has been restored to its original use as an orangery, the fountain in the garden below the castle repaired and replumbed, the southern walled garden redesigned and the vinery rebuilt on the original site based on its Victorian plan. Other structures being restored are the Swan Pond buildings, the beautiful bridge to the north and the spectacular pagoda. The Dolphin House has been turned into an environmental education centre.
▶ *Castle open. Park and gardens open all year – telephone or consult website for details*

7 Brodick Castle

One of the great plant-hunter's gardens of the past displays collections of tender plants in a wide variety of settings.

Isle of Arran, North Ayrshire KA27 8HY

Tel: 01770 302202 | www.nts.org.uk

Historic Scotland Inventory/
The National Trust for Scotland

LOCATION On Isle of Arran, 2 miles N of Brodick. Ferry from Ardrossan or Kintyre

Standing high above the shores of the Firth of Clyde and guarding the approaches to western Scotland is a castle of locally quarried sandstone. The garden was a jungle of rhododendrons until it was restored after the First World War.

From 1930, many trees and plants arrived by boat from Tresco in the Scillies, while others came from subscriptions to the second generation of great plant-hunters such as Frank Kingdon-Ward and George Forrest. Plants from the Himalayas, Burma, China and South America, normally considered tender, flourish in the mild climate, and there is a good display of primulas in the bog garden.

The walled formal garden to the east of the castle is more than 250 years old and has recently been restored as an Edwardian garden with herbaceous plants, annuals and roses. Among the many treasures in the woodland garden are some huge specimens in the lower rhododendron walk.
▶ *Gardens and country park open all year. Walled garden open main season – telephone or consult website for details*

SCOTLAND

8 Aiket Castle

A river separates the formal terraces around the castle from wilder areas, which feature meadow, quarry and cliff plantings.

Aiket Castle, Dunlop, Ayrshire KA3 4BW

Tel: 01560 483926

LOCATION 10 miles SW of Glasgow off A736 Barrhead-Irvine road. At Burnhouse turn left onto B706; after 1½ miles turn right

The 15th-century castle ruins provide a stunning backdrop for the undulating 7 acre garden. An avenue of handsome *Alnus rubra* underplanted with spring-flowering woodland plants leads to the front of the castle. Azaleas, hybrid rhododendrons, eucryphias, magnolias and hoherias, variegated cornus and hydrangeas thrive, with shelter provided by conifers.

The summer garden to the east slopes towards the burn with fine views across to Barr Hill. Two large oval ponds reflect the colours of the richly planted surrounding borders. These contain a good backbone of perennials, with masses of tulips in spring followed by cosmos, geraniums, nicotianas and dahlias. *Iris ensata* thrive in the moist conditions with a companion planting of phormiums, dieramas and many different grasses.

Behind the castle is a terraced area and a natural amphitheatre. The river divides the garden so that from the formal areas near the castle there are good views of the wilder and more natural landscape on the other side. Wooden bridges cross the river to extend the garden – one way leads to a wild-flower meadow, another to a quarry garden with a natural pond and cliff planted with tender plants thriving in the sheltered microclimate.

▶ *Open main season – telephone for details – and for parties by appointment*

9 Finlaystone

Unusual features here include a garden planted in a Celtic design and a paved maze, while woodland trails lead to waterfalls.

Langbank, Inverclyde PA14 6TJ

Tel: 01475 540505 | www.finlaystone.co.uk

Historic Scotland Inventory

LOCATION 8 miles W of Glasgow Airport, on A8 W of Langbank

Designed in 1900 and enhanced since the 1960s, this garden is imaginatively laid out over 10 acres. Spacious and elegant lawns are framed by long herbaceous borders, with shrubberies and mature copper beeches looking down over the River Clyde. John Knox's tree, a Celtic paving 'maze', a paved fragrant garden, a bog garden and a walled garden planted in the shape of a Celtic ring cross are other attractions. The 70 acres of mature woodland include unusual play areas for children.

▶ *Open all year – telephone or consult website for details*

10 Greenbank Garden

The wide range of plants on display showcases many varieties of narcissi and a National Collection of bergenia.

Flenders Road, Clarkston, Glasgow G76 8RB

Tel: 0141 616 5125/5126 or 0844 4932201

www.nts.org.uk

Historic Scotland Inventory/
The National Trust for Scotland

LOCATION From Clarkston Toll in S Glasgow take Mearns Road for 1 mile. Signposted

For gardeners seeking advice on planting small gardens, this is the place to visit. The 2½ acre walled garden has been divided into many different sections, offering diverse plantings. The colour combinations are especially appealing, and the plants are in good condition and well labelled.

A tennis court has been converted into an area full of ideas for disabled and infirm gardeners, with raised beds and a waist-high running-water pond, and wheelchair access to the glasshouse and potting shed where classes are held.

Woodland walks are filled with spring bulbs and shrubs, and there are usually Highland cattle grazing in the paddock. The garden also includes a National Collection of bergenias.

▶ *Open all year – telephone or consult website for details*

11 Colzium Lennox Estate

A walled garden on this country estate has a fine collection of rare trees, as well as an arboretum and a restored ice house.

Kilsyth, Glasgow G65 0PY | Tel: 01236 828150

www.northian.gov.uk

LOCATION 14 miles NE of Glasgow on A803

The combination of an unusual array of gardens and buildings, fine water features and outdoor activities make a visit to the 74 acre estate enjoyable for all ages. An outstanding collection

of conifers, including dwarf cultivars, and rare trees has been established in the beautifully designed walled garden. There are 100 varieties each of snowdrops and crocuses. An arboretum and a glen provide walks, and a curling pond, ice house and clock theatre are unusual features.
▶ *Estate open all year; walled garden open most of year – telephone or consult website for details*

12 Little Sparta

Poetry and sculpture blend with plants and the natural landscape in this unique garden, created by artist Ian Hamilton Finlay.

Dunsyre, Lanark, South Lanarkshire ML11 8NG

www.littlesparta.co.uk

Historic Scotland Inventory

LOCATION Turn off A721 at Newbiggin for Dunsyre. 1 mile W of Dunsyre turn up unmarked farm track signed to Stonypath and Little Sparta; garden is 1 mile walk uphill

The contemporary 5 acre garden, located 350m (1,148ft) above sea level in the Pentland Hills, was created by the late artist and poet Ian Hamilton Finlay. He believed that a garden should appeal to all the senses and provoke thought, both serious and light-hearted, and so revived the 17th-century art of emblematic gardening.

From 1966 the garden was gradually transformed from a hill farmstead into a garden full of sculpture, classical inscriptions and images, allusions and symbols, in a display that is both intellectual and witty. Trees, plants, beds and paths appear as if placed at random rather than as part of a coherent scheme.
▶ *Open main season – telephone or consult website for details*

13 Drumlanrig Castle

Four formal parterres display elaborate designs and elegant topiary, and an unusual pavilion in the woods has a heather roof.

Thornhill, Dumfries and Galloway DG3 4AQ

Tel: 01848 331555 | www.drumlanrig.co.uk

Historic Scotland Inventory

LOCATION 16 miles SW of M74 Junction 14, 18 miles NW of Dumfries, 3 miles N of Thornhill on A76. Signposted

The formal terraces and parterres around and below the house – one of Scotland's finest and most palatial residences, built in the late 17th

century – provide a suitably magnificent setting for the castle. The four parterres, all with different plants and colour themes and some featuring clipped box and yew topiary, are a stunning sight from the 200m (656ft) long terrace above. The Shawl Parterre has a pretty design using circles, ovals and hearts.

The parterres were first restored in the Victorian era, when heathers were used instead of bedding plants as infill. The Victorians also introduced foreign plants and shrubs as well as many of the exotic conifers still thriving in the woodland walk today, including one of the oldest Douglas firs in Britain, the tallest weeping beech (*Fagus sylvatica* 'Pendula') and an early fan-trained *Ginkgo biloba*. A charming heather-roof pavilion in the woodland walk overlooks the tumbling Marr burn. The 40 acre gardens were simplified during the two world wars and are now being restored again to a high standard.
▶ *Castle open. Gardens and country park open main season – telephone or consult website for details*

14 The Garden of Cosmic Speculation

Twisting landforms, water features and sculptures re-create aspects of the cosmos in this remarkable contemporary garden.

Portrack House, Holywood, Dumfries and Galloway DG2 0RW

LOCATION 5 miles N of Dumfries, 1 mile off A76

Covering 30 acres, this is one of the most exciting and important contemporary gardens in Britain. It was sculpted by the designer and architectural critic Charles Jencks and his wife, Maggie Keswick, and expanded by him after her death in 1995. In this garden innovative sculptures and landforms are used to explore some of the deeper ideas and laws of nature and several areas are devoted to fundamental discoveries. A water cascade tells the story of the universe, a terrace evokes the distortions caused by a black hole, a Quark Walk explores the building blocks of matter, and sinuous lakes and swirling landforms simulate fractal geometry.

Set in woodland, the front façade of the Nonsense Building was designed by renowned architect James Stirling, the rear by Jencks. The garden culminates in the Universe Cascade, a water feature set within a dramatic staircase which represents the story of the cosmos. This garden is a witty and intriguing interpretation of the laws that govern the universe.
▶ *Open for SGS and by written appointment*

FIFE AND SOUTHEAST SCOTLAND

Seasonal planting displays are a key feature of many of the region's gardens, while in others designers have succeeded in combining nature with art to create some extraordinary schemes.

1 Floors Castle

Colourful borders, vegetables and espaliered fruit trees are all part of a stately walled garden where Queen Victoria once took tea.

Roxburghe Estates Office, Kelso TD5 7SF

Tel: 01573 223333

www.floorscastle.com

Historic Scotland Inventory

LOCATION On outskirts of Kelso; well signposted

Floors is, architecturally, one of Scotland's grandest country houses. It is magnificently situated with glorious views across a huge sweep of open parkland towards the Cheviot Hills.

The walled kitchen garden, which Queen Victoria visited in 1867, ten years after its creation, is of equally stately proportions and contains the classic mix of glasshouses, herbaceous borders, fruit, vegetables and annuals. The long and broad borders, colour themed from cool to hot, are backed by original Victorian iron poles festooned with the pink rose 'American Pillar'

and purple clematis, while apple trees have been trained in the traditional French style as goblets and dwarf and full pyramids. A large children's playground and garden centre is also located here.

In a woodland garden, known as the Star Plantation, fine mature oaks, limes and sweet chestnuts tower above snowdrops in spring and carpets of colourful wild flowers in summer. Beyond lies a 2 acre formal garden, the Millennium Parterre, which features the intertwined initials of the present Duke and Duchess of Roxburghe. The design, similar to that used on the castle's linen in 1900, is picked out in traditional box, with contrast and highlighting provided by *Euonymus fortunei* 'Emerald 'n' Gold'.

Within the 25 acre gardens there are also enjoyable walks through woodland and along the banks of the Tweed, providing splendid views of the landscape. The parkland includes many fine trees, some dating back to the 18th century.

▶ *Castle open. Gardens and grounds open all year – telephone or consult website for details*

2 Kailzie Gardens

A walled garden, a wild garden and possibly Scotland's oldest larch are among the many attractions here.

Peebles, Scottish Borders EH45 9HT
Tel: 01721 720007 | www.kailziegardens.com

Historic Scotland Inventory

LOCATION 2½ miles SE of Peebles on B7062

The 25 acres of garden are situated in a beautiful part of the Tweed Valley, with breathtaking views. Although they lost their focal point in 1962 when the old mansion was pulled down, the vast walled garden still houses a magnificent greenhouse and has been transformed into meandering lawns and island beds filled with interesting shrubs and plants, most notably fuchsias and geraniums.

There are many delights, including drifts of snowdrops in the wild garden in early spring, a choice flower area, secret gardens, statuary and kissing seats beneath garlanded arbours. A fine fountain at the end of the herbaceous borders leads on to woods and stately trees, including a larch planted in 1725. From the woods, you can stroll down Major's Walk, which is lined with laburnum and underplanted with rhododendrons, azaleas, blue poppies and primulas. The grounds also include an 18 hole putting green, osprey viewing centre and fishing ponds.

▶ *Open all year – telephone for details*

3 Dawyck Botanic Garden

Set in a picturesque glen, the arboretum is renowned for its seasonal displays as well as a fine collection of rare and exotic species.

Stobo, Scottish Borders EH45 9JU
Tel: 01721 760254 | www.rbge.org.uk

Historic Scotland Inventory

LOCATION 20 miles SW of Edinburgh on B712

This is a specialist garden of the Royal Botanic Garden Edinburgh (see page 276). Its 60 acres has been planted with trees over a period of 300 years; they include rare Chinese conifers and the unique Dawyck beech.

The formal azalea terrace at the entrance leads into Scrape Glen, and from here paths cross Scrape Hill, where a burn tumbles down under a Dutch bridge. Mature specimen trees tower above the many varied flowering trees and shrubs, and there are magnificent views of the garden. Beech Walk is another attraction and Heron Wood includes an intriguing feature, the first sanctuary for 'cryptograms' – non-flowering plants, including fungi and lichen.

Dawyk's fine stonework and terracing on the balustrade, bridges and urns was produced by Italian craftsmen in the 1820s. Visit in February for the snowdrops, May and June for meconopsis and azaleas, and autumn for the glorious colours.

▶ *Open most of year – telephone or consult website for details – and by appointment*

ISLAND BEDS FILLED WITH INTERESTING SHRUBS

KAILZIE GARDENS

STOBO CASTLE WATER GARDENS

4 Stobo Castle Water Gardens

Magnificent Japanese water gardens with an impressive waterfall as their centrepiece are set in the castle's grounds.

Peebles, Scottish Borders EH45 8NX
Tel: 01721 760245
hugh.seymour@btinternet.com
Historic Scotland Inventory
LOCATION 7 miles SW of Peebles on B712, 12 miles E of Biggar

The appeal of Stobo Castle's peaceful 5 acres of gardens is the trees, lush plant life and a classic oriental landscape where clear water flows down a series of dramatic cascades. Here Japanese bridges and stepping stones invite visitors to zigzag from side to side, and peaceful streams meander away from the main torrent to create one huge water garden.

Its creators have manipulated nature to heighten the visual impact. A large earth dam has been built across a steep valley and faced with stone to create a spectacular waterfall – impressive in every season. The many fine mature trees include Japanese maples, which add glorious colour in autumn months.

▶ *Open for SGS and by appointment, but advisable to confirm*

5 Portmore

Replanted over the past 20 years, the grounds of this Edwardian house include a stylish walled garden and Italianate grotto.

Eddleston, Scottish Borders EH45 8QU
Tel: 01721 730383
LOCATION ½ mile N of Eddleston, on A703 Peebles-Edinburgh road

A long drive winds up through woods, fields and little lochs to the Edwardian mansion, which boasts a fine 1½ acre walled garden, designed and replanted with taste and flair. A soft mix of grey, blue, mauve, pink and dark red herbaceous plants fill its box-edged herbaceous borders. Beyond them, greenhouses are packed with colourful plants including geraniums, pelargoniums, streptocarpus and fuchsias.

Beside them is a fern-filled Victorian Italianate grotto. The rest of the garden is divided into squares with a potager, hawthorn walks and rose gardens. Elsewhere, a parterre has been laid out at the far side of the house, a recently developed water garden has been planted with shrubs and meconopsis, and woodland walks are being developed with rhododendrons, azaleas and shrub roses.

▶ *Open for SGS, and for parties by appointment*

6 Jupiter Artland

Leading artists, including Anish Kapoor and Antony Gormley, have created sculptures that complement the landscape.

Bonnington House, Steadings, Wilkieston, Edinburgh EH27 8BB

Tel: 0131 257 4170 | www.jupiterartland.org

LOCATION From Edinburgh city centre, take Dalry/ Gorgie Road to Sighthill, then follow A71 signed to Kilmarnock. Go through Wilkieston and take 2nd slip road on right (B7015), signed to East Calder; gates are 18m (60ft) on right

Set within the extensive grounds around the late 17th-century Bonnington House, this is one of Britain's most innovative sculpture parks. The challenging brief that artists received was to respond to the park's natural surroundings and fit their works into the spaces they have chosen.

As a result, visitors can wander through beech and oak woodland to view major sculptures by renowned artists including Anish Kapoor, Antony Gormley, Andy Goldsworthy, Marc Quinn, Laura Ford and Shane Walterner – there are also four works by the late Ian Hamilton Finlay. The centrepiece is an enormous landform, created by American landscape architect and critic Charles Jencks – walking through it and up to its apex is an experience to rival anything Europe or America has to offer in the genre.

Although open to the public three days a week, it is essentially a private collection. Entry fees go to the Jupiter Artland foundation which funds art education for children.

▶ *Open limited season – telephone or consult website for details*

7 Culross Palace

Re-created in Renaissance style, the grounds include terraces, raised vegetable beds and a delicately perfumed rose garden.

Culross, Dunfermline, Fife KY12 8JH

Tel: 01383 880359 | www.nts.org.uk

Historic Scotland Inventory/
The National Trust for Scotland

LOCATION 12 miles W of Forth Bridge off A985

Looking out on to the Firth of Forth, the ochre-walled palace stands at the heart of a picturesque historic village and is a rare example of an early 17th-century merchant's house. No one knows precisely what form the original garden took, but the National Trust for Scotland chose to give it a charming Renaissance-style setting, inspired by contemporary paintings and literature.

Eight raised beds planted with old varieties of vegetable lie nearest the house, with a vine-covered walkway to one side and a diminutive orchard where Scots Dumpy hens scratch and croon. Above lie terraces of mingled herbs, fruit and flowers, humming with bees on a hot summer's day.

As you wind upwards on crushed-shell paths, there are other period features, such as green-oak arbours, a turf bench and a tiny flowery mead. The Mary Luke garden at the top, heady with sweet-smelling old roses, commemorates the lady who inherited the house at the end of the 19th century and was determined that it should be preserved.

▶ *Palace open. Garden open all year – telephone or consult website for details*

8 Dowhill

Nine linked ponds form the spine of a remarkable garden, which features formal garden rooms and extensive woodland.

Kelty, Perth and Kinross KY4 0HZ

Tel: 01577 850207

LOCATION M90 Edinburgh to Perth, exit 5. Turn left to Cleish; house is ¾ mile on left

Over two decades, the garden's present owners have transformed the 6 acres surrounding the early Georgian house into a 'pleasure walk' based around nine linked ponds. The garden blends well with its rolling landscape, and has a natural feel and flow to it, enhanced by magnificent mature trees and many others planted more recently, with rhododendrons, primulas and blue poppies contributing additional colour. Generous lawns swirl and eddy around the traditionally planted borders, creating secluded areas that contrast with more formal garden rooms.

Visitors can explore the well-planted woodland, walking over decorative iron bridges and down manicured mown paths circling an unexpectedly expansive and beautiful lakeland area, where informal shrub and waterside plantings provide shelter for wildfowl and tame hens. The owners are now creating new attractions including a topiary walk and two quarry gardens.

▶ *Open for SGS, and by appointment*

9 Cambo Gardens

A walled garden includes rambling roses and a lilac walk. Beyond is a prairie and acres of woodland that lead to the sea.

Kingsbarns, St Andrews, Fife KY16 8QD

Tel: 01333 450313 | www.camboestate.com

LOCATION 6 miles SE of St Andrews on A917 between Kingsbarns and Crail

This romantic Victorian walled garden of 2½ acres was created around the Cambo burn with its weeping willows, waterfall and rose-clad wrought-iron bridges. Naturalistic plantings of rare and interesting herbaceous perennials add to the charmingly informal atmosphere. There are masses of spring bulbs, a lilac walk with 26 cultivars, more than 250 old-fashioned and rambling roses, and borders that glow with colour in early autumn.

A late-summer feature is the ornamental potager with its 2,500 eye-catching vegetables, which has evolved from a grid of geometric patterns into a dramatic and diffuse layout. Beyond the walled garden a former donkey paddock has been laid out as an American prairie, using 80 different species grown from seed in the garden, and a bog garden has been planted alongside a stretch of the burn. The 70 acres of woodland walks leading to the sea are carpeted in early spring with aconites and a spectacular display of snowdrops – a new woodland garden showcases part of a National Collection. In September a meadow is mauve with colchicums.
▶ *Open all year – telephone or consult website for details*

10 Kellie Castle

Old-fashioned varieties of vegetables and borders teeming with bees and butterflies enliven this small organic garden.

Pittenweem, Fife KY10 2RF | Tel: 01333 720271

www.nts.org.uk

Historic Scotland Inventory/ The National Trust for Scotland

LOCATION 3 miles NW of Pittenweem on B9171

The 1 acre garden, which is entered by a door in a high wall, appears to be 17th century in plan, but was embellished in late Victorian times.

Simple borders, such as one of nepeta, bustle with life as hundreds of bees and butterflies swarm around the flowers. Patches of lawn are contained within box hedges, and roses tumble over arches and trellises.

A small, romantic garden-within-a-garden is hidden behind a trellis in one corner, and a large commemorative seat provides a focus at the end of one of the main walks. An orchard, wall-trained fruit and a collection of old and unusual varieties of vegetables produced by organic gardening methods are other features.

Outside the walled garden, mown walks wind through a meadow and woodland, which is a haze of wild garlic in late spring.
▶ *Castle open. Garden and grounds open most of year – telephone or consult website for details*

11 Royal Botanic Garden Edinburgh

Created in 1670, this extensive garden boasts Britain's tallest palm house and outstanding collections of exotic plants.

Inverleith Row, Edinburgh EH3 5LR

Tel: 0131 552 7171

www.rbge.org.uk

LOCATION 1 mile N of city centre at Inverleith. Signposted

Established in the 17th century on an area the size of a tennis court, the Royal Botanic Garden now extends to 75 acres and has become one of the finest botanic gardens in the world. Rhododendrons and azaleas abound and, in spring, their flowers provide a blaze of colour and intriguing scents.

Its celebrated rock garden, which includes more than 5,000 alpine plants, is spanned by a long bridge over the stream. In summer, marsh orchids, lilies, saxifrages and bell-shaped campanulas give brilliant colour. There are also peat and woodland gardens and a stunning herbaceous border. The arboretum sweeps along the garden's southern boundary. There is also a Scottish heath garden, which replicates the landscape and plants of the Highlands.

A relatively recent addition to the botanic garden is the Chinese hillside on a south-facing slope. This includes a spectacular wild-water ravine crossed by bridges, the water tumbling down into a tranquil pond at the bottom of the

A CANOPY OF ARCHES IS
SHEPHERD HOUSE

hillside. There is a fine collection of Chinese plants – the largest collection outside China of plants that originate in the wild – and the *t'ing* (a traditional pavilion) is a perfect place to relax.

The glasshouses, featuring Britain's tallest palm house, lead the visitor on a trail of discovery through the temperate and tropical regions of the world, including passionflowers, cycads (some more than 200 years old) and species that help provide everyday necessities such as food, clothes and medicine. A garden in memory of the late Queen Mother opened in 2006.

▶ *Open all year – telephone or consult website for details. Garden tours April to Sept*

12 Landform UEDA

Architect Charles Jencks is responsible for a serpentine grass mound with crescent shaped pools – a mix of garden and art.

The Scottish National Gallery of Modern Art, 75 Belford Road, Edinburgh EH4 3DR

Tel: 0131 624 6200

www.nationalgalleries.org

National Galleries of Scotland

LOCATION Between Scottish National Gallery of Modern Art and Dean Gallery

Designed in 2002 by American architectural expert Charles Jencks for the Scottish National Gallery of Modern Art, the Landform Ueda (named for a Japanese scientist) is a serpentine stepped mound of mown grass with three crescent-shaped pools from which rise gentle spiral paths. The innovative design is based on the rhythmic patterns that occur in nature, such as weather systems. These create a series of curves that overlap but never repeat and are attracted to a point.

Jencks 'looked at the inherent principles of natural movement and designed the Ueda to reflect and heighten these natural forces'. Once you actually see the garden, the description can be perfectly understood. The Landform is 7m (23ft) high and occupies an area 300m² (360sq yd). From the paths there is also an elevated view over the two galleries' grounds, and their fine collection of sculptures, and towards the handsome Edinburgh skyline.

▶ *Open all year – telephone or consult website for details*

13 Shepherd House

An elegant stone rill that flows beneath rose-covered arches and columns is a central feature of this well-planted garden.

Inveresk, East Lothian EH21 7TH

Tel: 0131 665 2570

www.shepherdhousegarden.co.uk

LOCATION 7 miles E of Edinburgh. From A1 take A6094 exit, signed to Wallyford and Dalkeith, and follow brown tourist-signs to Inveresk Lodge Gardens

Developed over the past 50 years, the garden at Shepherd House is still evolving. Its dominant feature is a rill that springs from a fountain pond at its farthest end, flows down the centre, continues beneath a canopy of arches and pillars cloaked in flowering climbers, and ends in an oblong pool above the house terrace where running water washes the hair of a bronze nymphet.

Mirror potagers of decorative vegetables, underplanted with tulips and overlooked by blue obelisks of trained pears, stand on each side of the rill, while the planting on both sides of the pool is cleverly restricted to three fastigiate beeches interspersed with blue irises – a pleasing contrast to the colours of the terrace a few steps below.

The change of level is marked by an alpine-friendly wall topped by blue posts supporting espaliered *Malus* 'Red Sentinel', through which the upper garden can be glimpsed. The terrace, in perfect proportion to the charming 18th-century merchant's house above it, is lavishly enhanced by the gleaming colours of tulips and irises.

Nearest the house, the Millennium garden includes lavender, irises, salvias and oriental poppies. There are also informal but distinctly themed areas for meadow flowers, hellebores and snowdrops, a knot garden and a secluded cobbled arbour. Many decorative features are dotted around the garden – ornaments, pebble mosaics, topiary, keyholes – and a spiral, shell-shaped stone wall seat.

The charm of the 1 acre garden lies not only in its abundance of colour, but also the blend and balance achieved by ornamental trees and larger shrubs, and the mix of a certain formality with a cottage garden ambience.

▶ *Open for limited season – telephone or consult website for details – for SGS, and for parties by appointment*

SCOTLAND

CLOAKED IN CLIMBERS

14 Greywalls

This quintessentially Edwardian garden, attributed to designer Gertrude Jekyll, complements a fine house from the same era.

Gullane, East Lothian EH31 2EG

Tel: 01620 842144 | www.greywalls.co.uk

LOCATION 17 miles SE of Edinburgh on A198, 3 miles W of North Berwick. At east end of Gullane, signed to Greywalls; house is on right

The house, with views over Muirfield golf course and the Firth of Forth, was designed in 1901 by Sir Edwin Lutyens as a golfing holiday home. Its 6 acre formal gardens are believed to be the only gardens in Scotland created by Gertrude Jekyll. The main garden lying to the south, where a Yorkstone terrace opens onto the old rose garden, has recently been redesigned retaining the original design of 20 beds and using many of Jekyll's favourite plants – honeysuckles, clematis and roses climb ornamental metal pyramids.

An *œil-de-boeuf* in the stone wall provides a fine vista through to the Lammermuir Hills. Beyond this garden, box compartments with a central whitebeam underplanted with variegated vincas are backed by holly-hedged chambers containing cherry trees and sculptures. Next comes a single herbaceous border, a lavender border and a charming parterre of box, potentilla and hebes with sweet pea pyramids – all influenced by Jekyll in design and content. The garden combines the 'prettiness' of that particular era of English gardening with wonderful Scottish views and the tang of the sea.

▶ *Open by appointment*

15 Tyninghame Walled Garden

A lengthy apple walk leads to one of Scotland's oldest walled gardens, where classical statues are set into yew hedges.

Dunbar, East Lothian EH42 1XW

Tel: 01620 860559

Historic Scotland Inventory

LOCATION 25 miles E of Edinburgh N of A1. Take turning to North Berwick and Tyninghame on A198; after 1 mile turn right through archway

The gateways and the high brick walls, originally heated with fires to help ripen fruit, date from 1760, making this one of the oldest walled gardens in Scotland. Within are 4 acres of formal gardens redesigned in 1960. The wide grass walk with high yew hedges forms the backbone of the garden. Classical statues are set in alcoves cut in the yew, while pedestal urns and a fine Florentine fountain stand at the intersections of two paths that dissect the vista. One path, edged with nepeta, has arched supports for ornamental vines and climbing roses. The second is a beautifully planted rose walk.

Extensive borders of mixed plantings, a long border of peonies and an iris border are all impeccably maintained. There is also a knot garden, an apple orchard, a potager and a large woodland area where mature and unusual trees are underplanted with huge swathes of perennials.

The 90m (295ft) long apple walk outside the walls was planted in 1891 and formed the approach to the walled garden from the house.

▶ *Open for SGS, and by appointment*

16 Broadwoodside

Two courtyards are richly planted in formal designs while a kitchen garden features a doorway fashioned out of garden forks.

Broadwoodside, Gifford, East Lothian EH41 4JQ

Tel: 01620 810351

LOCATION On B6355, leaving Gifford towards golf course

The East Lothian farmstead was rescued from dereliction in 2000 and has been turned into something much grander, while its young garden is growing into a magical and intimate place.

An eye-catching door incorporating three garden forks forms the entrance to the kitchen garden and sets the atmosphere of this imaginative place. The centrepiece is a formal rectangular pond surrounded by willows that are cut back every winter, and vegetables in raised beds and flowers for cutting are arranged in symmetrical rectangular beds.

From the kitchen garden a covered pond leads to the first of the two courtyards, where a simple formal layout is richly and informally planted with scented pink and white roses, white foxgloves, astrantias, bronze fennel, macleayas, geraniums and violas.

The formality continues in the upper courtyard with a striking chequerboard design; alternate squares are occupied by standard mop-top *Acer platanoides* 'Globosum', each with a different underplanting – one has clipped box balls, another two varieties of allium and a third a solid block of clipped germander. Every detail is executed with perfection. The garden continues beyond the house and out into the beautiful East Lothian farmland with an iris canal, an *allée* of beech hedging, an orchard and an avenue lined with hornbeams. The wider landscape is dotted with a temple and several other follies.

▶ *Open for SGS, and for parties by appointment*

17 Manderston

Edwardian formal terraces give way to a picturesque landscape with a lake, Chinese-style bridge and woodland.

Duns, Scottish Borders TD11 3PP

Tel: 01361 883450

www.manderston.co.uk

Historic Scotland Inventory

LOCATION 2 miles E of Duns on A6105

Manderston is one of the last great classic houses to be built in Britain. It was described in 1905 as a 'charming mansion inexhaustible in its attractions'. This might equally well apply to the gardens, which remain an impressive example of gardening on the grand scale. Four magnificent formal terraces planted in the Edwardian style with a geometric design overlook a narrow serpentine lake, and a Chinoiserie bridge takes visitors over to the woodland garden on the far side and elegantly effects the transition from formal to informal.

The woodland garden – at its best in May – has an outstanding collection of azaleas and rhododendrons. The formal walled gardens to the north of the house are a lasting tribute to the best of the Edwardian era, when 24 gardeners were employed to do what two now accomplish to the same immaculately high standard.

Gilded gates open onto a panorama of colourful planting on different levels, with fountains, statuary and a charming rose pergola. Even the greenhouses were given lavish treatment, with the walls created from lumps of limestone to resemble a grotto and planted with exotic species. In all, there are 56 acres of formal and informal beauty.

▶ *House open. Gardens open main season – telephone or consult website for details – and all year by appointment*

BROADWOODSIDE

HUGE GRASSY SWARDS TILT, SPIRAL AND SNAKE AROUND THE GARDEN

THE GARDEN OF COSMIC SPECULATION

Sculpting the landscape

For centuries, earth has been moved and rivers dammed to create impressive landscapes and intriguing garden features.

Ever since squares of grass were beaten out with wooden mallets in medieval times to form the first English gardens, garden-makers have been digging out, levelling off and piling up the land around their homes to make their surroundings more interesting.

In a valley below a 19th-century farmhouse in Dumfriesshire, Scotland, the land has been whipped up into a series of huge grassy swards that tilt, spiral and snake their way around the garden and its network of curved pools. The Garden of Cosmic Speculation at Portrack is 'a spur to think about and celebrate some fundamental aspects of nature' according to its creator, leading landscape architect and critic Charles Jencks. Intriguing features such as the

Symmetery Break Terrace and Soliton Wave Gates explore concepts of time and space, while the Universal Cascade symbolises the story of life. One of the garden's most striking landforms is the conical Snail Mound, which has two spiralling paths that meet only at the top. Here, Jencks was inspired by the double helix of DNA and also by the viewing mounts that were a feature in Renaissance gardens.

Viewing mounts

Medieval gardeners first made these simple grassy mounds, called mounts, as a means of looking down at their enclosed gardens. By the 16th and 17th centuries, when garden owners were keen to have views out across the countryside,

ha-has in England from turf sods at Stowe in Buckinghamshire. It zigzagged around the house for nearly 4 miles. At Petworth in Sussex, the house enjoys magnificent views over the 700 acre deer park – one of the finest unspoilt examples of a 'Capability' Brown landscape – thanks to a 2.7m (9ft) deep ha-ha.

Shaping the land took place on a vast scale in the 18th century when renowned designers such as William Kent and 'Capability' Brown dispensed with much of the formality and geometrical aligning of Tudor and Elizabethan gardens. They wanted the landscape to look more natural but also to provide a succession of different views and viewpoints for their clients as they walked or rode around their estates. They damned streams and joined up small ponds to make huge irregular lakes and they moved tonnes of soil to create rolling hills and smooth valleys.

At Stowe, Lord Cobham employed a team of 30 gardeners to make these earthworks and he even moved an entire village so that the view down his newly created valley, the Elysian Fields, would not be spoiled. In the Grecian Valley, which 'Capability' Brown re-shaped into a series of undulating hills that looked as if they might have been smoothed naturally by glaciers, the gardeners dug out some 191m3 (250,000cu yd) of soil with their pickaxes and spades, wheeling it away to the waiting carts.

More recently, 17m (56ft) was sliced off the top of a 160-year-old china clay quarry to help to construct the Eden Project in Cornwall, a stunning millennium garden and landscape intended to bring visitors closer to nature. It took six months to shift the 1.8 million tonnes of dirt, before 83,000 tonnes of soil was added and the striking biomes constructed.

Grass amphitheatres

A more dramatic kind of shaping is the grass amphitheatre. In the 18th century, inspired by classical amphitheatres, Charles Bridgeman carved out the first grass amphitheatre in England on a 3 acre grassy slope at Claremont in Surrey. It makes a stunning sculptural feature and a superb viewing platform from which to admire the lake and the grounds beyond.

A smaller but equally striking amphitheatre can be seen at Great Fosters in Surrey. Created by landscape architect Kim Wilkie in 2003, it has formed a focal point at the end of a historic avenue of lime trees. The land has been sculpted with ramps rising up either side to enclose a series of seven grass terraces. The final circle has been sunk 1m (3ft) below the ground to provide a performance space with superb acoustics for musicians – a truly theatrical garden feature.

mounts had become much more elaborate and architectural, and were focal points in themselves. One at New College in Oxford started off as a rubbish tip before it was grassed over, grandiosely shaped like a four-sided pyramid and stone steps added. Some mounts were made of stone or brick and had a shelter or a banqueting house on top. Others, such as the one in the Privy Garden at Hampton Court, became elongated and were used as raised walks.

Like garden-makers more than 200 years before him, Jencks wanted to achieve a smooth transition from the house to an area on one side of the garden where cattle and sheep grazed, without having to break the view with a fence or railings. He made an undulating wall to form a kind of ha-ha – a sunken boundary wall with a sloping ditch at its base. For owners of big estates, this form of land shaping not only served as a foolproof barrier against livestock, it also opened up views across their parklands.

In the early 18th century, garden designer Charles Bridgeman made one of the first

CENTRAL AND NORTHEAST SCOTLAND

Himalayan ravines and picturesque landscapes around burns and glens have been created in the gardens of this region. Tender plants flourish in the fertile soil, high rainfall and climate tempered by the Gulf Stream.

1 Dun Ard

A cleverly designed garden full of surprises, featuring a hornbeam avenue, a lush box parterre and heritage vegetables.

Main Street, Fintry, Stirlingshire G63 0XE

Tel: 01360 860369

LOCATION 17 miles SW of Stirling, 17 miles N of Glasgow on B822

This inspirational 3 acre garden, which has evolved since 1988, is full of stimulating ideas and is now considered to be one of the best-designed gardens in Scotland. Situated on a north-facing slope behind a small village house in Fintry, surrounded by the beautiful Campsie Hill, hedges create a sequence of atmospheric garden rooms.

Nearest to the house is an organic garden filled with vegetables, many of them species first grown in the 19th century. Delights such as Panthers peas, Bull's Blood beetroot, crimson-flowered broad beans and different coloured salad leaves are all arranged in kaleidoscopic patterns. Further garden rooms reveal themselves slowly – rather like a theatrical performance unfolding – as you climb up the hill. One, with *Cornus kousa chinensis* as its centrepiece, displays an exuberance of unusual varieties, including tree peonies (a speciality of the garden), while another is planted with annuals and vegetables.

Halfway up the hillside is a superb pleached hornbeam avenue leading to a summerhouse set in an orchard meadow. Further up still, formality is introduced with a box parterre planted luxuriantly in four rectangles, each with *Rosa* 'William Lobb' cascading from a central obelisk. Then comes a serene space with a rectangular pond surrounded by grass and enclosed by beech hedges.

The water source at the top of the property is marked by a stone pyramid within a damp garden where meconopsis, primula, hostas and smilacina thrive. There are also three areas of meadow – one growing wild orchids – a late border planted in hot colours, a formal pond and, from most points, stunning views over the surrounding countryside to the mountains beyond.

▶ *Open by appointment only*

2 Glenarn

Winding paths cross a steeply sloping glen that is vibrantly coloured with acers, rhododendrons and towering magnolias.

Rhu, Helensburgh, Dunbartonshire G84 8LL

Tel: 01436 820493

www.gardens-of-argyll.co.uk

Historic Scotland Inventory

LOCATION On A814 between Helensburgh and Garelochhead. Go up Pier Road to Glenarn Road

Established in the 1920s and 1930s, the 10 acres of woodland garden here owe an incalculable debt to the Victorian plant hunters and 20th-

century expeditions. Well-kept paths meander round a sheltered bowl, sometimes tunnelling under superb giant species rhododendrons (including a *R. falconeri* grown from seed supplied by Joseph Hooker in 1849). Its collection of species rhododendrons was what first brought this garden to prominence.

As the paths continue across the glen, there are some glorious views over to the Clyde estuary and, on every side, there is plenty in the garden for visitors to admire, including huge magnolias, pieris, olearias, eucryphias and hoherias.

The owners, who are both professional architects, acquired Glenarn in 1983 and with almost no outside help have successfully replanted and restored where necessary, while retaining the special atmosphere created by such magnificent growth. The rock garden, built around the old quarry and natural outcrop, falls steeply down past the daffodil lawn to the house with its tall, twisting chimney pots. Work has been completed to expose the quarry face and is continuing on the restoration of the former scree bed.

▶ *Open main season for NGS – telephone or consult website for details*

BENMORE BOTANIC GARDEN

3 Linn Botanic Gardens

Collections of temperate plants, including ferns and bamboos, have transformed the gully of a burn into a jungle-like garden.

Cove, Helensburgh, Argyll and Bute G84 0NR

Tel: 01436 842084

www.linnbotanicgardens.org.uk

LOCATION 6 miles S of Garelochhead, ¾ mile N of Cove on shore of Loch Long

This unusual example of a private botanic garden covers 3 acres and includes large collections of bamboos, eucalyptus, magnolia and temperate ferns, trees, shrubs, as well as a glen with a rushing burn and abundant rhododendrons. The impression given is of a semi-tropical jungle packed with unusual and exotic plants.

Visitors follow well-signed paths on both sides of an intensively planted ravine. Ensuring year-round colour has been an important consideration, and a new area at the top of the garden is dedicated to plants from South Africa and New Zealand. There are sweeping views over the Firth of Clyde and the hills of Argyll.

▶ *Open all year – telephone or consult website for details*

4 Benmore Botanic Garden

This dramatic mountainside garden has 300 species of rhododendrons, Bhutanese and Chilean areas, and a giant redwood avenue.

Dunoon, Argyll, Argyll and Bute PA23 8QU

Tel: 01369 706261 | www.rbge.org.uk

Historic Scotland Inventory

LOCATION 7 miles N of Dunoon, W of A815

This regional offshoot of the Royal Botanic Garden Edinburgh is a mountainside area of 120 acres, set in the dramatic location of the Cowal Peninsula. Benmore is world-famous for its collections of flowering trees and shrubs.

Trails extend from Britain's finest avenue of giant redwoods (*Sequoiadendron giganteum*) planted in 1863. On the hillside beside the River Eachaig more than 300 species rhododendrons and an extensive magnolia collection shine out in their paintbox colours. Other features include a formal garden with stately conifers, an informal pond, the Glen Massan arboretum with some of the tallest trees in Scotland, a Chilean rainforest and a Bhutanese glade.

▶ *Open main season – telephone or consult website for details – and by appointment at other times*

SCOTLAND

5 Asgog Hall Fernery and Garden

A rare sunken Victorian fernery has been restored to its former glory, and is surrounded by enchanting gardens.

Ascog Hall, Isle of Bute, Argyll and Bute
PA20 9EU

Tel: 01700 504555

www.ascoghallfernery.co.uk

LOCATION Car ferry (35 mins) from Wemyss Bay to Rothesay (www.calmac.co.uk), 5 minute drive on A844

Although the restored fern house, built around 1875, is the star attraction here, the abundance of other choice plants in the 3 acre garden, including blue poppies in May and June and seductively perfumed old roses in midsummer, provide delightful surprises.

The present owners bought the house in 1986 and only then stumbled on hidden rustic steps leading down to a sunken, derelict interior with strangely fashioned walls and rotting vegetation. Thanks to a description and inventory in *The Gardeners' Chronicle* of 1879, help from Historic Scotland and a collection of ferns donated by the Royal Botanic Garden, Edinburgh, the glasshouse has been faithfully reconstructed.

Artfully planted in a grotto setting and sympathetically enhanced by a waterfall and pools, it now houses one of the most impressive collections to be found outside a botanic garden. Its star (and the only original survivor) is a 1,000-year-old *Todea barbara*.

▶ *Open main season – telephone or consult website for details*

6 Mount Stuart

A kitchen garden planted in striking colours and a garden displaying an extensive range of tender plants are the highlights here.

Rothesay, Isle of Bute, Argyll and Bute
PA20 9LR | Tel: 01700 503877

www.mountstuart.com

Historic Scotland Inventory

LOCATION Take ferry from Wemyss Bay (www.calmac.co.uk). Garden is 5½ miles S of Rothesay ferry terminal on A844

Within the 300 acres of designed landscape and waymarked woodland walks, there are a number of interesting horticultural features and a remarkable walk with a series of pools and cascades, designed as a kind of spiritual pilgrimage, replicating the Via Dolorosa. The gardens also contain a mature pinetum of 1860 and an old lime tree avenue leading to the shore – both restored over the past decade. With support from the Royal Botanic Garden Edinburgh, 100 acres have been set aside to grow endangered conifers from around the world.

Rock gardens provide decorative features near the house, but the two most important elements are the kitchen garden and the Wee Garden. The latter is, in fact, 8 acres of mixed and exotic plantings with emphasis on species from the Southern Hemisphere. It is set where conditions are mildest and grows some of the most tender plants to be found outside the glasshouse.

The kitchen garden has been redesigned, and six large beds planted with emphasis on bold colours. In the middle is the Pavilion Glasshouse sheltering rare flora from Southeast Asia.

▶ *House open. Garden open May to Sept, daily*

7 Achamore Gardens

The mild Gulf Stream climate of the Hebridean isle of Gigha enables many delicate plants to thrive here.

Isle of Gigha, Argyll and Bute PA41 7AD

Tel: 01583 505275 | www.gigha.org.uk

Historic Scotland Inventory

LOCATION Take A83 to Tayinloan then ferry to Gigha (check www.calmac.co.uk for details)

While woodland was established in the 19th century to shelter Achamore House from the strong sea winds, the magnificent gardens were planted from the 1940s by an owner who was particularly interested in growing rhododendrons.

The result is a collection unsurpassed in variety, quality and sheer visual magnitude, with fine specimens of tender species, and there are also many good varieties of camellias, cordylines, primulas and Asiatic exotica, all thriving in the mild climate.

The 54 acre landscape is delightfully varied because it has been sub-divided into 15 separate areas, each with its own character, and planted with species from around the world – few gardens outside the national botanic collections can claim such diversity and rarity. A fine *Pinus montezumae* stands in the walled garden, and drifts of Asiatic primulas feature around the pretty woodland pond.

▶ *Open all year – telephone or consult website for details*

8 Crarae Garden

This spectacular woodland garden, centred on the Crarae burn, is exotically planted with rare trees and rhododendrons.

Minard, Inveraray, Argyll and Bute PA32 8YA

Tel: 01546 886614

www.nts.org.uk

Historic Scotland Inventory/
The National Trust for Scotland

LOCATION 11 miles SW of Inveraray on A83

While set in a Highland glen, the rushing torrents, waterfalls and lush vegetation give this woodland garden – among the most important in Scotland – the appearance of a Himalayan ravine. The gardens were originally planned in the early 20th century, using surplus seed from the great plant expeditions, gifts from the owner's knowledgeable friends and the shared expertise of a network of famous horticulturists. A wide variety of rare trees was planted, together with exotic shrubs and species rhododendrons, which form great canopies above the winding paths.

This is a rare opportunity to see 600 different varieties of rhododendron, some exclusive to the garden, which, together with many other plants from the temperate world, create a magnificent spectacle of colour. The autumn leaves of sorbus, acers, prunus, cotoneasters and berberis are one of the great features of the 126 acre garden, which contains a National Collection of nothofagus, a tree from the Southern Hemisphere.

▶ *Open all year – telephone or consult website for details*

9 Arduaine Garden

Perched on an island promontory, this plant lover's paradise enjoys beautiful views and offers a dazzling spring display.

Oban, Argyll and Bute PA34 4XQ

Tel: 01852 200366

www.arduaine-garden.org.uk

Historic Scotland Inventory/
The National Trust for Scotland

LOCATION On A816, 20 miles S of Oban,
18 miles N of Lochgilphead

The 20 acre garden is set on a promontory bounded by Loch Melfort and the Sound of Jura, and enjoys a mild climate thanks to the North Atlantic Drift. It was conceived and begun in 1898, then restored when the Essex nurserymen

Edmund and Harry Wright acquired the property in 1971. They gave it to the National Trust for Scotland in 1992.

Although the garden's fame rests largely on its outstanding rhododendrons, azaleas, magnolias and other rare and tender trees and shrubs, it has far more than botanical interest to offer. Trees and shrubs, some over 100 years old and thickly underplanted, tower overhead as visitors climb up through the glen. At the lower level, hostas, ferns, candelabra primulas, meconopsis and numerous other flower and foliage perennials cluster around lawns and along the sides of the watercourses. Visitors who reach to the highest viewing point will enjoy the fine panorama of ocean, coast and islands.

▶ *Open all year – telephone or consult website for details*

10 An Cala

Planted in the romantic style of the 1930s, the garden has colourful borders, natural rockeries, ponds and a waterfall.

Easdale, Isle of Seil, Argyll and Bute PA34 4RF

Tel: 01852 300237

www.gardens-of-argyll.co.uk

Historic Scotland Inventory

LOCATION 16 miles SW of Oban. Signed to Easdale on B844 off A816 Oban-Campbelltown road

A charming garden in less than 5 acres, An Cala was designed in the 1930s in front of a row of old distillery cottages, nestling under the surrounding cliffs. The stream, with its ponds and waterfall, runs down the length of the garden through a series of different spaces filled with colourful species, which are especially attractive during the spring and summer months.

A small wooden temple lined with a mosaic of fir cones stands at the far end of one of the ponds, and local slate paths invite the visitor into each well-planned corner. It is a model example of how to plant azaleas and rhododendrons on a small scale – so that they enhance rather than dominate the landscape. Beyond the gate, in a different world, is the ocean and dramatic views across to the Hebrides.

▶ *Open main season – telephone or consult website for details*

SCOTLAND

11 Cawdor Castle

Three contrasting gardens – wild, walled and flower – make up the grounds around and below the historic 14th-century castle.

Cawdor, Nairn, Highland IV12 5RD

Tel: 01667 404401 | www.cawdorcastle.com

Historic Scotland Inventory

LOCATION Between Inverness and Nairn on B9090 off A96

Despite a latitude geographically north of Moscow, the castle's 20 acres of gardens enjoy the Gulf stream temperance and as many as 18 hours of sunshine daily in midsummer. The 1620 walled garden, the oldest part of the grounds, was originally an orchard. It was later planted as a kitchen garden with exotic vegetables and herbs before being remodelled in 1981 with a holly maze in a design taken from a mosaic of the Minotaur's labyrinth in a Roman villa. There are also Paradise, knot and thistle gardens, and an orchard of old Scottish fruit trees.

In the formal flower garden, influenced by French style and laid out in 1710, yew hedges are now festooned with the pretty climber *Tropaeolum speciosum*, the Scottish flame flower. Lavender borders and rose beds were added in 1850, and herbaceous borders have been given an extended season with bulbs, shrubs and ornamental trees.

A wild garden, planted with spring bulbs, azaleas and rhododendrons, was created in the 1960s, running from the castle down the hillside to the Cawdor Burn. Nature trails wind through a further 750 acres of woodland, with many varied trees and more than 100 species of lichen.
▶ *Castle open. Garden open main season – telephone or consult website for details*

12 Ballindalloch Castle

Set between the Spey and the Avon, the grounds showcase a rock garden, a walled garden and a spectacular lawn.

Ballindalloch, Moray AB37 9AX

Tel: 01807 500205

www.ballindallochcastle.co.uk

LOCATION Halfway between Grantown-on-Spey and Keith on A95. Signposted

One of the most attractive features of Ballindalloch is its 1937 rock garden, which comes tumbling down the hillside onto the most impressive lawn in the land – it takes three men two days to mow and edge it. The owners have renovated all the borders over the years and transformed the old walled garden into a rose and fountain parterre garden, which has matured most attractively.

The daffodil season and the river and woodland walks are a highlight at Ballindalloch. Other features include a grass labyrinth and a small parterre at the side of the house which displays humble nepeta and *Alchemilla mollis* to stunning effect.
▶ *Castle and garden open main season – telephone or consult website for details. Coaches by appointment*

13 Kildrummy Castle Gardens

Created in an ancient quarry, these romantic gardens feature brilliant maples and acers, exotic flowers and tranquil pools.

Alford, Aberdeenshire AB33 8RA

Tel: 01975 571203/563451

www.kildrummy-castle-gardens.co.uk

Historic Scotland Inventory

LOCATION 2 miles SW of Mossat, 10 miles W of Alford, 17 miles SW of Huntly. Take A944 from Alford, following signs to Kildrummy, and turn left onto A97. From Huntly turn right onto A97

The 20 acres of glorious gardens are set in a deep ravine between the ruins of a 13th-century castle and a Tudor-style house, which is now a hotel. The narrowest part of the ravine is crossed by a copy of the towering 14th-century Auld Brig O'Balgownie (Old Aberdeen Bridge), built in 1900.

The bridge affords a spectacular bird's-eye view of both sides of the water garden, which was commissioned from a firm of Japanese landscape gardeners in the same period. The planting was completed by a firm of renowned nurserymen, Backhouse of York, a few years later.

In April the reflections in the still water of pools enhance the impact of the luxuriant *Lysichiton americanus* and, later, the primulas, Nepalese poppies and a notable *Schizophragma hydrangeoides*. There are also fine maples, oaks and conifers and rhododendron species and hybrids. Although this is a severe frost pocket, the gardens can grow embothriums, dieramas and other choice plants. They are especially appealing in autumn, with colchicums in flower and acers in brilliant leaf.

The 1904 rock garden, also by Backhouse of York, occupies the site of the quarry that originally provided the stone for the castle.
▶ *Open daily April to Oct – telephone or consult website for details*

14 Leith Hall and Gardens

The grounds include a formal garden set apart from the house, a rock garden and way-marked woodland trails.

Huntly, Aberdeenshire AB54 4NQ

Tel: 01464 831216 | www.nts.org.uk

Historic Scotland Inventory/
The National Trust for Scotland

LOCATION 34 miles NW of Aberdeen, 1 mile W of Kennethmont on B9002

It is the old 6 acre garden at Leith Hall, remote from the house, that offers the greatest pleasure to the plant enthusiast. Rising on a gentle slope from the west drive, a series of small spaces sheltered by walls and hedges contains long borders and a large, well-stocked rock garden with a stream and gravel paths.

The rock garden's simple, romantic design allows a tremendous display of flowers during the whole of summer and early autumn. Especially fine are magenta *Geranium psilostemon* and an entire border of solid catmint. There are no courtyards or dominating architecture, just massive plantings of perennials and the odd rarity among the rocks. The circular moon gate leads to the old turnpike road, and woodland walks take in ponds and views down the garden.

▶ *House open. Garden and grounds open all year – telephone for details*

15 Pitmedden Garden

More than 5 miles of box hedging form six intricate parterres, which are filled with no fewer than 40,000 plants.

Pitmedden Village, Ellon, Aberdeenshire AB41 7PD

Tel: 01651 842352

www.nts.org.uk

Historic Scotland Inventory/
The National Trust for Scotland

LOCATION 14 miles N of Aberdeen, 1 mile W of Pitmedden, 1 mile N of Udny on A920

The Great Garden, originally laid out in 1675 as the centrepiece of the estate, reveals the tastes of 17th-century garden-makers and their love of geometric patterns that are made to be viewed from above. This rectangular parterre garden is enclosed by high terraces on three sides and a wall on the fourth, and simple topiary and box hedging abound.

The south and west-facing walls, lined by fine herbaceous borders, are covered by a great variety of old apple trees in both fan and espalier styles. These produce almost 2 tonnes of fruit at the end of the season. Ornamental patterns are cut in box on a grand scale, infilled with 40,000 annuals. The overall impact is especially striking when viewed from the original ogival-roofed ▷

PITMEDDEN GARDEN

stone pavilion at the north of the garden or when walking along the terraces. The old house was destroyed by fire in 1807, and when the National Trust for Scotland acquired the property in 1952, little of the original design was left in the 7 acres of garden. As a result, contemporary 17th-century plans for the garden at the Palace of Holyrood in Edinburgh were used to create what is seen at Pitmedden today.

▶ *Open main season – telephone or consult website for details*

16 Castle Fraser

One of Scotland's most elaborate castles overlooks a delightful walled garden, replanted to provide colour all season.

Sauchen, Inverurie, Aberdeenshire AB51 7LD

Tel: 01330 833463 | www.nts.org.uk

Historic Scotland Inventory/
The National Trust for Scotland

LOCATION 15 miles NW of Aberdeen, off B993 near Kemnay

The 328 acre grounds are notable as the historic setting for one of the most magnificent 'Castles of Mar' – built by the Earl of Mar in the 15th century. Extensive walks in the grounds include superb views of the house, which dominates the surrounding parkland.

The grounds are a happy marriage of landscape designed in the late 17th and early 18th century, and 18th-century agricultural improvements. The deep, south-facing herbaceous border, laid out in 1959, has been reworked to accommodate a greater selection of plants that can tolerate the climate. The old walled garden has been replanted with a traditional mix of herbaceous perennials, cut flowers, fruit, vegetables and herbs, and the original cross and perimeter paths have been reinstated. Around the walled garden, a woodland garden is being developed where children will enjoy the play area and its amphitheatre.

▶ *Castle open. Garden open all year – telephone or consult website for details*

17 5 Rubislaw Den North

This unusual, complex garden reflects the owner's passion for philosophy and science, as well as for unusual plants.

Aberdeen AB15 4AL | Tel: 01224 317345

LOCATION In W part of city centre off A90. Turn E into Queen's Road; turn left at next roundabout, then second left

Sculptural in design and complex in nature, this lovely 1 acre garden, sheltered by neighbouring trees, is densely planted with a wholly individual selection of plants and landscape features. Winding paths connect themed areas – a bamboo grove, a border illustrating the evolution of primitive plants, ferns, unusual herbaceous perennials, a cloud tree and woodland.

The owner describes himself as a retired natural philosopher, but he is also an academic gardener who, by incorporating elements of science and spirituality into the design, has created something both striking and personal. There is nothing else like it in Scotland.

▶ *Open main season – telephone or consult website for details*

18 Crathes Castle Garden

Colourful formal gardens are divided into themed areas by clipped Irish yew hedges dating from the early 18th century.

Banchory, Aberdeenshire AB31 5QJ

Tel: 08444 932166

www.nts.org.uk

Historic Scotland Inventory/
The National Trust for Scotland

LOCATION 3 miles E of Banchory, 15 miles SW of Aberdeen on A93

The romantic castle dates from 1596, and has changed little since the mid 18th century. Set in flowing lawns, it overlooks one of the finest enclosed gardens in Scotland. There is no record

ALTERNATING CHEQUERED NICHES DISPLAY A SERIES OF FASCINATING CARVED PANELS

EDZELL CASTLE

of how the 4 acres were laid out in earlier times, although the clipped Irish yew hedges are known to date from 1702. Sir James Burnett, who inherited the estate in the 1920s, was a keen collector, and his wife a talented garden designer. The grounds, set off by terraces and the sloping terrain, owe much to their enthusiasm and gifts.

Rare shrubs reflect Burnett's interest in the Far East, while the splendid wide herbaceous borders with clever plant associations were created by Lady Burnett; the most famous is the white border. In all there are eight themed gardens, each with a different character and varied planting schemes.

There are many specialist areas, such as the trough garden, and the large greenhouses contain a National Collection of Malmaison carnations. The extensive wild gardens and 20 acres of parkland have a number of picnic areas and marked trails. There is also a useful plant centre, which stocks alpines, herbaceous perennials and some of the old varieties of plants that can be seen in the garden.

▶ *Castle open. Garden and grounds open all year – telephone or consult website for details*

19 Arbuthnott House

A classical design makes clever use of the sloping site, with horizontal and diagonal paths dividing it into long garden rooms.

Laurencekirk, Aberdeenshire AB30 1PA

Tel: (01561) 361226

www.arbuthnott.co.uk

Historic Scotland Inventory

LOCATION 22 miles S of Aberdeen, 3 miles W of Inverbervie on B967 between A90 and A92

The enclosed 5 acre garden was laid out between 1685 and 1690 within the valley of the Bervie Water. The entrance drive crosses a fine bridge topped by imposing urns before reaching the house, which is set high on a promontory. Most of the 5 acre garden slopes steeply to the river below.

The 17th-century garden-makers came up with an ingenious way to cope with the difficult site – three main walks run horizontally across the contour of the slope, further connected by a series of diagonal grass paths. This fixed structure creates long garden rooms and vistas as the garden is explored. The intervals between the paths are mostly cultivated, and herbaceous perennials, a profusion of roses, shrubs

underplanted with hostas, primulas, meconopsis and lilies, lilacs and viburnums provide colour throughout summer.

The 2 acre garden next to the house has been planted in the style of a 17th-century French potager, with vegetables and soft fruit contained within beds bounded by herbaceous borders, rose beds and long strips for cut flowers. Espaliered fruit trees grow against the north wall, facing a row of greenhouses, with a 17th-century garden house positioned in the northwest corner. Further down the slope are two other large areas, one laid to lawn and the other planted as an orchard.

▶ *House open by appointment. Garden open all year – telephone or consult website for details*

20 Edzell Castle

Walls with chequered niches and wood panels carved in the 17th century give this garden a place in Renaissance art history.

Edzell, Brechin, Angus DD9 7UE

Tel: 01356 648631

www.historic-scotland.gov.uk

Historic Scotland Inventory

LOCATION 6 miles N of Brechin. Take A90 (A94) and after 2 miles fork left on B966

In 1604, within the walls of his red sandstone fortress, Sir David Lindsay created a curious and atmospheric 1 acre garden. The garden's enclosing walls of alternating chequered niches display a series of fascinating carved panels. These depict 21 sculpted symbolic figures representing the Seven Cardinal Virtues, the Seven Liberal Arts, and the Seven Planetary Deities and stand above large recesses, designed to hold flowers – the clear intent was to make a garden that would stimulate both the mind and the senses.

The whole is laid out to be viewed from a corner summerhouse and the windows of the castle. A central design of box parterres, lawns and bedding was created in the 1930s in the mannered layout typical of the early 17th century – after the castle and grounds had lain in ruins for 150 years. The garden is at its best when the bedding plants are in bloom.

▶ *Castle open. Garden open all year – telephone or consult website for details*

PITMUIES GARDENS

21 Pitmuies Gardens

Two semi-formal walled gardens shelter long borders of herbaceous plants that produce superb midsummer displays.

House of Pitmuies, Guthrie, By Forfar, Angus DD8 2SN

Tel: 01241 828245

www.pitmuies.com

Historic Scotland Inventory

LOCATION 1½ miles W of Friockheim, on A932

In the 20 acre grounds of an attractive 18th-century house and courtyard, these lovely walled gardens lead down towards a small river with an informal riverside walk and two unusual buildings – a turreted dovecote and a Gothic wash-house. There are also rhododendron glades with unusual trees and shrubs.

But pride of place must go to the spectacular semi-formal gardens behind the house. Here exquisite old-fashioned roses and a series of long borders containing a dramatic palette of massed delphiniums and other herbaceous perennials constitute one of the most memorable displays of its type to be found in Scotland during June and July.

Latterly the gardens have evolved with new plantings, vistas and focal points, and the conversion of a former tennis court has allowed for new habitats and a greater diversity of plants.

▶ *House open for parties by appointment. Garden open for Scottish Snowdrop Festival and main season, and at other times by appointment*

1790s in the style of 'Capability' Brown, but for today's gardeners, the key attraction is the yew-hedged Italian Garden, created in 1910 by the Queen Mother's mother, Countess Cecilia, which includes a raised terrace between two small gazebos that overlook parterres of formal beds.

Two spectacular long bowers of pleached beech – like green roofs on stilts – are its strongest elements, together with glorious borders that are a riot of alliums, roses, *Iris sibirica*, nepeta and geraniums, punctuated by obelisks bearing honeysuckles, golden hops or roses.

Nearby, the nature trail through the pinetum will soon include a new point of interest – the old walled garden is currently in the process of being transformed into an ornamental garden. This will combine flowers, herbs, vegetables and fruit – including 'Tower of Glamis' apple trees.
▶ *Castle open. Garden open most of year – telephone or consult website for details*

23 Glendoick Gardens

One family has built up an extensive collection of rhododendrons, which are displayed in the garden and adjoining nursery.

Glendoick, Glencarse, Perth and Kinross PH2 7NS

Tel: 01738 860205 (nursery); (01738) 860260 (garden centre)

www.glendoick.com

Historic Scotland Inventory

LOCATION 8 miles E of Perth, 14 miles SW of Dundee on A90

The gardens hold one of the most comprehensive collections of rhododendrons in the world. From 1919, three generations of one family developed the collection as they went, in their turn, on plant-hunting expeditions in the Himalayas and China to collect new specimens for the garden. In the adjoining nursery and garden centre, which are now known worldwide, the family business continues to flourish, breeding dozens of handsome new hybrid rhododendrons for the market.

In the gardens above the 18th-century mansion, fine trees and rhododendrons are enhanced by a dense understorey of perennials such as meconopsis, primulas, trilliums, lilies and nomocharis. Around the house itself you can study dwarf rhododendrons and azaleas at close quarters and visit the small arboretum and conifer collection.
▶ *Open for limited season – telephone or consult website for details – and for SGS*

22 Glamis Castle

The extensive grounds include the appealing Italian Garden, with bowers of pleached beech, as well as a nature trail and pinetum.

Glamis, Forfar, Angus DD8 1RJ

Tel: 01307 840393

www.glamis-castle.co.uk

Historic Scotland Inventory

LOCATION 5 miles W of Forfar on A94

The turrets and spires of the castle rise up dramatically at the end of a mile-long tree-lined avenue. As the childhood home of the late Queen Mother, Glamis Castle attracts hundreds of visitors but such is its scale that they rarely feel crowded. The park was landscaped in the

24 Branklyn Garden

Seeds collected from around the world helped to establish this garden, which boasts a fine collection of alpine plants.

116 Dundee Road, Perth, Perth and Kinross PH2 7BB | Tel: 01738 625535

www.branklyngarden.org.uk

Historic Scotland Inventory/
The National Trust for Scotland

LOCATION ½ mile from Friarton Bridge on A90, then A859 to Perth

Although less than 2 acres, the garden seems larger because of its many diminutive treasures, such as *Paraquilegia anemonoides* or *Shortia soldanelloides*. For lovers of alpines, this place is a particular treat, and everything in the great alpine scree rock garden, constructed with rock from the local Kinnoull Hill quarry, is painstakingly labelled for admirers.

The garden's creators began shaping and planting in 1922 in what was once an orchard. Contact with some of the great plant-hunters of the day, such as George Forrest and Frank Kingdon-Ward, enabled them to fill it with finds from Bhutan, Tibet and China, which they nurtured and recorded. The meandering paths are packed with Himalayan glories such as rhododendrons and meconopsis (Himalayan poppies), and several National Collections are held here, including cassiopes with their attractive, bell-shaped flowers.

▶ *Open main season – telephone or consult website for details*

25 The Hermitage

A dramatic waterfall is overlooked by an unusual folly in this woodland garden, created as part of a 'Picturesque' landscape.

Dunkeld, Perth and Kinross PH8 0HX

Tel: 01350 728641/0844 4932192

www.nts.org.uk

Historic Scotland Inventory/
The National Trust for Scotland

LOCATION 1 mile W of Dunkeld, 16 miles N of Perth off A9 (signposted)

The 37 acre woodland garden was created as part of a landscape designed in the Picturesque style by the 2nd Duke of Atholl in the 18th century. In the first half of the 19th century many of the conifers discovered by one of Scotland's foremost plant-hunters, David Douglas, were introduced and are now mighty specimens. Cutting through the woods, the River Braan becomes a broad, torrential waterfall that can be viewed from a platform projecting from a stone pavilion – the Hermitage, orginally named Ossian's Hall after the 1785 figure within it – beside the 18th-century bridge. A grotto hidden deep in the woods adds to the wild, romantic effect.

▶ *Open all year – telephone or consult website for details*

26 Scone Palace Gardens

The ancient crowning place of Scotland's kings is now part of an impressive garden, that has a five-pointed maze at its heart.

Perth, Perth and Kinross PH2 6BD

Tel: 01738 552300 | www.scone-palace.co.uk

Historic Scotland Inventory

LOCATION Just outside Perth on A93 Perth-Braemar road

It is hard to imagine, as you survey the wide green lawns and serene Georgian Gothic frontage of the palace, home to the Earls of Mansfield,

DRUMMOND CASTLE GARDENS

that this peaceful spot was once the capital of Scotland. The house was built on the site of Scone Abbey, and Scottish kings such as Macbeth and Robert the Bruce came here to be crowned on Moot Hill – still visible in the grounds, as are the picturesque remnants of the village, which was moved further away when the present palace was built in 1803.

The gardens offer scenic walks with panoramas of snowdrops, daffodils, primulas, bluebells, rhododendrons or roses appearing in their season. The trees are on an impressive scale too – a now-vast Douglas fir was grown from seed brought back by the plant-hunter David Douglas, who was born at Scone, and the 19th-century pinetum includes towering *Sequoia giganteum*.

There is also a laburnum tunnel and a butterfly garden, but the most original feature is probably the fiendish Murray Star maze in green and copper beech. Designed in the shape of a five-pointed star, the 2,000 beech trees used have been planted to create a tartan effect.

▶ *Palace and gardens open main season – telephone or consult website for details*

27 Drummond Castle Gardens

This garden is dominated by its stunning parterre – a St Andrew's Cross design surrounding an unusual sundial.

Muthill, Crieff, Perth and Kinross PH7 4HZ

Tel: 01764 681433

www.drummondcastlegardens.co.uk

Historic Scotland Inventory

LOCATION 2 miles S of Crieff on A822

This must count as one of gardening's greatest *coups de théâtre* – the moment when, having ascended the narrow beech avenue and entered the castle courtyard, you look over the balustrade on the right and take in the whole of the dazzling parterre laid out 20m (66ft) below. Designed in the shape of a St Andrew's Cross and with an unusual 17th-century multiplex sundial at its heart, it was made in the early 19th century.

There was a renewed interest in formal design at the time, and the garden was much admired by Queen Victoria and Prince Albert during a three day visit in 1842. Although lavender,

roses and simple summer bedding fill some of the box-edged compartments, most of the colour comes from the foliage of the many varied trees, immaculately pruned into lollipops and cones, umbrellas, spirals and drums – some of them tilted at crazy angles by the wind. Classical statuary and quartz stonework add further elegance and style to this unforgettable place.
▶ *Open main season – telephone or consult website for details*

28 Cluny House

Himalayan plants are a special feature of this wild woodland garden, which also includes the widest conifer in Britain.

Aberfeldy, Perth and Kinross PH15 2JT

Tel: 01887 820795

www.clunyhousegardens.com

Historic Scotland Inventory

LOCATION 32 miles NW of Perth. N of Aberfeldy, over Wade's Bridge, take A827 Weem-Strathtay road. House signed after 3 miles

If Cluny appears to be a wild woodland garden, that is a tribute to the present owners who work hard to make it look that way. But no wild woodland could ever contain such an exotic selection of plants – hellebores, trilliums and Asiatic primulas, erythroniums and cardamines, blue Himalayan poppies, martagon lilies and *Cardiocrinum giganteum*. It takes endless clearing, weeding and the clever insertion of new plants propagated with patience and skill.

The 6 acre garden was created from a patch of Perthshire hillside from 1951 onwards. Initially, a broad range of trees from the Himalayas and North America were added to the few already there, together with Japanese acers and a multitude of rhododendrons. Among the original trees are two impressive Wellingtonias, one of which – with a girth of 11m (36ft) – is Britain's widest conifer. The garden's paths can be steep,

so there are long and short routes to suit visitors with differing levels of fitness. Because the garden is managed organically, birds and red squirrels flourish here, too, adding to the pleasure.
▶ *Open main season – telephone or consult website for details – and for SGS*

29 Blair Castle

A statue of Hercules overlooks a vibrantly planted walled enclosure, which features landscaped ponds and a Chinese bridge.

Blair Atholl, Pitlochry, Perth and Kinross PH18 5TL | Tel: 01796 481207

www.blair-castle.co.uk

Historic Scotland Inventory

LOCATION 35 miles N of Perth on A9 at Blair Atholl. Signposted

Within the grounds of the dazzling white castle that is the ancestral home of the Dukes of Atholl and Scotland's most visited historic house, is a fine example of a lost garden brought back from the brink. The 9 acre Hercules Garden was named after the statue by John Cheere that overlooks it and is a relic of the landscaped park laid out in the 17th century by the 2nd Duke.

Upkeep declined in the 20th century, and it was only in the 1980s that the decision was made to restore the garden. Although the planting has been rationalised, the playful spirit of the original shines through. Broad slopes planted with lines of fruit trees dip down to a central waterway dotted with artificial peninsulas and islands supporting swan and duck huts, a herb garden and stands of trees. In the 275m (900ft) long herbaceous border, divided by yew buttresses, that runs the length of the south-facing wall, the summer planting scheme moves from vibrant reds and oranges to cooler pinks and blues. There are also ornamental vegetables, a Chinese bridge, a folly and a plethora of marble statues.
▶ *House and garden open most of year – telephone or consult website for details*

NO WILD WOODLAND WAS EVER SO COVERED WITH BEAUTIFUL PLANTS
CLUNY HOUSE

NORTH HIGHLANDS AND ISLANDS

Formal gardens, complete with water features, sculpture and statuary provide an elegant counterpoint to the rugged scenery beyond their walls, while clever planting brings exotic colour to the Highlands.

1 Dunrobin Castle Gardens

Inspired by the gardens of Versailles, the castle has two parterres laid out around circular pools in a formal Victorian design.

Golspie, Highland KW10 6SF

Tel: 01408 633177/633268

www.great.houses-scotland.co.uk

Historic Scotland Inventory

LOCATION 1 mile NE of Golspie on A9

The 5 acre Victorian formal gardens were designed in the grand French style by Sir Charles Barry in 1850 to echo the architecture of the castle. Descending the stone terraces, one can see the round garden, grove, parterre and herbaceous borders laid out beneath, together with round ponds, each one of which has its own fountain.

Earlier roses have been replaced with hardy geraniums, antirrhinums and *Potentilla fruticosa* 'Abbotswood'. Then come spring tulips through to hardy fuchsias, including *F.* 'Dunrobin Bedder'

and autumn-flowering dahlias. The shrubbery has been replaced by 20 wooden pyramids covered in roses, clematis and sweet peas and interplanted with small ornamental trees. An 18th-century summerhouse is now open to the public and there are many woodland walks in the grounds.
▶ *Castle open. Garden open main season – telephone or consult website for details*

2 Novar

This thriving estate between the Glass and Alness has a charming 18th-century walled garden and a delightful water garden.

Evanton, Highland IV16 9XL

www.novarestate.co.uk

LOCATION 7 miles NE of Dingwall off A9 and B817 between Evanton and junction with B9176

The walled garden and park were created to complement the Georgian mansion, and are a model of 18th-century garden-making. The ▷

DUNROBIN CASTLE GARDENS

walled garden covers 5 acres with charming arched entrances and an oval pond embellished with a contemporary bronze fountain.

In the mid 20th century a water garden was established with an attractive series of well-planted ponds, fed by streams gushing over stone steps and monumental waterfalls. To celebrate the millennium, the current owners planted a formal, semi-circular parterre overlooking the park. The whole estate covers 200,000 acres.

▶ *Open for SGS, and for parties of eight or more by appointment*

3 Torosay Castle and Gardens

An Italianate garden, with 19 magnificent statues, is among the many attractions in 12 acres of gardens and woodland.

Craignure, Isle of Mull, Argyll and Bute PA65 6AY

Tel: 01680 812421

www.torosay.com

Historic Scotland Inventory

LOCATION 1½ miles S from Craignure. Steamer from Oban to Craignure

The house, built in baronial castle style in 1858, is complemented by a formal Italianate main garden based on a series of descending terraces. The unusual statue walk features one of the richest collections of Italian rococo statuary in Britain.

The peripheral gardens around the formal terraces include a newly restored informal water garden, an Oriental garden looking out over Duart Bay, and a small rock garden. Rhododendrons and azaleas are less important here than in other west coast gardens, and are complemented by a collection of Australian and New Zealand trees and shrubs. A restoration is underway, and 2,000 species and cultivars have been planted over the past five years.

Outside the main garden, the owners, in conjunction with the Royal Botanic Garden Edinburgh, have created a 5 acre Chilean wood and underplanted another 2 acre wood with plants from the collection of the late award-winning plantsman Jim Russell.

Visitors can arrive by narrow-gauge railway, as steam and diesel-hauled trains run the short journey from the Craignure terminal to Torosay, alongside the Sound of Mull with views of Ben Nevis, the Glencoe hills, the island of Lismore and Ben Cruachan.

▶ *Castle open main season. Garden open all year – telephone or consult website for details*

4 Attadale

This artist's garden features gunneras and bamboo reflected in dark pools, while sculptures appear in surprising places.

Strathcarron, Highland IV54 8YX

Tel: 01520 722217 | www.attadalegardens.com

LOCATION 15 miles NE of Kyle of Lochalsh, on A890 between Strathcarron and Strome

Water and sculpture combine to give this 20 acre garden its considerable appeal – the present owner trained as a painter, and since the 1980s her energy and vision have given it new artistic dimensions. Inside the gate, a stream and ponds on one side of the drive are planted with candelabra primulas, irises, giant gunneras and bamboos. A bridge over a waterfall links the water garden with the upper rhododendron walk, commanding views of the sea and hills.

In the kitchen garden the conservatory contains a collection of sub-tropical plants naturalistically planted in beds supported by dry-stone walls, with a tiny stream and pond. Beyond, a geodesic dome houses exotic ferns and is surrounded by a dell of mature rhododendrons underplanted with meconopsis and lilies. The woodland path then leads on to a Japanese garden where rocks and gravel symbolise the River of Life and the Mystic Isles of the West.

The symmetrical sunken garden in front of the 1755 house (not open) provides a contrast, with *Rosa rugosa* hedges, herbaceous plantings and a fine obelisk. Sculpture from Zimbabwe and bronzes are reflected in the ponds, a crested eagle perches on a cliff and a life-sized bronze cheetah and giant slate-and-stone sundial can also be seen.

▶ *Open main season – telephone or consult website for details*

5 Dunvegan Castle

A landscape of delightful contrasting styles includes woodland glades, a formal round garden and an unusual walled garden.

Isle of Skye, Highland IV55 8WF

Tel: 01470 521206

www.dunvegancastle.com

Historic Scotland Inventory

LOCATION 14 miles NW of Portree, beyond A850/A863 junction

Framed against the backdrop of the oldest continuously inhabited castle in Scotland, the 5 acres of garden have three particular areas of interest. The woodland water garden is cool and colourful, with pools, streams, waterfalls, glades and a dell planted with rhododendrons, giant cardiocrinums and swathes of meconopsis – note the tiny maidenhair ferns, native wood sage and other treasures. Then comes a round garden with a boxwood parterre of 16 triangular beds, three mixed borders for summer and a fern house.

Finally, an exciting 2 acre walled garden was created on a long-derelict site during the 1990s. Laid out on a formal plan, the four quarters each have a different focus – a lawn with a sorbus avenue, a raised pool with gravel surround pierced by plants, a triangle with an internal yew triangle, and an unusual stepped 'temple' evocative of Mayan architecture. The surrounding paths spill over with helianthemums, cistus and other Mediterranean plants.

▶ *Castle open. Garden open main season – telephone or consult website for details – and by appointment*

6 Inverewe Garden

A tranquil garden, set on a craggy hillside with stunning views, is adorned with exotic species from around the world.

Poolewe, Highland IV22 2LG

Tel: 01445 781200 | www.nts.org.uk

Historic Scotland Inventory/
The National Trust for Scotland

LOCATION 6 miles NE of Gairloch on A832

This 62 acre garden on the shores of a sea loch, Loch Ewe, has covered the Am Ploc Ard peninsula with a spectacular tapestry of exotic plants. Planned as a wild garden around two dwarf willows on peat and sandstone, it has been developed since 1865 as a series of well-tended and way-marked walks through herbaceous and rock gardens, a wet valley, pond gardens and woodland.

It is a plant-lover's garden (plant labelling is discreet), containing nearly 6,000 different plants including many tender species from Australia, New Zealand, China and the Americas, sheltered by mature beech and pine trees. National Collections of olearias, brachyglottis and rhododendrons are also held here, and a meconopsis trail is developing nicely.

A sloping walled garden with fine sea views and colourful terraces is filled with a more traditional mixture of herbaceous plants, roses and vegetables. In all, the grounds here extend to 54 acres.

▶ *Open all year – telephone or consult website for details*

7 House of Tongue

Amid rugged scenery, the walled garden flourishes, protected from the winds and sea spray by a shelterbelt of tall trees.

Tongue, Lairg, Highland IV27 4XH

Tel: 01847 611209

Historic Scotland Inventory

LOCATION 1 mile N of Tongue off A838

Sheltered by tall trees, the 4 acre walled garden is a haven in an exposed environment, and especially colourful in high summer. Adjoining the 17th-century house, it is laid out with gravel and grass walks between herbaceous beds, hedged vegetable plots and orchard, and three beds filled with old and new rose varieties. The glasshouse has been restored, and a wild-flower meadow is in progress. A stepped beech-hedged walk leads up to a high terrace with fine views over the Kyle of Tongue. The centrepiece is a 1714 sundial, a sculpted obelisk of unusual design.

▶ *Open for SGS, and by appointment*

8 Dunbeath Castle

Constantly evolving, the two walled gardens at Dunbeath are imaginatively divided into a series of artistic garden rooms and parterres.

Dunbeath, Highland KW6 6EY

Tel: 01593 731308

www.dunbeath.co.uk

LOCATION 6 miles NE of Berriedale off A9

A 'keyhole' driveway descends through a tunnel of trees to the clifftop castle, outlined by steep grass banks on either side of which is a walled garden. The southern one has been beautifully refashioned, with well-clipped fuchsia hedges providing an outer frame for the eight inner compartments and parterres, divided by mown grass walks and paired to create an attractive pattern of vegetables, fruit and flowers. The outer walls have herbaceous planting at their base and are clad with climbers chosen for flower or foliage effect. A water feature with a cupola, a laburnum pergola, a gazebo, plant supports and border backdrops give structure, height and unity.

The northern walled garden is an imaginative and light-hearted water garden of formal ponds, rills and fountains, with three interconnecting round pools surrounded by relaxed plantings, including wild irises, grasses and silver birches. A turreted viewpoint looks over the whole area.

▶ *Open for parties by appointment*

SCOTLAND

Ireland

Most of the greatest gardens are clustered around Dublin and in the extreme north and south. Plenty of rainfall and a mild climate produce the perfect conditions for many acid-loving plants and tender species. Ferns and other exotics create striking displays, while fine collections of trees and shrubs include many rare species.

KEY
1 Garden location
— County boundary
Motorway
Principal A road

NORTHERN IRELAND

Magnificent displays of exotic ericaceous plants – a result of the wet, mild climate and acidic soil – feature in many of the gardens here, most of them set against a backdrop of dramatic scenery.

1 Rowallane

Informal plantings combine with a dazzling array of species, including rhododendrons, meconopsis and penstemons.

Saintfield, Ballynahinch, Co. Down BT24 7LH

Tel: 028 9751 0131 | www.nationaltrust.org.uk

Historic Garden/The National Trust

LOCATION ½ mile S of Saintfield on A7 Belfast-Downpatrick road

The 52 acre garden is famed for its displays of rhododendrons and blue meconopsis, but it has much more to offer. Its impressive collection of plants includes several which originated here, such as *Hypericum* 'Rowallane', *Primula* 'Rowallane Rose' and *Chaenomeles* x *superba* 'Rowallane'.

The walled garden exudes a quiet charm, with rhododendrons casting a carpet of petals in spring and hoherias a snowdrift of white blossom in summer. This area is also home to a National Collection of large-flowered penstemons.

Out in the pleasure grounds, plant enthusiasts will enjoy a wide range of fine trees and shrubs, an enormous *Davidia involucrata*, a rock garden and wild-flower meadows filled with wild orchids. Extensive woodland walks planted with snowdrops add winter interest.

▶ *Open all year – telephone or consult website for details*

2 Annesley

The National Arboretum boasts a fine collection of specimen trees and shrubs, with a historic walled garden at its core.

Castlewellan, Co. Down BT31 9BU

Tel: 028 4377 8664

www.forestserviceni.gov.uk

LOCATION 25 miles S of Belfast, 4 miles NW of Newcastle, in Castlewellan

Anyone with a love of trees and plants is sure to find inspiration in the 112 acres of garden and National Arboretum here. The walled garden, with its two restored fountain pools, contains an outstanding collection of trees and shrubs planted after 1849 – original specimens of some early cultivars are still flourishing. Rhododendrons and scarlet Chilean fire bushes (*Embothrium coccineum*) bloom in spring and early summer, followed by an impressive show of tropaeolums and a collection of eucryphias. There are 34 champion specimen trees, including 15 broad-leaved giants from the Southern Hemisphere. In addition, there are bulbs, herbaceous borders and Irish yews trimmed into decorative shapes.

Beyond the walls the arboretum extends for 85 acres in the Forest Park. Walks lead round a magnificent lake and the Cypress Pond. Here the largest and longest yew-hedge maze in the world represents the path to peace in Northern Ireland.

▶ *Open all year – telephone or consult website for details*

3 Mount Stewart

Vibrant rare plants flourish in the landscaped gardens of this historic house on the tranquil shores of Strangford Lough.

Portaferry Road, Newtownards, Co. Down BT22 2AD | Tel: 028 4278 8387

www.nationaltrust.org.uk

Historic Garden/The National Trust

LOCATION 15 miles E of Belfast, 5 miles SE of Newtownards on A20 Portaferry road

Their creator, Lady Londonderry, called these unmissable gardens her 'green fairyland'. They stretch down from the historic mansion, in front of which is a collection of statues depicting British political and public figures as animals. Beyond the formal terraces, with their rectangular beds of hot and cool colours, are dramatic informal gardens featuring a fine collection of mature trees and shrubs, together with spires of cardiocrinums, eucalyptus, banks of rhododendrons, ferns and blue poppies, a mass of candelabra primulas, and much more.

Rare tender shrubs such as *Metrosideros umbellata* from Australasia flourish along the lakeside path. To savour the rich, ever-changing tapestry of plants, water, buildings and trees, these gardens should be visited several times a year.

▶ *House open. Lakeside gardens and walk open all year. Formal garden open main season – telephone or consult website for details*

A RICH, EVER-CHANGING TAPESTRY OF PLANTS, WATER, BUILDINGS AND TREES

MOUNT STEWART

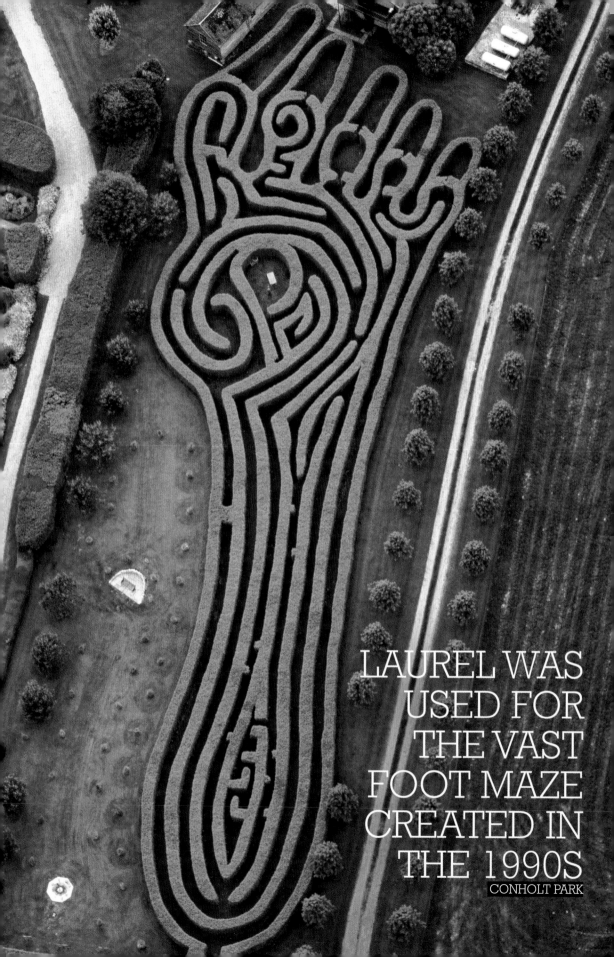

LAUREL WAS
USED FOR
THE VAST
FOOT MAZE
CREATED IN
THE 1990S
CONHOLT PARK

The twists and turns of mazes

The love of intricate designs and puzzles in gardens began in ancient times and maze-designers are still creating riddles today.

On one of their adventures in a boat, Jerome K. Jerome's three men visit the Great Maze at Hampton Court. Harris, one of the book's characters, has been before, alleging that 'it was so simple that it seemed foolish – hardly worth the twopence charged for admission'. The three men, however, wander for hours, eventually finding themselves 'in such a confused whirl that they were incapable of grasping anything'. Set in the Wilderness at Hampton Court, the oldest surviving hedge maze in Britain was laid out in 1691 for William of Orange and is still confounding visitors today.

The origins of mazes are lost in the mists of time. Perhaps the most famous classical labyrinth was designed by Daedalus (father of the high-flying Icarus) as a home for the half man/half bull Minotaur at King Minos's palace on Crete. Early turf mazes found in England showed similarity in design to those portrayed on Cretan coins.

An elaborate puzzle

Strictly speaking, a maze is a complex, branching puzzle, offering choices of direction. A labyrinth, meanwhile, has one route leading from a single entrance to the centre.

Pagan and subsequently Christian mazes were invested with symbolism, their elaborate pathways seen as representing man's journey through life, with all its twists and turns. Medieval builders laid mazes and labyrinths on the floors of their cathedrals. The narrow channel of the ancient turf maze (now kept defined by mattocks and spades) on St Catherine's Hill, south of Winchester, is thought to represent a penitential route.

From the 15th century, mazes became a key garden feature. Mostly these were knot gardens, designed to be seen from above. Their intricate, interlocking patterns, mixing pagan and religious symbols, were set out in low hedges of shrubs like hyssop, rosemary and thyme. Thomas Hill's book of 1577, *The Gardener's Labyrinth*, has charming illustrations and ideas for knots and mazes.

These elaborate knots were intended to amuse and delight, but not to confuse, unlike the head-high hedge maze, fashionable in the late 17th century. This enthusiasm was short lived, however, as the 18th-century taste for landscaped parks saw the destruction of virtually all early hedge mazes.

It was more than a century before a real interest in mazes took hold again. A 19th-century example is the yew maze at Somerleyton Hall in Suffolk. First planted by painter and garden designer William Nesfield in 1846, to conquer it involves a journey of 111m (365ft) – assuming no wrong turns are taken.

Mazes continue to appeal for the element of surprise they bring and the shrubs and materials that can be used. The maze at La Seigneurie on Sark is made of waxy leafed olearia or New Zealand holly. The Jubilee Maze at Symonds Yat, near Ross on Wye, was designed in 1981 with 12 routes to the centre but only one way out. It is formed of 1,039 Port Orford cedar bushes.

At Wyken Hall in Suffolk, the copper beech maze marks the boundary between the formal garden and the woodland beyond. The late Randoll Coate is responsible for the 1984 Beazer Maze in Bath, constructed of Bath stone paths among grass, and the symbolic Lunar Labyrinth and Sun Maze at Longleat in 1996. Laurel was used for the vast foot maze created at Conholt Park in Hampshire in the 1990s. Adrian Fisher designed the brick-and-grass pavement maze at Greys Court in Oxfordshire in 1980, inspired by Robert Runcie's enthronement sermon as Archbishop of Canterbury, relating mankind's search for understanding to being lost in a maze.

In 1991, the Duke of Marlborough commissioned Adrian Fisher to design the Marlborough Maze at Blenheim. The second largest symbolic maze in the world, it spells out 'Blenheim' in yew and reflects its history and architecture. Shapes in the maze include cannon, cannonballs, trumpets and banners, inspired by Grinling Gibbons' 18th-century wood carvings within the palace.

Designs in turf and grass

The wheel comes full circle: turf mazes have been made in the late 20th century at Leeds Castle in Kent and at Chenies Manor in Buckinghamshire, while at Little Court in Hampshire, spiralling grass paths were inspired by the labyrinth of Chartres Cathedral.

In 2000, individuals, groups and schools from all over Northern Ireland joined in the planting of the 6,000 yew trees that now form the Peace Maze in Annesley Gardens in County Down. Covering 2.7 acres, and taking an average of 40 minutes to solve, it is the longest and largest maze in the world. It was planted to represent the route taken by the people of Northern Ireland to achieve peace in the years following the 1998 Good Friday agreement.

REPUBLIC OF IRELAND

Ireland's westerly position and high rainfall ensure a warm, humid climate where tree ferns and Southern-Hemisphere conifers can flourish as well as many other plants too tender to grow elsewhere.

1 Belvedere

Amid rolling parkland dotted with follies is a charming walled garden, where herbaceous borders tumble down a slope.

Mullingar, Co. Westmeath

Tel: 00 353 44 934060www.belvedere-house.ie

LOCATION 5km (3 miles) S of Mullingar on N52

Set along the shores of Lough Ennell, Belvedere includes parkland, walled and formal gardens and wooded walks. The Jealous Wall, a sham ruin is one of a number of intriguing follies built in the 160 acres of romantic pleasure grounds.

The restored Victorian walled garden, which is divided into several sections and steeply sloped, holds beds of herbaceous perennials, a Himalayan garden around a small summerhouse, fine shrubs and statuary. There is also a glasshouse located beside the herb garden, a vegetable potager, a model farm laid out as a smallholding, a working apiary and an apple orchard of heritage apple varieties. From the terrace, magnificent views stretch out over the lake.
▶ *House open. Garden open all year*

2 Loughcrew Historic Gardens

Centuries of garden and landscape fantasy are reflected in this garden, which has a fern grotto, follies and an ancient yew walk.

Oldcastle, Co. Meath | Tel: 00 353 49 854 1922

www.loughcrew.com

LOCATION 85km (53 miles) NW of Dublin off N3

Architectural follies and features from different periods of garden history help to create Loughcrew's magical atmosphere. The long herbaceous border includes a section of grotesques – plants with weird, amusing and unusual historical connotations. There is a fine 17th-century yew walk and a strange fern grotto created out of pocked limestone. The ornamental canal is a replica of an original within the walled garden, yet to be restored. Outside its walls, the flower-filled stream garden is fed from a pond.
▶ *Open main season – telephone or consult website for details – and for parties by appointment*

3 Talbot Botanic Gardens

Australasian and Chilean trees and plants, including many rare and delicate species, are a highlight of these extensive gardens.

Malahide Castle, Malahide, Co. Dublin

Tel: 00 353 1 846 2456/1 890 5629

www.fingalcoco.ie

LOCATION 16km (10 miles) N of Dublin

This remarkable and well-displayed collection of plants was started in 1948 with seeds collected from Chile, Australia, Tasmania and New Zealand. Many rare and unusual plants now appear within the 290 acre grounds and 24 acres of gardens, including a National Collection of olearias.

About 19 acres are given over to the West Lawn and its fine trees, many from the Southern Hemisphere. Beyond the wooded walks and lawns is an extravagant 5 acre walled area, divided into separate gardens – a fine alpine garden, an intimate small garden dominated by a 17th-century hen house and dovecote, an exotic pond garden and a restored Victorian glasshouse containing Australian plants and auriculas.
▶ *Castle open. Gardens open main season – telephone or consult website for details. Walled garden open by appointment*

4 Primrose Hill

A key attraction is the spring garden, which is resplendent with snowdrops in February and includes varieties unique to the garden.

Lucan, Co. Dublin | Tel: 00 353 1 628 0373

LOCATION 13km (8 miles) W of city off N4

Approached up a beech avenue flanked by a 3 acre arboretum, the visiting season starts with a splendid display of snowdrops, including some 'Primrose Hill' seedlings, glorious in flower. In late spring and summer the generous borders feature irises, lobelias (two named ones originated here), lilies, kniphofias, *Primula auricula* 'Old Irish Blue' and many other border stars.
▶ *House open. Garden open for limited season – telephone or consult website for details – and by appointment*

5 The Dillon Garden

A striking canal runs through a walled garden in this tiny site, the imaginative creation of renowned plantswoman Helen Dillon.

45 Sandford Road, Ranelagh, Dublin 6

www.dillongarden.com

LOCATION 10 minute drive or 30 minute walk from city centre in cul-de-sac off Sandford Road just after Merton Road and church

This intriguing ½ acre town garden is the inspired creation of renowned plantswoman Helen Dillon. The front garden is a plain square of pink granite surrounded by *Betula* 'Fascination', and in the rectangular walled garden at the rear, which is typical of Dublin's Georgian town houses, the lawn has been replaced with a modern canal. In the mixed borders of shrubs and herbaceous perennials planted against the walls, each season brings new colour combinations.

Exploration reveals a series of linked secret rooms containing raised beds planted with rare species such as lady's slipper orchids and double-flowered *Trillium grandiflorum*. On the sunken terrace, terracotta pots sprout more rare plants. Clumps of *Dierama pulcherrimum* arch over the sphinxes, and a small alpine house and conservatory shelter the choicest species, including ferns, alpines, bulbs and foliage plants. Vegetables have recently been introduced into the garden, and a new area of dramatic foliage plants is being developed.

▶ *Open main season – telephone or consult website for details – and for parties of ten or more by appointment*

305

6 National Botanic Garden Glasnevin

A splendid array of plants includes more than 300 endangered species, and six species that are already extinct in the wild.

Glasnevin, Dublin 9

Tel: 00 353 1 804 0300/857 0909

www.botanicgardens.ie

LOCATION 1.5km (1 mile) N of city centre on Botanic Road close to cemetery

These gardens have been described as Ireland's 'brightest jewel'. Over their 50 acres along the River Tolka, many riches can be found among the 20,000 species arranged in seasonal display beds and scientific collections, an alpine yard and a fernery, a rockery and an arboretum. More than 300 endangered species can be seen here, including some that are already extinct in the wild.

When the aquatic house reopens, the restoration of the 19th-century glasshouses, including the great Curvilinear Range (an outstanding wrought and cast-iron building), the Great Palm House and the Turner conservatory, will be complete. Orchids, including many species recently collected in Belize, cacti, spurges, tender Vireya rhododendrons and a tropical rainforest collection are just a few of the housed displays. The most recent addition is a walled garden displaying the latest and most innovative organic methods of growing vegetables and fruit.

▶ *Open all year – telephone or consult website for details*

7 Powerscourt

Grand Italianate terraces, an impressive cascade and grottoes are dramatically framed by the Wicklow mountains beyond.

Enniskerry, Co. Wicklow

Tel: 00 353 1 204 6000 | www.powerscourt.ie

LOCATION 19km (12 miles) S of Dublin

This 47 acre garden reflects a triumph of art over the natural landscape. Although it has evolved over 250 years, the greatest changes to its layout and planting occurred in the mid 19th century.

The most arresting part of the design is the amphitheatre of Italianate terraces guarded by winged horses, and the great central axis formed by the ceremonial stairway leading down to the Triton Pond and jet, and stretching beyond to the Great Sugarloaf Mountain. The Pepper Pot Tower

has been restored and visitors can climb it to view 'the killing hollow' (where an Irish chieftain was said to have been murdered) and North American specimen trees in the tower valley. For a breathtaking view of Powerscourt, walk to the edge of the pond and look up along the staircase past the monumental terraces to the south façade of the house. Statuary, grottoes, a stunning cascade and an avenue of monkey puzzles are other fine features of the gardens.

▶ *Open all year – telephone or consult website for details*

8 Killruddery House and Gardens

The 17th-century formal gardens include original features such as an elaborate pattern of hedges running along two canals.

Southern Cross Road, Bray, Co. Wicklow

Tel: 00 353 128 63405 | www.killruddery.com

LOCATION 23km (14 miles) S of Dublin

One delight of Killruddery's 80 acres of gardens, is the formal hedging, known as 'The Angles', set beside canals, or 'long ponds', that lead to a ride into the distant hills.

The gardens date largely from the 17th century, with some 19th-century embellishments. There is a collection of 19th-century French cast statuary, a sylvan theatre created in sweet bay, and a fountain pool enclosed in a beech hedge. The fine 19th-century orangery has been re-roofed, its original dome replaced and its collection of statues conserved and restored.

Visitors can enjoy refreshments in a café set in an old ornamental dairy, which looks out over a sunken garden up to the Little Sugar Loaf.

▶ *House open. Garden open main season – telephone or consult website for details*

9 Tinode

A tranquil area of bamboos, grasses and ferns contrasts with beds profusely planted with a mix of cottage garden and rare species.

Blessington, Co. Wicklow

Tel: 00 353 1 45 82500/87 277 0399

www.juneblake.ie

LOCATION 10km (6 miles) S of Tallaght on N81

The 3 acre patch that surrounds this charming granite cottage (once the steward's house on the Tinode estate) is one of the most exciting gardens in Ireland. Started just a few years ago, it has developed at full tilt, and reflects its owner's sophisticated sense of design and energy.

As the garden developed, much of the space previously occupied by nursery stock was transformed into huge beds and borders. These are filled with an eclectic mix of plants – old cottage garden favourites such as aquilegias and dahlias are planted with rare and unusual plants from all over the world in dramatic combinations. In a space enclosed by mature beech and other hardwoods, locally sourced and salvaged materials are used to good effect, blending in with the surrounding terrain.

Welcome areas of calm are provided among the hurly-burly of the planting. These include a black reflecting pool and a meditation garden – a cool, green space with monumental boulders, ferns, bamboos, grasses and shade-loving plants, such as *Paris polyphylla* and *Deinanthe bifida*.

▶ *Open main season – telephone or consult website for details – and by appointment*

10 Hunting Brook

Bright colours and lush foliage combine in this contemporary garden, which has a vast collection of plants from around the world.

Lamb Hill, Blessington, Co. Wicklow

Tel: 00 353 8 728 56601

www.huntingbrook.com

LOCATION On N81 9km (5½ miles) from Tallaght exit towards Blessington

Panoramic views, an ancient woodland glen and fine planting make this 5 acre garden one of Ireland's most compelling modern gardens. The generous herbaceous borders below the house create a scene reminiscent of an Impressionist painting with a huge range of grasses and herbaceous perennials in shades of orange, purple and brown set off by a variety of foliage. The overall style is a modern combination of tropical and prairie planting.

The woodland walk has a very different character and style of planting. It winds down to the Hunting Brook, a shady haven of mature larches, interesting specimen trees, rhododendrons and bluebells. The woodland garden is set within the remains of a 7th-century ring fort and planted with species from around the world, including *Trochodendron aralioides* from Korea, *Diphylleia cymosa* from the Appalachian Mountains and *Deinanthe bifida* from Japan.

▶ *Open most of year – telephone or consult website for details – and by appointment*

11 Mount Usher

More than 5,000 different species of plants, including many native woodland varieties, can be found in this exuberant garden.

Ashford, Co. Wicklow

Tel: 00 353 404 40116/40205

www.mount-usher-gardens.com

LOCATION 50km (31 miles) S of Dublin, 6.5km (4 miles) NW of Wicklow, off N11 at Ashford

The Vartry River flows through this 22 acre garden, over weirs and under the bridges that allow visitors to meander through the collections. *Pinus montezumae* is always first port of call, a shimmering tree, magnificent when the bluebells are in flower.

The garden holds more than 5,000 different species. A striking grove of eucalyptus is among the fine trees and shrubs, many of which are difficult to cultivate outdoors in other parts of Britain and Ireland. A kiwi-fruit vine (*Actinidia chinensis*) cloaks the piers of a bridge, and beside the tennis court is the gigantic original *Eucryphia* x *nymansensis* 'Mount Usher'.

In spring, there are bulbs, magnolias and a procession of rhododendrons and camellias, in summer, eucryphias and leptospermums and in autumn the maples' russet and crimson leaves.

▶ *Open main season – telephone or consult website for details*

12 Heywood Garden

Within the grounds of an 18th-century park lies a fine formal garden, one of only a few designed by Edwin Lutyens in Ireland.

Ballinakill, Co. Laois | Tel: 00 353 502 33563

www.heritageireland.ie

LOCATION 5km (3 miles) SE of Abbeyleix. Turn E in Abbeyleix signed to Ballinakill

There are two garden types here – an early 20th-century gem designed by Edwin Lutyens and the remains of a romantic 18th-century park with lakes, woodland and architectural features. The Lutyens garden, one of the few he created in Ireland, comprises a pleached lime *allée*, a sunken oval pool garden, small garden rooms and the landscaping features typical of Lutyens' designs.

It is thought that Gertrude Jekyll had a hand in the design here, too. The hexagonal, octagonal and sunken pool areas are now being planted with species that may have featured in her original plans.

▶ *Open all year, daily, during daylight hours*

IRELAND

BALLYMALOE COOKERY SCHOOL GARDENS

13 Lismore Castle Gardens

Two gardens are set within the defensive walls of this great castle – one walled and one informal, with a stately avenue of yews.

Lismore, Co.Waterford | Tel: 00 353 58 54424

www.lismorecastle.com

LOCATION 57.5km (36 miles) SW of Waterford

The 7 acres of magnificent Lismore Castle, set high above the River Blackwater, include two beautiful gardens linked by the gatehouse entrance. The upper one, reached by a stairway in the gatehouse, leads to a Jacobean-style terrace with vegetables and flowers and an original Joseph Paxton glasshouse with a ridge-and-furrow roof. A fine view from the main axis to the church spire is enhanced by a new herbaceous border.

There are some attractive plants in the lower garden, but the principal feature is an ancient yew walk, where poet Edmund Spenser is said to have written parts of *The Faerie Queene*. Remarkable contemporary sculptures are dotted throughout the grounds.

▶ *Open main season – telephone or consult website for details*

14 Ballymaloe Cookery School

Managed organically, thoughtfully planted gardens include a herb garden, Celtic maze and shell-encrusted summerhouse.

Kinoith, Shanagarry, Co. Cork

Tel: 00 353 21 464 6785 | www.cookingisfun.ie

LOCATION 36km (22 miles) E of Cork, between Cloyne and Ballycotton

Geared to the needs of the burgeoning cookery school is this loosely linked series of gardens and garden rooms. The most memorable feature is a double herbaceous border leading to an octagonal summerhouse decorated with kaleidoscopic shell designs, which alone is well worth a visit.

A tree-arched path opens out onto a sheltered vegetable garden where old brick paths slice through vegetable and flowerbeds bursting with crops grown in tidy patterns. There is an arboretum with a reflecting pool and folly, herb garden, ornamental orchard and informal flower garden, with a summerhouse and viewing platform. Walks through wild-flower meadows add further interest to a charming, varied garden.

▶ *Open all year – telephone or consult website for details*

15 Annes Grove

Native and exotic species co-exist in this informal garden, which has stunning views over the Awbeg valley.

Castletownroche, near Mallow, Co. Cork

Tel: 00 353 22 26145

www.annesgrovegardens.com

LOCATION 2.5km (1½ miles) N of Castletownroche, between Fermoy and Mallow

At the heart of this tranquil 28 acre garden is a sweep of valley leading down to the River Awbeg – diverted and annexed into the garden – where trees and shrubs grown from seed obtained on plant-hunting expeditions to Tibet and Nepal in the early 20th century grow like native plants.

A maze of stone paths weaves through the different levels giving captivating views. Magnolias, hoherias and embothriums brighten a backdrop of mature conifers. A wide range of damp-loving plants, including primulas and gunneras, have colonised areas along a lush river walk, and trails pass impressive hydrangea and rhododendron plantations grown over great outcrops of rock. Inside the informal walled garden are herbaceous walks and box-hedged borders, and a fern-filled rockery hidden under a cherry, laburnum and eucryphia canopy.
▶ *Open main season – telephone or consult website for details – and by appointment*

16 Bantry House

A monumental staircase, formal terraces and parterres, adorned with statues, give the garden an Italian atmosphere.

Bantry, Co. Cork | Tel: 00 353 27 50047

www.bantryhouse.com

LOCATION On outskirts of Bantry on Cork road

The magnificent 45 acre garden, created around the house from 1844 to 1867, includes formal parterres, terraces and beds. A monumental staircase of 100 steps leads up the hillside, with views of the house, gardens and Bantry Bay below. Statues, urns and balustrading encircle and embellish the gardens, adding to its Italian air. As a result of the warm humid climate the plants that grow here include wisterias, magnolias, myrtles and *Trachelospermum asiaticum*.

Recently, the parterre surrounding the 19th-century wisteria circle and fountain have been completed, the round bed at the entrance to the house replanted, the woodland walk along the stream to the walled garden reclaimed, the 14 round beds to the north overlooking the bay re-created, and the old rose garden laid out afresh.
▶ *House and gardens open main season – telephone or consult website for details*

17 Derreen

Tree ferns from Australia and Tasmania thrive in abundance in the lush conditions here, as do rhododendrons and rare shrubs.

Lauragh, Killarney, Co. Kerry

Tel: 00 353 64 83588

LOCATION 24km (15 miles) SW of Kenmare on R571 road along S side of Kenmare Bay

Walks at Derreen weave through native woodlands and palisades of jade-stemmed bamboo. The evocatively named King's Oozy leads to a grove of tall, archaic tree ferns (*Dicksonia antarctica*) underplanted with species of hymenophyllum ferns. There's a large collection of rhododendrons, and rare, tender shrubs shelter among clipped *Gaultheria shallon*. This is one of the wettest places in these islands, which is reflected in the lushness of the plantings.
▶ *Open all year – telephone or consult website for details*

18 Ilnacullin

In a dramatic setting, this island garden boasts an Italianate garden adorned with wisteria and many tender species.

Glengarriff (Garinish Island) Co. Cork

Tel: 00 353 027 63040

www.heritageireland.ie

LOCATION On island in Bantry Bay

The boat trip across Bantry Bay reveals a superb garden dating from the early 1900s. Most visitors gather in the Casita – an Italianate garden covered in wisteria – to enjoy the spectacular scenery but walk beyond to the Temple of the Winds and you will pass through shrubberies filled with plants usually cultivated indoors – tree ferns, Southern-Hemisphere conifers, rhododendron species and cultivars. A flight of stone steps leads to the Martello tower, and then the path returns to the walled garden with its double-sided herbaceous border. Late spring to early summer sees the 37 acre gardens at their most colourful.
▶ *Open main season – telephone or consult website for details*

IRELAND

19 Lakemount

This garden cleverly combines neatly pruned trees and shrubs with a mass of low-level plantings for year-round interest.

Barnavara Hill, Glanmire, Co. Cork

Tel: 00 353 86 811 0241

www.lakemountgarden.com

LOCATION 8km (5 miles) E of Cork off R639

This has attracted garden visitors to Cork for many years, with virtuoso planting schemes, attention to detail and perfect maintenance. The garden is constantly evolving and while herbaceous plants once took centre-stage here, now larger structural shrubs and trees have come to the fore, many of them elegantly pruned to provide numerous views of the surrounding verdant landscape. Different layers of seasonal planting are used to good effect and beneath the trees and shrubs are a multitude of smaller, low-growing plants.

The 3 acre garden is divided into a formal pond garden, mixed shrub and perennial borders set around sweeps of lawn, a romantic apple orchard, a cottage flower garden and a greenhouse full of exotics.

▶ *Open all year, by appointment*

20 Terra Nova

The tiny, award-winning garden makes clever use of trellises, walls and bamboo to divide the site into even smaller areas.

Raymondstown, Dromin, Kilmallock, Co. Limerick

Tel 00 353 63 90744

www.terranovaplants.com

LOCATION 2km (1¼ miles) S of Bruff on R512 Kilmallock road. Signposted

Choice shrubs and trees, trellising, pergolas, dry-stone walls, tall gates and stands of bamboo divide this award-winning ½ acre plot effectively into a number of little gardens. The wide range of interesting and unusual species make it a magnet for plant lovers.

In one area grass paths cut through dense multi-storey schemes of dissected acers grown from seed, *Liriodendron tulipifera* and *Prunus serrula*, underplanted with variegated comfrey, hellebores, white violas, arisaema and even Italian black kale. Another area is given over to rare ferns in pots. A long curved pergola weighed down in summer by masses of yellow *Rosa* 'Teasing Georgia' and green *R. viridiflora* gives off an intoxicating scent.

Elsewhere a circle of *Betula jacquemontii* standing above sheets of lilies-of-the-valley is further evidence of the owners' inventiveness. Hidden in the middle of the garden is a large Thai tea house shaded by tree ferns.

▶ *Open main season – telephone or consult website for details*

21 Birr Castle

Hornbeam cloisters, a lake and a fernery are just some of the highlights in this garden, which is also home to a huge telescope.

Birr, Co. Offaly

Tel: 00 353 57 912036

www.birrcastle.com

LOCATION 130km (80 miles) SW of Dublin, 38km (24 miles) S of Athlone, on N52 in Birr

Scientists as well as garden visitors flock to the gardens at Birr for, alongside champion trees and exquisite plantings stands the 19th-century 'Leviathan', once the world's largest telescope. The river Camcor flows serenely through the grounds, past groves of Japanese acers, cornus and magnolias brought back from early plant-hunting expeditions, and past flower borders lying beneath the windows of the castle. Just up from the delicate suspension bridge, built around 1820, the river gathers into a waterfall as it cascades over a weir.

There are tree-lined lakeside walks, a fernery and a Gothic shell well. In the restored walled garden unusual hornbeam cloisters come with 'mullioned' windows, scented rose beds, *Paeonia* 'Anne Rosse' and elaborate box beds.

▶ *Open all year – telephone or consult website for details. Guided tours by arrangement*

22 Oakfield Park

Formal box parterres and lawns front the house while a train runs along a lake, giving views of the garden's wilder areas.

Oakfield Demesne, Raphoe, Co Donegal

Tel: 00 353 74 917 3068

www.oakfieldpark.com

LOCATION 10km (6 miles) SE of Letterkenny off R264.

This 100 acre garden, sensitively restored and redeveloped since 1996, is now reaching handsome maturity. The Georgian house (not open) lies at the top of a drive winding through parkland embellished by both established and newly planted trees. It is fronted by a box parterre and lawns sweeping down to a romantic, small lake, a former flax dam. In 2009, an elegant Nymphaeum surrounded by semi-formal planting, was completed beside the lake.

To the rear of the house is a large walled garden, encompassing a series of themed gardens. Six perfectly clipped yew sentinels guard a rill between the handsome traditional greenhouse and the manicured lawns on either side, which are edged by borders of shrubs and herbaceous perennials. Hidden behind hedges and red-brick walls, elegant gates open to reveal sheltered seating areas, a scented herb garden and an oriental garden, while a quieter enclosure has an oval, water-lily-filled pond with curving box hedging and shady evergreen shrubs.

In an area of woodland, pleached lime trees and gravel paths lead to a walled vegetable garden with a productive greenhouse. Small circular windows in the walls provide views of the extensive parkland.

On the opposite side of the road is a beautifully constructed railway station. At weekends a small train runs the 2½ mile route along the edge of a lake dominated by an eccentric folly – a pleasant trip which allows visitors to enjoy the extensive wetland and meadow plantings.

▶ *Open main season – telephone or consult website for details – and by appointment*

23 Glenveagh Castle

The rugged mountainous surroundings make a dramatic contrast with the formality of the gardens and pleasure grounds.

Glenveagh National Park, Churchill, Co. Donegal

Tel: 00 353 74 37090

www.glenveaghnationalpark.ie

LOCATION 24km (15 miles) NW of Letterkenny

The garden in Glenveagh National Park, is full of surprises, with each compartment given a different style. The 2 acre lawn in the pleasure grounds is fringed by rhododendron shrubberies, tree ferns, eucryphias and mass plantings of hostas, rodgersias and astilbes.

Beyond, pathways wind through oak woods in which grow scented rhododendrons and tender trees and shrubs. Here classical elements have been added, including terraced enclosures furnished with Italian statuary and massive terracotta pots. The potager, bounded by herbaceous borders, is planted with heritage vegetable varieties, Irish apple cultivars and rank upon rank of flowering herbs.

This is a paradise for garden enthusiasts. Tour the castle and walk the mountain sides, then take the last bus back to the remarkable heather-roofed visitor centre.

▶ *Castle open. Grounds and garden open all year – telephone or consult website for details*

LAKEMOUNT

Index

Page numbers in bold refer to main entries. Page numbers in italic refer to pictures.

317

Acknowledgments

Front Cover: The Garden Collection/Andrew Lawson (Cothay Manor); **Back Cover:** Andrew Lawson (Rousham House); **1-3** The Garden Collection/Jonathan Buckley (Great Dixter); **6-7** The Garden Collection/Derek Harris; **8-9** MMGI/Marianne Majerus (Trebah); **11** www.ntpl.org.uk/©NTPL/Andrea Jones; **12** Andrew Lawson; **15** www.ntpl.org.uk/©NTPL/Jerry Harpur; **18** Gap Photos Ltd/Jerry Harpur; **20-21** www.ntpl.org.uk/©NTPL/Stephen Robson; **25** Alamy Images/John Swithinbank; **26** www.ntpl.org.uk/©NTPL/Andrew Butler; **28-29** The Garden Collection/Jonathan Buckley; **30** www.ntpl.org.uk/©NTPL/Mark Bolton; **34-35** Gap Photos Ltd/Carole Drake; **36-39** Andrew Lawson; **41** www.ntpl.org.uk/©NTPL/Stephen Robson; **42-43** Clive Nichols Garden Photography (Mille Fleure); **44-45** The Garden Collection/Andrew Lawson (Heale House); **47** English Heritage Photo Library; **48** Clive Nichols Garden Photography; **51** www.ntpl.org.uk/©NTPL/Derek Croucher; **54-55** Clive Nichols Garden Photography; **56-57** www.ntpl.org.uk/©NTPL/Neil Campbell-Sharp; **60-61** The Garden Collection/Derek Harris The Garden Collection/Jonathan Buckley; **65** www.ntpl.org.uk/©NTPL/Jonathan Buckely; **68-69** MMGI/Marianne Majerus; **72-73** The Garden Collection/Derek Harris; **74** Country Life Picture Library/Clive Boursnell; **76-77** Andrew Lawson; **78** Clive Nichols Garden Photography; **80** John Parker; **82-83** Andrew Lawson; **85** www.ntpl.org.uk/©NTPL/Derek Croucher; **88-89** MMGI/Marianne Majerus; **90-91** MMGI/Marianne Majerus; **93** Andrew Lawson; **94** MMGI/Marianne Majerus; **96-97** www.ntpl.org.uk/©NTPL/Stephen Robson; **98** www.ntpl.org.uk/©NTPL/David Sellman; **102** Andrew Lawson; **105** www.ntpl.org.uk/©NTPL/Simon Tranter; **106-111** Andrew Lawson; **112-113** MMGI/Marianne Majerus (Hampton Court Palace); **114-115** Courtesy of the Inner Temple; **116-117** The Garden Collection/Liz Eddison; **121-123** Andrew Lawson; **126** MMGI/Marianne Majerus; **128-129** MMGI/Marianne Majerus (Helmingham Hall); **130** Country Life Picture Library/Clive Boursnell; **133** Gap Photos Ltd/Marcus Harpur; **136-137** MMGI/Marianne Majerus; **138-139** MMGI/Marianne Majerus; **140** Gap Photos Ltd/Jerry Harpur; **143** Andrew Lawson; **146-147** MMGI/Marianne Majerus; **148** MMGI/Marianne Majerus; **150** MMGI/Marianne Majerus; **154-155** MMGI/Marianne Majerus; **156-157** www.ntpl.org.uk/©NTPL/David Sellman (Packwood House); **159** Nick McCann/Heritage House Group; **162** MMGI/Marianne Majerus; **166-167** Andrew Lawson; **171** www.ntpl.org.uk/©NTPL/Andrew Lawson; **174-179** The Garden Collection/Jonathan Buckley; **181** MMGI/Marianne Majerus; **182-183** Andrew Lawson; **184-189** Country Life Picture Library/Val Corbett; **190** Andrew Lawson; **195** www.ntpl.org.uk/©NTPL/Jerry Harpur; **196-197** Country Life Picture Library/Val Corbett; **200** www.ntpl.org.uk/©NTPL/Andrew Butler; **203** Clive Nichols Garden Photography; **204-205** www.ntpl.org.uk/©NTPL/David Sellman; **208-209** www.ntpl.org.uk/©NTPL/David Noton; **212-213** Photolibrary.com/Britain on View/Alan Novelli (Arley Hall and Gardens); **214** Gap Photos Ltd/Fiona Lea; **217** John Parker; **220** Gap Photos Ltd/Mark Bolton; **222-227** Andrew Lawson; **230-231** Andrew Lawson/(Newby Hall); **232-233** The Garden Collection/Jane Sebire; **237** Country Life Picture Library/Val Corbett; **238-239** John Parker; **240** www.ntpl.org.uk/©NTPL/Andrea Jones; **244-245** Gordon Ratcliffe; **247** The Garden Collection/Jane Sebire; **250-251** www.ntpl.org.uk/©NTPL/Derek Croucher (Bodnant); **253** Charles Hawes; **257** www.ntpl.org.uk/©NTPL/Stephen Robson; **258-259** The Garden Collection/Derek Harris; **260** Andrew Lawson; **264-265** Andrew Lawson/(Crathes Castle); **267** Scottish Viewpoint/Allan Devlin; **268** Scottish Viewpoint/VisitScotland; **272-279** Country Life Picture Library/Val Corbett; **280-281** © Charles Jencks, from The Garden of Cosmic Speculation, Frances Lincoln 2003; **282-283** Scottish Viewpoint/Mike Clarke; **287-295** Andrew Lawson; **298-299** Photolibrary.com/Garden Picture Library/Michael Diggin (Mount Usher); **301** www.ntpl.org.uk/©NTPL/Joe Cornish; **302** www.lastrefuge.co.uk/Dae Sasitorn; **305** Andrew Lawson; **308** MMGI/Marianne Majerus; **311** MMGI/Marianne Majerus

Contributors

Project Editors Caroline McDonald, Diane Cross
Art Editors Austin Taylor, Conorde Clarke
Consultants Katherine Lambert, Anne Gatti
Cartographic Consultant Alison Ewington
Feature Writers Vanessa Berridge, Liz Friedrich, Anne Gatti, Katherine Lambert
Additional Editing Jo Bourne, Lisa Thomas, Rachel Warren Chadd
Picture Editor Christine Hinze
Proofreader Barry Gage
Indexer Marie Lorimer
Maps European Map Graphics Limited

READER'S DIGEST GENERAL BOOKS
Editorial Director Julian Browne
Art Director Anne-Marie Bulat
Managing Editor Nina Hathway
Head of Book Development Sarah Bloxham
Picture Resource Manager Sarah Stewart-Richardson
Pre-press Account Manager Dean Russell
Product Production Manager Claudette Bramble
Production Controller Katherine Tibbals

Colour origination by FMG
Printed in China

The Most Amazing Gardens in Britain & Ireland is published by The Reader's Digest Association Limited, 11 Westferry Circus, Canary Wharf, London E14 4HE

Copyright © 2010 The Reader's Digest Association Limited
Copyright © 2010 Reader's Digest Association Far East Limited
Philippines Copyright © 2010 Reader's Digest Association Far East Limited
Copyright © 2010 Reader's Digest (Australia) Pty Limited
Copyright © 2010 Reader's Digest India Pvt Limited
Copyright © 2010 Reader's Digest Asia Pvt Limited

The Most Amazing Gardens in Britain & Ireland is based on material taken from **The Good Gardens Guide 2010/2011**. Text copyright © Katherine Lambert and Anne Gatti 2010

We are committed both to the quality of our products and the service we provide to our customers. We value your comments, so please do contact us on **08705 113366** or via our website at **www.readersdigest.co.uk**

If you have any comments or suggestions about the content of our books, email us at **gbeditiorial@readersdigest.co.uk**

ISBN 978 0 276 44586 6
Book Code 400-472 UP0000-1
Oracle Code 250014439S.00.24